a or an before h? use an only if the h is silent: an hour, an heir, an honourable man, an honest woman; but a hero, a hotel, a historian (but don't change a direct quote if the speaker says, for example, "an historic") • **abattoir** • **abbeys** cap up, eg Rievaulx Abbey, Westminster Abbey • **Aborigines, Aboriginal** cap up when referring to native Australians • **aborigines, aboriginal** lc when referring to indigenous populations • **accents** use on French, German, Spanish and Irish Gaelic words (but not anglicised French words such as cafe, apart from exposé, resumé) • **access** has been known as contact since the 1989 Children Act • **acknowledgment** not acknowledgement • **acronyms** take initial cap, eg Aids, Isa, Mori, Nato • **act** uc when using full name, eg Criminal Justice Act 1998, Official Secrets Act; but lc on second reference, eg "the act", and when speaking in more general terms, eg "we need a radical freedom of information act"; bills remain lc until passed into law • **acting** always lc: acting prime minister, acting committee chair, etc • **actor** male and female: avoid actress except when in name of award, eg Oscar for best actress. One 27-year-old actor contacted the Guardian to say "actress" has acquired a faintly pejorative tinge and she wants people to call her actor (except for her agent who should call her often) • **AD, BC** AD goes before the date (AD64), BC goes after (300BC); both go after the century, eg second century AD, fourth century BC • **adaptation** not adaption • **addendum** plural addendums • **addresses** 119 Farringdon Road, London EC1R 3ER

> **This stuff matters. Rules do not limit; they liberate**
>
> **John Humphrys**

> **Valuably insists on the writing of good English**
>
> **Tom Paulin**

MediaGuardian

In Print

A Career in Journalism

Edited by **Chris Alden**

Copyright in text © Chris Alden
Copyright in database © Guardian Newspapers Ltd 2005
Austin Cartoons © David Austin

The Guardian and MediaGuardian are
trademarks of the Guardian Media Group plc
and Guardian Newspapers Ltd.

Guardian Books is an imprint of
Guardian Newspapers Ltd.

A CIP record for this book is available from
the British Library

ISBN: 1-84354-206-4

Distributed by Atlantic Books
An imprint of Grove Atlantic Ltd
Ormond House
26–27 Boswell Street
London WC1N 3JZ

Cover Design: Two Associates
Text Design: www.carrstudio.co.uk

Data researched and updated on behalf of Guardian Newspapers Ltd
by Toni Hanks

Disclaimer
*We have taken all steps possible to ensure the accuracy of the data in
this directory. If any information
is incorrect, please send an email with updated
details to* mediadirectory@guardian.co.uk

Printed by Cambridge University Press

Contents

How to use this book

Many people dream of a career in newspapers and magazines, but not everyone succeeds. This book gives you the lowdown on how to tip the odds in your favour: how to target and find the role for you, and how to go about getting it.

To help you, we have split the book into four sections. One, what journalism is: this gives you an introduction to the world of newspapers and magazines. Two, the jobs: read this section to get a comprehensive sense of the different kinds of people who make a newspaper or a magazine work. Then three, how to get the job: we suggest you read this once you have worked out what job it is you want. Finally, we list all the phone numbers and websites you need to get there, in section four.

Section 1: what journalism is

Before you start looking for a job in newspapers or magazines, you need to know what you are letting yourself in for. So in this section, we tell you exactly that.

What skills and personality do you have to have to work in newspapers or magazines? The answer, of course, is that there are many different jobs for different kinds of people, some within journalism and some allied to it. So on page 10, you will find a summary "career flowchart" to help you get a sense of what skills and personality you might need to do each job. You can use this flowchart to help you decide what career is right for you. We also offer a guide to the major employers.

Section 2: the jobs

In this section, we explain what these different jobs are – from reporting and feature writing to subediting, picture editing, photography and design. We tell you in greater depth what specific skills you need to do them, with examples of different kinds of writing; and we provide tips on how your career might progress. But don't just take our word for it: we include first-hand experiences of working journalists, many from the Guardian, but also many who work on other newspapers, websites and magazines.

Section 3: how to get the job

When you have a good idea of what job you want, then it is time to turn to Section 3: the 10-step plan on getting it. The plan is not long: we have cut out the self-help padding as far as we can, to leave you with simple, step-by-step practical advice on research, networking, portfolios, CVs, interviews and more – in short, everything existing journalists have painstakingly done before they stumbled into the jobs they have now.

To get the most out of the plan, follow it in conjunction with the advice in Section 2 that relates to the job you want: there will be more specific information on many parts of it there.

Section 4: press contacts

Finally, we offer the meat and drink on which every journalist thrives: contacts. At the back of the book are phone numbers and websites for every newspaper and magazine in the country, plus names of the people in authority: the editor of course, but also where appropriate the news editor, features editor and the production editor or chief sub. We also include the names of ancillary organisations that can help you in your career – unions, diversity associations, and of course the trade press.

Follow the advice in this book, and we confidently predict that you will land that career in newspapers, magazines or journalism – if you are talented enough, hard-working enough and lucky enough too. And if you still haven't succeeded after approaching the task in an organised and practical way, then take our advice: turn to page 78 of this book.

What journalism is

What journalism is

What is journalism? The answer, of course, will depend on who you are. It is the fourth estate, it is grub street, or it is the gutter press. It is the writing of articles in the public interest that expose the iniquity of the powerful and rich; or it is the scribbling of salacious gossip about the same. It is a business, it is a political movement, or an end in itself; it is sold, it is a vehicle for advertising, or it is transmitted as a free public service. It is words, it is pictures, and it is sound; it is digital information being communicated down a wire. It is hard news, it is soft news, views, reviews, interviews; it is sport, it is travel, it is fashion; it is local, it is national, it is international. For someone just starting out in the industry, journalism can be almost anything you want.

The landscape of journalism

First, you should have an idea of what different kinds of journalism there are. The best way to do this is to have a flick through the contacts at the back of the book. There you will find national newspapers, broadsheet and tabloid, daily and Sunday. You will find daily regional newspapers in every major town, and weekly local newspapers serving every village. You will find weekly trade newspapers covering almost every industry, from finance and shipping to travel and health. There are glossy consumer magazines covering almost any subject, which can be anything from weekly to quarterly. There are customer magazines, aimed at different groups from supermarket shoppers to frequent flyers to mobile phone customers. There are also TV and radio stations, in analogue and digital, national and regional. There is access radio; there is hospital radio. There are online news services, online magazines, email services and text message alerts. There are agencies, who sell news and features to most of these markets, often many at the same time. And there are freelance journalists, who do the same. You could be in any one of these workplaces: but each one will demand a different mix of personality and skills.

Think about yourself

So what skills or personality do you have? Think about yourself, in order to work out what you want to do. You could start out in a "content creation" role, such as writing, presenting and photography; or a more production-based job, such as subbing, editing and design.

Career Flowchart

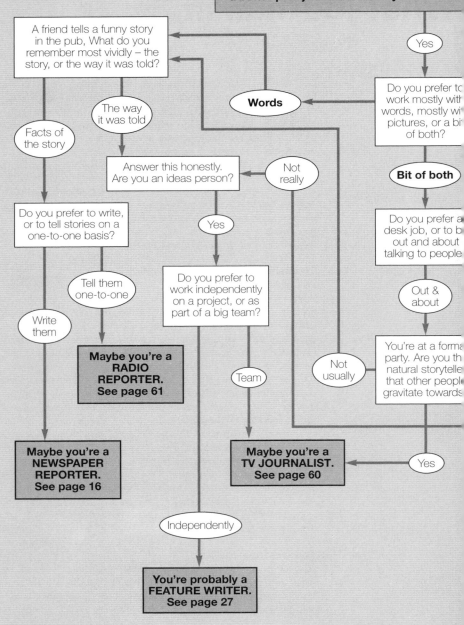

Are you prepared to work for very little pay, often for long hours, in the hope of getting a better-paid job further on in your career?

Yes

A friend tells a funny story in the pub, What do you remember most vividly – the story, or the way it was told?

Do you prefer to work mostly with words, mostly with pictures, or a bit of both?

Words

The way it was told

Facts of the story

Answer this honestly. Are you an ideas person?

Not really

Bit of both

Do you prefer a desk job, or to be out and about talking to people?

Do you prefer to write, or to tell stories on a one-to-one basis?

Yes

Tell them one-to-one

Do you prefer to work independently on a project, or as part of a big team?

Out & about

Write them

Maybe you're a RADIO REPORTER. See page 61

Team

Not usually

You're at a formal party. Are you the natural storyteller that other people gravitate towards?

Maybe you're a NEWSPAPER REPORTER. See page 16

Maybe you're a TV JOURNALIST. See page 60

Yes

Independently

You're probably a FEATURE WRITER. See page 27

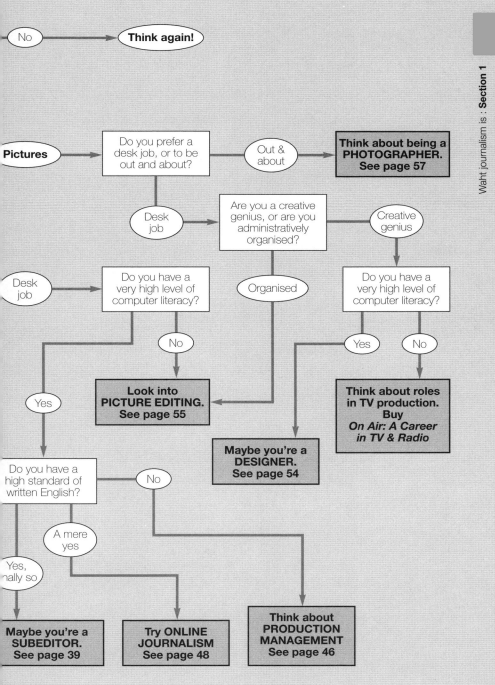

No → **Think again!**

Pictures → Do you prefer a desk job, or to be out and about? → Out & about → **Think about being a PHOTOGRAPHER. See page 57**

Desk job → Are you a creative genius, or are you administratively organised? → Creative genius

Desk job → Do you have a very high level of computer literacy?

Organised

Do you have a very high level of computer literacy?

No

Yes   No

Look into PICTURE EDITING. See page 55

Think about roles in TV production. Buy *On Air: A Career in TV & Radio*

Yes

Maybe you're a DESIGNER. See page 54

Do you have a high standard of written English? → No

A mere yes

Yes, nally so

Maybe you're a SUBEDITOR. See page 39

Try ONLINE JOURNALISM See page 48

Think about PRODUCTION MANAGEMENT See page 46

Main journalism employers

	What they publish	Turnover	Ownership	No. of staff	UK offices	More details
Archant	Regional newspapers including Eastern Daily Press	£158m	Privately owned	2,800	London & South-east, East Anglia, South-west, Scotland	page 86
BBC Worldwide	Magazines including BBC brands, Radio Times	£500m	BBC	2,000	London	page 135
Condé Nast UK	Magazines including Vogue, Glamour, GQ, Condé Nast Traveller	£20–30m	Advance Magazine Group, USA	550	London	page 135
Daily Mail & General Trust	Daily Mail, Mail on Sunday, Evening Standard, regional newspapers	£1.9bn	Lord Rothermere (63% of shares)	18,000 worldwide	London & nationwide	page 86
DC Thomson	Scots regional newspapers, Beano, other magazines	not available	Family owned	2,000	Dundee, Glasgow, Manchester & London	page 86
Dennis Publishing	Maxim, Jack, Viz, The Week, 15 other magazines	£200m	Privately owned by Felix Dennis	350	London	page 135
Emap	FHM, Zoo and more than 60 other titles	£1bn	Plc	5,300	London & Peterborough	page 135
Future Publishing	Consumer magazines	£183m	Plc	1,000 worldwide	London & Bath	page 135
Guardian Media Group	Guardian, Observer, Manchester Evening News & other regional papers, AutoTrader	£526m	Scott Trust	3,200	Manchester, London & nationwide	page 86
Hachette Filipacchi	Elle, Red, Sugar, other magazines	£2.2bn worldwide	Hachette Filipacchi Médias, France	8,000 worldwide	London	page 135
Haymarket	More than 100 titles	£160m	Privately owned	1,500 worldwide	London, Middlesex	page 135
Independent News and Media	Independent titles, regional papers including Belfast Telegraph	£930m	Plc	11,500	London, Belfast	page 86
IPC Media	Nearly 100 titles including Nuts, Marie Claire, Woman's Own	£400–500m	Time Inc, USA	2,200	London, Croydon, Poole	page 135
Johnston Press	Lancashire Evening Post, Yorkshire Post, other regional newspapers	£492m	Plc	7,800	Edinburgh, Lancashire, Midlands, Yorkshire, Eastern England & Hampshire	page 86
National Magazine Company	Cosmopolitan, Company and 15 other magazines	about £300m	Hearst Corporation, USA	700	London	page 135
News International	Sun, Times, News of the World	£1.4bn*	News Corporation (Rupert Murdoch)	4,000	London	page 86
Newsquest	Local newspapers	£530m	Gannett, USA	9,300	Nationwide	page 86
Northern & Shell	Express Newspapers, OK!, other magazines	£425m	Richard Desmond	2,000	London	page 82
Pearson	Financial Times, Penguin	£4bn	Plc	30,900	London	page 83
Press Association	News agency	£65m	Limited company	1,200 - just over half journalists	London, Bristol, Yorkshire, Scotland	page 179
Reed Elsevier	Business and science magazines	£4.9bn	Anglo-Dutch plc	35,000 worldwide	London, Surrey, Oxford, Cambridge	page 136
Reuters	News agency	£3.2bn	Plc	17,300	London	page 179
Telegraph Group	Telegraph, Sunday Telegraph, Spectator	£310m	Barclay brothers	1,200	London	page 82
Trinity Mirror	Mirror Group Newspapers, regional newspapers	£1.1bn	Plc	11,500	Nationwide	page 86

*News Corporation worldwide newspaper revenues

There may be even the opportunity to start in a hybrid writing/ editing role, for example on a small magazine or website. Perhaps you think more visually than verbally; perhaps you don't like the sound of your own voice. This chapter outlines all the jobs in turn, so you can find a job that suits you.

To help you, the previous page carries a career flowchart that you can use to find your niche: simply start at the top and work down, where you will find short explanations of the kinds of job you might do. The chart then refers you to the in-depth guides to each role that form the bulk of this chapter. Note that the jobs won't always fall under the strict definition of "journalism"; but they are included here because they might be suitable: an art editor for a national newspaper, for example, might not strictly be a journalist, but has a vital role in the presentation of the information as it ultimately appears on the page. But we would recommend that whatever the result of the flowchart, you do read this entire chapter to get an idea of the different kinds of work that go into making journalism happen.

Frequently asked questions

Who can work in journalism? In principle, anyone who is talented or hard-working enough, or some happy combination of the two. In practice, though, discrimination and a "cottage industry" appointments process still make it hard for some people to pursue their chosen career. In a column in the Guardian in December 2002, the Guardian columnist Gary Younge was moved to conclude that racism still "impedes your advancement" in the media: there are no current studies into the number of non-white journalists working in British national papers, but the number is still thought to be no more than a few dozen out of 3,000. Ageism is also rife: jobs are often aimed specifically at younger people who cost less, and ask fewer questions, than their more experienced counterparts. It is hard to apply for any job if your advancement is going to be impeded because of who you are; the only advice can be to aim high and prove the doubters wrong. Thankfully, the institutionalised sexism of the newspaper is a thing of the past: women in newspapers are no longer consigned to the bottom rung on the reporting ladder or the "women's pages" as they once mostly were, and journalism is definitely seen as a women-friendly career. Nevertheless, many women reporters still complain they have to work harder to be as successful as a man, and salaries are still not always equal. Turn to page 181 for a list of media diversity groups.

Where can you work in journalism? In theory, anywhere in the country – but you are at a huge advantage if you live near London, where most journalists are based. Outside London, the best opportunities for newcomers to journalism are in local papers, radio and TV stations, and regional news agencies; the larger regional papers are almost as hard to get a job on as a national. In London, you have all these options – plus an abundance of magazine companies, trade publishers, contract publishers and websites, which enormously increases your chances of finding a job. There is also the option of freelancing, which may mean working at home or doing shifts in an office; if you are working from home you can in theory do it from anywhere, but if you are doing shifts then you need to live as close to as many different publishers as you can.

Why work in journalism? For some, it is a vocation in itself; for others, it is just a way to sound off about their pet subjects; for others, it is just a way to pay the rent. Reporters in particular often catch the bug, working hard for absurdly low salaries just to do the job they love; some subs traipse into the office at 9am with a hangover and disappear to the pub on the dot of five, barely uttering a word in between. Different people get a kick out of different things. Many of the questions on the previous page's flowchart are about issues such as money and work-life balance, as well as your career skills.

Finally, if you do end up in the wrong career, either inside or outside journalism, remember that it is never too late to move. Journalists tend to switch jobs more frequently than other professions, particularly early in their career, so an editor won't hold it against you for not sticking your last job out for more than a year. If you have experience in the "real" world, meanwhile, it could be useful background knowledge for working in magazines or the trade press.

The jobs

Writing

So, you want to be a hack. The low pay and the grubby image haven't put you off: you want to earn your keep slumped in front of your laptop, living for the intermittent joy of seeing your name in print.

A laudable dream – but now is the time to stop dreaming.

In this part of the book, the key thing to do is decide what kind of writer you want to be. Are you a hardnosed newshound with a passion for the scoop? Are you a feature-writer with a talent for getting under the skin of your subject? Are you a film, theatre or sports buff? Are you a columnist, leader writer, or reviewer in the making? Is journalism even for you? This chapter will help you decide.

News reporter

Of all the jobs that go to make up a newspaper, only one is the *sine qua non*. Not the editor: every bigwig has a deputy who's nearly as good at the same job. Nor the star columnist, the film critic, the feature-writer, the leader writer, the photographer, subeditor, nor even – some might disagree – the crossword compiler. Remove any one of these from any given paper and, although what was left might not sell so many copies, it would still be a newspaper tomorrow. Not so, though, if you take away the news – or rather, the person that spends all day finding it, asking about it, and scribbling it down. The reporter.

Because it is so crucial, being a reporter is the most demanding and competitive branch of journalism. Editors, and news editors, expect great things from those who try. They want someone who is passionate about the newspaper and the community it serves. Someone who is so steeped in people, so curious about the world around them, that they can sniff out an angle in the most anodyne remark – and keep asking questions till they stand the story up. Someone, at local level, who is prepared to turn their life over to the community they work for, at any time of day or night: to attend court cases, inquests, council meetings, press conferences, crime scenes, crash scenes and worse; to develop a book of contacts for every eventuality; to have ideas on how to follow up every lead. Someone who is able to tell a story: who can write a grab-me intro and include all the who, what, when, where and above all, why, on deadline, in a maximum 800 words. And on top of that, they want you to do it for money that would be insulting to a self-respecting nurse, fireman, policeman or teacher.

Many people have some, but not all, of what it takes. You might not be able to handle the pressure of deadlines; you might not like talking to difficult people; you might not, for all your efforts, be able to write. You might just not fancy slogging your guts out for not very much cash. Many people, successful journalists among them, realise their limitations soon enough. If that's you, don't worry: there are other rewarding jobs you can do, many of them in this chapter.

But for those who do take it on, reporting gives job satisfaction in a way that few other jobs do. You could start out on the internet or at a news agency, but working for a local paper is the traditional route. Many successful reporters say they wouldn't have started any other way; those who move on to better-paid things often miss the rough and tumble of working a patch. And in the world of newspapers,

⬆ Glossary of terms

ABC Audit Bureau of Circulations; body that accredits newspaper circulations.

bulks Copies of a paid-for title that are distributed free, often promotionally.

byline Your name on the article you've written. Make sure you get one if you deserve it.

circulation How many copies a newspaper or magazine sells.

contempt Short for "contempt of court", a criminal offence. Journalists may commit it by flouting court reporting rules, thus prejudicing a trial.

copy Main text of an article.

copy approval When a source asks to see your article prior to publication. Refuse politely.

cuttings Previously written articles – either your own for your portfolio, or other people's for an article you're about to write.

cuttings job Article cobbled together from someone else's cuttings. Give credit where it's due.

death-knock Interviewing someone who's recently bereaved – in person.

defamation Something you write that injures someone's reputation.

distribution How many copies a free newspaper or magazine gives away.

DPS Double-page spread; often just called a spread.

intro All-important first paragraph. In the US they call it a "lead"; in Britain a lead is the main piece on a page, though on the front page that might be a splash.

leader Article representing the opinion of a newspaper.

libel A civil "tort"; generally you commit it by publishing a defamation, unless you can mount a defence on the basis that it was true, or fair comment, or an accurate, contemporaneous report of something said in parliament or court. Read up further.

NCTJ National Council for Training of Journalists; accredits journalism courses.

news agency Company that sells news stories to a newspaper or magazine. Usually delivered electronically to your desktop over the wires, for you to rewrite.

NUJ National Union of Journalists; trade union.

off-diary Story you can't predict.

off the record When a source tells you something that is not for publication; you might go on to use it without attribution. Be prepared to defend the anonymity of such sources.

on-diary Story you know is going to happen, that you prepare for.

on spec Article submitted without a guarantee that it's going to be used. Only if you're desperate.

on the record When a source tells you something for publication.

scoop (noun) An exclusive story, or one published first.

(transitive verb) To beat [a rival paper] by getting a scoop.

source Anyone who tells you anything that leads to a story.

sub, subeditor Person who edits your work. See next chapter.

Teeline Best form of shorthand to learn.

wires Electronic delivery of news and pictures, sent by agencies to your desktop.

there is little substitute for the respect you achieve by having been a local reporter: years later, it could even be the experience that decides whether or not you get that bigwig job. If you get that far, today's long hours and low pay will have been worth the pain.

A final point: even if you plan to write for magazines instead of newspapers, news reporting is still a useful skill. You might not need to do it every day of the week, and you might not need shorthand at 100wpm, but it is a rare publication that does not have a news section of some length. Even more importantly, the skills of a news reporter – research, interviewing, and writing to the point – are the basic skills you need to do other kinds of writing too.

A word about news

So what is a reporter? A reporter, primarily, is someone who finds out the news. But what is news? The answer depends on two things: who you are, and who your readers are.

This chapter isn't the place for an academic discussion about what is newsworthy – newsrooms rarely are – but, for the sake of all our souls, it is worth pointing out this: news is nothing without its audience. Every article you write will be read by someone else: and that person could be a businessman; a sandal-wearing academic; a home-owning pensioner; a Surrey housewife; or a driver of a white van. It won't take you too long to match a national newspaper to each of those stereotypes. So before you even begin working on a story, you need to ask yourself: to whom am I writing? Why do my stories matter to them? If you can't imagine that typical reader, you will find being a reporter, and in fact all journalism, impossibly hard.

If you were to go on a journalism course (page 74), you would be taught that many other factors also decide whether a story makes a paper. These include topicality, locality, how the story confounds or confirms expectations (asylum seeker bites dog), whether or not the story is an exclusive, editorial balance, quality of pictures, and in the worst cases, how much the newspaper is prepared to pay. There are more. You need to be able to understand them, and to be able to pitch a story to an editor on the basis of them – or even despite them. It's your career: it's up to you whether you want to be John Pilger or a 3am Girl, after all. But if it's not relevant to *someone*, you might as well give up now.

More on reporting: finding the story

Whatever kind of reporter you are, finding news is essentially a simple process. It happens in two ways: you ask people questions and you do research of your own. You need to be good at both.

First, you need the research skills. This cannot be under estimated: it is often said that reporters are not necessarily an expert about a subject, but they always know someone who is. Keep up to date: read the local and national papers every day, to get up to speed with the personalities and issues that affect your patch. If you have access to wire services or cuttings files, learn how to use them. Then

The reporter

Name: Allison Martin
Current job: **deputy editor, the Wharf (free local paper, London)**

What was your first job in journalism?
Junior reporter, the Wharf.

How did you get the job?
I did a week of work experience at the Wharf while working as a legal secretary in November 2000, as I'd always wanted to be a newspaper reporter. The editor offered me a job, soon after which I started in January 2001.

What did the job involve? What was it like?
The most important thing to a local reporter is contacts; they are the key to bringing in strong, exclusive stories.

The first few months were about getting out and meeting people. Having had no formal training it was a steep learning curve at first but I'd recommend on-the-job training to anyone. It was a baptism of fire but I had the time of my life doing what I always wanted .

What were your educational qualifications at the time?
I have five A-levels and a degree in English language and literature from Lancaster University .

What journalism did you do before starting work?
Other than my week at the Wharf, I have had work experience at the Sheffield Star local newspaper and Yorkshire TV newsroom.

How did your career progress after your first job?
Although I'm still in my first job, I've worked my way up to be deputy editor – responsible for two reporters and producing a news list every week. For the last year I have also been shifting regularly at both the Daily Mirror and the Sunday Mirror.

What are you doing at work this week?
Not the sexiest of weeks. On Monday morning I checked the weekend papers and updated the news list while chasing Paul McCartney's people for pictures of him rehearsing at the Millennium Dome. In the afternoon I got out and about on the hunt for news. Tuesday was one of those frustrating days – I spent a large chunk of time chasing lawyers to do a progress check on a compensation case. I also chased a local bar for a picture of a waitress for a story on how Canary Wharf workers are leaving restaurants without paying their bill – surprising lack of would-be models among the bar staff. Also chased Canary Wharf cleaners to find out how they felt about their new pay rise following a campaign by the Wharf: proof local papers can make a difference!

We go to press on Wednesday at 1pm so the morning is a fraught and frantic bid to meet deadline while making sure nothing's missed – would have been helpful if 2012

> The best advice is just don't give up – as I tried to break into the industry, so many people said: "Crap pay, long hours, difficult to get into"

Olympic bid boss Barbara Cassani had stepped down at 10.30am rather than noon! Thursday and Friday are for getting out and meeting contacts, so lots of coffee drinking and chatting with everyone from financial press officers to the local fire chief.

What advice would you have for anyone thinking of a career in journalism?
I didn't follow the formal path into journalism, so am proof that if you are enthusiastic and relentless, then anything's possible. Work experience is a brilliant way to get a foot in the door, as is calling your local newspaper with story ideas. The best advice is just don't give up – as I tried to break into the industry, so many people said: "Crap pay, long hours, difficult to get into." I was lucky enough to find a editor who said: "Crap pay, long hours BUT it's the best job in the world."

is also the web: you should be familiar not only with Google, but also all the newsgroups, chatrooms and gossip sites where people discuss the issues you cover. Use Google News or its less well-known equivalent, worldnews.com, to get a sense of what the competition is covering. Learn how to do advanced searches to drill down to the specific information you require.

You will have to start developing contacts. This can be difficult at first. In this case a journalism course is helpful, because it gives you an overview of how public life works, the difference between primary and secondary sources (see box) and which public officials do what; if

The news editor

Name: **Albert Scardino**
Current job: **executive editor (news), the Guardian**

What was your first job in journalism?
Summer intern, the Weekly News, Atlanta, Georgia USA.

How did you get the job?
My brother-in-law owned the paper.

What did the job involve?
Emptying the trash, pasting up all the classifieds, driving the paper to the printer, returning bundles to the office and the post office, in exchange for freedom to write a column about state politics. $40/week plus room.

What were your educational qualifications at the time?
Completed school, going on to university in the autumn.

What journalism did you do before starting work?
Summer university programme for school journalists, five weeks.

How did your career progress after your first job?
Different American daily every summer as an intern, general assignment reporter; Associated Press reporter after university; returned to postgraduate university study in journalism; then documentary film work; founded a weekly newspaper, helped put 37 elected officials in jail through campaigning against corruption in state and local government; won a Pulitzer Prize for leader writing; joined the New York Times as an editor and columnist; became press secretary for the mayor of the city of New York; moved to London when my wife became chief exec of the Economist; joined The Guardian 10 years later as executive editor.

What are you doing at work this week?
Strategic planning, newsroom personnel issues, designing a summer internship programme and a post-graduate training

> Travel. Read about journalism but develop knowledge about other subjects

programme, redesigning and relaunching the Guardian Weekly.

What advice would you have for anyone thinking of a career in journalism?
Write for any outlet possible, as often as possible. Complete as much education in any subject as you can possibly force yourself to do. Travel. Read about journalism but develop knowledge about other subjects – law, art, healthcare, transportation, finance, sports – then write about what you know best.

not, learn as much as you can by visiting government, court and local websites. Don't be afraid to ask fellow reporters for contacts as you need them; unless there is a good reason, they shouldn't say no. Remember, everyone is a potentially useful contact: so if you know a friend who knows a friend who knows what you want, don't be afraid to ask. You can always buy the latest copy of the MediaGuardian Media Directory; its Contacts Book at the back lists 6,000 phone numbers for journalists, including every major public institution

The foreign editor

Name: **Francis Harris**
Current job: **deputy foreign editor, the Daily Telegraph**

What was your first job in journalism?
Reporter, South Wales Argus.

How did you get the job?
I applied to become a trainee reporter, after the postgraduate journalism course at Cardiff University.

What did the job involve? What was it like?
It was a standard local newspaper reporting job: lots of silver weddings, local council meetings, court cases and county fairs during the day, lots of drinking with reporters at night.

What were your educational qualifications at the time?
A BA in history and a postgraduate diploma from Cardiff.

What journalism did you do before starting work?
I spent a few weeks getting (unpaid) work experience on local newspapers in East Anglia.

How did your career progress after your first job?
Erratically. Depressed by the news that I was being sent to the district office in the new town of Cwmbran for 18 months ("Good experience boy, everyone does it"), I resigned and took a job with a financial paper in London. That turned out to be even less fun than Cwmbran, so after a year I wrote to The Daily Telegraph offering to work as a freelance in Prague. It was October 1989. The Telegraph's foreign editor called the next day and asked me in. He was desperate for stringers in eastern Europe and offered me £100 a month (£100 was almost as pisspoor then as it is now) plus lineage and a

copy of the paper. By the time I arrived, communism was in a bit of trouble. I started to write.

What are you doing at work this week?
Working. The Iraq prisoner scandal now appears to be threatening senior members of the US administration, the Shia are under assault from US forces, bombs are exploding all over the place and there's a very obvious need to counteract the misery by digging up stories that aren't soaked in blood.

What advice would you have for anyone thinking of a career in journalism?
Consider accountancy. Newspaper circulation is in trouble across the board. That's partly because people prefer to read Metro than splash out 60p on a paper, and partly because they imagine television news covers the same ground as newspapers (it doesn't). The only sensible answer is to become a bean counter, or in extremis, a television news reporter.

around the country, plus charities, campaign bodies, unions and FTSE 100 companies.

Second, there is the asking. You need to be comfortable doing it. For anyone with a healthy level of self-awareness, it seems arrogant to get on the phone and start asking someone you have never met about how badly they are doing their job. To be a reporter, you need to get over that. With experience, you become better at coaxing answers out of people: if a contact is not used to dealing with the media, for example, you can start by asking them where they were born, how old they are, or other background questions to put them at their ease. If your contact is a press officer, conversely, they will have a practised line to feed you, and it will take firmer questioning to get to the point. If you cannot see yourself arguing the toss about hospital car parking with the defensive communications director of a part-privatised NHS trust, reporting might not be your ideal job.

So you need to be thick-skinned – but you also need your persuasive side, if you are to get people to talk to you. That's not easy when you need comment from an individual and the paper goes to

The trade editor

Name: Jane King
Current job: Editor, Personnel Today and editorial director, Personnel Today Group

What did the job involve? What was it like?
It was great fun: on-the-job training combined with formal classroom training, as part of the NCTJ three-year apprenticeship.

What were your educational qualifications at the time?
O-levels only – I left school at 17. Got an NCTJ qualification in 1980.

What journalism did you do before starting work?
None.

How did your career progress after your first job?
Well ... senior reporter, chief reporter, deputy news editor, news editor etc.

What was your first job in journalism?
Trainee reporter at the East Grinstead Observer, a paid-for local weekly, in 1977.

How did you get the job?
I wrote to the editor and asked for a work placement.

What are you doing at work this week?
Speaking at an industry conference; writing a leader; managing the team; heading up a company-wide project to improve the editorial content across all our magazines.

What advice would you have for anyone thinking of a career in journalism?
Be ambitious for yourself and for your product. Grab whatever opportunities come along – and have a lot of fun.

press within the hour. One method is to say that you want to include their views "for the sake of balance"; a note of desperation or flirtation in your voice sometimes does the trick. Get in touch with that inner charmer. At a local paper, such skills will also be useful when you come to do your first "death-knock" – that is, doorstep someone who has been recently bereaved. No reporter enjoys it, but the usual approach is to say you want to include some words about the departed "from those who knew them best"; you might be sent packing, but at least you tried.

Interviews can be face-to-face, which is preferable but time-consuming; on the phone, which is less personal but convenient; or by email, for when you are on deadline, feeling idle, dealing with an obstreperous press office, or all three. In any interview situation, prepare enough open-ended questions to get to the point in the time you have – in a press conference, for example, you might only get one chance. Once the subject is talking, you need to be able to keep your mouth shut, unless they are disappearing off at a tangent; if they are, you could wait for a natural break and then interrupt firmly and politely with another open-ended question. Remember, interviewing is all about listening: if the tangent comes up with an interesting lead, you can usually follow it up before coming back to the point.

Finally, you need the skills to get those juicy quotes down. So for any serious reporter, shorthand is essential. Teeline is the method of choice, because it is the easiest to pick up: you can learn it on any NCTJ newspaper journalism course, you can take evening shorthand classes, or (if you are both disciplined and poor) you can buy a coursebook and practise at home. Whichever method you choose, learn it as early as you can – and practise, practise, practise. It's a faff; but the day you have three interviews to do in quick succession, one on the phone and two out of the office, all to be written up by 2pm this afternoon, you will be grateful for that hard work.

That's not to say that other interviewing methods don't have a place. Tapes, MiniDiscs or MP3s are a useful back-up and handy for the irregular interviewer, but they are no substitute for the real thing: they take longer to transcribe, so they aren't very useful if you are writing more than one story at a time. Even more importantly, every so often they fail to work. It will happen, and when it does, it makes your heart fall through your shoes. If you want to be a reporter, then learn shorthand now and avoid the stress.

Telling the story

It almost goes without saying: to be a reporter, you need to be able to write. To qualify that: to be a reporter, you need to be able to write concisely. The reader has a limited attention span. She might only read the headline and your intro, before going on to the crossword or the letters page. You want to ensure that if she spends only a few seconds on your story, she can still tell her mother tomorrow what it was about.

So you need to be familiar with the most common system of news reporting: the "inverted pyramid" story structure. Its principle is this: tell the most important bit of the story first, then back it up with the less important bits. Each paragraph contains more crucial information than the one below it. The top paragraph, or intro, is the bit that holds the structure together: hence the inverted pyramid.

Imagine you attend the inquest of a woman who died after her appendicitis was misdiagnosed as a stomach bug. The coroner records a verdict of unlawful killing. What is your first paragraph?

There are a few possible angles here. As a first effort, you might go with this:

A coroner recorded a verdict of unlawful killing yesterday at an inquest into a Hampshire woman whose doctor failed to spot she had appendicitis.

This gets the main facts in, but it doesn't inspire. It's not long, which is good, but there is too much information to keep in your head; too many bits hanging off bits. The coroner is centre stage, but the real drama – the death of the woman – is hanging off the end. So if you are working for a typical, midmarket local paper, you might rewrite by focusing on the woman instead; that is, mentioning her first:

A Hampshire woman who died of a ruptured appendix was unlawfully killed, an inquest ruled yesterday.

This is better. There are fewer words; better still, the difficult subclause about the inquest is cordoned off after the comma, bringing dynamism to everything that goes before. And – joy – because of the increased focus, the rest of the story starts to write itself. Who was she? Why was she unlawfully killed? How long ago did this happen? What did the doctor say? All of these necessary questions can be answered in the second paragraph:

A Hampshire woman who died of a ruptured appendix was unlawfully killed, an inquest ruled yesterday.
Stacey Devereux, from Little Wishing near Portsmouth, went to see her GP, Dr Maik Kryzo, on October 24 last year, suffering from severe pains in her stomach. But Dr Kryzo thought she had a stomach bug, and told her to take a packet of Rennies.

From there, all you have to do is include the statement of the coroner, the reaction of the family and the reaction of the doctor, and you're almost done.

But what if you're writing for a trade newspaper aimed at busy doctors? The situation is completely different. You'd want to get the doctor upfront:

A Hampshire GP faces being struck off the medical register today, after giving indigestion tablets to a woman who later died of appendicitis.

Dr Maik Kryzo, from Great Wishing near Portsmouth, will face the General Medical Council's professional conduct committee next month.

An inquest yesterday decided that …

And so on. The new intro pushes the story off on a completely different angle, so the second par is different too. Ms Devereux will be named somewhere in the story, but nowhere near the top. Know your market, focus the intro, and the story writes itself. It just takes practice.

There are pitfalls to be aware of. Law is one. If you want to be a reporter and you haven't been on an NCTJ journalism course, then go to a bookshop now and buy McNae's Essential Law for Journalists. You don't want to be libelling anyone on your first day, and you certainly don't want to find yourself in contempt of court. Read that book, and the chances of such a disaster befalling you will be slim.

As you write, try to remember your integrity. The US has been rocked by scandals in the past two years about high-profile journalists who have plagiarised or concocted their news stories. Jayson Blair, a New York Times reporter, was caught ripping off quotes and stories from other newspapers in America, a scandal that cost the editor his job; it was later discovered that Jack Kelley, a Pulitzer-prize-winning writer at USA Today, had been faking major foreign news stories for several years. If you use quotes from a rival newspaper, credit them; and, please, don't go making stuff up. It's not what reporting is about.

Do remember some of the grammar tips you learned at school – but forget some of the others. So: don't use a long word when you can use a short one (never "commented" when you can use "said"). Use as few words as possible. Always use a colon before reported speech. Keep straight news in the past tense. It's fine to begin a paragraph with "But" or "And". Prefer active verbs to passive ones. Delete as many adjectives and adverbs as you can. And if you don't know what verbs, adjectives and adverbs are, find out!

Finally, a good tip is always to make a point of comparing what you wrote with what actually appears in print. You'll soon get a sense of what is required.

Up the career ladder

A successful reporter will often go on to be a **chief reporter** and then a **news editor**. The news editor is the journalist responsible for managing reporters and deciding the relative importance of news stories – including which make the splash (the front page) and which don't make the cut. So, to progress in the job, you need to be a strong decision-maker with a highly developed news sense and experience of reporting. Again, you'll need to be good at working to deadlines – but this time you'll be managing the work of a number of different reporters as they file to the subeditors at the same time. If you're a hands-on editor, you'll also make sure all the headlines and intros are spot-on before they go to press. On most newspapers or news-led magazines, the news editor is ahead of the features editor in the queue for the editor's chair.

Alternatively, if you don't fancy the idea of moving into management, you could do freelance reporting shifts (see page 78) or apply for a job at a bigger publication, such as a national newspaper.

☑ Get the Job

Employers
Every national and regional newspaper and magazine, some websites

Qualifications
- Minimum: five Cs at GCSE including English
- More than half of entrants have a degree
- About half of entrants do an NCTJ course (page 74)

Before the interview
- Read the last three months' editions of the publication; visit the websites of people or bodies who are frequently mentioned and write down what you think could be improved
- Type the publication name into a search engine
- Work on your writing portfolio, to bring to the interview
- Come up with five ideas for news angles and features

What you need to demonstrate at interview
- Curiosity – so ask questions
- Enthusiasm
- Willingness to work hard
- For a first job, experience of writing at any level
- Ability to write concisely and on deadline
- *Reporters*: Good Teeline shorthand: NCTJ demands 100wpm

What to discuss at interview
- The compact revolution: will broadsheet journalism survive?
- Week that was: what's in the news at the moment

Questions to ask
- Office bound: is this a desk job or not?
- Creative soul: will I get the chance to do other kinds of writing too?
- Learning on the job: what formal training is available?
- How much will I be paid?

Feature writing

Are you someone who likes to focus on how or why something has happened, beyond noting the simple fact that it has? Someone who wants to find out more about the personalities in the media and the news? Who wants to explore how health problems, political crises or public events affect people from day to day? Who has a consuming interest in the arts, culture or travel? Who likes to write creatively, or to inject greater personality into your prose? If you answer yes to most of these questions – and many journalists do – then you will no doubt have considered a career as a feature writer, either on a newspaper or on a magazine.

The feature writer

Name: **Simon Hattenstone**
Current job: **staff writer, the Guardian**

What did the job involve? What was it like?
Laying out and subbing pages of incomprehensible computer programming.

What were your educational qualifications at the time?
A degree in English, and a PGCE (education qualification).

What journalism experience did you have before starting work?
I worked on a student paper at Leeds University.

What was your first job in journalism?
Subeditor for Europress, computer magazine producers in Hazel Grove, Stockport.

How did you get the job?
I sent hundreds of job applications.

How did your career progress after your first job?
It didn't exactly set me back, but it hardly helped. I had to spend another six months writing off for jobs before being offered a subbing job with GP, a magazine for GPs owned by Michael Heseltine's Haymarket.

Don't write things you don't believe

What are you doing at work this week?
I am finishing off an interview with an actor, and writing up a long-term piece about an asylum family we have been following for more than year.

What advice would you have for anyone thinking of a career in journalism?
Don't give up. Be passionate. Find yourself a subject, or more than one. Don't write things you don't believe. Make people trust you, and don't betray that trust. Be honest.

The section editor

Name: **Lynne Michelle**
Current job: **health & beauty editor, the Sunday Mirror**

What was your first job in journalism?
Wire editor, World Entertainment News Network (WENN)

How did you get the job?
It was my work experience placement on my postgraduate journalism course (I did a nine-week diploma in magazine journalism with PMA). At the end of a two-week stint I was asked to come back permanently when my course finished.

What did the job involve? What was it like?
I worked one of three shifts (6am-1pm, 1-8pm, through the night) writing up and sending out showbiz stories to various media, from newspapers to radio stations. At the time, I loathed the job – it was dismal pay for antisocial hours, I had to work virtually every weekend for free and felt constantly jet-lagged due to the shift rotation. Looking back now, I admit it

was good training – I learned a lot about working to tight deadlines, following house style, and showbiz journalism in general, and I also made some good contacts (and mates) in the six months I was there.

What were your educational qualifications at the time?
I had a 2:1 in history and my postgrad qualification.

What journalism did you do before starting work?
As a student, I wrote for several Hobsons titles (educational publishers) and even got paid for some of it, which I remember being pathetically pleased about.

How did your career progress after your first job?
I left WENN to work in on a trade magazine, Soap, Perfumery & Cosmetics, as assistant editor (I later became deputy). As a sideline, I freelanced for newspapers and magazines to avoid being pegged as a "trade journalist", and eventually started writing for the Sunday Mirror magazine – having been recommended to the editor by a former WENN colleague, funnily enough. Two months later, their then beauty editor was poached by the News Of The World so I just happened to be in the right place at the right time. I wrote the beauty column freelance for

a few weeks and was then taken on as a full-time member of staff. Six months later, the magazine relaunched as a celebrity title and I was informed I was now the health editor too.

What are you doing at work this week?
Interviewing nutritionists for a feature on the Atkins diet, writing a piece on beach beauty, sorting out an interview and shoot with Leah Woods, setting up a piece with Kirsty Gallagher, researching a piece on travel health, editing a freelance make-up feature and planning my features list for autumn.

What advice would you have for anyone thinking of a career in journalism?
Do as much work experience as you can and be proactive - don't just sit there expecting people to come up with ground-breaking features for you to do. The work experience people who've got jobs and freelance commissions here are those who've been enthusiastic, used their initiative, come up with ideas of their own and just got on with it. I would also suggest budding journalists consider developing their knowledge in an area of personal interest to them, whether it's nutrition, cars or food, as it can be helpful to have a niche.

Don't, however, get carried away too soon. Feature writing is not easy: in order to be successful, you will need to have the basic skills of a news reporter (page 16), and more besides. You still need to do your research, still need to be good at securing interviews and getting quotes, still need to know how to be concise. As a result, some

The travel editor

Name: **William Ham Bevan**
Current job: **deputy editor, Sunday Times Travel Magazine**

What was your first job in journalism?
Trainee newswire editor, World Entertainment News Network (WENN).

How did you get the job?
An advert had been placed on the noticeboard in my journalism training college. I applied, and was awarded the job after coming in for a trial shift.

What did the job involve? What was it like?
It involved compiling and editing showbiz stories for the WENN newswire, from our reporters and from monitored sources, then transmitting the news feeds to our subscribers. As a 24-hour operation, it meant shift and night work.

What were your educational qualifications at the time?
BA in English and MPhil in general linguistics from Oxford University, and a diploma in journalism from the Centre for Journalism Studies, Cardiff.

What journalism did you do before starting work?
I contributed to the Oxford Student newspaper, and was editor of the Oxford Handbook - a 300-page guide to the city and university that was published each year.

How did your career progress after your first job?
I initially went freelance as a writer and subeditor. I had long-term arrangements with Radio Times (as a copywriter) and the Daily Express (as a sub). All the while, I did shorter term subbing work and feature commissions, for technology, lifestyle and men's magazines. Through friends I made at Cardiff, I also began to write a few ski and travel features each year. After a stint as a sub on the features desk of the Daily Mail, I was offered the deputy editorship of Sunday Times Travel, then on only its third issue.

What are you doing at work this week?
Compiling the front-of-book news section for Travel magazine with the help of our staff writers, revising and passing pages, and checking proofs from the repro house.

What advice would you have for anyone thinking of a career in journalism?
A course is very useful, as on-the-job training is pretty much non-existent these days; but work experience is crucial, to get your name known and to meet people. We filled our last writing vacancy only from the pool of people who had done unpaid internships at the magazine. And keep in contact with as many people as you can who are at the same stage of their career as you are – these can be more useful than contacts further up the editorial ladder, as they will be willing to swap tips, share freelance opportunities, and give you an honest inside track on where they've worked. Having the ready-made network of my year-group at Cardiff made the difference between sinking or swimming as a freelance.

journalists get into feature writing by starting their career as a news reporter – often on a small local paper or specialist desk, where journalists work across news and features at the same time. This makes sense: few people are better placed to write an analysis piece about an issue than the reporter who has just been covering it for news; similarly, when you are working a patch, ideas for features will suggest themselves. The job will be demanding but rewarding, and editors respect the experience it provides.

But it's also possible to go straight into feature writing either as a freelance, or as a first job on a magazine. If this is the case, then you need to immerse yourself in the kinds of feature writing that appear in newspapers and magazines. The following tips should therefore be helpful.

Get to the point – and find examples

What is a feature? The answer is that it can be many things. These include the "news feature", probably a slightly off-diary news story written in some depth; a profile or interview; a discussion about an issue that might arise from the news; or a discussion about an issue of importance to the readership, often in a field such as careers, education, transport, travel, personal relationships or health. What the best features have in common, though, is that they have a single identifiable point.

Take these spreads from the Guardian's G2 features section, on April 13, 2004. Reading the headlines, standfirsts and intros (opposite), it's possible to sum up the point of each article in seven words or less:

Have we stopped worrying about nuclear weapons? (Laura Barton)

Late for an interview with Judi Dench (Simon Hattenstone)

My difficulty walking with multiple sclerosis (Nicky Broyd)

No more vitamin supplements for me (Bill Parry)

"Art from Islamic lands" exhibition (Jonathan Jones)

How much theatre can I see for £50? (Leo Benedictus)

Volvo S40 (Giles Smith)

US soldiers claiming asylum in Canada (Anne McIlroy)

In these eight articles, it is possible to identify six different treatments. One article is a political debate with a news hook; one is an interview (that happened to go pear-shaped); two are personal features about health; two are in-depth reviews, of an exhibition and of a car; one is a personal take on discount theatre tickets; one is a news feature about a legal issue abroad. All that in just one supplement – excluding even the shorter columns, think pieces, quizzes and regular fillers.

With so many types of feature, who is a good feature-writer? Simply this: someone who is incisive enough to see the point of the

article even as they are writing it, and lateral enough to see the everyday details that will help get that point across. In most cases, to do this best, you need to be out on the road, and you might ideally have a photographer with you as well. Take Laura Barton's intro to her piece on nuclear weapons:

> Easter Monday drifts slowly over Aldermaston, a haze of through traffic and dog walkers and loafered day-trippers enjoying ice creams by the canal. As the 13.51 train from Reading draws gently into the station, a handful of anoraked pensioners and art students incongruously clad in pink leggings and glittery eyeshadow tumble on to the platform and begin the trek to the Atomic Weapons Establishment building, an hour or so's walk from the station.

This isn't, of course, an "inverted pyramid" structure like news reporting. Instead, everything in the first paragraph – from the inglorious weather to the "handful" of protesters on the train –

reinforces the point that, compared to the heyday of protests against nuclear weapons, these days there ain't much going on. The article is accompanied by photographs contrasting a quiet Aldermaston today against a busy Aldermaston 50 years ago, adding a visual flavour to the spread. Working from the specific to the general, Barton moves from seemingly everyday observations to the main issues of the piece nuclear weapons and the culture of protest; with interviews with people who protested then and are protesting now.

Less orthodoxly, on the next page, Simon Hattenstone is late for an interview with Dame Judi Dench, and has been forced to conduct the best part of it by phone on the way, with a PR officer calling time in the background:

> ... I run out of the car, tape recorder in one hand, mobile phone in the other. The same voice in the background says, "You've got one minute left."
>
> I run and run, and somehow find myself in Dench's sitting room, panting. She looks smart and sombre in her dark suit and cravat and trademark Joan of Arc crop.
>
> I apologise again, tell her how useless I am, ask if there's any possibility of meeting up after the talk. "No, that will be impossible," she says.
>
> "Thirty seconds left," the PR says.

The writer uses the story of his minor professional crisis to get a serious point across about the actor: that she is punctual, firm doesn't have a lot of time for hacks, and is prepared to let the PR team end the interview at the original allotted time – even though it gives Hattenstone only 30 seconds' audience. Are these the disciplined qualities, we ask ourselves, that led to Dame Judi's theatrical success

Because feature writing is so much about personal observation there are no strict rules on what should go into a feature intro. It could be a revealing anecdote or quote, or an aspect of someone's daily routine. It could be a statistic. It could be something about an interviewee's house, a detail in a painting, a little-known coffee shop in a destination that seems to encapsulate the spirit of the place Work from the specific to the general, and the reader will follow you everywhere you go.

Come up with ideas for short features
In the features pages of both magazines and newspapers, much space is devoted to short, regular "spot" features – often written by different writer each day, week or month. In Guardian supplements these include Pass notes, Why I love..., Webwatch ... and others; if you examine the opening pages of a consumer magazine, you will find countless other examples, each targeted to their particular readership. Readers love them because they take only seconds to digest; editors love them because they take away some of the pain of filling pages. Writers love them because coming up with ideas for them can be a route into a career.

Why not practise? Buy a few magazines you are interested in working for, and give it a go: come up with a list of treatments that make good spot features, and also some subject ideas to match existing spots. The challenge, of course, is to reinvent the wheel: to make the same old subject seem bold and refreshing and new. If you are happy with the result, write them up, and perhaps add the package to your portfolio (see page 73). Many would-be feature writers have landed jobs this way.

Up the career ladder

At many newspapers or magazines, the successful feature writer will go on to be the **features editor**. The features editor is the journalist

The assistant editor, magazines

Name: **Kate Collyns**
Current job: **assistant editor, Greece magazine; production assistant, Portugal magazine; production assistant, Antiques & Collectables magazine**

What was your first job in journalism?
Freelancing at BBC Worldwide for a children's magazine, as junior writer and editorial assistant.

How did you get the job?
Through a week's work experience.

What did the job involve? What was it like?
It involved admin work (calling in products for review, typing up readers' letters, answering letters, keeping database etc) and writing (cartoon strips, competition pages, subscriptions pages, giveaway pages etc.)

What were your educational qualifications at the time?
A degree in English and philosophy.

What journalism did you do before starting work?
Books editor of student newspaper at university, plus the week's work experience.

How did your career progress after your first job?
Got more work experience at Merricks Media and helped to launch Greece magazine; got job as staff writer of A&C and assistant editor of Greece; then also took on role of production assistant for Portugal.

What are you doing at work this week?
Writing an article on Athens and Olympics after trip there last week; researching properties for sale in Greece and Portugal; looking for news stories; sorting out flatplans; subbing articles; arranging giveaways.

What advice would you have for anyone thinking of a career in journalism?
Have a broad range of interest that you can draw on for all the different kinds of newspaper and magazine; also keep abreast of new publications and launches in the media world.

responsible for managing feature-writers and commissioning features from freelances; so to progress in your career, you need to be a strong ideas person who can visualise how features will look on the page. Depending on the length of the features, you'll then work with the writer on any necessary changes — and work with the subeditors designers and picture editors to make your vision a reality. On a magazine or features-led paper, the features editor is usually ahead of the news editor in the queue for the editor's chair.

Alternatively, if you don't fancy the idea of moving into management, you could become a freelance feature writer (see page 26) or apply for a writer's job at a bigger publication, such as a national newspaper or glossy consumer magazine.

The glossy editor

Name: **Marie O'Riordan**
Current job: **editor, Marie Claire**

What was your first job in journalism?
subeditor on Communications Magazine, published by International Thompson. Subscriber-only title.

How did you get the job?
It was advertised in the Guardian, and I applied, but I was considered too junior so I didn't get an interview. However, the "successful" candidate was fired during their probation and the editor went back to the rejected CVs, found mine and gave me an interview

based on the fact I was a Scrabble fan and so was she! How embarrassing that I'd mentioned this on my list of hobbies.

What did the job involve? What was it like?
Being production editor of a monthly magazine – pre-Apple Mac, so it involved old-fashioned cutting, pasting and designing, writing heads and sells and cutting copy to fit.

What were your educational qualifications at the time?
A BA in English and history, and an MA in modern Irish and American literature.

What journalism did you do before starting work?
A student mag.

How did your career progress after your first job?
I got a job as a production editor on More! magazine, and worked my way up the greasy

pole to deputy editor and then editor. I then got editor of Elle, from there publishing director of Emap's youth group, and from there to editor of Marie Claire.

What are you doing at work this week?
Individual performance development reviews with my staff (there are about 40 of them); planning my October and November issues; some lunches with advertisers; appearing on a TV show.

What advice would you have for anyone thinking of a career in journalism?
Be dogged – take any job in any sector, and you can move about till you land your ideal position. Always buy and read the magazine or paper before your interview. It still amazes me how interviewees don't even bother reading the mag before an interview.

Specialist writing: columns, reviews, leaders and the rest

Beyond general features, there are many specialised kinds of writing that appear in magazines or particularly newspapers – including columns, reviews, leaders and match reports. If you want to do any of these, the best advice is to try to add them to your portfolio as soon as you can; but be aware that they can be very hard to break into as a first job.

The arts writer

Name: **Alexis Petridis**
Current job: **rock and pop critic, the Guardian**

What was your first job in journalism?
Production manager/news editor/staff writer at Mixmag.

How did you get the job?
I went there on work experience while studying at City University for my postgraduate diploma in periodical journalism.

What did the job involve? What was it like?
The job involved a bit of everything, from making the tea to writing cover features. At the time, Mixmag was a small, privately-owned magazine with a tiny staff. It was incredibly hard work – I once worked a shift that started at 9am on Tuesday and ended at 6am the next morning – but it was really good experience, better than anything you could be taught at journalism school.

What were your educational qualifications at the time?
I had a BA in English and a postgraduate diploma in periodical journalism.

What journalism experience did you have before starting work?
Student newspaper stuff – music critic, arts ed, columnist. I'd done a couple of weeks work experience on a local paper when I was 16 as well.

How did your career progress after your first job?
I worked my way up at Mixmag for three-and-a-half years, and ended up as deputy editor. I quit, then went freelance - writing for Q, Mojo, Daily Telegraph, Evening Standard etc - then became editor of Select. That closed, so I went to work at a small TV company as a researcher, which I hated. I started writing for the Guardian while I was there, then eventually, after a few months, they offered me my current job. I've been there almost three years.

What are you doing at work this week?
Reviewing PJ Harvey's album, going to Spain to see Paul McCartney live as part of a feature, commissioning the album reviews and sorting out the live reviews, writing a piece for the comment page about i-Pods, writing up an interview about Glastonbury, sorting out some forthcoming features.

What advice would you have for anyone thinking of a career in journalism?
Do as much writing as you possibly can, for whoever – free sheets, student papers, anything. It's the only way you'll get better as a writer.

The review

Reviewing is a job for the specialist. If you're only dabbling in arts, books or film, then editors won't usually be keen to use you: they want well-informed experts who can be called upon to produce sparkling reviews on demand. For this reason, reviewers are either staff journalists who work on an arts desk across news and features (in both newspapers and magazines), or freelances who can devote time to immersing themselves in the creative world. To get into reviewing, you should build up your knowledge, get work experience in an arts journalism environment, and include a mix of reviews and arts features in your portfolio. With that in mind, see page 71 for the 10-step plan.

The columnist

Name: **Richard Tomkins**
Current job: **columnist, the Financial Times**

What was your first job in journalism?
Reporter, Walsall Observer – then a local paid-for weekly.

How did you get the job?
It was my local paper. I applied for a job, was interviewed twice and submitted a sample article.

What did the job involve?
Reporting local news: from diary stories such as council meetings, magistrates courts, inquests and golden weddings to breaking news such as sudden deaths, accidents and crime. I was never bored – you learned so much about people and their surprising lives.

What were your educational qualifications at the time?
O- and A-levels. (This was a long time ago! You would probably need to be a graduate now.)

What journalism did you do before starting work?
None.

How did your career progress after your first job?
After a couple of years I obtained my NCTJ proficiency certificate, mostly through training on the job but also through eight weeks' attendance at college. I then started looking for short cuts to Fleet Street. Hearing the FT was looking for subeditors, I trained myself how to sub by doing unpaid Saturday shifts on the Birmingham Evening Mail (a sister paper to the Walsall Observer), then obtained casual shifts as an FT sub. Eventually I obtained a staff job as an FT sub and, a couple of years after that, a move to the reporting side. After gathering experience in several different FT posts, I became a New York correspondent, then consumer industries editor in London. I became a full-time columnist last year.

What are you doing at work this week?
Working on Friday's column. I also contribute leaders.

What advice would you have for anyone thinking of a career in journalism?
Get something published – if nowhere else, then on the web. And if you're not 100 per cent certain you're going to be a journalist, forget about it. Fortune favours the determined.

The sports report

Most sports reporting is similar to news reporting – it consists of a similar mix of news and features, though there is often a more laid-back atmosphere about the desk. The extra element on newspapers, of course, is the match or race report. Such reports are half news, half feature, but often have a formulaic rhythm of their own: to familiarise yourself with this rhythm, you need to have read a lot of sports reports and, once again, know an extraordinary amount about your field. Knowledge about sports other then football is always a plus.

Be aware that sports reports in national newspapers are written to very tight deadlines: the writer might file some background copy at the beginning of a match, then file other paragraphs in dribs and drabs as the match progresses; parts of the final article will often appear in reverse order to that in which they were written. Although there is a subeditor back at the office pulling it all together, to write like this remains a testing skill – and even experienced hacks are often caught out, as a flurry of late goals appears in the first few paragraphs, followed by a languorous, incongruous account of the scoreless early exchanges. Once again, the only key is to start building your knowledge and experience early.

The column

Many dream of having a column: few get to live their dream. If you want to be a columnist in a newspaper or magazine, you usually need to establish yourself as a journalist or expert in some other field first; no editor will give a half-page of comment each week to an inexperienced hack.

But that doesn't mean you shouldn't start practising. Writing a good column is about finding your voice; so while you are getting started in journalism, why not keep an online journal, or blog, in which you can record your thoughts each day? Sure, there are a lot of bad blogs about – but why not be a good one? Go to Blogger.com and find out how. You'll soon find yourself grappling with the same issues that face columnists everywhere: that is, how much of your private life you should allow the outside world to glimpse; how provocative you should be; how often you should return to your pet subjects; whether you should get involved in arguments with readers who don't take kindly to your point of view. This experience could be invaluable later. When you are happy with what you are writing, you could add parts of your blog to your writing portfolio.

The leader

The leader is the voice of a newspaper or magazine; that part of the publication where the editorial team reveals their position on any given issue. At a small local paper or magazine, the editor or a senior deputy will write the leader themselves; but on a national, there are teams of specialist writers who work with editors to thrash out where the paper stands.

Good leader writing is another difficult skill. It is relatively easy to run a news story saying Something Must Be Done; far harder to sustain an analysis of what in fact should be done, as news or political events change. Accordingly, national leader writers are often a mix of experienced political journalists, who are familiar with the culture of the paper, and intelligent young policy geeks who are destined for careers in political thinktanks. If you are an Oxbridge graduate with good contacts and an encyclopaedic knowledge of foreign policy, it might just be an in – the rest of us will just have to wait our turn.

The freelancer and novelist

Name: **Matthew Lewin**
Current job: **former editor, Hampstead & Highgate Express. Now freelance journalist and novelist.**

What was your first job in journalism?
Trainee "cub" reporter on an evening daily in Johannesburg, South Africa.

How did you get the job?
I applied for a place on the training course.

What did the job involve? What was it like?
It was very disappointing. Not much training, and lots of late night work and attending magistrates courts for days on end. I left.

What were your educational qualifications at the time?
I had a first degree in social anthropology and psychology.

What journalism did you do before starting work?
None.

How did your career progress after your first job?
I moved to a weekly news magazine where I was given much more responsibility and on-the-job training. I later freelanced for the magazine during a year travelling through South America before coming to live permanently in London. I joined the staff of the Ham & High in 1973 and moved up through the ranks becoming news editor then deputy editor and then editor during 1994–2000.

What are you doing at work this week?
I have written two short book reviews for the Guardian, a restaurant review for the Ham & High, an interview piece for the Ham & High on the author of a new book and working on a story about a local man who has found a letter and musical manuscript by the composer Edward Elgar (who lived in Hampstead). I am also working on my fourth novel.

What advice would you have for anyone thinking of a career in journalism?
Think of something else – unless you are really and truly determined that this is what you want to do and prepared to put in the effort. Then get some formal training and proper experience and prepare yourself for the greatest job on earth.

Production

To anyone who has never visited the office of a newspaper or magazine, the production side of the business might seem a mystery. Who puts a publication together? Who keeps the picture archives, designs and lays out pages, and rewrites reporters' carefully crafted copy? What strange power do they wield?

The reply is, of course, that they are many different people – and between them, they are vital to any publication's success. There are the subeditors, or "subs", who edit pages and have day-to-day control over the production process; there are art editors and picture editors, who concentrate on the look and feel; and finally there are production managers, who understand the complex business of getting the whole thing to press. Each of these roles is a career in its own right, but usually only the subeditors are considered part of the "journalistic" hierarchy.

The subeditor

The subs, broadly speaking, are a publication's presentation team. Their role is to take the copy as written by the reporter, and turn it into a product that is accessible to the reader. They edit articles into concise, grammatical and comprehensible English; they craft headlines, picture captions and other page furniture to help guide the reader; and they work with the designer and picture editor to make the page look as it should. This means a good subeditor has an unusual mix of skills: part wordsmith, part designer, part Apple Mac wizard. In all these roles, the key is to be a perfectionist even while working at speed.

Chief among these roles is the **wordsmith's**. No sub will survive long without impeccable spelling and grammar: when an article comes across to you, you need to be able to read it to ensure that it makes unambiguous sense, all the while subbing it into "house style" – the publication's conventions on spellings, capitalisations, italicisation and other grammar points, as laid down in a style guide — for the Guardian's version, see the new publication, The Guardian Stylebook (Guardian Books) or www.guardian.co.uk/styleguide. At this stage, you keep an eagle eye out for potentially serious pitfalls. Is the piece usable, or does it need a rewrite? Is the news angle right? Are the facts correct? As a sub, you might not be writing a news story or a feature from scratch – but you should know what works best. If anything needs to go back to the writer or editor, you need the confidence to raise it – and enough tact to put your point across. Or are there legal problems? You should have read McNae's Essential Law for Journalists, and be prepared to call the lawyer if anything seems amiss.

If all is well, then the piece is ready to be dropped in the page. At this stage, more crafting is needed. Can you cut copy to fit, so it still

Adobe InDesign Desktop publishing program. Originally a design tool; now becoming system of choice for some subs desks, thus superseding Quark.

back bench Senior journalists on a daily newspaper.

byline Name of the reporter, or reporters, on an article.

cap Capital letter.

caption Bit of text describing a picture.

chief sub Your boss.

copy Main text of an article.

coverline Line on the cover of a magazine, to flag up articles and attract the reader. It's a key subbing skill to write one well.

crosshead Words used to break up text. A design thing: often bears only subliminal relation to the narrative sense.

cut To remove part of a story.

deck Horizontal line of words in a headline ("this headline runs to three decks").

endnote Bit at the end of the feature or opinion piece, where you say what the author's credentials are.

flatplan Page-plan of a publication, showing what articles and adverts go where.

font Typeface.

hard copy Copy that's been printed out on to paper.

headline Title of an article. It's a key subbing skill to write one well.

house style A publication's individual take on alternative forms of punctuation and spelling. Usually a combination of common sense, pandering to the target readership and the last chief sub's whim. More important than the law of the land.

kerning Adjustment of horizontal space between two written characters.

lay out (verb) To design a page, deciding what stories to put where.

layout (noun) How a page is designed.

layout sub Sub who is skilled at laying out pages.

leading Adjustment of vertical space between two lines.

mark Correction.

masthead The bit with the title at the top of the front page.

nib News in brief.

orphan First line of a paragraph appearing on the last line of a column of text. Traditionally avoided, because it looks ugly.

PhotoShop (noun) Program for editing images. Impress a chief sub by putting the cap S on a CV.

(verb) To edit a picture. Now almost a generic term.

point size How big the typeface is.

production editor Responsible for everything the chief sub does

proof (noun) Copy of a laid-out page, for corrections.

(verb) To proofread.

pull-out quote (or pullquote) Quote separated from the rest of the text, and made bigger for emphasis.

Quark XPress Desktop publishing program. Threatened by Adobe InDesign.

quote What someone is quoted as having said. Not to be tinkered with.

sans serif Font without little horizontal lines on all the characters. (Like this.)

serif Font with little horizontal lines on all the characters (eg. at the top and bottom of the I).

standfirst Bit below the headline that tells you a bit more about an article. It's a key subbing skill to write one well.

style guide Copy of a publication's house style. Dog-eared and coffee-stained.

tracking Adjustment of overall space between letters in, say, a paragraph. Lazy way to get words to fit; often banned (and then used anyway) by chief subs.

widow Last line of a paragraph appearing on the first line of a column of text. Traditionally avoided, because it looks ugly. Often OK if it runs to full width of column, but check house style.

wob White on black (and often white on any other colour).

reads as well as (or better than) the original? Can you write news headlines that tell the story in a nutshell, and features headlines that sum up the point of the article – all in the tiny space the design allows? Can you write pithy standfirsts, captions, slugs, pull-outs and sells (see glossary) that guide the reader along? You need all these skills to be a sub.

As far as revising pages is concerned, different publications work in different ways – but at some stage you will have to insert corrections made by another journalist, or make such corrections on hard copy (ie paper) yourself. Accordingly, you should learn how to make and read standard proofreading marks. Comprehensive

☑ Get the Job: **subeditor**

Employers

Every national and regional newspaper and magazine, some websites

Before the interview

- Check up on commonly misspelled words
- Read the style guide, if it's publicly available

Skills you need to demonstrate

- Concise, impeccable English
- Accurate eye for factual and legal pitfalls
- Knowledge of common subbing marks and terms
- A flair for headlines and coverlines
- Knowledge of Quark or InDesign, and PhotoShop
- On technical titles, knowledge of the subject matter
- Tact and diplomacy

What to discuss at interview

- Eats, Shoots & Leaves: what do you think of Lynne Truss's book? (And what's your view of s-apostrophe-s?)
- Battle of the software: which do you prefer, Quark or InDesign?

If you're set a subbing test

- Remember to read through the whole article first; you might be tested on your rewriting skills, not just your spelling and punctuation

Questions to ask

- Seen and not heard: how influential are the subs?
- Separate lives: are the subs in the same office as the reporters?
- Clocking off: is there a shift system?
- How much will I be paid?

use of such marks has dwindled with the rise of computers, but knowledge of the most commonly used ones (see below) remains essential.

Sometimes, and particularly on magazines, the page will be laid out by a designer or experienced sub; but on a newspaper or small publication, you might have to lay it out yourself. Either way, you need an **eye for page design**. Design is a complex skill and not generally taught to subs – but as a general rule, elements of the page

---

Commonly used proofing marks

My first day as a freelance subeditor, ~~I have to confess~~ was a bewildering experience.	⁊ omit
I had/left university and, although I would never have admitted it at the time, I didn't	**just** ⅄ insert
know any proofreading marks and I couldn't	⌒ close up
tell one end of Quark/from the other. I was	# space
left to sub the <u>Dulwich News</u> letters page –	**ital/** italic
which I thought was because it was the least important Page to do, but I later realised was	**lc/** lower case
because it was one of the most *challenging*.	**rom/** roman
Cutting a letter to half its length without distorting its meaning/and writing a headline	⟨,⟩ comma
to match, I now realise, is a good way of showing a sub/chief your skills. Fortunately,	**tr/** transpose
I was able to ask another young sub about the rudiments of quark, so my subbing skills	**cap/** cap up
didn't go to waste/Probably because they	⊙ full point
were short-staffed and I was cheap, the chief sub invited me back next day.	**stet/** ignore correction

---

> You should learn how to make and read standard proofreading marks. Comprehensive use of such marks has dwindled with the rise of computers, but knowledge of the most commonly used ones remains essential

should not compete for the reader's attention; it should be clear from the positioning of pictures and size of the fonts, for example, where the reader is to look first. You will need diplomacy when working with art editors and designers, who generally think that journalists don't understand the first thing about good design – and with a few exceptions, are probably right.

All this is happening, of course, within a **desktop publishing system** that you need to be able to use. Traditionally, this has been Quark XPress (or, at larger companies, its big brother production system, QPS), but increasingly publishers are turning to Adobe InDesign for its "integrated" approach to pictures and other design features. As things stand, you need to be expert in both these programs – plus Adobe PhotoShop, which is used for editing pictures. Ideally, you should go on a course to learn them: but courses are expensive, so you might well be able to pick up the basics when on work experience or at a student paper or magazine. Either way, make sure you learn the keyboard shortcuts, which can cut the time you spend on an article by as much as a half.

If you think that is a lot to do in one job, you would be right. Partly because of this, and because subbing is often considered unglamorous, publishers often complain that good subeditors are hard to recruit. Of course, if you *do* have the skills – and don't mind the fact that other journalists' bylines are appearing on articles that you may have substantially rewritten – this can work in your favour, and you can consider it as a good way to get into writing, or as a long-term career in itself.

The subbing culture

If you do decide to be a sub, you need to be prepared for the culture of the subs desk. This is not the antiquated, smoke-filled bastion of bachelordom it once was – but it can retain some of that feel. It is usually an informal, but studious, place to work – apart from the odd gaggle of people who crowd around a desk as deadlines approach, the atmosphere is often one of intense industry. Perhaps as a result, subs also often have quite a geeky image, particularly among reporters, that can be hard to live down. They also remain almost exclusively deskbound – so if you want a job that involves getting out of the office every once in a while, you should consider another career.

On some newspapers and magazines, subs can be quite distant from editorial decision-making. Some people would be frustrated by this; others actively seek it. Generally speaking, subs have more power at national tabloid newspapers, where presentation is considered a vital part of the editorial process, and news stories can be almost totally rewritten to suit; national broadsheets are more reporter-led culture; while magazines tend to have fewer subs, but a greater emphasis on art editing and design.

A recent trend among local newspaper groups has to been to "centralise" the production process among neighbouring – or even not so neighbouring – newspapers. Subs fear that in such offices, it is less easy to communicate with reporters and editors, and editorial standards can fall.

Subs are usually paid more than reporters of equivalent experience, often – thanks to a prevalent "shift" culture at many offices – while putting in fewer hours.

Up the career ladder

Usually, the successful sub will go on to be a **chief sub**. As a chief sub, your role is to manage the subs desk, assigning pages to each member of the team, and booking in freelance cover. As a chief sub you are the linchpin of the production process: you will get involved in the

The freelance sub

Name: **Jon Crampin**
Current job: **freelance subeditor, for Sunday Times, Man United matchday programme, FourFourTwo, and African Soccer**

What was your first job in journalism?
Eight years ago, I started as a reporter on a transport magazine, Local Transport Today. It was a subscription-only industry magazine run by a small publishing company in south London.

How did you get the job?
It was advertised in the media jobs pages of the Guardian (always a good place to start looking!) I had an interest in the subject, and at the time was working as an office assistant at Centaur Publishing based in central London.

What did the job involve? What was it like?
It mainly involved reporting on news in the transport industry and writing features for the magazine. There were also press conferences and news briefings with the prominent government figures at the time, including Brian Mawhinney, Steven Norris and John Prescott, which could be quite entertaining. It was a fairly small editorial team, which meant some late press nights, but on the up side, there was plenty of opportunity to share tasks. I found myself being drawn towards rewriting my colleagues' work – that's when my subediting career began!

What were your educational qualifications at the time?
I left university with a degree in politics and economics. When I got the job a few years later, I had done a few postgrad courses such as desktop publishing and could demonstrate good use of English through a couple of years I spent working as an English teacher abroad, but I hadn't really done any media-specific courses.

What journalism did you do before starting work?
Very little. If I was starting out on the career ladder now, I certainly wouldn't wait for a lucky break into journalism. Whether it's unpaid work, such as writing for a university paper, a club newsletter or football fanzine, or work experience at a newspaper, it's important to get out there and get media experience. A few years ago, I was responsible for organising work experience at a football magazine; naturally it was a popular place to work and places were limited – applicants who already had relevant experience generally stood out a mile, and were far more likely to be offered a place.

How did your career progress after your first job?
Though I began as a writer, I soon realised my main skills and interests lay in putting the magazine together, including sub-editing copy. After three years on LTT, I moved to become production editor on Autosport.

I'd been there for about a year, when a similar role came up on a monthly football magazine in the same publishing company. I was delighted to get a job working on a magazine about my first love, football. In four years there, I built up enough contacts in sports media to take the plunge and go freelance. Since doing so, my job has become a lot more varied, and I've been lucky enough to have taken on a range of different subbing roles, including the Sunday Times sports desk, Man United's matchday programme United Review, African Soccer and UEFA Champions mag, while still doing occasional writing for magazines such as FourFourTwo.

production process at an early stage, attending features and news meetings to help decide how commissioned articles could be best presented; and you will check each page before it passes, with particular attention to the front page or cover. Chief subs are usually calm and unflappable, but will still get a "buzz" from putting the last few pages of a publication to bed.

Having been a chief sub is good experience for working at an editorial level. Perhaps because of their experience of rewriting features and coming up with ways to present them, former chief subs sometimes make the sideways move into features editing.

Other chief subs will often either go freelance (see below, and page 78) or apply for a sub's job at a bigger publication, such as a national newspaper, where pay rates are higher.

Many publications have a **production editor**, either in addition to or instead of the chief sub. This is a similar but more senior role: the production editor will be responsible for everything the chief sub does, and may also handle production management issues.

Working as a freelance sub

Because subbing is such a skills-based role – either you have the requisite skills, or you don't – freelancing can be a very good way to land yourself a job. Many subs desks use freelances on a regular basis, so when jobs come up, they may offer it to an established freelance without even conducting an open interview. You need to be aware of this.

If you are job-seeking as a freelance sub, some other tips can be useful. Take the house style guide home with you and read it on the evening of your first day: it can be difficult to remember every point to start with, but the extra effort will help you to impress. Conversely, don't be discouraged if you think you are making a lot of style errors in the first few days; this is normal, just as long as they are style errors and not outright editorial mistakes. Keep asking questions and you should be fine.

Next, don't forget the importance of headline-writing. Ask the chief sub what kind of headline is required on each article: otherwise you could waste a lot of time working on a witty pun when a more direct effort is needed – or vice versa. A lot of your headlines might be changed to start with; this is only to be expected as you gain experience. Always compare your efforts to the final version, and try to work out why the chief sub thought it was better.

Finally, it can be helpful to keep a portfolio, in a similar way to a writer. Many subs keep photocopies of their best headlines, standfirsts and layout work; send them along every time you apply for a freelance gig or a job. Just because there is no byline on your work, it doesn't mean you can't take the credit.

What are you doing at work this week?

I'm currently dividing my time between subbing features for United Review and UEFA Champions. I'm also the editor of the World Football and Reviews sections of FourFourTwo, which involves commissioning people to write news and reviews. On Saturday, I'll be working for the Sunday Times to subedit their football match reports. Each sub gets two or three matches, and a tight deadline to do it in – the first editions of the Sunday papers have to be completed by 6pm, just over an hour after the final whistle has blown.

What advice would you have for anyone thinking of a career in journalism?

Don't underestimate the importance of having an interest or knowledge in the subject matter, and try to get as much relevant experience as possible early on. Not everyone is cut out to be a top writer, so it's worth bearing in mind that there are plenty of other rewarding careers in journalism out there, whether it's writing, subbing, design or production.

Production management

There is more to editorial production than journalism and design. In larger newspapers or magazines, there is at least one person whose job it is to manage day-to-day production processes, such as flatplan management and negotiating with repro houses and the printworks. They may be a non-journalist production manager or executive, or the job may be done by the production editor.

One of the most important of these roles, on a print publication, is to manage the "flatplan"; that is, the plan of the publication on which

The production supremo

Name: **David Marsh**
Current job: **assistant editor (production), the Guardian and Observer**

What were your educational qualifications at the time?
Eight O-levels, three A-levels (A, A, B), 2:1 in history from Sheffield University. I later got an MA at UCL in English language and linguistics.

What journalism did you do before starting work?
Worked extensively for Darts, Sheffield student newspaper.

What was your first job in journalism?
Trainee reporter, Kent Messenger Group.

How did you get the job?
I applied for their graduate training scheme.

What did the job involve? What was it like?
Reporting for several local weekly papers, then moving on to the evening paper. It was fantastic training and most of what I know about journalism I learned in Kent during those years.

How did your career progress after your first job?
Worked my way up KM Group, becoming news editor of the evening paper, then moved away and became editor of the Redditch Indicator series in Worcestershire. Another editorship followed, before I joined the Independent as part of the launch team in 1986. I stayed there 10 years, becoming night editor and production editor, then worked for South China Morning Post in Hong Kong, returned to UK as sub on the FT, finally joining the Guardian in 1996 and have held a number of senior jobs here.

What are you doing at work this week?
Getting the paper, and its various sections, out on time. Putting the finishing touches to the extended and updated style guide, which is being published in book form for sale to the general public next month. Working out how we can publish a sport tabloid, and G2, and the G3s, during Euro 2004 and the Olympics this summer. Attending numerous meetings to plan and organise stuff. Sorting out various subbing problems including rotas, training, recruitment, pastoral stuff. Giving a talk to Sheffield University journalism postgraduate students. And lots more.

What advice would you have for anyone thinking of a career in journalism?
Don't be discouraged when people try to put you off. Don't try to specialise too soon – be open-minded. Read the Guardian stylebook and follow its excellent advice.

all adverts – and consequently, all the editorial space that has to be filled – are clearly marked. To do this, you need to be an intelligent and effective organiser, who is calm under pressure: creating a flatplan that fulfils the wishes not only of both the ad sales departments but also the editorial team can be akin to doing a crossword puzzle, with tact and diplomacy thrown in. Calmness is also essential as you negotiate with the outside agencies who put a publication together, such as printers and repro houses; they might let you down now and again, but you should know when to be firm and when to exercise some give and take. If your editorial team misses a deadline, you might well need the printer or repro house to get you out of a hole.

As a production executive, you will need to be expert in whatever desktop publishing software the subs desk uses – normally Quark or Adobe InDesign, plus Adobe PhotoShop.

Further reading

McNae's Essential Law for Journalists

Online journalism

Dotcom, dotgone, dotbackagain. After the collapse of dozens of internet ventures in 2000 and 2001 which cost hundreds of online journalists their jobs, confidence in the web is back. In 2003, according to the Advertising Association, internet advertising was again the fastest-growing media sector, and was again bigger than cinema advertising in terms of total spend. Since 2004, according to Ofcom, more British homes now have internet access than do not. With money starting to come back in, online journalism is once again a serious career option for the would-be journalist – and as a career starting-point, a viable alternative to a news agency, magazine or local paper.

Most online journalism is similar to print journalism. At an online news service, for example, the tried and tested "inverted pyramid" story (page 24) remains the primary method of telling the news: this is as true of broadcasters' websites as it is of those run by newspapers and magazines. In other words, online editors are looking for similar writing skills to their print counterparts, with one proviso – on the

---

↑ Glossary of terms

banner Advert on the top of a web page.

blog Online web journal. Short for "web log" or "weblog".

cascading stylesheets Technique for designing web pages, in which you make a file with a defined "style" and let the other pages refer to that. Cuts download time.

dHTML Dynamic HTML. Allows exciting things to happen when you mouse over a word.

download To get a file from somewhere else on to your computer, via the internet.

Flash Program used to view design-heavy content.

gif Type of picture file, most useful for images that include text.

home page (often homepage). Front page of a website.

HTML Hypertext mark-up language. Language used to write most web pages.

JavaScript Web language, often used to launch other windows.

JPeg Type of picture file most commonly used on the web.

navigation Page furniture used to guide the user around the website.

page impressions Number of times someone views a page on the internet.

PDA Personal digital assistant. A hand-held computer.

pop-under Advert that appears under a page you're surfing, so you only notice it when you close the window you're using. Sneaky.

pop-up Little square advert that "pops up" at you as you surf the web.

post To add a comment to a blog.

pulldown Text menu that you activate by pressing on a little down arrow.

traffic Amount of users who use a website.

upload To send a file out toward the internet; hence, to add an article to a website.

URL Web address.

Webmonkey Useful resource with HTML tips and tricks (including a character list).

web, it is even more important to be concise. On a computer screen, only a small amount of text can be seen at one time; in an email or on a handheld (PDA), there is even less. Tell a good news story in a few words, and you will thrive in online journalism – and, of course, anywhere else.

The web offers further challenges. There is the opportunity to offer breaking news, in much the same way as 24-hour radio and television broadcasters. So not only do you need to be able to write to deadline: you need be able to write multiple updates to multiple stories, all due as soon as possible, and faster than your rivals. So you need to be able to handle and prioritise many different tasks at the same time; and you might well be expected to work nights.

There is also a greater incidence of "background" journalism – forms of writing that do appear in newspapers or magazines, but less frequently because of limitations in space. British news websites carry a high proportion of profiles, timelines, press reviews, reactions in quotes, galleries, original speeches (subbed into house style), interactive guides, minute-by-minute match reports – the list goes on. If a bomb goes off in Tel Aviv, for example, you could provide links to a history of the Middle East crisis, maps of the region, even off-site links to Ha'aretz and the Jerusalem Post. For the journalist, that means you are not only reporting, but you are also engaged in a perpetual process of contextualisation. It's more powerful than just supplying a potted update in the last few pars of your story – and it's why so many websites charge for the use of their archived news.

From your point of view, that leads to a problem that is increasingly true of journalists, but especially online: what with all that Googling you're doing, you do tend to get tied to your desk. You might not even get the bylines you feel you deserve for the work you're putting in. This is a fact of life. Most news websites have grown out of existing print and broadcast newsgathering operations; these teams are extremely good at their jobs, and don't necessarily need their own online arm to show them how it's done. Possible result: the print team gets the high-profile interviews and trips out of the office, while the web team stays at their desk to write the sidebars, cuttings jobs and the updates from the wires, that make the web product the wonderful thing it is. For a young reporter starting on the web, it might mean you have to work even harder to get the reporting, door-knocking or feature writing experience you need to progress.

But there are other forms of expression that can compensate. The web gives you the chance to explore more innovative forms of journalism: things that a newspaper or a broadcaster couldn't hope to provide. The Guardian, for example, was the first British newspaper to have its own blog: using similar technology, an online journalist might be able to travel to a set-piece conference or event and cover it from their PDA or laptop almost in real time. Editors might turn to the web team to offer this kind of coverage. Readers would get regular and frequent updates that they couldn't get from the traditional news report; and with the help of the existing site, they get more context than they would

The online journalist

Name: **Jane Perrone**
Current job: **assistant news editor, Guardian Unlimited**

What was your first job in journalism?

As a reporter at a local paper, the Citizen in Milton Keynes, after a year as a researcher working on an online journalism project at a university.

How did you get the job?

I'd done work experience at the paper during my NCTJ postgraduate course.

What did the job involve?

I worked as the sole reporter for an edition that covered a town, in competition with two other newspapers. I did everything from reviewing plays and working with photographers to court reporting and local politics. It was hard work but I did get the splash every week, and it was interesting to be in the unusual position in the UK regional press of having two other papers to beat to the scoops.

Fortunately I worked in the same office as the journalists working for another title of the same parent company. There was a generally friendly atmosphere, enhanced by the fact that most of the reporters were a similar age to me, although the subs were a more mature bunch. The only bad things about the job were the appallingly low pay and the fact that after a couple of years, the subject matter tended to become a little monotonous and the tight focus on a small geographical area frustrating.

What were your educational qualifications at the time?

I had an undergraduate degree in English literature, a masters degree in mass communication which I took in the US (a combination of media theory and practice), and the postgraduate NCTJ. Which, considering I could have been earning more working in Tesco than at a local paper, was galling.

What journalism did you do at university?

Very little at undergraduate level, but I got involved with a lot of journalism while studying for my masters degree in the US: I wrote for the campus newspaper (as a reporter and later as a columnist), I was news editor of the campus radio station and I wrote for the university's magazine. It was invaluable in helping me decide what type of journalism I wanted to do, and great fun too.

How did your career progress after your first job?

I got my job as a reporter at Guardian Unlimited.

What are you doing at work this week?

Editing front pages; commissioning content; writing the Guardian Unlimited weblog; writing stories about technology; helping to manage a team of reporters and subs.

What advice would you have for anyone thinking of a career in journalism or online journalism?

Don't bother doing an undergraduate degree in journalism: it's preferable to get your degree in a subject that could be a valuable skill or develop into a specialism, such as politics, a foreign language or technology. Stack up as much work experience as you can and read as many newspapers as you can get your hands on: it's amazing the number of students I've met who claim to want a career in journalism who have never picked up a copy of Private Eye, do not know which newspaper Julie Burchill writes for and cannot identify their favourite columnist.

> Stack up as much work experience as you can and read as many newspapers as you can get your hands on

Jane Perrone

from the TV. With the rise in the number of broadband connections, you might even become half-writer, half-broadcaster: doing video voxpops or even a short piece to camera, for example, to supplement your written story. Wireless internet access from a laptop might soon liberate many online journalists from their desks altogether. The possibilities are limitless, and as ever it falls to the pushy and most innovative journalists to break the boundaries where they can.

That brings us to the third and fourth main challenges for online journalists: technology and money. They come together, of course, because technology costs money – and since the bottom fell out of the technology sector in 2001, there hasn't been a lot of money about. Despite a recent upturn in revenues, funds for online journalism are still tight; and that means not only are journalists generally less well

The online reporter

Name: **Polly Curtis**
Current job: **reporter, EducationGuardian.co.uk**

What was your first job in journalism?
Freelance TV researcher.

How did you get the job?
I hassled the director I wanted to work with until they gave me a job.

What did the job involve? What was it like?
It involved researching ideas for documentaries, setting up interviews and planning shoots.

What were your educational qualifications at the time?
I had a degree and postgraduate training in journalism.

What journalism did you do before starting work?
I did work experience, worked on the student paper and won a Guardian Student Media award for travel in the year that I graduated.

How did your career progress after your first job?
I spent a year working in TV while freelancing for magazines and newspapers. But I wanted something more permanent and felt I should chose between TV and writing. I started doing shifts on the Guardian Unlimited, which eventually turned into a staff job.

What are you doing at work this week?
This week I am writing daily news for EducationGuardian.co.uk – I have to come up with around six stories a day spanning the university and schools sectors. I'll attend a meeting for the Education Guardian supplement to plan ideas for next week, and I'm writing the cover piece for the Guardian's annual university guide supplement

What advice would you have for anyone thinking of a career in journalism?
Blinker yourself to the competition and make sure it's what you really want.

paid than their print and TV counterparts, but headcounts are lower and editorial budgets are slimmer too. Conversely, when headcounts are low and editorial budgets are slim, journalists need that much more technical knowledge to land themselves a job. Online reporters bound to their desks as they are, might then find themselves doing more than a little production on the side.

So what technical knowledge do you need? Basic HTML and web skills are a minimum, and it's a rare online journalist who doesn't have rudimentary PhotoShop as well. That should do it if you just want to write. On the production side, basic audio- and video-editing skills are helpful – essential if the site you work for is a broadcaster – and if you're on a newspaper website, it's useful to know your way around Quark and InDesign. Better PhotoShop skills are also needed on the production side. Knowledge of how to build a basic website is also good to have, even if you don't have a site yourself – the BBC has been known to test for such knowledge at interview. If you don't know what cascading stylesheets are, tap "Webmonkey" into Google and find out now.

More than ever, though, writers and subs in online journalism will have similar levels of technical skills – which makes it a good career if you're one of those journalists who is lost in the career no man's land between reporter and sub. It is a common breed: the journalist with the perfect grammar and spelling who can't bear to spend all day every day reading other people's stuff, but whose writing is hampered by the perpetual need to self-edit. For these hybrid hacks, a job on a website might suit. There's enough production to please your sense of order, but enough writing to quench your creative lust.

Finally, it's impossible not to mention that old journalistic bete noir: age. Perhaps because of the relatively low pay, perhaps because of the technological skills required, or perhaps because of discrimination, most people in online journalism are young. The result is that online is quickly becoming an alternative route into the industry, next to the local paper and the journalism course – with the exception that, unlike at the local papers, there aren't any older hacks moaning in the corridors about the breaks they never had. Yet. Looking forward 50 years, it's tempting to think that some of today's young web go-getters will be in the top jobs at whatever newspaper-cum-TV online behemoth is ruling the media world; tempting also to view their current 20-something colleagues, slumped in the corners over their antiquated 2005 Apple Macs, whingeing. Aaah, them were the days.

Resources

dotjournalism
www.journalism.co.uk

Online Journalism Review
www.ojr.org

The jobs : **Section 2**

Art & design

Art and design are vital to the success of any newspaper or magazine. It includes the designer or art editor, who will help establish and maintain a publication's visual identity, to help differentiate it from its rivals; and often picture editors, illustrators and photographers, who together add an essential element to that identity: the pictures. These people work together as part of the same team – but they follow very different career routes.

Designer

As a designer, you are one of the most important people on a newspaper or magazine. It is your job to work out the look and feel of each page of a publication, both to attract as much of the target audience as you can, and to establish the publication's unique "brand". To do this, you will usually design templates and styles to which the production team can operate; and on more complex features, you will design individual pages yourself. This means the job is varied: it involves periods of strategic thinking, particularly when you work on a launch or redesign; but there is also the regular creative challenge of putting each issue of the publication together.

The tools of your trade are text, pictures, space, and the computer software with which to manipulate them on the page. In Quark or InDesign, for example, a single paragraph of text can be in one of hundreds of different fonts, scripts and sizes; it can be tracked, kerned and leaded; and it can be any colour you like. By changing these settings, you establish a style for different types of page furniture, such as headlines ("Greeks win Euro 2004"), standfirsts ("Do Greeks really make the best lovers? Our roving correspondent reports") or sells ("2004 ways to drive your man wild") – so that when the subeditors come to write them, they know exactly how they should look as they try to find something that fits. As far as illustrations are concerned, you design graphics, and may also commission illustrations; and you work with the picture editor to select the best photographs and, using Adobe PhotoShop, get them looking as attractive as you can.

Design is of course a complex and individual thing, but some principles are worth mentioning. First, you should think of the reader at all times – in newspapers, this means not only choosing the right fonts and breaking up text with pictures, but also making it absolutely clear which part of the page should be read first. Similarly design has to marry with the kind of publication you work on: if you work for a medical publication which uses phrases like "ultra II-beta inhibitors" in a typical headline, for example, there is no point designing short headlines in snazzy, colourful fonts. Finally, a good design is a living thing: it needs to be ordered enough to maintain

A good design is a living thing: it needs to be ordered enough to maintain readers' familiarity with the brand, but flexible enough to be tweaked as circumstances dictate

readers' familiarity with the brand, but flexible enough to be tweaked as circumstances dictate. Best to let the design control the rules, not the other way around.

The most important attributes are, of course, design ability and technical skills. Design ability is about good visualisation, and is to a certain extent innate; software skills can be learned on an undergraduate, postgraduate or training course, after which you can try to get work experience, freelance, or apply for a job as a **design assistant** or **assistant designer**.

The most senior designer is sometimes known as the **art editor**.

Web design

Web design is once again a flourishing area, after the dotcom crash of 2000 and 2001. The general design principles are, of course, similar to print; but there are also specific challenges, because a website will typically carry a huge amount of information but only a tiny "front page", if you count the screen area before the reader starts to scroll down. So you need to be even more of a technical wizard: you should certainly know HTML, Adobe Illustrator and Adobe PhotoShop, and be familiar with the latest web authoring techniques; and you might be expected to use other software such as Flash or DreamWeaver. Whether you are considered a "pure" designer or a "technical" designer, though, will often vary from site to site. To get into the profession, the best way forward is to spend as much time as possible designing websites – either at home, or by doing a web design course.

Picture editor

Picture editing is partly a creative role, but is mostly organisational. As a picture editor, you are responsible for sourcing and managing the thousands of pictures that your newspaper and magazine uses each year.

The first part of the job, sourcing the pictures, is perhaps the fun bit. If budgets allow, this means using commercial photographic and picture libraries, most of which keep electronic databases; it could also mean commissioning freelance photographers to cover a story or do a shoot. To do the job, you will need to have a good sense of what pictures will work and what won't; you need to be able to use Adobe PhotoShop to tweak pictures into shape; and you need to know copyright law.

The organisational side of the job is the painstaking part. Any publication that has been around a while will have thousands of pictures lurking in filing cabinets, on CDs or in computer databases; as a picture editor, you must ensure these can be accessed quickly by journalists and designers. This means each photograph the publication stores – whether print, slide or digital – needs to be marked with its date, subject matter and copyright status: without

The picture editor

Name: **Sian Parry**
Current job: **picture editor, Red magazine**

What was your first job in newspapers or magazines?
I joined Red as a picture assistant.

How did you get the job?
I saw the job advertised in MediaGuardian.

What did the job involve? What was it like?
It involved assisting the picture editor with all aspects of the running of a picture desk, as well as all the admin, print orders and returns. I got involved pretty quickly with picture research for specific features as well as looking after regular sections like art and entertainment and fashion and beauty news pages.

What were your educational qualifications at the time?
I had nine O-levels, three A-levels, a BA in history of design from Manchester Metropolitan University, and had done a one-year postgrad course in works of art at Sotheby's, the auctioneers.

What experience did you have before starting work?
Before my magazine break I had worked for three years as senior researcher at the British Film Institute stills posters and designs collection. This meant that I was undertaking specific picture research projects for various magazines, newspapers and books, as well as documentary and TV programmes. When I decided I wanted to become a picture editor, I started taking freelance research jobs to gain more experience working on titles rather than from a library angle.

How did your career progress after your first job?
I was promoted to deputy picture editor after a year, and picture editor two years later. I have been head of the department for a year now, and manage a deputy and a freelance assistant.

What are you doing at work this week?
This week I'm finding a London location and getting production under way for a celebrity cover shoot (can't say who!). As well as big productions, I've got to organise a one-hour shoot slot in a hotel room with an American musician, a fashion and beauty makeover shoot with real people, a "this life" at-home interiors shoot and lots of other bits too numerous to mention!

What advice would you have for anyone thinking of a career in picture editing?
You have to really love magazines and photography, buy all the magazines you like, make tears of the features and images that you like and see why they really work. Take a note of all the photographers you admire and follow their work. If you can, get some work experience on a picture desk: nothing beats hands-on learning. Gaining experience in a picture library can be a way to get into pictures, but the crossover from library researcher to picture desk is often a very competitive one.

Get the Job: **picture editor**

Employers

Every national newspaper, most regionals and magazines

Before the interview

- Read the last three months' editions of the publication and its competitors; look at the pictures used, and write down what you think works and what could be improved
- Type the publication name into a Google image search – you never know what might crop up

What you need to demonstrate at interview

- Love of pictures
- Experience of picture research, often at a library
- Knowledge of picture libraries, photographers and resources
- Knowledge of different picture file formats
- Willingness to work hard
- Knowledge of computer databases and filing systems
- Tact and diplomacy
- Problem-solving skills

What to discuss at interview

- London loves: what's on at the Photographers' Gallery?

Questions to ask

- Money talks: what's the typical picture budget per page?
- Front row: what's the story behind a recent cover you like?
- How much will I be paid?

> Take a note of all the photographers you admire and follow their work
>
> Sian Parry

the first two, it is of course worthless; and without the last, an angry photographer or illustrator will soon be on the phone. To be a good picture editor, it is therefore essential to be equally on terms with the filing cabinet and the computer database.

A job as an **assistant picture editor** on a small title is the usual way in.

Photographer

With the possible exception of news reporting, photography must be one of publishing's toughest jobs. First up, there's also the problem of reputation: press photographers in particular are held in low esteem, mainly because of the antics of the tabloid paparazzi. Then there is the fact that there are hardly any staff jobs any more: almost all photographers these days are freelances. This means you have to

The jobs : **Section 2**

The photographer

Name: **Murdo Macleod**
Current job: **freelance photographer**

What was your first paid job as a photographer?
Photographing geese supposedly defending whisky for the Observer.

How did you get the job?
I did a tour of London desks just as the Observer fell out with the person they used in my geographical area.

What did the job involve?
It was a human interest "stand alone" photo-op cooked up by a desperate PR seeking publicity for a whisky brand. It was a new and puzzling experience for me as it did not fit with what I then imagined journalism to be. But it was fine – it got used and I got paid.

What were your qualifications at the time?
O-levels; a couple of highers and a three-year diploma in photography from Napier College, Edinburgh.

What photography did you do before starting work?
I taught myself from books as a teenager as a hobby. I was a crofter's son on a rural Hebridean island, and photographed my surroundings using a Soviet camera and enlarger.

How did your career progress after your first job?
Slowly. I was unambitious and clueless. I shaped up a bit once I had a lovely partner and children, and now I work for the Guardian, the Observer and various magazines.

What are you doing at work this week?
So far: peat cutting in the Hebrides; last small boatyard on the Clyde; Glasgow plastics factory explosion; D-Day veteran, James Gibson; Frank Gehry-designed building, Dundee; Michael Howard Tory leader speech to Scottish conference … then opening a bottle of wine.

What advice would you have for anyone thinking of a career as a photographer?
I only know about newspaper and magazine work, but remember: even if you are rubbish – like me – you can succeed if you want to. A passion and a desire are what you need. If you are young and unsure how to proceed, college is the route. If you are lean, mean and dogged, then maybe try to get work with regional and local papers or agencies. Research what your view will be about the copyright in the photos you take, as this has a bearing on how you will be employed.

Do not be discouraged. Study the competition closely and look at a lot of pictures, even from years gone by. If you are freelance, follow the money unless you love being poor. Remember everyone is just trying to get through the day, so be nice but do not be a doormat. Good pictures talk for themselves so concentrate on getting them.

Organisational infrastructure is valuable. If freelance, get VAT registered; get a good accountant that does book-keeping rather than one who likes to do lunch. Avoid investment and business shortcuts. Always agree terms with clients in advance. Always get a receipt.

Lastly, when you get a good bylined show in a respected publication – spread it out on the passenger seat and take it for a drive round town.

train yourself (on a course such as a City & Guilds), pay for your own expensive equipment, compete for work, network, build up your portfolio, fill in tax returns, and combat wage deflation – all while you are still getting yourself on your feet, with a significant chance that you won't make it in the end. Unless photography is something you love doing, you are unlikely to succeed.

There are two main types of photography "job" for which you might be paid. The first is the news story or shift, where you take pictures for a newspaper – with or without a journalist, on the instruction of the news, features or picture editor. Apart from being able to take photographs, you will need to be mobile and flexible, good at following the brief, have a rapport with the general public, and to work to tight deadlines; but above all, it is important to realise that the job is really photojournalism. Thinking creatively will often give you an unusual photographic angle on a news story; thinking journalistically will get you in the right place at the right time when the photograph is the news story. The better your communication with the reporters you are working with, of course, the better the photographs you are likely to take.

The second type is the shoot, when you might photograph a public figure or celebrity for a newspaper or magazine; in this type of work, the main focus is on designing a picture that suits the mood that either the artist and publication are trying to project – though these two might be entirely different. Apart from technical knowledge about photography and lighting, it is again important to maintain a rapport with the subject and work to deadlines.

Photographers do tend to pick particular kinds of work and stick to it, developing relationships with editors and picture editors in either the newspaper or magazine worlds. For this reason, it can be useful, especially when starting out, to develop a niche. If you are known as the "golf photographer" or the best photographer in a particular part of the country, for example, then that is a good reason for an editor to call you; build up a good series of stock photos, meanwhile, and you have a photographic library business as well.

Finally, to survive as a photographer, you should also have a good understanding of copyright law; or at least, the fact that copyright in a picture rests with you unless you sign it away. For this reason, publishers and picture agencies will often try to claim rights in any work you do for them; resist this if you can, as it will hit your earnings in the long run.

> " Do not be discouraged. Study the competition closely and look at a lot of pictures, even from years gone by
> Murdo Macleod

Broadcast journalism

So you want to be a broadcast journalist? Congratulations: you've been seduced by the most demanding, most competitive part of the media there is. Wherever you want to work – in radio or TV, local journalism or national, for a commercial broadcaster or for the BBC – it will be a tough challenge for you to break in.

Why is broadcast journalism so hard to get into? Because broadcast journalism is really two jobs: journalism, and broadcasting. This means that not only do you have to be brilliant at finding and researching stories – a people person, in other words, with an insatiable curiosity about the world you live in, and a growing contacts book of everyone you've ever come across at work – but you also need to be a good storyteller, who is comfortable on air or on camera, and can find the language, sound and pictures to get your points across. Most people find it hard enough to do one well; but to do both takes rare talent – not to mention the commitment and determination to do it all again the next day and the day after that. Little wonder that editors and producers are picky about those who apply.

Ways in

If you want to get on in broadcast journalism, your first major goal should be to find a job as a **reporter**. This is because most production in broadcast journalism is done by the people who find the stories themselves – so there is no separate journalistic "production route" other than becoming a radio researcher or similar (see radio production). The traditional way to start off is as a reporter in local radio; this is probably still the best grounding for a career in TV, as it gives you the chance to get the broadest possible experience as early as possible in your career. Other entry points these days include 24-hour news channels and news agencies; and of course many broadcast journalists are in fact experienced newspaper reporters.

To get yourself that coveted reporter's job, you have two main options: you can find work experience, and you can do a course accredited by the BJTC (Broadcast Journalism Training Council). Of these, only the work experience is absolutely essential: editors and producers are looking for signs that you have been in a broadcast environment before, and can also demonstrate your passion and commitment to radio or TV. To maximise your chances of getting work experience, the best thing to do is start small: hospital radio is the traditional starting point, but in recent years there has been a marked increase in the number of student and community radio stations too. You could also apply for a placement at a BBC local radio station (see www.bbc.co.uk/jobs); but remember, the larger the broadcaster, the greater the competition, so the more formal the process you will normally have to get through. See page 73 for how to get the best out of work experience when you get it.

A BJTC course also comes highly recommended, not only because it teaches you basic broadcast journalism skills, but because it will help you get work experience. There is a wide range of courses available: turn to page 205 of this book to have a flick through what is on offer, and to page 74 for a guide to getting the best out of it. Remember that new courses are always appearing: City University, for example, started a "current affairs journalism" course in 2002, for students who want to produce more in-depth, analytical reports. Whichever course you choose, make sure it covers enough of the basic vocational skills that you think you will need.

There is also a highly competitive BBC broadcast journalist trainee scheme.

Radio reporting

Although radio and TV reporting are very different worlds, they share important common ground. Most of the basic skills you need to be a reporter will enable you to get by in both – so if you want to be a TV reporter, you should certainly read this section too.

The first skill you need in any local radio job – and indeed, when applying for any job in journalism – is to understand the needs of the audience. So you need to be **steeped in media**. So keep up to date: you need to be someone who reads all the local newspapers and catches all the local news bulletins; this way you will know what issues are exercising local people most. Make a point of recording all the different local radio bulletins in your area; that way you will get a sense of who the typical listener to each programme is. Follow the national press too: many story ideas that you come up with may be local takes on issues of national concern.

In order to initiate and follow up story ideas, you also need good **research skills**. You should know how to use wire services, cuttings files, libraries, the internet and more, so that you are reading not just today's news but the archives of what has gone before. Even more importantly, you need to be constantly building personal contacts, be they on the phone, over lunch or in the pub: so keep a contacts book, and keep it backed up. Remember everyone is a potential contact; whether they are a friend of a friend, or someone a colleague may know. You can buy the latest copy of the MediaGuardian Media Directory, which lists 6,000 of the everyday phone numbers that journalists and researchers need. A BJTC course may also be helpful with contacts, as it gives you an overview of how public life works, and which public officials do what.

One of the most important skills you need in local radio reporting is the ability to **conduct an interview**. Before you get any job, you should be well practised at interviewing using simple equipment such as a portable microphone and digital recorder. This could be done over the phone, but people tend to open up more if you have time to interview them in person. Before conducting any interview, though, you should

The radio reporter

Name: **Jonathan Swingler**
Current job: **reporter, BBC Radio Cleveland, on board the BBC Bus**

What was your first job in broadcasting?
The first time I ever got paid for hanging about a radio station was at Scot FM. I'd been sent out to report on anticapitalist protestors kicking up a fuss on the streets of Edinburgh. So what did I find? Nothing. But as I was about to phone the editor, the bomb squad were kind enough to turn up and close off the main street. One of the shops had received a suspicious package and so within a few minutes I was doing a live report on the lunchtime news programme. Looking back on it I probably sounded a bit overexcited – a good imitation of Alan Partridge on speed. Of course the "bomb" turned out to be nothing.

How did you get the job?
I'd done some work experience so I'd been given a few paid shifts. Working freelance is a little like treading water, but it does give you the opportunity to work in a few different places.

What did the job involve? What was it like?
I'd only worked a few shifts there. At the same time I managed to get a bit of freelance work at BBC Radio Scotland, which was all good experience.

What were your educational qualifications at the time?
I was doing a politics degree at Edinburgh University so it wasn't anything specifically aimed at broadcast news. After the freelance work I did a postgraduate course in journalism at Cardiff University.

What experience did you have before starting work?
I mucked about on student publications for a while. It was a good laugh interviewing bands playing at the student union. I had no formal training at first but you quickly pick up skills on the job.

How did your career progress after your first job?
During my postgraduate course I worked as a reporter for BBC Radio Newcastle, and after that I worked as a TV reporter for Tyne Tees Television. I was then offered a job on the BBC Bus at BBC Radio Cleveland. It's absolutely mad but great fun. Over the last few months I've been accosted by the American secret service, had my hair set on fire by a hot air balloon and got stuck down Europe's deepest mine.

What are you doing at work this week?
Being hyper! We've just won two Sony Awards, one of which was a gold for our coverage of George W Bush's visit here in November 2003. Plus I've been doing a bit of research on stories I'll be reporting on next week.

What advice would you have for anyone thinking of a career in broadcasting?
Get to know the industry well, make contacts, listen to lots of radio, watch lots of TV news and know what you want to do. Editors receive stacks of vague emails from students saying they want to work in the media, so you need to be precise on what you can offer a station.

Over the last few months I've been accosted by the American secret service, had my hair set on fire by a hot air balloon and got stuck down Europe's deepest mine

Jonathan Swingler

do as much research as you can about your subject, and then prepare open-ended questions that will get your subject talking. During the interview, you need to be good at coaxing out interesting answers: so if the subject is reticent, you need to be good at putting them at their ease with background questioning; but if they are evasive, you need to be strong enough to ask the incisive follow-up questions. If the interview is recorded, you should be thinking at this stage about what the final broadcast is going to sound like: you need to be a good listener, so that you can ask further questions as they suggest themselves to you. Whenever the interviewee says something interesting enough to use later, note the position on the disc or tape; and try not to wrap up the interview until you have the material you need.

You probably won't have good enough recording equipment to do it at home, but to be a good radio reporter, you also need to be good at identifying the background sounds that illustrate the point of your piece – such sounds will enliven even short pieces of radio journalism.

Once you have recorded an interview, you need to be able to edit it. Editing is primarily about selecting those passages of the audio that get the subject's point across faithfully, in the shortest possible time. This can be time-consuming work: but it is also instructive, because it is inevitably when you edit a piece of audio that you begin to notice the questions you should have asked. On the technical side, it is useful when looking for work experience to have practised editing interviews on your computer at home: to do this, you could download an audio editor from a website such as Download.com. Connect your digital or analogue recorder to your computer with a cable from any hardware store.

Although not all broadcast journalists have the skill, it is also useful to have shorthand. Sure, most of your interviews will be on tape – but there may be times when a contact either refuses to be recorded, or you don't have the right equipment with you. In these cases, having a good standard of Teeline shorthand is an invaluable backup. The downside is that shorthand takes a long time to learn properly – many journalism courses or evening classes teach it, or you can buy a coursebook and practise at home.

The final skills, and the most high-profile, are writing, editing and talking; in short, the **storytelling**. To be a good writer for radio, you need to be able to sum up the point of any story – the who, what, where, when, how and above all why – in as few words as possible. Unlike in newspapers, these might not necessarily be in the first words of your report – it is usually better to "set up" your key points to maintain interest right through to the end, as you would when telling a story in conversation; and also, just as in conversation, it is good to use lots of short sentences instead of one long one. Remember, good journalism is about putting the listener first – so you must always ask yourself: if I were the listener, what would I want to know? Never underestimate the listener's intelligence. Links and cues, meanwhile, are a skill of their own: you need to write them in such a way that whet the appetite of the listener, without giving away the point of what is to be broadcast next. In each case, you may only have a few seconds to get your point across: so your English must be concise and direct. Use active verbs when you can, cut out the adjectives and adverbs, and don't say anything that doesn't need to be said, or raises questions to which you can't give a satisfactory answer.

Finally, you need to be comfortable on the radio, and have a good broadcasting voice. When presenting, the key is to know who your typical listener is, and always have him or her in mind both when writing and when on air. If you have a voice creamy enough to drag a cat from its food, so much the better; but even if you don't, your listeners will appreciate it if you take the time to speak with poise and clarity. This, of course, means you have to be even better at editing your words down to make your broadcast fit the time available: but it is far better than rushing or garbling your broadcast, which will only confuse your listener.

TV reporting

TV reporting has one very significant difference to radio reporting pictures. To be a good TV reporter, you need to be good at telling stories in images as well as in language; which means you are not merely reporting on the news, but you are often also showing the news and setting it in context with your report.

This emphasis on pictures will have a great effect on your working life as a TV reporter. First, you may find that your news values alter from those of a newspaper or radio reporter: put simply, a story is less of a story if you do not have the pictures to tell it with. Second, you have to be prepared to work long hours: if you are going to get the pictures you need, then you always need to be in the right place at the right time – and then you may have to spend time editing your packages or doing live pieces to camera. Third, you need to be good at working in a team: you may have a camera crew working with you, in which case you need to be able to both lead them journalistically and take advice from them too; but even if you are shooting your own pictures, you still need to be in constant communication with the programme editor to make sure you are getting the kind of sequence he or she wants.

Visual storytelling is not an easy skill to learn. Before working in TV news, it is helpful to have had some experience operating some kind of lightweight camera yourself; at least this will give you a sense of the complexity of the job. Broadly speaking, you need to find the pictures that at best show the news first-hand, or at least illustrate the story you are trying to tell. Then, you will employ different kinds of shot in order to give your sequence a sense of visual development. So a wide shot of a location will set the scene for the viewer, and give sense of perspective to your piece; a close-up will give a sense of immediacy, so the viewers feel as if they are experiencing the scene almost at first hand; and a medium shot, somewhere in between, will give enough width to show individual action. The skill, which you must master to be a good TV reporter, is to build these different kinds of shot into a unified whole.

Pictures, of course, are nothing without context. So in TV as in radio, you need to have clear, concise writing skills and a good broadcasting voice; but this time your words must work in conjunction with the images the viewer sees. Your writing does not have to be as explicit as it would be for a radio report; you can let the pictures tell the story where they can, but you must never keep the viewer guessing as to what a picture is or means. Other than that, reread the section on radio reporting: many of the same principles apply to TV.

Needless to say, to be a TV reporter, you also need to be confident in front of the camera. That doesn't mean you have to have a pretty face: it just means you have to be an effective on-screen communicator, who is just as happy reporting on live TV as you are

The reporter/presenter

Name: **Caroline Richardson**
Current job: **assistant editor, BBC South Today, reporting and presenting bulletins for TV**

What was your first job in broadcasting?
Broadcast journalist, BBC Radio Stoke.

How did you get the job?
I went there on a college placement - they then gave me freelance shifts which soon became a permanent staff post.

What did the job involve?
Mainly reporting to start, then bulletin reading. It was very hard work, for low pay, for an editor with very high standards. An excellent training ground – and one that has set me up with the stamina and skills that keep me going today!

What were your educational qualifications at the time?
I had just finished my postgrad diploma in broadcast journalism at the London College of Printing. I also had a degree in French and politics.

What broadcasting experience did you do before starting work?
Apart from the college attachment at BBC Radio Stoke, I had done some work experience at BBC Midlands Today and at the commercial radio station in Birmingham, BRMB. I was also a trainee researcher on DayTime TV for the year before my postgrad course, to earn money to pay for the course.

How did your career progress after your first job?
I stayed at Radio Stoke for three years, then saw adverts for journalists at BBC South. I went to BBC Radio Solent as a radio journalist reading bulletins – then had an attachment in the TV newsroom for South Today (they share the same building). I went back to Solent as news editor for three months, then back to TV to start production

shifts of smaller lunchtime and late-night bulletins. I became a district reporter and starting presenting news bulletins. I have recently been promoted to assistant editor, newsgathering.

What are you doing at work this week?
Presenting live from Portsmouth in the run-up to the D-Day commemorations in France.

What advice would you have for anyone thinking of a career in TV?
Get plenty of work experience. Listen to criticism and feedback. Be tenacious and thick-skinned.

Don't plot your entire career – doors will open in unusual places, and unexpected opportunities will present themselves, so don't let them pass you by. Remember, not everyone can be the Washington correspondent!

65

The regional correspondent

Name: **Michelle May**
Current job: **north of England correspondent, Sky News**

What was your first job in broadcasting?
Freelancing for Channel One TV in Liverpool, briefly. I think freelancing is good way in. My first contract job was as a part-time journalist for Lite AM radio in Manchester.

How did you get the job?
For Lite AM, I was living in Liverpool looking for work and sent my CV to lots of radio stations. They took me on quite quickly.

What did the job involve? What was it like?
It was very early morning till around 2.30pm. It was a very small radio station with few news resources. I would work alone writing a few stories up from wires, IRN and from local sources – then read the national and local news on the hour and sport on the half-hour. It was good money and helped me develop news judgement and improve my voice. It started as just a weekend job, but gradually I got more shifts. The early starts were painful, especially as I was commuting from Liverpool – but I really enjoyed it.

What were your educational qualifications at the time?
Nine GCSEs, three A-levels; BA in journalism, film and broadcasting from Cardiff University; postgraduate diploma in broadcast journalism from Cardiff Journalism School, Cardiff University.

What broadcasting experience did you do before starting work?
The Cardiff diploma organised great work experience opportunities during the course. I spent time at BBC Wales and Channel One London where I worked as a VJ (video jockey) for two weeks. The course was very practical with lots of package making.

How did your career progress after your first job?
I started freelancing for regional Granada TV news whilst also working for Lite AM. After six months I got a job as an off-screen journalist for Granada. This was all the responsibilities of a reporter, but my face wasn't allowed on TV! After 18 months I applied successfully as on-screen Liverpool reporter. I gave up Lite AM and Granada moved me to the main Manchester office where I stayed for another three years doing lots of major stories and occasionally newsreading. I particularly enjoyed live TV, and answered a Guardian ad for Sky News. I was thrilled to be taken on as north of England correspondent in January 2004.

What are you doing at work this week?
Very varied. So far, reports and lives in Oldham on Gordon

> Know that it's not glamorous! It's hard work and long hours but extremely rewarding

Brown's comprehensive spending review, and a fun piece on Harrison Ford's canal holiday in Wales!

What advice would you have for anyone thinking of a career in TV?
If you're sure, then start as young as you can. My first job was as a teenage runner at my local newspaper – a background in print media is well respected. There are so many people wanting to get into TV – you need to get as much experience as possible.
Be flexible: I moved to the north of England without work because I knew it was a busy news patch and was prepared to risk it.
Although it is not always essential, I would recommend a journalism qualification.
Know that it's not glamorous! It's hard work and long hours but extremely rewarding, and everyone you know will quiz you about your job!

putting a recorded package together. Above all, you need to be yourself. Acting naturally on live TV can be nerve-racking, so if you don't think you can do it, maybe broadcast journalism isn't for you: consider working in print journalism or documentary production instead. Conversely, don't love the camera too much: being on screen day after day can give you authority, but it can also be irritating to the viewer. Use pieces to camera only where you or the editor want that first-hand, walk-me-through touch.

Finally, one of the best ways to understand TV news is to watch a lot of it – so again, you need to be **steeped in TV**. Get to know its strengths, its weaknesses, and its absurdities. Set your video to record all tonight's evening news bulletins, on all the major radio and television channels, including those broadcasting 24-hour news; then tomorrow morning, watch and listen to them all. Look out for how different channels make different decisions about what the stories are, according to the markets they face; but also try to pick out which reports were too bloated, or so short they left you wanting to know more.

Up the career ladder

In TV or radio news, there are two or three ways for your career to progress. First, you can keep reporting for as long as you can: if you love reporting and don't want to get into middle management, this is the way to go. Your goal, on this career route, is both to become a **correspondent** – which means you will be reporting on an individual specialism such as business news or international news – and to join a major broadcaster. If you choose this route, you can do the job as long as editors or viewers can stand the your face: but remember, ageism is rife in the media, so you may one day find yourself ousted by cheaper, less experienced talent. The goal is to make yourself indispensable.

Your second option is to climb the news chain. If you do this, you could become the **editor** of a programme or bulletin – in other words, the person who decides what stories or issues to cover. As an editor, you need to be able to manage breaking news, direct presenters and shuffle running orders as you see fit. You will usually spend the eight to 12 hours before your bulletin advising your reporters and correspondents, reviewing packages shortly before they go out, and editing presenters' scripts. To do the job, you need to be a hard-working and experienced news journalist with good leadership and organisation skills. If you excel as an editor, you could go on to be a **series editor** or **executive editor** or join a large broadcaster – or both, in which case your job will be as much about budgets and policy as it is about hard news.

How to get the job

The 10-step plan

Once you have read through the job descriptions in Section 2 and settled on your career path – be it as feature writer, reporter, sub or whatever – then it is time to work out what you need to do to get into the business as soon as possible. Here are the 10 steps to launching yourself on a career in journalism.

1 Research

This first step is the most basic – and the most overlooked. Editors being busy people, they resent it when they encounter prospective journalists who do not know their stuff. So if you want a career in journalism, you need to research until you do. This means regular trips to the library, or to one of those bookshops that lets you read their stock for the price of a coffee, to read plenty of newspapers and magazines; and it also means time spent surfing the web.

First, of course, you need to know where the jobs are. MediaGuardian on a Monday and MediaGuardian.co.uk are the place to start; after that, try the trade press, such as Press Gazette or Broadcast. Try the websites of individual employers: the BBC has a comprehensive section on job opportunities, as do other media companies. Not all jobs are advertised, though, which is why you need to build your contacts (step two).

Second, get your background knowledge about the industry. The best place to find this is in the trade press – that is, the newspapers about journalism itself. There is a list on page 166, but the most useful are usually MediaGuardian, its website MediaGuardian.co.uk, and the weekly trade newspaper Press Gazette. Follow the media sections of other newspapers too. Within a few months – or if you are short of time, by going to the library or online and reading a few months' worth of back issues – you will have the minimum background knowledge you need.

Third, immerse yourself in whatever media you want to work in. Read not only the newspapers, magazines and websites you can see yourself working for, but their competitors as well. As you read, concentrate on two key areas: the subject matter, and the target market. So if you want a career as a reporter, you need to read a lot of newspapers and know a lot about current affairs, regionally, nationally and internationally; but you also need a good sense of who

71

is the typical reader of each publication. If you can't tell from the writing style, look at the ads. Similarly, if you want a career in a specialist area such as reviewing or magazines, then you need to know the subject matter inside out – but you also need to imagine yourself writing features in a similar style, to a similar readership.

Finally, remember that research is as much about good note-taking as the reading you do. Imagine you have a job interview tomorrow. Who was that photographer whose work you liked in that architecture magazine? What did you make of that competitor newspaper you saw that day in the library? Why did that website go with one lead feature rather than another? Record your thoughts now, and you won't be struggling to find the information when you need it.

2 Build contacts

OK, so you're not Victoria Coren. You don't go to the best parties; none of your friends are in journalism; in fact, your family is wondering why you don't drop this media lark and find yourself a proper job. But that doesn't mean you can't network with the best of them.

Networking is about enlisting everyone you know to your cause. And that means everyone – friends, family, work contacts – because everyone might know someone in newspapers or magazines who could be in a position to help you in a career. You don't need to be too pushy – but it's no sin to talk about your ambitions, and to ask people you know if they know someone in journalism. If everyone on the planet is connected to everyone else by six degrees of separation, it won't take you too many steps to find yourself a hack.

When you find someone who seems promising, call them or send them an email, mentioning the person you know in common. Ask them if they can make time for a 10-or 15-minute chat. Most people won't begrudge you this. Try to call at a convenient time; no one wants to be disturbed five minutes before deadline. When you get through, don't ask them right out if they can land you a job; chances are they aren't in a position to do so, and will be embarrassed by having to decline. Instead, try to ask them about themselves: how they got into the business, what their working week is like, what advice they have you. As in a journalism interview, that should relax them. If things are going well, ask them if they take people to do work experience (step four). Finally, ask if they know anyone else who can talk to you. Being in the industry already, they should know a lot of people who will be able to tell you about your particular interest or niche. When you're done, make sure they have your details – and drop them a note thanking them for your time.

Using this contact-building method landed me my first job in journalism. Someone at my dad's running club turned out to be a publisher at a well-known trade press group. After a brief conversation at a family barbecue – in which the publisher told me quite correctly, that I'd make much more money if I got into sales – he asked his chief sub, who was short-staffed, if he'd try me out on a trainee rate as a freelance. My career started from there.

Finally, do keep a contacts book, even if you are not a reporter: you never know when you might need that phone number again. Most people keep one book in hard copy and one on a PC.

3 Build your portfolio

It sounds obvious, but if you are not producing good work, you will never cut it in the publishing world. So now is the time to prove how good you are, by building a portfolio of your journalism, design or your photography.

This doesn't mean wasting time and money on buying an expensive presentation case or building a pretty website – not at this stage, at least. Instead, it means working for whatever publications you can – newsletters, student newspapers and magazines, local papers, websites, whoever will print your work. Aim to build a portfolio that reflects the kind of work you want to do in future. Try to get bylines or credits if you can, as this is the best evidence that the work is indeed yours; however, if you do any work that isn't credited, don't be afraid to include it in your portfolio in any case (this applies to subs as well). Then, when you are applying for a job or a work placement, simply select your best and most appropriate work, and send that along too.

A course (step six) will help you get into print, usually on a student publication; and if you are lucky, you might get a byline when you do work experience (step four). If you're still struggling to get yourself published even at student level, read the advice on freelancing for some tips (step 10).

4 Get work experience

Nothing, employers argue, prepares you better for working in the media than doing the job. As a result, work experience – that is, free labour – is an established way to make yourself stand out from the crowd.

Like anything else, getting work experience is mostly about research and networking. First, check the websites of larger organisations that you would consider working for – they may have formal training schemes. Otherwise, focus again on building your contacts as outlined in step two; meet enough people, asking them if there are work experience opportunities available, and sooner or later you will be offered a stint or two. If all else fails, get a copy of a reference book about journalism – the MediaGuardian Media Directory is one – and, using it as a guide, cold-call the editors of the six magazines or newspaper desks you would most like to work for. The smaller and the more understaffed the magazine is, the greater your likelihood of success. I chose this method, and was offered experience at a fairly highbrow magazine in London. I spent it fact-checking articles and making trips to the local sandwich bar – experience that was enough to land me that first job.

Make sure you get the best out of your work experience. If you're bitter about having to work for free, don't show it. So look fairly smart, put on a plausible manner, and try to be as helpful as you can: don't look disappointed at being asked to do a boring job like filing the papers or photocopying. Whenever you get the chance, ask questions. And if anyone invites you for a trip out to the sandwich bar or the pub, make sure you go along; it is your chance to be more searching, and it will mean people remember who you are.

Some people think work experience is a bit of a con. True, it does seem a bit rich when a FTSE-listed publisher asks you to work for them free; in this case, be sure to push for your expenses. From a small publisher with tight margins, the practice of free labour is more understandable. But looking at it from the long-term perspective, the money is immaterial: what work experience gives you is the chance to sample life in a different working environment, without having to make any commitment beyond a week or two of your time. Take it with both hands.

Consider a niche

If you have a particular interest in and knowledge about a subject – be it arts, books, film, health, technology, sport or whatever – you should certainly consider making it your niche. This applies to writers, subs and photographers alike. Genuine expertise about a subject is a bankable phenomenon in journalism, because so few people can combine such knowledge with the ability to write about it clearly and concisely. Where the subject is something most journalists don't know much about, such as science, you could find yourself very much in demand.

Be creative about what your niche may be. Are you interested in health, social issues or education? These issues command endless column inches in papers and magazines. Don't worry about being pigeonholed too early: many journalists start out in niche areas who have gone on to broader things. Remember that the narrower the subject matter, the more types of writing you will be expected to do: while a news reporter on a national newspaper might just write news, for example, an education or science writer will often write both news and features at the same time. This will help you to put together a better portfolio.

Consider a course

You have two main career paths if you want to be a journalist: go straight into work, be it at a local paper, magazine, website or news agency; or do an NCTJ journalism course.

It is certainly tempting to go straight into work: it pays the rent, it gets you on the career ladder early, and it teaches you how to do the job in the fastest possible way. On the other hand, unless you are on one of a very few schemes run by large employers, formal on-the-job training is almost non-existent. So if you don't want to be left with gaps in your knowledge, you might gain confidence from doing an NCTJ.

An NCTJ will not turn you into a journalist if you do not have the skills. It will certainly not teach you how to write – although it will help you turn your writing into journalistic writing, favouring concision and straightforwardness over gaseous prose. What a good course will do is give you specific skills such as shorthand, law and knowledge of the workings of public life; it will also help you get work experience; and almost above all else, it will provide you a readymade network of contacts in journalism. Which is useful when you're looking for a job in years to come.

7 Get the tech skills

seven

Technology has transformed the way publishers work even in the past decade. To progress in any role in newspapers and magazines, you should keep ahead of the game by getting as many technical skills as you can.

The closer to the production side of the business you are, the more technology you will be using. A sub needs a working knowledge of Adobe Indesign, Adobe PhotoShop and Quark XPress; a designer should have in even more in-depth knowledge of all these programs, and should also know Adobe Illustrator. Online journalists should be familiar with any of a myriad internet publishing packages. Even writers should keep abreast of their tech skills: word processing, email and Googling skills are all you really need.

It pays to spend a few minutes each month finding a bit more about the programs you use every day. In particular, learn keyboard shortcuts, such as ctrl-S to save or ctrl-W to close a window: not only will they help you avoid RSI (repetitive strain injury), but they will save you vital minutes when you are up against deadline.

8 Target your CV

eight

The traditional CV and covering letter are not always required to get a job in publishing, as jobs are often won informally by word of mouth. But if you do apply for a job through open competition, then you need to stand out from the crowd.

The secret is to prepare a different CV and covering letter for each job for which you are applying. This is time-consuming; but just as journalists target stories to a typical reader, so you need to target your CV to the editor who will read it. So go over your experience to date, work out what is most relevant, and give most space to that. Under each bit of experience you have gained, bullet-point two or three things you did or learned that are especially relevant; try to keep these down to one line each. Don't devote too much space to your educational achievements; instead emphasise the journalism experience you have gained – including student journalism or a journalism course. List all relevant tech skills. At the bottom, mention a few interests that you would be willing to talk about at interview. Make sure you include the names of your referees (or, if you haven't decided who they are, the words "References available on request"), and you are done.

Writing a covering letter is much harder. Its role is to explain why the experience outlined in your CV is so relevant. The classic approach is to write three short paragraphs: one, who you are and a little about your background; two, why your experience makes you appropriate for the position, with bullet-points of essential skills; three, why you want the job so much, with evidence that you have read the publication and know what it is about. The golden rule is not to over-write.

If you are suffering from the "empty CV" syndrome – that is, you haven't got enough career or work experience to fill a page of A4 – then there is an emergency alternative: move parts of the covering letter into the CV. Using this system, you write a concise summary of who you are at the top of the CV, with your most relevant general skills bullet-pointed underneath. Next you write the heading "Experience" and carry on with your usual CV. Your covering letter, in this case, will merely state that you are applying for the job. This approach is less formal, so is useful when applying for work experience or freelance gigs.

In publishing, how you present your application is of course a reliable indicator of how you would do your job in practice. Remembering this, don't give editors any excuses to put your application on the "no" pile. Ensure your spelling and grammar are perfect: no prospective sub who makes a spelling error on a CV will get a second chance, and few reporters will get away with it either. Where words have alternative spellings, take your lead from the publication itself. Similarly, keep CV and covering letter to one page each if you can: as either sub or writer, you need to show evidence that you can present information concisely. If you need more space for the CV, try reducing the margins instead of going for a smaller font. Design should be clean and simple; don't attempt to be too flashy unless you are going for a flashy design job. Finally, use a well-known font such as Times or Arial, at a readable point size.

Other CV points are more general. Editors are as impressed as anyone if you can demonstrate evidence of a well-rounded character or unusual interests, especially if they are useful to your job (see step five). Language skills are more likely to come in handy on a national; they may also be useful if you are a sub. You can't do much about your education other than to get the best grades you can, and to consider a journalism course (step six). Finally, get references from people in journalism if you can (step two); that way they will still score for you even if they are not actually checked.

Prepare for the interview

If you get an interview for a job at a newspaper or magazine, congratulations. It means you have the potential to get a job, and will probably land one in a matter of time. Whether it happens this time depends on your interview technique.

Remember that interviews, primarily, are about the stories you tell, and how you tell them. You are presenting a version of yourself. So when preparing for interview, look over your written application again, to remind yourself what your relevant skills and experience are. Then take time to remember something that happened that backs this up. If you are applying for a job as a reporter, for example, your CV might mention the work experience you did at a local paper, and your letter might say that you fitted well into the small team there. In the interview, you might be asked to expand on this further. So don't mention the fact that you spent every spare second with the reporters in the pub: instead recount how you met a particular challenge while working on a piece, and how the support of the team helped get you through. The implied message here is that you are enthusiastic, you take the initiative, and are willing to learn – essential skills for working in a small team.

With this technique in mind, you should be able to come up with answers to almost every interview question you are asked, including the classics. Why do you want the job? How would you cope with difficult colleagues? What would you do if you came across a contact who was unwilling to talk? How do you cope when the intro of a feature needs completely rewriting? As long as you have done all your research (step one) and got enough experience (steps three and four), you should have a story that tells the answer.

After that, it is all about getting the basics right. So dress smartly, even if you will be in T-shirt and jeans when you do the job. Try to moderate your nervous instincts: if you are an extrovert, practise speaking slowly and formally, and thinking before you open your mouth; if an introvert, practise making good eye contact and projecting your voice. Expect the unexpected: you might have an active interviewer who grills you with searching questions, in which case you need to be able to think on your feet; or they might be passive and apparently uninterested in you, in which case you need to take control if you are to get across the points you want to make. You might be in a plush meeting room, a tiny office, even the company canteen. Be prepared for all these scenarios, and you should be able to fight off the nerves.

Finally, it will be your turn to ask the questions. Prepare these in advance, but remember that interviewers will often be rushing to get you out of the room, so you need to interest them too. First, ask about opportunities for career progression: this shows ambition, which is always good. Second, try to ask something about the editor's plans for their publication, that is relevant to the job you are going to do. Then there is money. If salary has not been raised, you should mention that it hasn't been raised yet – an indirect way of asking what it is. Whatever the answer, keep your poker face. You might have to negotiate a pay rise at a later date.

If you don't get the job this time, don't be downhearted – getting an interview is good experience in itself. After a few days, you might call or email the editor and ask what it was that made you fall short by comparison to the candidate who got the job. The chances are it is something you can fix next time.

10 Consider freelancing

What happens if you find it hard to get a job? If you have done a journalism course, built up your portfolio, got your CV sorted out, done more work experience than you ever want to again – and still can't pay the bills? Do you give up on your journalism dream?

Not necessarily. There is a halfway house, and that is freelancing.

Freelancing means being paid only for the work you do. That might mean being paid only for the articles you write; or it might mean being paid only by the day to work as a sub, reporter, editor or designer. Of these two options, the second is perhaps more likely to land you a job – because if you are knocking around the office all the time, you stand a pretty good chance of filling a vacancy by default.

If you want to work shifts in this way, simply send your CV and portfolio to a selection of chief subs or news editors, telling them that you are available to provide freelance cover. At this stage, the scattergun approach is probably best: it will take a particularly overworked and short-staffed editor to call you, so you need to widen your search as much as you can. If you are lucky, the phone will ring and you have an in.

If, on the other hand, you want to freelance by selling articles you write from home, then good on you – and good luck. You will need luck, because it is even more difficult to survive in this way as a newcomer. There are any number of freelance writers who have been in journalism for years; so editors will be particularly circumspect about commissioning you. Consider it mainly as a short-term career move, which will help you improve your portfolio while you are looking for a job.

Whichever approach you take, you need to be organised and to market yourself. You need to keep a database of contacts, and to keep records of every conversation you have with an editor. If you are writing from home, keep organised files of ideas, and do plenty of market research as outlined in step one. Whenever a good idea suggests itself to you, work out the best treatment for it with an eye on the target reader; and then write a printed query letter to a specific editor, outlining the piece, including the length and when it can be finished. Explain why you are the best person to write it. If an editor replies, they may reject it outright; they may say they will "take a look at it", which means they want you to write it but they are not promising to use it (a poor deal for you, but worth doing if you are desperate enough); or they may commission it. If you are lucky and it is commissioned, then you will need to negotiate about the fee – and also about the rights you are selling. Ask for a written contract, but try not to sign forms that hand over "all rights" to the publisher, because this means you won't ever be paid for those same words again.

Whether you are working shifts or working from home, freelancing means you have to be in close control of your financial affairs. On shifts this is easier, because usually you will be treated as a "casual employee", and taxed at source; you will also be entitled to holiday pay. Working from home, though, you will be paid gross, which means you need to fill in a tax return and be treated as a self-employed business. Get in touch with the Inland Revenue as soon as you can for advice. At the moment, for example, you get 100 per cent tax relief on computer equipment in the first year – which knocks a good 25 per cent off the price.

All freelances should make sure they are members of the NUJ, if only because it means being sent the Freelance Fees Guide every year. This useful document sets out minimum recommended rates for all kinds of journalistic work; while the Freelance newsletter tells you what other journalists are getting for the work they do. These rates are also collected at http://media.gn.apc.org/feesguide.

11 Persevere

OK, so we said there would be 10 steps. But the 11th is perhaps the most important. In any career, there will be ups and downs – sometimes it will seem as if you are in control of your future, and at other times you will feel stuck in a rut. Just keep persevering and thinking positively. If you can't find work – keep making those contacts and building your skills. If you feel stuck, don't be afraid to make new contacts and new skills. It's your life – make the most of it.

Press
contacts

National press Contacts

Daily Express
Express Newspapers
Ludgate House
245 Blackfriars Rd
London SE1 9UX
020 7928 8000
www.express.co.uk
firstname.surname@express.co.uk
Editor: Peter Hill

- *Deputy editor: Hugh Whittow;
news editor: Howard Smith;
home affairs correspondent: James
Slack; political editor: Patrick
O'Flynn; chief political
correspondent: Alison Little*
- *Section editors – city: Stephen Kahn
(deputy: Peter Cunliffe; associate city
editor: Robert Lindsay; markets:
David Shand); comment:
Jennifer Selway; Express Woman:
Tina Moran; defence: John Ingham;
features: Fergus Kelly; foreign:
Gabriel Milland; health:
Julia Wheldon/Rachael Baird;
personal finance: David Prosser;
showbusiness: Mark Jagasia;
sport: Bill Bradshaw; transport:
John Ingham; TV & radio:
Charlotte Civil*
- *Production editor: Bob Smith;
chief sub: Keith Ging*
- *Publicity: Brian MacLaurin
Associates, 020 8834 1034*

Daily Mail
Associated Newspapers
Northcliffe House, 2 Derry St
Kensington, London W8 5TT
020 7938 6000
www.dailymail.co.uk
firstname.surname@dailymail.co.uk
Editor: Paul Dacre

- *Deputy editor: Alistair Sinclair;
news editor: Tony Gallagher
(assistant: Chris Evans); political
editor: David Hughes (deputy:
Paul Eastham); chief reporter:
David Williams*
- *Section editors – city:
Alex Brummer; diplomatic:
Richard Kay; features:
Leif Kalsayan; Money Mail:
Tony Hazell; royal: Richard Kay;
sport: Peter Ferguson; transport:
Ray Massey; TV: Tara Conlan*

- *Correspondents – consumer
affairs: Sean Poulter; education:
Sarah Harris; health: Beezy Marsh;
industry: Darren Behar; political:
James Chapman, Graeme Wilson;
social affairs: Steve Doughty*
- *Production editor: Hugh Dawson;
chief subs: Gerry Williams (news);
Robin Popham (features)*
- *Publicity: Laurence Sear,
020 7938 6000*

Daily Mirror
Trinity Mirror
1 Canada Square, Canary Wharf
London E14 5AP
020 7293 3000
www.mirror.co.uk
firstname.surname@mirror.co.uk
Editor: Richard Wallace

- *Deputy editor: Conor Hanna;
news editor: Chris Boffey (deputy:
James Mellor); political editor:
Oonagh Blackman (group political
editor: David Seymour)*
- *Section editors – 3am columnists:
Jessica Callan, Eva Simpson,
Caroline Hedley; business:
Clinton Manning; consumer:
Ruki Sayid; fashion: Ollie Picton
Jones (deputy: Amber Graafland);
features: Alison Phillips
(assistant editor – features, Matt
Kelly); foreign: Mark Ellis;
health: Caroline Jones;
letters: Fiona Parker; money:
John Husband; sport: Dean Morse;
TV: Nicola Methven*
- *Executive editor (production):
Jon Moorhead; chief news sub:
Pratima Sarwate; chief features sub:
James Rettie; assistant editor
(pictures): Ian Down;
picture editor: Greg Bennett*
- *Publicity: Sarah Vaughan-Brown,
020 7293 3222*

Daily Sport
Sport Newspapers
19 Great Ancoats St
Manchester M60 4BT
0161 236 4466
www.dailysport.net
firstname.surname@
sportsnewspapers.co.uk
Publicity: Jane Field, 0161 238 8135

Daily Star
Express Newspapers
Ludgate House,
245 Blackfriars Rd
London SE1 9UX
020 7928 8000
www.dailystar.co.uk
firstname.surname@dailystar.co.uk
Editor: Dawn Neesom

- *Deputy editor: Jim Mansell;
news: Kieron Saunders; political:
Macer Hall; features:
Samantha Taylor; sport:
Howard Wheatcroft; Cashpoint:
Michelle Carter*
- *Production editor: Bob Hadfield
(deputy: Brian Kelly)*
- *Publicity: Brian MacLaurin
Associates, 020 8834 1034*

Daily Telegraph
Telegraph Group
1 Canada Square, Canary Wharf
London E14 5DT
020 7538 5000
www.telegraph.co.uk
firstname.surname@
telegraph.co.uk
Editor: Martin Newland

- *Deputy & Saturday editor:
Sarah Sands; news: Fiona Barton;
political: George Jones (chief
political correspondent: Toby Helm);
home affairs: Philip Johnston;
managing editor: Sue Ryan;
executive editor: Neil Darbyshire;
night editor: David Lucas*
- *Section editors – arts & books:
Tom Horan; city: Kate Rankine
(deputy); Alistair Osborne &
Andrew Cave (associate editors);
diplomatic: Anton La Guardia;
environment: Charles Clover;
fashion: Hilary Alexander;
features: Richard Preston; foreign:
Alan Philps; health/medical:
Celia Hall; health & style:
Rachel Forder; legal: Joshua
Rozenberg; personal finance:
Ian Cowie; science: Roger Highfield;
sport: David Welch; Weekend:
Rachel Simhom*
- *Production editor: Steve Greaves*
- *Publicity: Victoria Higham,
020 7538 6259*

Financial Times

The Financial Times Group
1 Southwark Bridge
London SE1 9HL
020 7873 3000
www.ft.com
firstname.surname@ft.com
Editor: Andrew Gowers

- *Deputy editor: Chrystia Freeland;
  news: Edward Carr; political:
  James Blitz*
- *Section editors – Asia:
  John Ridding; FT magazine:
  John Lloyd; FT Weekend:
  Emma Tucker; Europe: Brian Groom;
  features: Andrew Hill; media:
  Tim Burt; public policy:
  Nicholas Timmins*
- *Production editors: Jo Russ,
  Ken Tough (day); Andy Anderson,
  Matthew Pettipher (night).
  Chief subs: Jeremy Hart (news),
  Andrew Hill (features)*
- *Communications director:
  Jo Manning-Cooper, 020 7873 3829*

The Guardian

Guardian Media Group
119 Farringdon Rd
London EC1R 3ER
020 7278 2332
www.guardian.co.uk
firstname.surname@guardian.co.uk
Editor: Alan Rusbridger

- *Deputy editor (news): Paul Johnson;
  home affairs: Alan Travis; home
  news: Ed Pilkington, Andrew Culf;
  political: Michael White (chief
  political correspondent:
  Patrick Wintour)*
- *Section editors – arts: Charlie English
  (Friday Review: Merope Mills);
  books: Claire Armistead; city:
  Julia Finch (deputy: Jill Treanor);
  economics: Larry Elliott; education:
  Will Woodward; environment:
  John Vidal; features: Ian Katz;
  foreign: Harriet Sherwood;
  health: Sarah Boseley; media:
  Charlie Burgess; northern:
  Martin Wainright; obituaries:
  Phil Osborne; Online: Vic Keegan;
  regional affairs: Peter Hetherington;
  social affairs: John Carvel; sport:
  Ben Clissit; travel: Andy Pietrasik;
  Weekend magazine: Katherine Viner;
  women's page: Clare Margetson*
- *Assistant editor (production):
  David Marsh; production editor,
  G2: Paul Howlett; production
  editor, Weekend: Bill Mann;
  chief sub, city: Rob Firth*
- *Publicity: Anna Sinfield,
  020 7239 9818*

The Independent

Independent News and Media (UK)
Independent House
191 Marsh Wall
London E14 9RS
020 7005 2000
www.independent.co.uk
firstletter.surname@
independent.co.uk
firstname.surname@
independent.co.uk
Editor: Simon Kelner

- *Deputy editor: Ian Burrell; news
  editor: Danny Groom; political
  editor: Andrew Grice (deputy:
  Colin Brown; chief political
  correspondent: Marie Woolf)*
- *Section editors – business:
  Michael Harrison; city:
  Damian Reece; diplomatic:
  Mary Dejevsky; education:
  Richard Garner; environment:
  Michael McCarthy; features:
  Lisa Markwell; foreign:
  Leonard Doyle (international news:
  Anne Penketh); health:
  Jeremy Laurance; labour:
  Barrie Clement; media: Ian Burrell;
  science: Steve Connor; sport:
  Paul Newman; technology:
  Charles Arthur; transport:
  Barrie Clement*
- *Production editor: Louis Jebb;
  chief news sub: Andrew Webster*
- *Marketing manager: Johnathan
  Grogan, 020 7005 2000*

The Sun

News Group Newspapers
1 Virginia St, London E98 1SN
020 7782 4000
www.thesun.co.uk
firstname.surname@the-sun.co.uk
Editor: Rebekah Wade

- *Deputy editor: Fergus Shanahan;
  assistant editor (news):
  Graham Dudman; political editor:
  Trevor Kavanagh (deputy:
  George Pascoe-Watson; Whitehall
  editor: David Wooding);
  chief reporter: John Kay*
- *Section editors – Bizarre:
  Victoria Newton; business: Ian King;
  crime: Mike Sullivan; defence:
  Tom Newton Dunn; deputy features
  editor: Ben Jackson; motoring:
  Ken Gibson; sport: Steve Waring;
  Sun Woman: Sharon Hendry;
  TV: Emily Smith*
- *Chief production editor (night):
  John Perry; chief sub, news:
  Jim Holgate*
- *Publicity: Lorna Carmichael,
  020 7782 5000*

The Times

Times Newspapers
1 Pennington St, London E98 1TT
020 7782 5000
www.timesonline.co.uk
firstname.surname@thetimes.co.uk
Editor: Robert Thomson

- *Deputy editor: Ben Preston;
  news: John Wellman; home:
  Ian Cobain; political:
  Philip Webster (deputy:
  Rosie Bennett; assistants:
  Peter Riddell, Tom Baldwin;
  Whitehall: Jill Sherman;
  chief political correspondent:
  David Charter)*
- *Section editors – business:
  Patience Wheatcroft (international
  business: Carl Mortished);
  comment: David Finkelstein;
  countryside: Valerie Elliott;
  defence: Michael Evans;
  diplomatic: Richard Beeston;
  education: Tony Halpin; fashion:
  Lisa Armstrong; features:
  Michael Harvey; financial:
  Graham Searjeant; foreign:
  Bronwen Maddox; health:
  Nigel Hawkes; personal
  finance: Anne Ashworth;
  sport: David Chappell*
- *Executive editors/chief subs:
  Chris McKane, Simon Pearson*
- *Communications director:
  Anoushka Healy, 020 7782 5000*

Press contacts : **Section 4**

83

The Business
Sunday Business Publishing
PA News Centre
292 Vauxhall Bridge Rd
London SW1V 1AE
020 7961 0000
www.thebusinessonline.com
firstinitialsurname@
thebusinesspress.net
Also published on Monday
Publisher: Andrew Neil
- *Deputy editor: Ian Watson*
- *Economics: Allister Heath;
technology: Tony Glover;
transport: Tracey Boles*
- *Production: Graham Penn;
chief sub: Phil Swift*
- *Publicity: Grant Clelland,
020 7961 0029*

Daily Star Sunday
Express Newspapers
Ludgate House, 245 Blackfriars Rd
London SE1 9UX
020 7928 8000
www.megastar.co.uk
firstname.surname@dailystar.co.uk
Editor: Gareth Morgan
- *Deputy editor: David Harbord;
news editor: Michael Booker;
political editor: Macer Hall*
- *Features: Julia Etherington;
sport: Ray Ansbro*
- *Chief sub: Mike Woods; picture
editor: Tomassina Brittain*
- *Publicity: Brian MacLaurin
Associates, 020 8834 1034*

The Independent on Sunday
Independent News and Media (UK)
Independent House,
191 Marsh Wall
London E14 9RS
020 7005 2000
www.independent.co.uk
initial.surname@independent.co.uk
Editor: Tristan Davies
- *Deputy editor: Michael Williams;
news editor: Robert Mendick;
political editor: Andy McSmith
(deputy): Francis Elliott)*
- *Sections – education:
Richard Garner; environment:
Geoffrey Lean; features:
Nick Coleman; sport: Neil Morton;
Time Off: Simon O'Hagan;
women's: Elizabeth Heathcote*
- *Production editor: Keith Howitt*
- *Marketing manager: Johnathan
Grogan, 020 7005 2000*

The Mail on Sunday
Associated Newspapers
Northcliffe House
2 Derry St, Kensington
London W8 5TT
020 7938 6000
www.mailonsunday.co.uk
firstname.surname@
mailonsunday.co.uk
Editor: Peter Wright
- *Deputy editor: Rod Gilchrist;
news: Sebastian Hamilton;
home affairs: Christopher Leake;
political: Simon Walters*
- *Sections – education: Glen Owen;
defence: Christopher Leake;
environment: Jo Knowsley;
features: Sian James;
showbusiness: Katie Nicholl;
sport: Malcolm Vallerius*
- *Production editor: Tim Smith;
chief sub: Nick Petkovic*
- *Managing editor: John Wellington,
020 7938 7015*

News of the World
News Group Newspapers
1 Virginia St
London E98 1NW
020 7782 4000
www.thenewsoftheworld.co.uk
firstname.surname@notw.co.uk
Editor: Andy Coulson
- *Deputy editor: Neil Wallis;
news editor: James Weatherup;
assistant editor (news): Greg Miskiw;
associate news editors:
Ian Edmondson, Gary Thompson;
political editor: Ian Kirby;
investigations: Mazher Mahmood;
senior associate editor: Harry Scott*
- *Production editor:
Richard Rushworth*
- *Publicity: Hayley Barlow,
020 7782 4000*

The Observer
Guardian Media Group
119 Farringdon Rd
London EC1R 3ER
020 7278 2332
www.observer.guardian.co.uk
firstname.surname@observer.co.uk
Editor: Roger Alton
- *Deputy editors: John Mulholland,
Paul Webster; executive editor,
news: Andy Malone; political
editor: Kamal Ahmed; chief
political corr: Gaby Hinsliff*
- *Sections – business: Frank Kane;
comment: Mike Holland; foreign
news: Andy Malone; health:
Jo Revill; media: Vanessa Thorpe;
Observer Magazine: Allan Jenkins;
Observer Food Monthly: Nicola Jeal;
Observer Music Monthly:
Caspar Llewellyn Smith; Observer
Review: Louise France; personal
finance: Maria Scott; public affairs:
Anthony Barnett; Scottish editor:
Stephen Khan; social affairs:
Jamie Doward; sport: Brian Oliver;
travel: Jeannette Hyde*
- *Production editor: Bob Poulton;
chief news sub: David Pearson*
- *Publicity: Anna Sinfield,
020 7239 9818*

The People
MGN, 1 Canada Square
Canary Wharf
London E14 5AP
020 7293 3000
www.people.co.uk
firstname.surname@people.co.uk
Editor: Mark Thomas
- *Deputy editor: Alan Edwards;
news editor: Ian Edmondson;
deputy news editor: Ben Proctor;
associate news editor: David Jeffs;
political editor: Nigel Nelson*
- *Features: Katie Weitz;
investigations: Roger Insall;
showbiz: Sean O'Brien;
sport: Lee Horton*
- *Chief sub: Trisha Harbord;
night editor: Matt Clarke;
picture editor: Paula Derry*
- *Publicity: Sarah Vaughan-Brown,
020 7293 3222*

The Sunday Express

Express Newspapers
Ludgate House, 245 Blackfriars Rd
London SE1 9UX
020 7928 8000
www.express.co.uk
firstname.surname@express.co.uk
Editor: Martin Townsend
*Deputy editor: Richard Dismore;
news: James Murray; political:
Julia Hartley-Brewer*
▪ *Sections – arts: Rachel Jane;
business: David Parsley; crime:
Andrea Perry; defence &
diplomatic: Tim Shipman;
environment: Stuart Winter;
features: Janie Lawrence;
health: Hilary Douglas; royal:
Keith Perry; sport: Scott Wilson;
travel: Jane Memmler*
▪ *Night editor: Andy Hoban;
assistant night editor (features):
Stuart Kershaw; chief news sub:
Keith Ging*
▪ *Publicity: Brian MacLaurin
Associates, 020 8834 1034*

Sunday Mirror

MGN, 1 Canada Square
Canary Wharf
London E14 5AP
020 7293 3000
www.sundaymirror.co.uk
firstname.surname@
sundaymirror.co.uk
Editor: Tina Weaver
*Associate editor: Mike Small;
assistant editor (news):
Nick Buckley; news editor:
James Scott; political editor:
Paul Gilfeather; chief reporter:
Euan Stretch*
▪ *Sections – features: Nicky Dawson
(deputy: Deborah Sherwood);
investigations: Graham Johnson;
show business: Ben Todd;
sport: Craig Tregurtha*
▪ *Chief subs: Brian Hancill (news/
features); Phil Davies (sport);
Picture editor: Mike Sharp*
▪ *Publicity: Sarah Vaughan-Brown,
020 7293 3222*

Sunday Sport

Sport Newspapers
19 Great Ancoats St
Manchester M60 4BT
0161 236 4466
www.sundaysport.com
firstname.surname@
sportsnewspapers.co.uk
Publicity: Jane Field, 0161 238 8135

The Sunday Telegraph

Telegraph Group,
1 Canada Square
Canary Wharf
London E14 5DT
020 7538 5000
www.telegraph.co.uk
firstname.surname@
telegraph.co.uk
Editor: Dominic Lawson
*Deputy editor: Matthew d'Ancona;
news editor: Richard Ellis
(chief reporter: Andrew Alderson);
home affairs: David Bamber;
political: Patrick Hennessy
(deputy: Melissa Kite)*
▪ *Sections – city: Robert Peston;
features: Emma Gosnell; foreign:
Topaz Amoore; sport: Jon Ryan*
▪ *Chief subs: Justin Williams (news),
John Morgan (features)*
▪ *Publicity: Victoria Higham,
020 7538 6259*

The Sunday Times

Times Newspapers
1 Pennington St,
London E98 1ST
020 7782 5000
www.sunday-times.co.uk
redirected to timesonline.co.uk
firstname.surname@
sunday-times.co.uk
Editor: John Witherow
*Deputy editor: Martin Ivens;
managing editor: Richard Caseby;
news: Charles Hymas; associate
editor: Bob Tyrer; managing editor,
news: Mark Skipworth; political
editor: David Cracknell (deputy:
Andrew Porter)*
▪ *Sections – business: William Lewis;
city: Paul Durman; culture:
Helen Hawkins; economics:
David Smith; environment:
Jonathan Leake; foreign:
Sean Ryan; medical: Lois Rogers;
money: Naomi Caine; News Review:
Eleanor Mills; science:
Jonathan Leake; sport: Alex Butler;
Sunday Times magazine:
Robin Morgan; travel:
Christine Walker*
▪ *Managing editor (production):
Ian Coxon; chief subs: David Paton;
Denise Boutall (features)*
▪ *Publicity: Mary Fulton (Townhouse
Publicity), 020 7226 7450*

Regional press Contacts

Archant

Prospect House, Rouen Rd
Norwich NR1 1RE
01603 628311
www.archant.co.uk

Daily Mail & General Trust

www.dmgt.co.uk
Associated Newspapers
Northcliffe House, 2 Derry St
London W8 5TT
020 7938 6000
www.associatednewspapers.co.uk
Northcliffe Newspapers Group
31–32 John St
London WC1N 2QB
020 7400 1100
www.thisisnorthcliffe.co.uk

DC Thomson

185 Fleet St
London EC4A 2HS
020 7400 1030
www.dcthomson.co.uk

Guardian Media Group

164 Deansgate
Manchester M3 3RN
0161 832 7200
www.gmgplc.co.uk

Independent News and Media

2023 Bianconi Avenue
Citywest Business Campus
Naas Road
Dublin 24, Ireland
00 353 1 466 3200
www.independentnewsmedia.com

Johnston Press

53 Manor Place
Edinburgh EH3 7EG
0131 225 3361
www.jptalk.co.uk

Midland News Association

51–53 Queen St
Wolverhampton WV1 1ES
01902 313131
www.expressandstar.com

Newsquest Media

58 Church Street, Weybridge
Surrey KT13 8DP
01932 821212
www.newsquest.co.uk

Scotsman Publications

Barclay House
108 Holyrood Road
Edinburgh EH8 8AS
0131 620 8620
www.scotsman.com

Trinity Mirror

4th Floor, Rear Wing
191–197 North Circular Rd
Dublin 7
00 353 1 868 8600
www.trinitymirror.com
UK head office
Chronicle House
Commonhall Street
Chester CH1 2AA
01244 687000

Regional newspapers – England

Main regionals

Birmingham Evening Mail
Weaman St, Birmingham
West Midlands B4 6AT
0121 236 3366
www.icbirmingham.co.uk
Daily. Editor: Roger Borrell
News editor: Andy Richards
Features editor: Alison Handley
Bristol Evening Post
Temple Way
Bristol BS99 7HD
0117 934 3000
www.thisisbristol.co.uk
Daily. Editor: Mike Lowe
News editor: Kevin Blackadder
Features editor: Bill Davis
Chief sub-editor: Helen Lawrence
Coventry Evening Telegraph
Corporation St
Coventry CV1 1FP
024 7663 3633
www.iccoventry.co.uk
Daily. Editor: Alan Kirby
News editor: John West
Features editor: Steven Chilton
Derby Evening Telegraph
Northcliffe House, Meadow Rd
Derby, Derbyshire DE1 2DW
01332 291111
www.thisisderbyshire.co.uk
Daily. Editor: Mike Norton
News editor: Nicola Hodgson
Features editor: Cheryl Hague
Chief sub-editor: Peter Pheasant
Eastern Daily Press
Archant Norfolk, Prospect House
Rouen Rd, Norwich NR1 1RE
01603 628311
www.edp24.co.uk
Daily. Editor: Peter Franzen
Evening Chronicle
Groat Market
Newcastle Upon Tyne NE1 1ED
0191 232 7500
www.icnewcastle.co.uk
Daily (Mon–Fri)
Editor: Paul Robertson
News editor: Mick Smith
Features editor: Richard Ord
Chief sub-editor: Adrian Hogg

Evening Standard
Associated Newspapers
Northcliffe House, 2 Derry St
020 7938 6000
www.thisislondon.co.uk
Daily. Editor: Veronica Wadley
News editor: Ian Walker
Features editor: Guy Eaton

Express & Star
51–53 Queen St, Wolverhampton
West Midlands WV1 1ES
01902 313131
www.expressandstar.com
Daily. Editor: Adrian Faber
News editor: Mark Drew
Features editor: Dillion Evans
Chief sub-editor: Tony Reynolds

Leicester Mercury
St George St
Leicester LE1 9FQ
0116 251 2512
www.leicestermercury.co.uk
Daily. Editor: Nick Carter
News editor: Richard Bettsworth

Liverpool Post & Echo
Old Hall St, Liverpool L3 9JQ
0151 227 2000
www.icliverpool.co.uk
Daily. Editor: Mark Dickinson
News editor: Alison Gow

Manchester Evening News
164 Deansgate
Manchester M3 3RN
0161 832 7200
www.manchesteronline.co.uk
Daily. Editor: Paul Horrocks
News editor: Ian Woods
Chief sub-editor: John Whittaker

The News (Portsmouth)
Portsmouth Publishing & Printing
The News Centre, Military Rd
Hilsea, Portsmouth
Hampshire PO2 9SX
023 9266 4488
www.thenews.co.uk
Daily. Editor: Mike Gilson
News editor: Colin McNeill
Features editor: John Millard
Chief sub-editor: Steve Matthews

Northern Echo (Darlington & South West Durham)
Priestgate, Darlington
County Durham DL1 1NF
01325 381313
www.thisisthenortheast.co.uk
Daily. Editor: Peter Barron
News editor: Nigel Burton
Features editor: Nick Morrison
Chief sub-editor: Ken Farrier

The Sentinel (Stoke-On-Trent)
Staffordshire Sentinel Newspapers
Sentinel House, Etruria
01782 602525
www.thesentinel.co.uk
Daily. Editor: Sean Dooley
News editor: Robert Cotterill
Features editor: Charlotte Little-Jones

Shropshire Star
Shropshire Newspapers, Ketley
Telford, Shropshire TF1 5HU
01952 242424
www.shropshirestar.com
Daily. Editor: Sarah Jane Smith
News editor: John Simcock
Features editor: Carl Jones
Chief sub-editor: Lisa Bailey

Southern Daily Echo
Newsquest (Southern)
Newspaper House, Test Lane
Redbridge, Southampton
SO16 9JX
023 8042 4777
www.dailyecho.co.uk
Daily. Editor: Ian Murray
News editor: Gordon Sutter
Chief sub-editor: Colin Jenkins

The Star (Sheffield)
York St, Sheffield
South Yorkshire S1 1PU
0114 276 7676
www.sheffieldtoday.net
Daily. Editor: Peter Charlton
News editor: Bob Westerdale
Features editor: John Highfield
Head of content: Paul License

Sunday Mercury
Weaman St, Birmingham
West Midlands B4 6AT
0121 236 3366
www.icbirmingham.co.uk
Sunday. Editor: David Brookes
News editor: Tony Larner
Features editor: Paul Cole

Sunday Sun (Newcastle)
Groat Market
Newcastle Upon Tyne NE1 1ED
0191 232 7500
www.icnewcastle.co.uk
Sunday. Editor: Peter Montellier
News editor: Mike Kelly
Chief sub-editor: Lesley Oldfield
Production editor: Colin Patterson

Yorkshire Evening Post
PO Box 168, Wellington St
Leeds LS1 1RF
0113 243 2701
www.leedstoday.net
Daily. Editor: Neil Hodgkinson
News editor: Gillian Howorth
Features editor: Anne Pickles
Production editor: Howard Corry

Yorkshire Post
PO Box 168, Wellington St
Leeds LS1 1RF
0113 243 2701
www.yorkshireposttoday.co.uk
Daily. Editor: Rachael Campey
News editor: Hannah Start
Features editor: Catherine Scott
Head of production: Dick Porter

Other local and regional papers

London

Barnes, Mortlake & Sheen Times
020 8940 6030
www.richmondandtwickenham
times.co.uk
Weekly (Fri). Editor: Paul Mortimer
News editor: Andrew Raine

Barnet & Potters Bar Times
020 8203 0411
Weekly (Thu). Editor: John Killeen
News editor: Ian Lloyd

Barnet & Whetstone Press
020 8367 2345
Weekly free (Thu).
Editor: Simon Jones
News editor: Jonathan Lawn

Brent & Wembley Leader
020 8427 4404
www.trinitymirrorsouthern.co.uk
Weekly free (Fri).
Editor: Jo Makosinski
News editor: Caroline Lord
Features editor: Victoria Prewer
Production editor: Andre Erasmus

Brentford, Chiswick & Isleworth Times
020 8940 6030
www.richmondandtwickenham
times.co.uk
Weekly (Fri). Editor: Paul Mortimer
News editor: Andrew Raine

Bromley & Beckenham Times
020 8269 7000
Weekly (Thu). Editor: Melody Ryall
Production editor: Mick Taylor

Bromley & Orpington Express
020 8269 7000
Weekly free (Wed).
Editor: Melody Ryall
Production editor: Mick Taylor

Bromley News
01959 564766
www.bromley-today.co.uk
Weekly (Thu). Editor: Bridger Hogan

Bromley News Shopper
020 8646 6336
www.newsshopper.co.uk
Weekly (Thu). Editor: Andrew Parkes
News editor: Matthew Ramsden
Chief sub-editor: Tim Miles
Camden Chronicle
020 8340 6868
Weekly (Thu). Editor: Tony Allcock
Camden New Journal
020 7419 9000
www.camdennewjournal.co.uk
Weekly (Thu). Editor: Eric Gordon
News editor: Dan Carrier
Features editor: Claire Davies
Chief sub-editor: Obi Jilani
Production editor: Sarah Roberts
Camden Times
020 8962 6800
Weekly (Wed). Editor: Tim Cole
Caterham & District Advertiser
020 8763 6666
www.icsurrey.co.uk
Weekly (Fri). Editor: Ian Carter
News editor: Mike Hawkins
Chingford Guardian
020 8498 3400
Weekly (Thu). Editor: Pat Stannard
The Chiswick
020 8940 6030
Weekly (Wed). Editor: Paul Mortimer
News editor: Andrew Raine
City of London & Dockland Times
07957 961520
Fortnightly (Mon)
Editor: Richard Alvin
Croydon Advertiser
020 8763 6666
www.iccroydon.co.uk
Weekly (Fri). Editor: Ian Carter
News editor: Mike Hawkins
Croydon Borough Post
020 8763 4433
Weekly (Wed). Editor: Ian Carter
News editor: Mike Hawley
Croydon Guardian
020 8774 6565
www.croydonguardian.co.uk
Weekly (Wed).
Editor: Alison Hepworth
News editor: Helen Barnes
Docklands & City Recorder
020 8472 1421
Weekly (Wed). Editor: Colin Grainger
News editor: Pat Cougherey
Chief sub-editor: John Finn
Docklands News
020 7473 2488
www.docklandsnews.co.uk
Weekly (Thu). Editor: Richard Alvin

Ealing & Acton Gazette
020 8579 3131
Weekly (Fri). Editor: Linda Coulson
News editor: Sarah Graham
Features editor: Victoria Prewer
Chief sub-editor: Joyce McKim
Ealing & Uxbridge Times
01494 755000
www.hillingdontimes.co.uk
Weekly free (Thu).
Editor: Steve Cohen
News editor: Kelly Clayton
Ealing Informer
020 8579 3131
Weekly (Wed). Editor: Linda Coulson
News editor: Sarah Graham
Features editor: Victoria Prewer
Chief sub-editor: Joyce McKim
Ealing Leader
01895 451000
Weekly (Fri). Editor: Linda Coulson
News editor: Sarah Graham
Features editor: Victoria Prewer
Chief sub-editor: Joyce McKim
Ealing Times
01494 755000
www.ealingtimes.co.uk
Weekly (Thu). Editor: Steve Cohen
News editor: Kelly Clayton
East End Life
020 7364 3059
Sunday free. Editor: Lorraine Clay
News editor: Helen Watson
East London Advertiser
020 7790 8822
Weekly (Thu).
Editor: Richard Tidiman
East London Enquirer
01277 627300
Weekly (Thu). Editor: Carol Driver
Edgware & Mill Hill Press
020 8367 2345
Weekly free (Thu).
Editor: Simon Jones
News editor: Jonathan Lawn
Edgware & Mill Hill Times
020 8203 0411
Weekly (Thu). Editor: John Killeen
News editor: Ian Lloyd
Eltham and Greenwich Times
020 8269 7000
Weekly (Wed). Editor: Melody Ryall
Production editor: Mick Taylor
Enfield Advertiser
020 8367 2345
Weekly (Wed). Editor: Simon Jones
News editor: Jonathan Lawn
Enfield Gazette
020 8367 2345
Weekly (Thu). Editor: Simon Jones
News editor: Jonathan Lawn

Enfield Independent
020 8362 1431
www.enfieldindependent.co.uk
Weekly (Wed). Editor: Kate Russell
Erith & Crayford Times
020 8269 7000
Weekly (Wed). Editor: Melody Ryall
Production editor: Mick Taylor
Evening Standard
020 7938 6000
www.thisislondon.co.uk
Daily. Editor: Veronica Wadley
News editor: Ian Walker
Features editor: Guy Eaton
Fulham Chronicle
020 8572 1816
Weekly (Thu). Editor: Kim Chapman
News editor: Janice Raycroft
Features editor: Gerri Besgrove
Fulham Gazette
020 8579 3131
Weekly (Fri). Editor: Sarah Graham
News editor: Lindsay Coulson
Greater London Advertiser
024 7625 1627
Weekly (Wed). Editor: Sam Lee
Greenford & Northolt Gazette
020 8579 3131
Weekly (Fri). Editor: Sarah Graham
News editor: Lindsay Coulson
Greenwich Borough Mercury
020 8769 4444
Weekly (Wed)
Editor-in-chief: Hannah Walker
Editor: Douglas Nel
Hackney Gazette
020 7790 8822
Weekly (Thu). Editor: Mick Ferris
News editor: Ross Lawrence
Hammersmith & Fulham Chronicles
020 8572 1816
Weekly (Thu). Editor: Kim Chapman
News editor: Janice Raycroft
Features editor: Gerri Besgrove
Hammersmith & Shepherd's Bush Gazette
020 8579 3131
Weekly (Fri). Editor: Sarah Graham
News editor: Lindsay Coulson
Hammersmith Times
020 8962 6800
Weekly (Wed). Editor: Tim Cole
Hampstead and Highgate Express
020 7433 0000
www.hamhigh.co.uk
Weekly (Fri). Editor: Geoff Martin
News editor: Bridget Galton
Features editor: Melanie Smith

Harefield Gazette
01895 451000
Weekly (Wed). Editor: Adrian Seal
News editor: Liz Bellchambers
Features editor: Neil Dhot

Haringey Advertiser
020 8367 2345
Weekly (Wed). Editor: Simon Jones
News editor: Jonathan Lawn

Haringey Independent
020 8359 5959
www.haringeyindependent.co.uk
Weekly (Fri). Editor: Kate Russell

Harrow & Sudbury Chronicle
020 8962 6800
Weekly (Wed). Editor: Tim Cole

Harrow Leader
020 8427 4404
www.trinitymirrorsouthern.co.uk
Weekly free (Fri).
Editor: Jo Makosinski
News editor: Caroline Lord
Features editor: Victoria Prewer
Production editor: Andre Erasmus

Harrow Observer
020 8427 4404
Weekly (Thu). Editor: Jo Makosinski
News editor: Caroline Lord
Features editor: Victoria Prewer
Production editor: Andre Erasmus

Harrow Times
01923 216216
www.harrowtimes.co.uk
Weekly (Thu). Editor: Charlie Harris

Havering Herald
01708 771500
Weekly (Wed)
Editor: Mark Sweetingham

Hayes and Harlington Gazette
01895 451000
Weekly (Wed). Editor: Adrian Seal
News editor: Liz Bellchambers
Features editor: Neil Dhot

Hendon & Finchley Press
020 8367 2345
Weekly free (Thu).
Editor: Simon Jones
News editor: Jonathan Lawn

Hendon Times
020 8359 5959
www.hendontimes.co.uk
Weekly (Thu). Editor: John Kileen
News editor: Colin O'Toole

Highbury & Islington Express
020 7433 0000
www.islingtonexpress.co.uk
Weekly (Fri). Editor: Geoff Martin
News editor: Bridget Galton
Features editor: Melanie Smith

Hillingdon Times
01494 755000
www.hillingdontimes.co.uk
Weekly (Thu). Editor: Steve Cohen

Hornsey & Crouch End Journal
020 8340 6868
Weekly (Thu). Editor: Tony Allcock

Hounslow, Brentford & Chiswick Informer
020 8572 1816
Weekly free (Fri).
Editor: Kim Chapman
News editor: Ben Harvey

Hounslow Chronicle
020 8572 1816
Weekly (Thu). Editor: Kim Chapman
News editor: Ben Harvey
Features editor: Gerri Besgrove

Hounslow Guardian
020 8940 6030
www.hounslowguardian.co.uk
Weekly (Thu). Editor: Paul Mortimer
News editor: Andrew Raine

Hounslow Informer
020 8572 1816
Weekly free (Fri).
Editor: Kim Chapman
News editor: Janice Raycroft
Features editor: Gerri Besgrove

Hounslow, Feltham & Hanworth Times
020 8940 6030
Weekly (Fri). Editor: Paul Mortimer
News editor: Andrew Raine

Hoxton & Stamford Hill Express
020 7790 8822
Weekly (Thu).
Editor: Clara Wiseman

Ilford Recorder
020 8478 4444
www.recorderonline.co.uk
Weekly (Thu). Editor: Chris Carter
News editor: Antigone Forder
Production editor: Mike Cubitt

Islington Gazette
020 8340 6868
Weekly (Thu). Editor: Tony Allcock

Islington Tribune
020 7419 9000
Weekly (Thu). Editor: Eric Gordon
News editor: Dan Carrier
Features editor: Claire Davies
Chief sub-editor: Obi Jilani
Production editor: Sarah Roberts

Kensington & Chelsea Informer
020 8572 1816
Weekly (Fri). Editor: Kim Chapman
News editor: Janice Raycroft
Features editor: Gerri Besgrove

Kensington Times
020 8962 6800
Weekly (Wed). Editor: Tim Cole

Kilburn Times
020 8962 6800
Weekly (Wed). Editor: Tim Cole

Kingston & Surbiton Times
020 8940 6030
Weekly (Fri). Editor: Paul Mortimer
News editor: Chris Briddon

Kingston Guardian
020 8940 6030
www.kingstonguardian.co.uk
Weekly (Thu). Editor: Sean Duggan

Kingston Informer
020 8572 1816
www.trinitymirrorsouthern.co.uk
Weekly (Fri). Editor: Kim Chapman
News editor: Janice Raycroft
Features editor: Gerri Besgrove

Lewisham and Greenwich Mercury
020 8769 4444
www.icsouthlondon.co.uk
Weekly free. Editor: Hannah Walker
News editor: Shujal Azam

Lewisham Borough Mercury
020 8692 1122
Weekly (Wed). Editor: Douglas Nel

Lewisham News Shopper
020 8646 6336
www.newsshopper.co.uk
Weekly (Thu). Editor: Andrew Parkes
News editor: Matthew Ramsden
Chief sub-editor: Tim Miles

Leyton & Leytonstone Guardian
020 8498 3400
www.leytonguardian.co.uk
Weekly (Thu). Editor: Pat Stannard

Marylebone & Paddington Informer
020 8572 1816
Weekly (Fri). Editor: Kim Chapman
News editor: Janice Raycroft
Features editor: Gerri Besgrove

Marylebone & Paddington Mercury
020 8572 1816
Weekly (Fri). Editor: Kim Chapman
News editor: Janice Raycroft
Features editor: Gerri Besgrove

Mayfair Times
020 7839 2455
Monthly free (1st Mon)
Editor: Eric Brown

Metro London
020 7651 5200
www.metro.co.uk
Daily. Editor: Kenny Campbell
News editor: Mark Dorman
Features editor: Kieran Meeke
Production editor: Jason Kent

Mitcham, Morden & Wimbledon Post
020 8769 4444
www.icsouthlondon.co.uk
Weekly free (Fri)
Editor: Hannah Walker
News editor: Shujal Azam

Muswell Hill Journal
020 8340 6868
Weekly (Thu). Editor: Tony Allcock
New Addington Advertiser
020 8763 6666
www.icsurrey.co.uk
Weekly (Fri). Editor: Ian Carter
News editor: Mike Hawkins
Newham Recorder
020 8472 1421
www.recorderonline.co.uk
Weekly (Thu). Editor: Colin Grainger
News editor: Pat Cougherey
Chief sub-editor: John Finn
North London Herald
020 8340 6868
Weekly (Thu). Editor: Tony Allcock
Paddington Times
020 8962 6800
Weekly (Wed). Editor: Tim Cole
Pinner Observer
020 8427 4404
Weekly (Thu). Editor: Jo Makosinski
News editor: Caroline Lord
Features editor: Victoria Prewer
Production editor: Andre Erasmus
Potters Bar Press
020 8364 4040
Weekly free (Thu)
Editor: Jonathan Lawn
News editor: Joseph Lee
Richmond & Twickenham Informer
020 8572 1816
Weekly (Fri). Editor: Kim Chapman
News editor: Janice Raycroft
Features editor: Gerri Besgrove
Richmond & Twickenham Times
020 8940 6030
www.richmondandtwickenham times.co.uk
Weekly (Fri). Editor: Paul Mortimer
News editor: James Adlam
Richmond Borough Guardian
020 8940 6030
www.kingstonguardian.co.uk
Weekly (Thu). Editor: Paul Mortimer
News editor: James Adlam
Ruislip & Northwood Gazette
01895 451000
Weekly (Wed). Editor: Adrian Seal
News editor: Liz Bellchambers
Features editor: Neil Dhot
Ruislip & Northwood Informer
01895 451000
Weekly free (Fri). Editor: Adrian Seal
News editor: Liz Bellchambers
Features editor: Neil Dhot
South London Press
020 8769 4444
www.icsouthlondon.co.uk
Twice-weekly (Tue, Fri)
Editor: Hannah Walker
News editor: Shujal Azam

Southall Gazette
020 8579 3131
Weekly (Fri). Editor: Sarah Graham
News editor: Lindsay Coulson
Southwark News
020 7231 5258
Weekly (Thu). Editor: Chris Mullany
News editor: Kevin Quinn
St John's Wood & Maida Vale Express (Wood & Vale)
020 7433 0000
Weekly (Fri). Editor: Geoff Martin
News editor: Bridget Galton
Features editor: Melanie Smith
Stanmore Observer
020 8427 4404
Weekly (Thu). Editor: Jo Makosinski
News editor: Caroline Lord
Features editor: Victoria Prewer
Production editor: Andre Erasmus
The Star
01494 755000
Weekly free (Thu).
Editor: Steve Cohen
News editor: Julie Voyce
Features editor: Clare Bourke
Stratford & Newham Express
020 7790 8822
Weekly (Wed).
Editor: Richard Tidiman
Streatham Guardian
020 8646 6336
www.streathamguardian.co.uk
Weekly (Thu).
News editor: Dave Tilley
Features editor: June Simpson
Streatham, Clapham & West Norwood Post
020 8769 4444
www.icsouthlondon.co.uk
Weekly free (Thu)
Editor: Hannah Walker
News editor: Shujal Azam
Teddington & Hampton Times
020 8940 6030
Weekly (Fri). Editor: Paul Mortimer
News editor: James Adlam
Tottenham & Wood Green Journal
020 8340 6868
Weekly (Thu). Editor: Tony Allcock
Tower Hamlets Recorder
020 8472 1421
www.recorderonline.co.uk
Weekly (Thu). Editor: Colin Grainger
News editor: Pat Cougherey
Chief sub-editor: John Finn
Uxbridge & Hillingdon Leader
01895 451000
Weekly free (Thu).
Editor: Adrian Seal
News editor: Liz Bellchambers
Features editor: Neil Dhot

Uxbridge & W Drayton Gazette
01895 451000
Weekly (Tue). Editor: Adrian Seal
News editor: Liz Bellchambers
Features editor: Neil Dhot
Uxbridge Informer
01895 451000
Weekly (Wed). Editor: Adrian Seal
News editor: Liz Bellchambers
Features editor: Neil Dhot
Uxbridge Leader
01895 451000
Weekly free (Wed).
Editor: Adrian Seal
News editor: Liz Bellchambers
Features editor: Neil Dhot
Walthamstow Guardian
020 8498 3400
www.walthamstowguardian.co.uk
Weekly (Thu). Editor: Pat Stannard
Wandsworth Guardian
020 8646 6336
www.wandsworthguardian.co.uk
Weekly (Thu). News editor: Dave Tilley
Features editor: June Simpson
Wembley & Kingsbury Chronicle
020 8962 6800
Weekly (Wed). Editor: Tim Cole
Wembley Leader
020 8427 4404
Weekly (Thu). Editor: Jo Makosinski
News editor: Caroline Lord
Features editor: Victoria Prewer
Production editor: Andre Erasmus
Wembley Observer
020 8427 4404
Weekly (Thu). Editor: Jo Makosinski
News editor: Caroline Lord
Features editor: Victoria Prewer
Production editor: Andre Erasmus
West End Extra
020 7419 9000
Weekly (Fri). Editor: Eric Gordon
News editor: Dan Carrier
Features editor: Claire Davies
Chief sub-editor: Obi Jilani
Production editor: Sarah Roberts
Westender
020 7607 6060
Monthly free (last week in month)
Editor: Eileen Martin
News editor: Bina Gowrea
Features editor: Eileen Duff
Production editor: Jason Kent
Westminster & Pimlico News
020 8572 1816
Weekly (Fri). Editor: Kim Chapman
News editor: Janice Raycroft
Features editor: Gerri Besgrove
Westminster Independent
020 8961 3345
www.londonlocals.co.uk
Weekly (Fri). Editor: Jan Mappin

Westminster Times
020 8962 6800
Weekly (Wed). Editor: Tim Cole
The Wharf
020 7510 6306
www.icthewharf.co.uk
Weekly free (Thu)
Editor: Ann Stenhouse
Willesden & Brent Chronicle
020 8962 6800
Weekly (Wed). Editor: Tim Cole
Willesden Observer
020 8427 4404
Weekly (Thu). Editor: Jo Makosinski
News editor: Caroline Lord
Features editor: Victoria Prewer
Production editor: Andre Erasmus
Wimbledon Guardian
020 8646 6336
www.wimbledonguardian.co.uk
Weekly (Thu).
News editor: Dave Tilley
Features editor: June Simpson
Wimbledon News
020 8646 6336
Weekly (Wed).
News editor: Dave Tilley
Features editor: June Simpson

South-east England

Bedfordshire, East Sussex,
Hertfordshire, Kent, Surrey,
West Sussex

Addlestone and Byfleet Review
01483 508700
www.surreyad.co.uk
Weekly (Wed).
Editor: Marnie Wilson
Adscene – Ashford & Tenterden
01227 767321
Weekly (Thu). Editor: Lesley Finlay
News editor: Julia Rogers
Chief sub-editor: Mark Silva
Adscene (Canterbury)
01227 767321
Weekly (Thu). Editor: John Nurden
News editor: Ian Reed
Features editor: Julia Rogers
Chief sub-editor: Paul Taylor
Production editor: Mark Silva
Adscene (Folkestone & Dover)
01227 767321
Weekly (Thu). Editor: Simon Finlay
Adscene (Maidstone)
01622 690339
www.kent-online.co.uk
Weekly free (Thu).
Editor: Diane Nicholls

Adscene (Medway)
01227 767321
Weekly (Thu). Editor: Diane Nicholls
News editor: Nicola Jordan
**Adscene (Sittingbourne &
Sheppey)**
01227 767321
Weekly (Thu).
Editor: Christine Rayner
News editor: Steve Waite
Adscene (Thanet)
01227 767321
Weekly (Thu). Editor: Mike Pearce
Aldershot News
01483 508700
www.aldershot.co.uk
Weekly (Tue). Editor: Marnie Wilson
Ashford KM Extra
01233 623232
Weekly (Tue). Editor: Brian Lewis
News editor: Leo Whitlock
Features editor: Leo Whitlock
Chief sub-editor: Claire Stevens
Production editor: Gary Barker
Baldock Crow
01763 245241
Weekly (Thu). Editor: Les Baker
Barnet & Potters Bar Times
020 8359 5959
www.barnettimes.co.uk
Weekly (Thu). Editor: John Kileen
News editor: Colin O'Toole
Bedford Times & Citizen
01234 405060
www.bedfordtoday.co.uk
Weekly (Fri). Editor: Chris Hall
News editor: Mark Lewis
Features editor: Olga Norford
Bedfordshire on Sunday
01234 300888
www.seriousaboutnews.com
Sunday. Editor: Steve Lowe
News editor: Liz Ashton
Production editor: Phil Umney
Bexhill AdNews
01424 730555
www.bexhilltoday.co.uk
Weekly free (Wed).
Editor: Michael Beard
Deputy editor: John Dowling
News editor: Rob Hustwaype
Bexhill-On-Sea Observer
01424 730555
www.bexhilltoday.co.uk
Weekly (Fri). Editor: Michael Beard
Deputy editor: John Dowling
News editor: Rob Hustwaype
Bexley & Eltham Express
020 8269 7000
Weekly free (Wed).
Editor: Melody Ryall
Production editor: Mick Taylor

**Bexley Dartford & Gravesham
News Shopper**
01689 885701
Weekly (Wed). Editor: Andrew Parkes
Bexley Mercury
020 8769 4444
www.icsouthlondon.co.uk
Weekly free. Editor: Hannah Walker
News editor: Douglas Mill
Bexleyheath & Welling Times
020 8269 7000
Weekly (Wed). Editor: Melody Ryall
Production editor: Mick Taylor
Biggin Hill News
01959 564766
www.biggin-hill-today.co.uk
Weekly (Thu). Editor: Bridger Hogan
Biggleswade & Sandy Comet
01462 420120
www.thecomet.net
Weekly (Thu). Editor: Darren Isted
News editor: John Adams
Biggleswade Advertiser
01462 441020
www.hitchinadvertiser.co.uk
Weekly (Wed)
No editorial
Biggleswade Chronicle
01767 222333
www.biggleswadetoday.co.uk
Weekly (Fri). Editor: Jim Stewart
Bishops Stortford Citizen
01992 572285
Weekly (Thu).
Editor: David Jackman
Bishops Stortford Herald
01279 624331
Weekly (Thu). Editor: Peter Jeffery
News editor: Tracey Hubbard
Features editor: James Wilmore
Bognor Regis Guardian
01243 534133
Weekly free (Wed).
Editor: Alicia Denny
Bognor Regis Observer
01243 828777
www.chichester.co.uk
Weekly (Thu).
Editor: Keith Newberry
Features editor: Kevin Smith
Borehamwood & Elstree Times
020 8359 5959
www.borehamwoodtimes.co.uk
Weekly (Fri). Editor: John Kileen
News editor: Colin O'Toole
Brighton & Hove Leader
01273 544544
www.thisisbrightonandhove.co.uk
Weekly (Fri). Editor: Chris Chandler
News editor: Mike Dunford

Brighton Evening Argus
01273 544544
www.thisisbrightonandhove.co.uk
Daily. Editor: Simon Bradshaw
News editor: Simon Freeman
Features editor: Jacqui Phillips
Chief sub-editor: Pat Lewis
Production editor: Chris Heath

Camberley Courier
01252 339760
www.camberley.co.uk
Weekly free (Wed).
Editor: James Taylor
News editor: Adam Clark

Camberley News & Mail
01252 339760
www.camberley.co.uk
Weekly (Fri). Editor: James Taylor
News editor: Adam Clark

Canterbury KM Extra
01227 768181
Weekly (Tue). Editor: Bob Bounds
News editor: Trisha Jaimeson
Production editor: Gary Barker

Cheshunt & Waltham Mercury
01992 414141
Weekly (Fri). Editor: Ian Rogerson
News editor: Pat Roberts

Chichester & Selsey Journal
01243 534133
www.chichester.co.uk
Weekly free (Wed).
Editor: Alicia Denny

Chichester Observer
01243 539389
www.chiobserver.co.uk
Weekly (Thu).
Editor: Keith Newberry
Features editor: Peter Homer

Chislehurst Times
020 8269 7000
Weekly (Thu). Editor: Melody Ryall
Production editor: Mick Taylor

Cranleigh Times
01483 508700
Weekly free (Wed).
Editor: Marnie Wilson

Crawley News
01737 300300
www.icsurrey.co.uk
Weekly (Wed). Editor: Ian Carter
News editor: John Keeble

Crawley Observer
01293 562929
www.crawleyobserver.co.uk
Weekly (Wed).
Editor: Graham Campbell
News editor: Allan Norbury
Chief sub-editor: Mark Dunford

Crowborough Courier
01892 681000
www.thisiskentandeastsussex.
 co.uk
Weekly (Fri). Editor: Giles Broadbent
News editor: Melanie Whittaker
Features editor: Lucia Blash
Chief sub-editor: Lindsey Jones
Production editor: Richard Page

Croydon Advertiser
01737 732000
www.iccroydon.co.uk
Weekly (Fri). Editor: Mike Hawkins

Croydon Guardian
020 8774 6590
www.croydonguardian.co.uk
Weekly (Wed).
Editor: Alison Hepworth
News editor: Helen Barnes
Chief sub-editor: Ali Mased

Croydon Post
01737 732000
Weekly (Thu). Editor: Mike Hawkins

Dartford & Swanley Extra Informer
01322 220791
Weekly (Thu).
Editor: Sandra Hembury
News editor: Teresa Gaines

Dartford Express
020 8269 7000
Weekly free (Wed).
Editor: Melody Ryall
Production editor: Mick Taylor

Dartford Messenger
01322 220791
www.kent-online.co.uk
Weekly (Thu).
Editor: Sandra Hembury
News editor: Denise Eaton

Dartford Times
020 8269 7000
Weekly (Thu). Editor: Melody Ryall
Production editor: Mick Taylor

Dover & Deal Extra
01233 623323
Weekly (Wed). Editor: Brian Lewis
News editor: Leo Whitlock
Features editor: Leo Whitlock
Chief sub-editor: Claire Stevens
Production editor: Gary Barker

Dover Express
01227 767321
Weekly (Thu). Editor: Simon Finlay

Dover Mercury
01304 240380
Weekly (Thu). Editor: Graham Smith

Downs Mail
01622 630330
www.downsmail.co.uk
Monthly (variable)
Editor: Geoff Manners

Dunstable Gazette
01582 526000
www.lutontoday.co.uk
Weekly (Wed).
Editor: John Buckledee

Dunstable On Sunday
01582 707707
www.seriousaboutnews.com
Sunday. Editor: Aylia Fox
News editor: Gaynor Selby
Production editor: Phil Umney

Eastbourne & District Advertiser
01323 722091
www.eastbournetoday.co.uk
Weekly free (Thu).
Editor: Peter Lindsay
News editor: Robin Emanuel
Features editor: Andrew Bennett

Eastbourne Gazette
01323 722091
www.eastbournetoday.co.uk
Weekly (Wed). Editor: Peter Lindsay
News editor: Robin Emanuel
Features editor: Andrew Bennett

Eastbourne Herald
01323 722091
www.eastbournetoday.co.uk
Weekly (Fri). Editor: Peter Lindsay
News editor: Robin Emanuel
Features editor: Andrew Bennett

East Grinstead Courier
01892 681000
Weekly (Thu).
Editor: Giles Broadbent
News editor: Melanie Whittaker
Features editor: Lucia Blash
Chief sub-editor: Lindsey Jones
Production editor: Richard Page

East Grinstead Observer
01737 732000
www.icsurrey.co.uk
Weekly (Wed). Editor: Ian Carter
News editor: Catherine Simmons

East Kent Gazette
01227 767321
Weekly (Thu).
Editor: Christine Rayner
News editor: Steve Waite

East Kent Mercury
01304 365526
Weekly free. Editor: Graham Smith
Production editor: Gary Barker

Edenbridge Chronicle
01959 564766
Weekly (Thu). Editor: Signid Sherr

Edenbridge County Border News
01959 564766
www.edenbridge-today.co.uk
Weekly (Thu). Editor: Kevin Black

Edenbridge Courier
01892 681000
www.thisiskentandeastsussex.
co.uk
Weekly (Fri). Editor: Giles Broadbent
News editor: Melanie Whittaker
Features editor: Lucia Blash
Chief sub-editor: Lindsey Jones
Production editor: Richard Page
Edgware & Mill Hill Times
020 8359 5959
www.edgwaretimes.co.uk
Weekly (Thu). Editor: John Kileen
News editor: Colin O'Toole
Elmbridge Guardian
020 8646 6336
Weekly (Thu). Editor: Sean Duggan
Epsom Guardian
020 8646 6336
www.epsomguardian.co.uk
Weekly (Thu). Editor: Sean Duggan
Epsom, Ewell & Banstead Post
020 8763 6666
www.icsurrey.co.uk
Weekly (Fri). Editor: Ian Carter
News editor: Mike Hawkins
Esher News & Mail
01483 508700
www.esher.co.uk
Weekly (Fri). Editor: Marnie Wilson
Farnham Herald
01252 725224
www.farnham-herald-today.co.uk
Weekly (Fri). Editor: Vic Robbie
News editor: James Bowman
Chief sub-editor: Sandy Baker
Farnham Post
01420 88949
Fortnightly free (Mon)
Editor: Alan Wooler
Faversham KM Extra
01227 768181
Weekly (Tue). Editor: Bob Bounds
News editor: Trisha Jaimeson
Production editor: Gary Barker
Faversham News
01227 475901
www.faversham.org/GENERAL
/favnews.htm
Weekly (Thu). Editor: Bob Bounds
News editor: Trisha Jaimeson
Production editor: Gary Barker
Faversham Times
01227 767321
Weekly (Thu).
Editor: Christine Rayner
News editor: Steve Waite
Features editor: Julia Rogers
Folkestone & Hythe Extra
01303 850676
Weekly (Wed). Editor: Brian Lewis
Production editor: Gary Barker

Folkestone Express
01233 623232
Weekly (Wed). Editor: Brian Lewis
News editor: Leo Whitlock
Features editor: Leo Whitlock
Chief sub-editor: Claire Stevens
Folkestone Herald
01227 767321
Weekly (Thu). Editor: Simon Finlay
Friday-Ad
0870 162 9999
www.friday-ad.co.uk
Weekly (Fri).
Editor: David Sommerville
Gatwick Skyport
01932 561111
Weekly free (Fri). Editor: Liz Billings
Godalming Times
01483 508700
Weekly free (Wed)
Editor: Marnie Wilson
Gravesend Express
020 8269 7000
Weekly free (Wed).
Editor: Melody Ryall
Production editor: Mick Taylor
Gravesend KM Extra
01474 333381
www.kent-online.co.uk
Weekly (Fri).
Editor: Sandra Hembury
News editor: Denise Eaton
Gravesend Messenger
01474 333381
www.kent-online.co.uk
Weekly (Thu).
Editor: Sandra Hembury
News editor: Denise Eaton
Gravesend Reporter
020 8269 7000
Weekly (Thu). Editor: Melody Ryall
Production editor: Mick Taylor
Guildford Times
01483 508700
www.surreyad.co.uk/news
/guildford-times.html
Weekly free (Wed)
Editor: Marnie Wilson
Hailsham Gazette
01323 722091
Weekly (Wed). Editor: Peter Lindsay
News editor: Robin Emanuel
Features editor: Andrew Bennett
Harpenden Observer
01727 834411
Weekly (Wed).
Editor: Deborah Williams
Haslemere Times & Mail
01252 716444
Weekly free (Tue). Editor: Jean Parrat

Hastings & St Leonards Observer
01424 854242
www.hastingstoday.co.uk
Weekly (Fri). Editor: Michael Beard
News editor: Ann Terry
Associate editor: Russell Claughton
Hastings AdNews
01424 854242
www.hastingstoday.co.uk
Weekly (Fri). Editor: Michael Beard
News editor: Ann Terry
Associate editor: Russell Claughton
Hemel Hempstead Gazette
01442 262311
www.hemelonline.co.uk
Weekly (Wed).
Editor: David Feldstein
News editor: Ann Traynor
Hendon & Finchley Times
020 8359 5959
www.hendontimes.co.uk
Weekly (Thu). Editor: John Kileen
News editor: Colin O'Toole
Herne Bay Gazette
01227 475901
Weekly. Editor: Bob Bounds
News editor: Trisha Jaimeson
Production editor: Gary Barker
Herne Bay KM Extra
01227 768181
Weekly (Tue). Editor: Bob Bounds
News editor: Trisha Jaimeson
Production editor: Gary Barker
Herne Bay Times
01227 771515
Weekly (Thu). Editor: John Nurden
News editor: Ian Reed
Features editor: Julia Rogers
Chief sub-editor: Paul Taylor
Production editor: Mark Silva
Hertford Times
01727 327551
www.hertsad.co.uk
Weekly (Wed).
Editor: Terry Mitchinson
Hertfordshire Mercury
01992 526625
www.herts-essex-news.co.uk
Weekly (Fri). Editor: Paul Winspear
Hertfordshire News
01926 431601
Weekly (Mon).
Editor: Funsho Ajibade
Hertfordshire on Sunday
01582 700800
Sunday. Editor: Liz Reilly
Hertfordshire Star
01992 526625
www.herts-essex-news.co.uk
Weekly (Wed). Editor: Chris Bristow

Herts & Essex Observer
01279 866355
www.herts-essex-news.co.uk
Weekly (Thu). Editor: Val Brown
News editor: Sandra Perry
Herts Advertiser
01727 865165
www.hertsad.co.uk
Weekly (Thu). Editor: Noel Cantillon
Hitchin Advertiser
01462 441020
www.hitchinadvertiser.co.uk
Weekly (Wed)
General manager: Ricky Allan
Hitchin Comet
01462 420120
www.thecomet.net
Weekly (Thu). Editor: Darren Isted
News editor: John Adams
Hoddesdon & Braxbourne Mercury
01992 414141
Weekly (Fri). Editor: Ian Rogerson
News editor: Pat Roberts
Horley Life
01273 544544
Weekly (Thu). Editor: Chris Chandler
News editor: Mike Dunford
Horsham Advertiser
01403 751200
www.horshamtoday.co.uk
Weekly (Fri). Editor: Gary Shipton
Chief sub-editor: Steve Payne
Production editor: Jonathan Taylor
Hythe Herald
01227 767321
Weekly (Thu). Editor: Simon Finlay
Isle of Thanet Gazette
01227 767321
Weekly (Thu). Editor: Mike Pearce
Kent & Sussex Courier
01892 681000
www.thisiskentandeast
sussex.co.uk
Weekly (Fri). Editor: Giles Broadbent
News editor: Melanie Whittaker
Features editor: Lucia Blash
Chief sub-editor: Lindsey Jones
Production editor: Richard Page
Kent Messenger
01622 695666
www.kent-online.co.uk
Weekly (Fri). Editor: Ron Green
News editor: Cathy Tyce
Kent on Sunday
01227 732223
www.kentonsunday.co.uk
Sunday. Editor: Ian Patel
News editor: Gary Wright
Chief sub-editor: Dave Hobday
Production editor: Jason Pyne

Kentish Express
01233 623232
Weekly (Thu). Editor: Brian Lewis
News editor: Leo Whitlock
Features editor: Leo Whitlock
Chief sub-editor: Claire Stevens
Production editor: Gary Barker
Kentish Gazette
01227 768181
Weekly (Thu). Editor: Bob Bounds
News editor: Trisha Jaimeson
Production editor: Gary Barker
Kentish Times Newspapers
020 8269 7000
Weekly (Thu). Editor: Melody Ryall
Production editor: Mick Taylor
Kingston Guardian
020 8646 6336
www.kingstonguardian.co.uk
Weekly (Thu). Editor: Sean Duggan
Lea Valley Star
01992 526625
Weekly (Wed). Editor: Chris Bristow
Leatherhead Advertiser
01737 732000
www.icsurrey.co.uk
Weekly (Thu). Editor: Ian Carter
News editor: Monica Hawley
Leatherhead Guardian
020 8646 6336
Weekly (Thu). Editor: Sean Duggan
Leighton Buzzard & Linslade Citizen
01908 651200
www.miltonkeynestoday.co.uk
Weekly free (Thu). Editor: Alan Legg
Leighton Buzzard Observer
01525 858400
www.miltonkeynestoday.co.uk
Weekly (Tue). Editor: Nick Wormley
News editor: Mike King
Leighton Buzzard On Sunday
01908 809000
www.seriousaboutnews.com
Sunday. Editor: Liz Aston
Letchworth & Baldock Comet
01462 420120
www.thecomet.net
Weekly (Thu). Editor: Darren Isted
News editor: John Adams
Limited Edition – Hertfordshire
01923 216220
Monthly (1st Tue)
Editor: Deborah Aspinall
Littlehampton Gazette
01903 230051
www.littlehamptontoday.co.uk
Weekly (Thu). Editor: Roger Green
Luton Herald & Post
01582 700600
www.lutontoday.co.uk
Weekly (Thu). Editor: John Francis

Luton News
01582 526000
www.lutontoday.co.uk
Weekly (Wed).
Editor: John Buckledee
Assistant editor: Geoff Cox
Luton on Sunday
01582 707707
www.seriousaboutnews.com
Sunday. Editor: Aylia Fox
News editor: Gaynor Selby
Maidstone KM Extra
01622 695666
www.kent-online.co.uk
Weekly free (Fri). Editor: Ron Green
News editor: Cathy Tyce
Medway Messenger (Rochester Chatham, Maidstone, Gravesend)
01634 830600
www.kent-online.co.uk
Weekly. Editor: Bob Diamond
News editor: Nikke White
Features editor: Lynn Cox
Chief sub-editor: Digby Kennard
Medway News
01227 767321
Weekly (Thu). Editor: Diane Nicholl
News editor: Nicola Jordan
Medway Standard
01227 767321
Weekly (Fri). Editor: Diane Nicholls
News editor: Nicola Jordan
The Messenger (Haslemere)
01428 653999
www.messenger-online.co.uk
Weekly free (Wed).
Editor: Guy Butchers
News editor: Sheila Checkley
Mid Sussex Citizen
01444 452201
www.midsussextoday.co.uk
Weekly free (Wed).
Editor: Paul Watson
Mid Sussex Leader
01273 544544
www.thisismidsussex.co.uk
Weekly (Thu). Editor: Chris Chandl
News editor: Mike Dunford
Mid Sussex Times
01444 452201
www.midsussextoday.co.uk
Weekly (Thu). Editor: Paul Watson
Midhurst & Petworth Observer
01730 813557
www.midhurstandpetworth.co.u
Weekly (Thu).
Editor: Keith Newberry
News editor: Jane Hurt
News in Focus
01732 228000
www.thisiskentandeastsussex.
co.uk
Weekly (Tue). Editor: Frank Baldw

News & Mail
01483 508900
www.surreyad.co.uk/aboutus.htm
Weekly (Wed).
Editor: Marnie Wilson
News Shopper Guide
020 8646 6336
Weekly (Thu). Editor: Andrew Parkes
News editor: Matthew Ramsden
Chief sub-editor: Tim Miles
Orpington & Petts Wood Times
020 8269 7000
Weekly (Thu). Editor: Melody Ryall
Production editor: Mick Taylor
Paddock Wood Courier
01892 681000
www.thisiskentandeastsussex.
co.uk
Weekly (Fri). Editor: Giles Broadbent
News editor: Melanie Whittaker
Features editor: Lucia Blash
Chief sub-editor: Lindsey Jones
Production editor: Richard Page
Redhill & Reigate Life
020 8646 6336
Weekly (Wed).
Editor: Alison Hepworth
News editor: Helen Barnes
Chief sub-editor: Ali Mased
Reigate Post
020 8770 7171
Weekly (Thu). Editor: Ian Carter
News editor: Helen Backway
Reigate, Redhill & Horley Post
01737 732000
www.icsurrey.co.uk
Weekly (Wed). Editor: Ian Carter
News editor: Glen Mitchell
Romney Marsh Herald
01227 767321
Weekly (Wed). Editor: Diane Nicholls
News editor: Nicola Jordan
Royston & Buntingford Mercury
01992 526600
Weekly (Fri). Editor: Paul Winspear
News editor: Paul Brackley
Features editor: Bridget McAlpine
Royston Crow
01763 245241
Weekly (Thu). Editor: Les Baker
Rye & Battle Observer
01424 854242
www.ryeandbattletoday.co.uk
Weekly (Fri). Editor: Michael Beard
News editor: Ann Terry
Associate editor: Russell Claughton
St Albans & Harpenden Review
01727 834411
www.stalbansobserver.co.uk
Weekly free (Wed)
Editor: Deborah Williams

St Albans Observer
01727 834411
www.stalbansobserver.co.uk
Weekly (Thu).
Editor: Deborah Williams
Seaford Gazette
01323 722091
Weekly (Wed). Editor: Peter Lindsay
News editor: Robin Emanuel
Features editor: Andrew Bennett
Sevenoaks Chronicle
01732 228000
www.thisiskentandeastsussex.
co.uk
Weekly (Thu).
Editor: Frank Baldwin
Sheerness Times Guardian
01795 580300
Weekly (Thu). Editor: Duncan Marsh
News editor: Linda Mitchell
Sheppey Gazette
01227 767321
Weekly (Thu).
Editor: Christine Rayner
News editor: Steve Waite
Shoreham Herald
01903 230051
www.shorehamtoday.co.uk
Weekly (Thu).
Editor: Michelle Neville
Sidcup & Blackfen Times
020 8269 7000
Weekly (Wed). Editor: Melody Ryall
Production editor: Mick Taylor
Sittingbourne KM Extra
01795 580300
Weekly (Wed).
Editor: Duncan Marsh
News editor: Linda Mitchell
South Coast Leader
01273 544544
www.thisisbrightonandhove.co.uk
Weekly (Fri). Editor: Chris Chandler
News editor: Mike Dunford
Staines & Ashford News
01932 561111
www.trinitymirrorsouthern.co.uk
Weekly free (Wed).
Editor: Kim Chatman
News editor: Judy Parsons
Staines & Egham News
01932 561111
www.trinitymirrorsouthern.co.uk
Weekly free (Wed).
Editor: Kim Chatman
News editor: Judy Parsons
Staines Guardian
020 8940 6030
www.stainesguardian.co.uk
Weekly (Thu). Editor: Paul Mortimer
News editor: James Adlam

Staines Informer
01932 561111
www.trinitymirrorsouthern.co.uk
Weekly free (Thu).
Editor: Kim Chatman
News editor: Judy Parsons
Staines Leader
01932 561111
www.trinitymirrorsouthern.co.uk
Weekly free (Thu).
Editor: Kim Chatman
Star Classified (Bishops Stortford)
01279 866355
www.herts-essex-news.co.uk
Weekly (Thu). Editor: Val Brown
News editor: Sandra Perry
Stevenage Advertiser
01462 441020
www.hitchinadvertiser.co.uk
Weekly (Wed)
General manager: Ricky Allan
Stevenage Comet
01462 420120
www.thecomet.net
Weekly (Thu). Editor: Darren Isted
News editor: John Adams
Stevenage Herald
01462 420120
www.thecomet.net
Weekly free (Wed).
Editor: Darren Isted
News editor: John Adams
Stevenage Mercury
01992 526600
Weekly (Fri). Editor: Paul Winspear
News editor: Paul Brackley
Features editor: Bridget McAlpine
Surrey & Hants News
01252 716444
Weekly free (Tue). Editor: Jean Parrat
Surrey Advertiser
01483 508700
www.surreyad.co.uk
Weekly (Fri). Editor: Marnie Wilson
Surrey Comet
020 8646 6336
Weekly (Wed). Editor: Sean Duggan
Surrey Hants Star
01252 316311
www.shstar.co.uk
Weekly free (Thu).
Editor: Alan Franklin
Surrey Herald
01932 561111
Weekly (Wed). Editor: Kim Chatman
Surrey Mirror
020 8770 7171
www.icsurrey.co.uk
Weekly (Wed). Editor: Ian Carter
News editor: Glen Mitchell
Features editor: Caroline Harrap
Chief sub-editor: Sherif El Alfay

Sussex Express
01273 480601
www.sussexexpress.co.uk
Weekly (Fri). Editor: Peter Austin
Deputy editor: Kevin Penfold
Sutton Advertiser
020 8763 6666
www.icsurrey.co.uk
Weekly (Fri). Editor: Ian Carter
News editor: Mike Hawkins
Sutton Borough Post
020 8763 6666
www.icsurrey.co.uk
Weekly (Wed). Editor: Ian Carter
News editor: Mike Hawkins
Sutton Guardian
020 8646 6336
www.suttonguardian.co.uk
Weekly (Thu). Editor: Marie Jackson
Swanley Messenger
01322 220791
www.kent-online.co.uk
Weekly (Thu).
Editor: Sandra Hembury
News editor: Teresa Gains
Swanley Times
020 8269 7000
Weekly (Thu). Editor: Melody Ryall
Production editor: Mick Taylor
Tandridge Chronicle
01959 564766
www.tandridge-today.co.uk
Weekly (Thu). Editor: Signid Sherrell
Tandridge County Border News
01959 564766
www.tandridge-today.co.uk
Weekly (Thu). Editor: Kevin Black
Tenterden Express
01233 623232
Weekly (Tue). Editor: Brian Lewis
News editor: Leo Whitlock
Features editor: Leo Whitlock
Chief sub-editor: Claire Stevens
Tenterden KM Extra
01233 623232
Weekly (Tue). Editor: Brian Lewis
News editor: Leo Whitlock
Features editor: Leo Whitlock
Chief sub-editor: Claire Stevens
Thanet KM Extra
01843 221313
Weekly (Fri). Editor: Rebecca Smith
News editor: Sarah Munday
Production editor: Gary Barker
Thanet Times
01227 767321
Weekly (Thu). Editor: Mike Pearce
News editor: Sarah Murdey

Tonbridge Courier
01892 681000
www.thisiskentandeast
sussex.co.uk
Weekly (Fri). Editor: Giles Broadbent
News editor: Melanie Whittaker
Features editor: Lucia Blash
Chief sub-editor: Lindsey Jones
Production editor: Richard Page
Tunbridge Wells Courier
01892 681000
www.thisiskentandeast
sussex.co.uk
Weekly (Fri). Editor: Giles Broadbent
News editor: Melanie Whittaker
Features editor: Lucia Blash
Chief sub-editor: Lindsey Jones
Production editor: Richard Page
Tunbridge Wells Extra
01892 525111
Weekly (Fri). Editor: Ron Green
News editor: Nigel Jarrett
Virginia Water Villager
01753 523355
Fortnightly (Thu).
Editor: Martin Biddle
News editor: Mike Sim
Walton & Weybridge Informer
01932 561111
www.trinitymirrorsouthern.co.uk
Weekly free (Thu).
Editor: Kim Chatman
News editor: Abbi Dornan
Watford Free Observer
01923 216216
www.watfordobserver.co.uk
Weekly (Thu)
Editor: Peter Wilson-Leary
News editor: Frazer Ansell
Watford Review
01727 834411
www.stalbansobserver.co.uk
Weekly free (Wed)
Editor: Deborah Williams
Watford Times
01788 543077
Weekly free (Wed)
Editor: Stephen Williams
News editor: Stuart Platt
Weald Courier
01892 681000
www.thisiskentandeast
sussex.co.uk
Weekly (Fri). Editor: Giles Broadbent
News editor: Melanie Whittaker
Features editor: Lucia Blash
Chief sub-editor: Lindsey Jones
Production editor: Richard Page
Wealden Advertiser
01580 753322
www.wealdenad.co.uk
Weekly free (Fri).
Editor: Graham Thorn

Weekend Herald (Crawley, Horsham, Horley)
01293 562929
www.crawleyobserver.co.uk
Weekly free (Fri)
Editor: Graham Campbell
News editor: Allan Norbury
Chief sub-editor: Mark Dunford
Welwyn & Hatfield Review
01727 834411
www.stalbansobserver.co.uk
Weekly (Thu).
Editor: Deborah Williams
Features editor: Paul Collins
Welwyn & Hatfield Times
01727 327551
www.whtimes.co.uk
Weekly (Wed).
Editor: Terry Mitchinson
Westerham County Border News
01959 564766
www.westerham-today.co.uk
Weekly (Thu). Editor: Kevin Black
West Sussex County Times
01403 751200
www.horshamonline.co.uk
Weekly (Fri). Editor: Gary Shipton
Chief sub-editor: Steve Payne
Production editor: Jonathan Taylor
West Sussex Gazette
01243 534155
www.chichester.co.uk
Weekly (Wed).
Editor: Dorothy Blundell
News editor: Jeannie Knight
Chief sub-editor: Tony Jackman
Weybridge Villager
01753 523355
Fortnightly (Thu).
Editor: Martin Biddle
News editor: Mike Sim
Whitstable Gazette
01227 768181
Weekly (Thu). Editor: Bob Bounds
News editor: Trisha Jaimeson
Production editor: Gary Barker
Whitstable KM Extra
01227 768181
Weekly (Tue). Editor: Bob Bounds
News editor: Trisha Jaimeson
Production editor: Gary Barker
Whitstable Times
01227 771515
Weekly (Thu). Editor: John Nurden
News editor: Ian Reed
Features editor: Julia Rogers
Chief sub-editor: Paul Taylor
Production editor: Mark Silver

Woking Informer
01932 561111
www.trinitymirrorsouthern.co.uk
Weekly free (Thu).
Editor: Kim Chatman
News editor: Irlene Watchmore
Woking News & Mail
01483 755755
www.woking.co.uk
Weekly (Thu). Editor: Penny Bray
News editor: Lisa Porter
Woking Review
01483 508700
www.surreyad.co.uk
Weekly (Wed). Editor: Penny Bray
News editor: Lisa Porter
Worthing Advertiser
01903 230051
www.worthingtoday.co.uk
Weekly (Wed). Editor: Tony Mayes
Worthing Guardian
01903 282398
www.worthingtoday.co.uk
Weekly (Fri). Editor: Nikki Jeffrey
Worthing Herald
01903 230051
www.worthingtoday.co.uk
Weekly (Thu). Editor: John Buss
News editor: Harriet Shelley

South England

Berkshire, Buckinghamshire, Hampshire, Oxfordshire, Wiltshire

Abingdon Herald
01865 425262
www.thisisoxfordshire.co.uk
Weekly (Thu). Editor: Derek Holmes
The Advertiser (Newbury)
01635 524111
www.newburynews.co.uk
Weekly (Tue). Editor: Brian Beharrell
News editor: Martin Robertshaw
Aldershot Courier
01252 339760
www.aldershot.co.uk
Weekly free (Wed).
Editor: James Taylor
News editor: Adam Clark
Aldershot Mail
01252 339760
www.surreyad.co.uk
Weekly (Tue). Editor: James Taylor
News editor: Adam Clark
Aldershot News
01252 339760
www.aldershot.co.uk
Weekly (Fri). Editor: James Taylor
News editor: Adam Clark

Alresford Advertiser
01252 716444
Weekly (Tue)
Editor: Christine McDermott
News editor: Paul Ferguson
Alton Gazette
01420 84446
Weekly (Wed)
Editor: Christine McDerment
News editor: Paul Ferguson
Alton Times & Mail
01252 716444
Weekly free (Tue). Editor: Jean Parrat
Amersham & Chesham Free Press
01494 755081
Weekly (Fri). Editor: Steve Cohen
News editor: Julie Voyce
Features editor: Clare Bourke
Amersham Examiner
01753 888333
Weekly (Thu). Editor: Peter Krinks
News editor: Estelle Sinkins
Features editor: Rachael Double
Andover Advertiser
01264 323456
www.andoveradvertiser.co.uk
Weekly (Fri). Editor: Joe Scicluna
News editor: Judy Belbin
Features editor: Simon Reeve
Chief sub-editor: Judith Hughes
Andover Advertiser Midweek
01264 323456
www.andoveradvertiser.co.uk
Weekly (Wed). Editor: Joe Scicluna
News editor: Judy Belbin
Features editor: Simon Reeve
Chief sub-editor: Judith Hughes
Ascot News
01344 456611
Weekly (Wed). Editor: Paul Ryan
Features editor: James Osborne
Ash & Farnham Mail
01252 339760
Weekly (Tue). Editor: James Taylor
News editor: Adam Clark
Banbury Cake
01295 256111
www.thisisoxfordshire.co.uk
Weekly (Thu). Editor: Derek Holmes
News editor: Stephanie Preece
Banbury Citizen
01295 227777
www.banburyguardian.co.uk
Weekly free (Fri).
Editor: Bridget Dakin
News editor: Ben Kendall
Banbury Guardian
01295 227777
www.banburyguardian.co.uk
Weekly (Thu). Editor: Bridget Dakin
News editor: Ben Kendall

Basingstoke Extra
01256 461131
www.thisishampshire.net
Weekly free (Wed).
Editor: Mark Jones
News editor: Simon Pluckrose
Chief sub-editor: Jonathan Lee
Production editor: Alan Cranham
Basingstoke Observer
01256 694121
www.basingstoke.co.uk
Weekly (Thu). Editor: Steve Davies
Beaconsfield Advertiser
01753 888333
www.buckinghamtoday.co.uk
Weekly (Thu). Editor: Peter Krinks
News editor: Estelle Sinkins
Features editor: Rachael Double
Bicester Advertiser
01865 425262
www.thisisoxfordshire.co.uk
Weekly (Fri). Editor: Derek Holmes
Bicester Review
01280 813434
Weekly (Fri). Editor: Rob Giddard
Assistant editor: Mark Pendred
Deputy editor: Clare Wale
Bordon Post
01730 264811
Weekly (Wed). Editor: David Garlant
Features editor: Will Parsons
Bordon Times & Mail
01252 716444
Weekly free (Tue). Editor: Jean Parrat
Bracknell & Ascot Times
0118 936 6180
www.getbracknell.co.uk
Weekly (Thu).
Editor: Keith Redbourn
News editor: Matt Blackman
Brackley & Towcester Advertiser
01280 813434
Weekly (Fri). Editor: Rob Giddard
Assistant editor: Mark Pendred
Deputy editor: Clare Wale
Bracknell & Wokingham Standard
0118 936 6180
www.getbracknell.co.uk
Weekly (Thu). Editor: Adam D Smith
Bracknell Midweek News
01344 456611
Weekly (Wed). Editor: Paul Ryan
News editor: James Osborne
Bracknell News
01344 456611
Weekly (Wed). Editor: Paul Ryan
News editor: James Osborne

Buckingham & Winslow Advertiser
01280 813434
Weekly (Fri). Editor: Rob Giddard
Assistant editor: Mark Pendred
Deputy editor: Clare Wale
Buckinghamshire Advertiser
01753 888333
www.buckinghamtoday.co.uk
Weekly (Thu). Editor: Peter Krinks
News editor: Estelle Sinkins
Features editor: Rachael Double
Buckinghamshire Echo
0116 233 3635
Weekly (Tue). Editor: Paul Clark
Buckinghamshire Examiner
01753 888333
www.buckinghamtoday.co.uk
Weekly (Thu). Editor: Peter Krinks
News editor: Estelle Sinkins
Features editor: Rachael Double
Bucks Free Press
01494 755000
www.bucksfreepress.co.uk
Weekly (Fri). Editor: Steve Cohen
News editor: Julie Voyce
Bucks Herald
01296 318300
www.bucksherald.co.uk
Weekly (Wed).
Editor: David Summers
Chippenham, Corsham Advertiser
01225 760945
www.wiltshirepublications.com
Weekly (Thu). Editor: David Gledhill
News editor: Paul Wiltshire
Features editor: George McCready
Production editor: Marion Wild
The Citizen
01908 371133
Twice-weekly free (Tue/Thu)
Editor: Jan Henderson
Crowthorne & Sandhurst Times
0118 936 6180
Weekly (Wed).
Editor: Keith Redbourn
News editor: Matt Blackman
Crowthorne, Sandhurst, Owlsmoor Newsweek
01344 456611
Weekly (Wed). Editor: Paul Ryan
News editor: James Osborne
Devizes, Melksham and Vale of Pewsey News
01793 528144
www.thisisswindon.co.uk
Weekly free (Wed).
Editor: Mark Waldron
Didcot Herald
01865 425262
www.thisisoxfordshire.co.uk
Weekly (Thu). Editor: Derek Holmes

Eastleigh News Extra
01962 841772
www.thisishampshire.net
Weekly free (Thu).
Editor: Mary Payne
Eton Observer
01753 523355
Weekly (Fri). Editor: Martin Biddle
News editor: Mike Sim
Evening Advertiser
01793 528144
www.thisisswindon.co.uk
Daily. Editor: Mark Waldron
News editor: Cath Turnbull
Fareham & Gosport Journal
023 9266 4488
www.thisisportsmouth.co.uk
Weekly free (Thu).
Editor: Mike Gilson
News editor: Colin McNeill
Features editor: John Millard
Fareham & Gosport News
023 9266 4488
www.thisisportsmouth.co.uk
Daily. Editor: Mike Gilson
News editor: Colin McNeill
Features editor: John Millard
Farnborough News & Mail
01252 339760
www.farnborough.co.uk
Weekly (Tue). Editor: James Taylor
News editor: Adam Clark
Fleet News & Mail
01252 339760
www.fleet-online.co.uk
Weekly (Tue). Editor: James Taylor
News editor: Adam Clark
Gazette Extra
01256 461131
www.thisishampshire.net
Weekly (Wed). Editor: Mark Jones
News editor: Simon Pluckrose
Chief sub-editor: Jonathan Lee
Production editor: Alan Cranham
Hamble Valley Journal
023 9266 4488
www.thisisportsmouth.co.uk
Weekly free (Thu).
Editor: Mike Gilson
News editor: Colin McNeill
Features editor: John Millard
Hampshire Chronicle
01962 841772
www.thisishampshire.net
/hampshire/winchester
Weekly (Fri). Editor: Alan Cleaver
News editor: Kit Neilson
Hants & Dorset Avon Advertiser
01722 426500
Weekly (Wed). Editor: Bill Browne
News editor: David Vallis
Features editor: Lesley Bates
Chief sub-editor: Sarah Elderkin

Hants and Surrey Post Dispatch
01420 88949
Fortnightly free (Mon)
Editor: Alan Wooler
Hart Courier
01252 339760
www.surreyad.co.uk
Weekly (Fri). Editor: James Taylor
News editor: Adam Clark
Havant & Waterlooville Journal
023 9266 4488
www.thisisportsmouth.co.uk
Weekly free (Thu).
Editor: Mike Gilson
News editor: Colin McNeill
Features editor: John Millard
Havant & Waterlooville News
023 9266 4488
www.thisisportsmouth.co.uk
Daily. Editor: Mike Gilson
News editor: Colin McNeill
Features editor: John Millard
Hemel Hempstead Herald & Express
01442 262311
www.hemelonline.co.uk
Weekly (Thu).
Editor: David Feldstein
News editor: Ann Traynor
Sports editor: Graham Caygill
Henley Standard
01491 419444
www.henleystandard.co.uk
Weekly (Fri).
Editor: George Tuckfield
News editor: David Dawson
Isle of Wight County Press
01983 521333
www.iwcp.co.uk
Weekly (Fri). Editor: Brian Dennis
News editor: Phil Wolsey
Liphook Times & Mail
01252 716444
Weekly free (Tue). Editor: Jean Parr
Lymington Times
01425 613384
Weekly (Fri). Editor: Charles Curry
Maidenhead Advertiser
01628 680680
www.maidenhead-advertiser.co.uk
Weekly (Fri). Editor: Martin Trepte
Marlow Free Press
01494 755081
Weekly (Fri). Editor: Steve Cohen
News editor: Julie Voyce
Features editor: Clare Bourke
The Midweek (Reading)
01494 755081
Weekly (Tue). Editor: Steve Cohen
News editor: Julie Voyce
Features editor: Clare Bourke

Meon Valley News
023 9263 2767
Monthly (Mon).
Editor: Christine Miller
Melksham Independent News
01225 704761
www.melkshamnews.com
Fortnightly free (Thu).
Editor: Ian Drew
News editor: Loraine Ward
Mid Hampshire Observer
01962 859559
www.hantsmedia.co.uk
Weekly (Wed). Editor: Pete Harvey
Milton Keynes Citizen
01908 651200
www.miltonkeynes.co.uk
Weekly free (Thu)
Editor: Jan Henderson
Milton Keynes Journal
0116 233 3635
Weekly (Tue). Editor: Paul Clark
MK News
01908 809000
www.seriousaboutnews.co.uk
Weekly (Wed). Editor: David Gale
Monday Gazette
01256 461131
www.thisishampshire.net
Weekly (Mon). Editor: Mark Jones
News editor: Simon Pluckrose
Chief sub-editor: Jonathan Lee
Production editor: Alan Cranham
New Forest Post
01590 613888
www.thisishampshire.net/
Weekly (Thu). Editor: Sue Edwins
New Milton Advertiser
01425 613384
Weekly (Fri). Editor: Charles Curry
Newbury & Thatcham Chronicle
01635 32812
www.icberkshire.co.uk
Weekly free (Wed).
Editor: Brian Mustoe
Newbury Weekly News
01635 524111
www.newburynews.co.uk
Weekly (Thu).
Editor: Brian Beharrell
News editor: Martin Robertshaw
The News (Portsmouth)
023 9266 4488
www.thenews.co.uk
Daily. Editor: Mike Gilson
News editor: Colin McNeill
Features editor: John Millard
Chief sub-editor: Steve Matthews
Oxford Courier
01235 553444
www.courier-newspapers
-oxford.co.uk
Weekly (Thu). Editor: Lawrence Web
Production editor: Howard Taylor

Oxford Journal
01235 553444
www.courier-newspapers
-oxford.co.uk/journal.htm
Weekly (Fri). Editor: Lawrence Web
Production editor: Howard Taylor
Oxford Mail
01865 425262
www.thisisoxfordshire.co.uk
Daily. Editor: Simon O'Neil
Oxford Star
01865 425262
www.thisisoxfordshire.co.uk
Weekly (Thu). Editor: Simon O'Neil
Oxford Times
01865 425262
www.thisisoxfordshire.co.uk
Weekly (Fri). Editor: Derek Holmes
News editor: Stephanie Preece
Chief sub-editor: Marc Evans
Oxfordshire Guardian
01926 431601
Weekly (Thu). Editor: Paul Gleeson
Oxfordshire Weekly
01865 425262
www.thisisoxfordshire.co.uk
Weekly (Wed). Editor: Derek Holmes
Petersfield Mail
01252 716444
Weekly free (Tue). Editor: Jean Parrat
Petersfield Post
01730 264811
www.petersfield.co.uk
Weekly (Wed). Editor: David Garlant
Features editor: Will Parsons
Portsmouth & Southsea Journal
023 9266 4488
www.thisisportsmouth.co.uk
Weekly free (Thu).
Editor: Mike Gilson
News editor: Colin McNeill
Features editor: John Millard
Property Chronicle (Berkshire)
0118 950 3030
www.icberkshire.co.uk
Weekly (Wed, Thu)
Editor: Anthony Longden
News editor: Maurice O'Brien
Features editor: Paul Kirkley
Production editor: Jeremy Drakes
Reading Central
0118 918 3000
www.readingcentral.co.uk
Weekly (Thu). Editor: Hiliary Scott
Chief sub-editor: Keir Rithie
Reading Chronicle
0118 950 3030
www.icberkshire.co.uk
Weekly (Thu).
Editor: Anthony Longden
News editor: Maurice O'Brien
Features editor: Paul Kirkley
Production editor: Jeremy Drakes

Reading Evening Post
0118 918 3000
www.getreading.co.uk
Daily (Mon–Fri).
Editor: Andy Murrill
News editor: Lucy Rimmer
Features editor: Kate Magee
Chief sub-editor: Alan Blayney
Romsey Advertiser
023 8042 4777
www.thisishampshire.net
/hampshire/romsey
Weekly (Fri). Editor: Ian Murray
News editor: Gordon Sutter
Chief sub-editor: Colin Jenkins
Salisbury Avon Advertiser
01722 426500
www.thisiswiltshire.co.uk
Weekly (Wed). Editor: Bill Browne
News editor: David Vallis
Features editor: Lesley Bates
Salisbury Journal
01722 426500
www.thisissalisbury.co.uk
Weekly (Thu). Editor: Bill Browne
News editor: David Vallis
Features editor: Lesley Bates
Sandhurst & Crowthorne Mail
01252 339760
Weekly (Tue). Editor: James Taylor
News editor: Adam Clark
Sandhurst & Crowthorne News
01252 339760
Weekly (Fri). Editor: James Taylor
News editor: Adam Clark
Slough Express
01753 825111
www.icberkshire.co.uk
Weekly (Thu). Editor: Paul Thomas
News editor: Francis Batt
Features editor: Sarah Larch
Slough Observer
01753 523355
www.thisisslough.com
Weekly (Wed). Editor: Martin Biddle
News editor: Mike Sim
**South Bucks, Wycombe &
Chiltern Star**
01494 755000
www.hillingdontimes.co.uk
Weekly (Thu). Editor: Steve Cohen
News editor: Clare Bourke
South Oxfordshire Courier
01235 553444
www.courier-newspapers
-oxford.co.uk
Weekly (Thu). Editor: Lawrence Web
Production editor: Howard Taylor
Southampton Advertiser
023 8042 4777
Weekly (Thu). Editor: Ian Murray
News editor: Gordon Sutter
Chief sub-editor: Colin Jenkins

Southern Daily Echo
023 8042 4777
www.dailyecho.co.uk
Daily. Editor: Ian Murray
News editor: Gordon Sutter
Chief sub-editor: Colin Jenkins
Surrey & Hampshire Guardian
02476 631911
Daily. Editor: Jag Basra
News editor: Keith Brailford
Features editor: Andrew Woods
Swindon Star
01793 528144
www.thisisswindon.co.uk
Weekly free (Thu).
Editor: Mark Waldron
News editor: Cath Turnbull
Tadley Gazette
01256 461131
www.thisishampshire.net
Weekly free (Wed).
Editor: Mark Jones
News editor: Simon Pluckrose
Chief sub-editor: Jonathan Lee
Production editor: Alan Cranham
Thame Gazette
01296 318300
www.aylesburytoday.co.uk
Weekly (Fri). Editor: David Summers
Thames Valley Weekly
01235 553444
www.courier-newspapers
-oxford.co.uk/tvw.htm
Weekly (Fri). Editor: Lawrence Web
Production editor: Howard Taylor
Thatcham News
01635 524111
www.newburynews.co.uk
Weekly (Thu).
Editor: Brian Beharrell
News editor: Martin Robertshaw
Trowbridge, Melksham,
Bradford-On-Avon Advertiser
01225 760945
www.wiltshirepublications.com
Weekly (Thu). Editor: David Gledhill
News editor: Paul Wiltshire
Features editor: George McCready
Production editor: Marion Wild
Twyford Times
0118 936 6180
Weekly (Wed).
Editor: Keith Redbourn
News editor: Matt Blackman
Wallingford Herald
01865 425262
www.thisisoxfordshire.co.uk
Weekly (Thu). Editor: Derek Holmes
Wantage Herald
01865 425262
www.thisisoxfordshire.co.uk
Weekly (Thu). Editor: Derek Holmes

Warminster Journal
01985 213030
Weekly (Fri).
Editors: RC Shorto, DJ Watkins
Weekend Express
01753 825111
www.icberkshire.co.uk
Weekly (Fri). Editor: Paul Thomas
News editor: Francis Batt
Features editor: Sarah Larch
West & North Wilts Star
01225 777292
www.thisiswiltshire.co.uk
Weekly free (Thu)
Editor: Toby Granville
News editor: Holly Robinson
Features editor: Claire Waring
Westbury, Warminster
Advertiser
01225 760945
www.wiltshirepublications.com
Weekly (Thu). Editor: David Gledhill
News editor: Paul Wiltshire
Features editor: George McCready
Production editor: Marion Wild
White Horse News
01225 704761
www.wiltshirepublications.com
Fortnightly free (Thu)
Editor: Ian Drew
News editor: Loraine Ward
Wilts & Gloucestershire
Standard
01285 642642
www.thisiscirencester.com
Weekly (Thu). Editor: Jeff Eames
News editor: Lindi Roberts
Production editor: Mark Jones
Wiltshire Gazette and Herald
01793 528144
www.thisisswindon.co.uk
Weekly (Thu). Editor: Mark Waldron
News editor: Gary Lawrence
Wiltshire Guardian
024 7663 1911
Weekly free (Thu). Editor: Jag Basra
News editor: Keith Brailford
Features editor: Andrew Woods
Wiltshire Times
01225 777292
www.thisiswiltshire.co.uk
Weekly (Fri). Editor: Toby Granville
News editor: Holly Robinson
Features editor: Claire Waring
Winchester News Extra
01962 841772
www.thisishampshire.net
Weekly free (Thu). Editor: Mary Page
Winchester Shopper
023 8042 4777
Sunday. Editor: Ian Murray
News editor: Gordon Sutter
Chief sub-editor: Colin Jenkins

Windsor Express
01753 825111
www.icberkshire.co.uk
Weekly free (Thu)
Editor: Paul Thomas
News editor: Francis Batt
Features editor: Sarah Larch
Windsor, Ascot & Maidenhead
Observer
01753 523355
www.thisiswindsor.com
Weekly (Fri). Editor: Martin Biddle
News editor: Mike Sim
Witney & West Oxfordshire
Gazette
01865 425262
www.thisisoxfordshire.co.uk
Weekly (Wed). Editor: Derek Holmes
Wodley Times
0118 936 6180
Weekly (Wed).
Editor: Keith Redbourn
News editor: Matt Blackman
Wokingham News
01344 456611
Weekly (Wed). Editor: Paul Ryan
News editor: James Osborne
Wokingham Times
0118 366180
www.getwokingham.co.uk
Weekly (Wed).
Editor: Keith Redbourn
News editor: Matt Blackman
Woodley & Earley Chronicle
0118 963 3151
www.icberkshire.co.uk
Weekly (Thu).
Editor: Anthony Longden
News editor: Maurice O'Brien
Features editor: Paul Kirkley
Production editor: Jeremy Drakes
Yateley Mail
01252 339760
Weekly (Tue). Editor: James Taylor
News editor: Adam Clark
Yateley News
01252 339760
Weekly (Fri). Editor: James Taylor
News editor: Adam Clark

South-west England

Cornwall, Devon, Dorset,
Somerset & Avon

Bath Chronicle
01225 322322
www.thisisbath.co.uk
Daily. Editor: David Gledhill
News editor: Paul Wiltshire
Features editor: George McCready
Chief sub-editor: Graham Holburn
Production editor: Marion Wild

Bath Times
01225 322322
www.thisisbath.co.uk
Weekly (Wed). Editor: David Gledhill
News editor: Paul Wiltshire
Bournemouth Advertiser
01202 554601
www.thisisdorset.net
Weekly free (Thu)
Editor: Neal Butterworth
News editor: Andy Martin
Features editor: Kevin Nash
Bridgwater Mercury
01823 365151
www.thisisthewestcountry.co.uk
Weekly (Tue).
Editor-in-chief: Ken Bird
News editor: Bob Drayton
Bridgwater Star
01823 365151
www.thisisthewestcountry.co.uk
Weekly (Thu).
Editor-in-chief: Ken Bird
News editor: Bob Drayton
Bridgwater Times
01749 672430
www.thisissomerset.co.uk
Weekly (Thu). Editor: Carol Deacon
News editor: Juliette Auty
Bridport & Lyme Regis News
01308 425884
www.thisisdorset.net/dorset
/bridportandlyme
Weekly (Fri).
Editor: Margery Hookings
Bristol Evening Post
0117 934 3000
www.thisisbristol.co.uk
Daily. Editor: Mike Lowe
News editor: Kevin Blackadder
Features editor: Bill Davis
Chief sub-editor: Helen Lawrence
Bristol Observer
0117 934 3401
www.thisisbristol.co.uk
Weekly free (Fri).
Editor: Peter O'Reilly
News editor: Sharon Kelly
Chief sub-editor: Mike Chart
Brixham News
01584 856353
www.thisisthewestcountry.co.uk
Weekly (Thu). Editor: Gina Coles
Bude & Stratton Post
01566 772424
Weekly (Thu). Editor: Geoff Secombe
News editor: Keith Whitford
Burnham & Highbridge Mercury
01823 365151
www.thisisthewestcountry.co.uk
Weekly (Tue).
Editor-in-chief: Ken Bird
News editor: Bob Drayton

Burnham & Highbridge Times
01749 672430
www.thisissomerset.co.uk
Weekly (Thu). Editor: Carol Deacon
News editor: Juliette Auty
Burnham & Highbridge Weekly News
01823 365151
www.thisisthewestcountry.co.uk
Weekly (Thu).
Editor-in-chief: Ken Bird
News editor: Bob Drayton
Camborne and Redruth Packet
01326 213333
www.thisisthewestcountry.co.uk
Weekly (Wed).
Editor: Terry Lambert
News editor: Stephen Ivall
Chief sub-editor: David Robinson
Camelford & Delabole Post
01566 772424
Weekly (Thu). Editor: Geoff Secombe
News editor: Keith Whitford
Camelford & Delabole Journal Gazette
01566 772424
Weekly (Fri). Editor: Geoff Secombe
News editor: Keith Whitford
Central Somerset Gazette
01749 832300
www.thisissomerset.co.uk
Weekly (Fri). Editor: Philip Welch
Chard & Ilminster News
01823 365151
www.thisisthewestcountry.co.uk
Weekly (Wed).
Editor-in-chief: Ken Bird
News editor: Bob Drayton
Chard & Ilminster News (Somerset)
01460 67474
www.thisisthewestcountry.co.uk
Weekly (Wed).
Editor: Bryan Armstrong
News editor: Alan Hall
Chard Advertiser
01935 471764
www.chard-today.co.uk
Weekly free (Fri).
Editor: Philip Edwards
Cheddar Valley Gazette
01749 832300
www.thisissomerset.co.uk
Weekly (Thu). Editor: Philip Welch
Chew Valley Gazette
01275 332266
www.chewvalleygazette.co.uk
Last monthly (Fri)
Editor: Rowland Janes
Features editor: Anne Collier

Clevedon Mercury
01275 335142
www.thisissomerset.co.uk
Weekly (Thu). Editor: Carol Deacon
News editor: Juliette Autey
Chief sub-editor: Kevin Lee
Cornish & Devon Post
01566 772424
Weekly (Thu). Editor: Geoff Secombe
News editor: Keith Whitford
Cornish Guardian
01208 78133
www.cornishguardian.co.uk
Weekly (Thu). Editor: Alan Cooper
News editor: Ian Sheppard
Chief sub-editor: Anne Witney
Cornish Times
01579 342174
www.liskeard-today.co.uk
Weekly (Fri). Editor: John Noble
The Cornishman
01736 362247
www.thisiscornwall.co.uk
Weekly (Thu). Editor: Jeremy Ridge
Features editor: Joyce Channon
Crewkerne Advertiser
01935 471764
www.crewkerne-today.co.uk
Weekly free (Fri).
Editor: Philip Edwards
Culm, Crediton & Tiverton Gazette
01884 252725
Weekly (Tue)
Editor: Mary-Ann Bloomfield
Daily Echo
01202 554601
www.thisisbournemouth.co.uk
Daily. Editor: Neal Butterworth
News editor: Andy Martin
Features editor: Kevin Nash
Dartmouth Chronicle
01548 853101
www.dartmouth-today.co.uk
Weekly (Fri). Editor: Gina Coles
Chief sub-editor: Lucy Baker-Kind
Dawlish Gazette
01626 353555
www.dawlish-today.co.uk
Weekly (Fri). Editor: Ruth Davey
News editor: John Belment
Chief sub-editor: Steven Taylor
Dawlish Post
01626 353555
www.dawlish-today.co.uk
Weekly (Fri). Editor: Ruth Davey
News editor: John Belment
Chief sub-editor: Steven Taylor

Dorchester Advertiser
01305 830930
www.thisisdorset.net
Weekly (Thu).
Editor: David Murdock
News editor: Paul Thomas
Features editor: Dirmaid Macdonagh
Chief sub-editor: Nick Horton
Dorset Echo
01305 830930
www.thisisdorset.net
Weekly (Thu).
Editor: David Murdock
News editor: Paul Thomas
Features editor: Dirmaid Macdonagh
Exeter Express & Echo
01392 442211
www.thisisexeter.co.uk
Daily. Editor: Steve Hall
News editor: Sue Kemp
Features editor: Lynne Turner
Production editor: Jerry Charge
Exeter Leader
01392 442211
www.thisisexeter.co.uk
Weekly free (Wed). Editor: Steve Hall
News editor: Sue Kemp
Features editor: Lynne Turner
Exmouth Herald
01392 888444
www.archantdevon.co.uk
/exmouthherald.asp
Weekly free (Fri)
Chief sub editor: Mary Evans
Falmouth Packet
01326 213333
www.thisisthewestcountry.co.uk
Weekly (Thu). Editor: Terry Lambert
News editor: Stephen Ivall
Chief sub-editor: David Robinson
Frome Times
01225 704761
www.frometimes.com
Fortnightly free (Thu).
Editor: Ian Drew
News editor: Loraine Ward
Hayle Times
01736 795813
www.thisiscornwall.co.uk
Weekly (Fri). Editor: Toni Carver
News editor: Paul Popcock
Features editor: Tricia Carver
Helston Gazette
01326 213333
www.thisisthewestcountry.co.uk
Weekly free (Wed)
Editor: Terry Lambert
News editor: Stephen Ivall
Chief sub-editor: David Robinson
Holsworthy Post
01566 778220
Weekly (Fri). Editor: Keith Whitford

Honiton Advertiser
01297 33034
www.pulmansweekly.co.uk
Weekly (Wed). Editor: Philip Evans
News editor: Tony Woodman
Production editor: Jacqui Evans
Ivybridge, South Brent and South Hams Gazette
01548 853101
www.ivybridge-today.co.uk
Weekly (Fri). Editor: Gina Coles
Chief sub-editor: Lucy Baker-Kind
Journal (Exmouth)
01392 888444
www.archantdevon.co.uk/
journal.asp
Weekly (Thu). Editor: Mary Evans
Kingsbridge and Salcombe Gazette
01548 853101
Weekly (Fri). Editor: Gina Coles
Chief sub-editor: Lucy Baker-Kind
Launceston Journal Gazette
01566 772424
Weekly (Fri). Editor: Geoff Secombe
News editor: Keith Whitford
Liskeard Gazette & Journal
01579 342174
Weekly (Wed).
Editor: Mary Richards
Mid Cornwall Advertiser
01726 66755
www.midcornwall-today.co.uk
Monthly (middle of month)
Editor: Fiona Jolley
Mid Devon Advertiser
01626 353555
www.dawlish-today.co.uk
Weekly (Fri). Editor: Ruth Davey
News editor: John Belment
Chief sub-editor: Steven Taylor
Mid Devon Star
01823 365151
www.thisisthewestcountry.co.uk
Weekly (Fri).
Editor-in-chief: Ken Bird
News editor: Bob Drayton
Mid Somerset Times
01749 672430
www.thisissomerset.co.uk
Weekly (Thu). Editor: Philip Welch
Midweek Herald
01392 888444
www.archantdevon.co.uk
Weekly (Wed). Editor: Andre Gibbons
North Cornwall Advertiser
01208 815096
www.northcornwall-today.co.uk
First week of month
Editor: Tony Gregan

North Devon Gazette & Advertiser
01392 888444
www.northdevongazette.co.uk
Weekly (Wed). Editor: David Tanner
North Devon Journal
01271 347420
www.thisisnorthdevon.co.uk
Weekly (Thu). Editor: Andy Cooper
News editor: Richard Best
Features editor: Sue Robinson
Chief sub-editor: Chris Machin
North Somerset Times
01934 422622
www.thewestonmercury.co.uk
Weekly (Wed).
Editor: Heather Pickstock
News editor: Andy Ridgeway
Newquay Voice
01637 878298
www.newquayvoice.co.uk
Weekly (Wed).
Editor: Andrew Laming
News editor: Matt Bond
North Cornwall Advertiser
01208 815096
www.northcornwall-today.co.uk
Monthly (first wed) free
Editor: Tony Gregan
Okehampton Times
01822 613666
www.okehampton-today.co.uk
Weekly (Thu). Editor: Colin Brent
Ottery Advertiser
01297 33034
Weekly (Wed). Editor: Philip Evans
News editor: Tony Woodman
Production editor: Jacqui Evans
Penwith Pirate
01326 213333
www.thisisthewestcountry.co.uk
Weekly free (Wed)
Editor: Terry Lambert
News editor: Stephen Ivall
Chief sub-editor: David Robinson
Plymouth Evening Herald
01752 765529
www.thisisplymouth.co.uk
Daily. Editor: Alan Qualtrough
News editor: John Casey
Features editor: Mike Bramhall
Plymouth Extra
01752 765525
www.thisisthewestcountry.co.uk
Weekly free (Thu).
Editor: Paul Atkins
News editor: Pam Guyatt
Plympton Plymstock & Ivybridge News
01548 853101
Weekly (Fri). Editor: Gina Coles
Chief sub-editor: Lucy Baker-Kind

Poole Advertiser
01202 675413
Weekly free (Thu)
Editor: Neal Butterworth
News editor: Andy Martin
Features editor: Kevin Nash

Post Advertiser
01305 830900
Monthly free (Mon).
Editor: Bob Conway

Princetown Times
01822 613666
www.thisisthewestcountry.co.uk
Weekly (Thu). Editor: Colin Brent

St Ives Times & Echo
01736 795813
www.thisiscornwall.co.uk
Weekly (Fri). Editor: Toni Carver
News editor: Paul Pocock
Features editor: Tricia Carver

Shepton Mallet Journal
01749 832300
www.thisissomerset.co.uk
Weekly (Thu). Editor: Philip Welch

Sidmouth Herald
01392 888444
www.archantdevon.co.uk
Weekly (Fri).
Editor: Emma Silverthorne

Somerset County Gazette
01823 365151
www.thisisthewestcountry.co.uk
Weekly (Fri).
Editor-in-chief: Ken Bird
News editor: Bob Drayton

Somerset Guardian
01225 322322
www.thisissomerset.co.uk
Weekly (Thu).
Editor: Joanne Roughton
Features editor: Pip Larkham

Somerset Standard
01225 322322
www.thisissomerset.co.uk
Weekly (Thu).
Editor: Joanne Roughton
Features editor: Pip Larkham

South Devon & Plymouth Times
01584 856353
www.thisisthewestcountry.co.uk
Weekly (Thu). Editor: Gina Coles

Sunday Independent
01752 206600
www.thisisthewestcountry.co.uk
Sunday. Editor: John Noble
News editor: Nikki Rowland

Swanage and Wareham District Advertiser
01929 427428
www.thisisdorset.net
Weekly free (Thu)
Editor: Neil Butterworth
News editor: Paula Tegerdine

Taunton Star
01823 365151
www.tauntonstar.co.uk
Weekly (Wed).
Editor-in-chief: Ken Bird
News editor: Bob Drayton

Taunton Times
01823 250500
www.thisissomerset.co.uk
Weekly free (Thu).
Editor: Debbie Rundle
News editor: Matt Chorley

Tavistock Times Gazette
01822 613666
www.tavistock-today.co.uk
Weekly (Thu). Editor: Colin Brent

Teignmouth News
01626 353555
www.dawlish-today.co.uk
Weekly (Fri). Editor: Ruth Davey
News editor: John Belment
Chief sub-editor: Steven Taylor

Teignmouth Post & Gazette
01626 353555
www.dawlish-today.co.uk
Weekly (Fri). Editor: Ruth Davey
News editor: John Belment
Chief sub-editor: Steven Taylor

Torbay Weekender
01803 676000
www.thisissouthdevon.co.uk
Weekly (Thu)
Editor: Bendan Hanrahan
News editor: Jim Parker
Features editor: Nick Pannell
Chief sub-editor: Nigel Lines

Torquay Herald Express
01803 676000
www.thisissouthdevon.co.uk
Daily. Editor: Bendan Hanrahan
News editor: Jim Parker
Features editor: Nick Pannell
Chief sub-editor: Nigel Lines

Totnes News
01548 853101
Weekly (Fri). Editor: Gina Coles
Chief sub-editor: Lucy Baker-Kind

Totnes Times Gazette
01584 856353
www.thisisthewestcountry.co.uk
Weekly (Thu). Editor: Gina Coles

Trader News (West Somerset)
01984 632731
Weekly free (Wed).
Editor: Gareth Purcell

Truro Packet
01326 213333
www.thisisthewestcountry.co.uk
Weekly (Wed). Editor: Terry Lambert
News editor: Stephen Ivall
Chief sub-editor: David Robinson

Wellington Weekly News
01823 250500
www.thisissomerset.co.uk
Weekly (Wed). Editor: Debbie Rundle
News editor: Matt Chorley

Wells Journal
01749 832300
www.thisissomerset.co.uk
Weekly (Thu). Editor: Philip Welch

The West Briton
01872 271451
www.thisiscornwall.co.uk
Weekly (Thu)
Editor: Richard Vankinsbergh
News editor: Mark Binnersley

West Somerset Free Press
01984 632731
www.west-somerset-today.co.uk
Weekly (Fri). Editor: Gareth Purcell

Western Daily Press (Bristol)
0117 934 3223
www.westpress.co.uk
Daily. Editor: Terry Manners
News editor: Cathy Ellis
Features editor: Steve White
Chief sub-editor: Dave Web
Production editor: Tony Wills

Western Gazette
01935 700500
www.westgaz.co.uk
Weekly (Thu). Editor: Martin Heal
News editor: Zena O'Rourke
Features editor: Carla Gale

Western Morning News
01752 765500
www.thisisplymouth.co.uk
Daily. Editor: Barrie Williams
News editor: Philip Reynolds
Features editor: Sue Carroll

Weston and Worle News
01275 335140
www.thisissomerset.co.uk
Weekly (Thu). Editor: Carol Deacon
News editor: Juliette Autey
Chief sub-editor: Kevin Lee

Weston Mercury
01934 422622
www.thewestonmercury.co.uk
Weekly (Fri). Editor: Judy Kisiel
News editor: Andy Ridgeway

Weston Super Mare Admag
01934 422622
www.thewestonmercury.co.uk
Weekly (Wed). Editor: Judy Kisiel
News editor: Andy Ridgeway

Weymouth & Dorchester Advertiser
01305 830930
www.thisisdorset.net
Weekly (Thu).
Editor: David Murdock
News editor: Paul Thomas
Features editor: Dirmaid Macdonagh

Yeovil Express
01823 365151
www.thisisthewestcountry.co.uk
Weekly (Thu).
Editor-in-chief: Ken Bird
News editor: Bob Drayton
Yeovil Independent Clarion
01935 471764
www.yeovil-clarion-today.co.uk
Weekly free (Fri).
Editor: Philip Edwards
Yeovil Times
01935 700500
Weekly free (Wed).
Editor: Martin Heal
News editor: Zena O'Rourke
Features editor: Carla Gale

East of England

Cambridgeshire, Essex,
Lincolnshire, Norfolk, Suffolk

Alford Standard
01754 897120
Weekly (Wed). Editor: John Coupe
Axholme Herald
01427 874417
Weekly (Fri). Editor: Ron Shipley
Barking & Dagenham Post
020 8491 2000
Weekly (Thu). Editor: Dave Russell
News editor: Scott Morrow
Chief sub-editor: Graham Whitmore
Barking & Dagenham Recorder
020 8478 4444
www.recorderonline.co.uk
Weekly (Thu). Editor: Chris Carter
News editor: Antigone Forder
Production editor: Mike Cubitt
**Barking & Dagenham
Weekender**
020 8491 2000
Weekly (Fri). Editor: Dave Russell
News editor: Scott Morrow
Chief sub-editor: Graham Whitmore
**Barking & Dagenham
Yellow Advertiser**
01268 503400
www.trinitymirrorsouthern.co.uk
Weekly (Thu). Editor: Graham Allen
News editor: Paula Dady
Features editor: Pat Jones
**Basildon and Wickford
Recorder**
01268 522792
www.thisisessex.co.uk
Daily. Editor: Martin McNeil
News editor: Chris Hatton
Features editor: Sally King
Chief sub-editor: Neal Reeve

Basildon Yellow Advertiser
01268 503400
www.trinitymirrorsouthern.co.uk
Weekly (Thu). Editor: Graham Allen
News editor: Paula Dady
Features editor: Pat Jones
Beccles & Bungay Journal
01603 628311
www.edp24.co.uk
Weekly (Fri). Editor: Terry Redhead
Billericay & Wickford Gazette
01277 219222
www.thisisessex.co.uk
Weekly (Wed). Editor: Roger Watkins
News editor: Sheelagh Bree
Features editor: Josie Stephenson
Boston Citizen
01205 311433
www.bostontoday.co.uk
Weekly (Fri). Editor: Julia Ogden
News editor: Pam Browne
Chief sub-editor: Warren Moody
Boston Focus
01205 354547
Monthly free. Editor: Irene Kettle
News editor: Sally Tetheridge
Features editor: Iris Clapp
Chief sub-editor: Will Bramhill
Boston Standard
01205 311433
www.bostontoday.co.uk
Weekly (Wed). Editor: Julia Ogden
News editor: Pam Browne
Chief sub-editor: Warren Moody
Boston Target
01522 820000
www.thisislincolnshire.co.uk
Weekly (Wed). Editor: Glynn Belsher
Braintree & Witham Times
01376 343344
www.thisisessex.co.uk
Weekly (Thu). Editor: Neil Thomas
News editor: Veronica Balls
Braintree Chronicle
01245 600700
www.thisisessex.co.uk
Weekly (Wed/Thu)
Editor: Stuart Rawlins
News editor: Matt Adams
Features editor: Darryl Webber
Brentwood Gazette
01277 219222
www.thisisessex.co.uk
Weekly (Wed). Editor: Roger Watkins
News editor: Sheelagh Bree
Features editor: Josie Stephenson
Brentwood Weekly News
01268 522792
www.thisisessex.co.uk
Weekly (Thu). Editor: Martin McNeil
News editor: Chris Hatton
Features editor: Sally King
Chief sub-editor: Neal Reeve

Brentwood Yellow Advertiser
01268 503400
www.trinitymirrorsouthern.co.uk
Weekly free (Fri).
Editor: Graham Allen
News editor: Paula Dady
Features editor: Pat Jones
**Brentwood, Billericay &
Havering Recorder**
01708 771500
www.recorderonline.co.uk
Weekly (Fri).
Editor: Mark Sweetingham
News editor: Ross Hindley
Bury Free Press
01284 768911
www.buryfreepress.co.uk
Weekly. Editor: Barry Peters
News editor: Lesley Anslow
Features editor: Claire Brown
Bury St Edmunds Citizen
01284 768911
www.edp24.co.uk
Weekly. Editor: Barry Peters
News editor: Lesley Anslow
Features editor: Claire Brown
Bury St Edmunds Mercury
01284 702588
www.edp24.co.uk
Weekly (Fri). Editor: James Mortlock
News editor: David Desilva
Cambridge Crier
01223 434434
www.cambridge-news.co.uk
Weekly (Fri). Editor: Nigel Brookes
Features editor: James Fuller
Cambridge Evening News
01223 434434
www.cambridge-news.co.uk
Daily. Editor: Colin Grant
News editor: John Deex
Features editor: Debbie Tweedie
Cambridge Weekly News
01223 434434
www.cambridge-news.co.uk
Weekly (Wed). Editor: Nigel Brookes
Cambridgeshire Times
01354 652621
Weekly (Thu). Editor: Brian Asplin
News editor: John Elworthy
Features editor: Maggie Gibson
Castle Point Yellow Advertiser
01268 503400
www.trinitymirrorsouthern.co.uk
Weekly free (Thu).
Editor: Graham Allen
News editor: Paula Dady
Features editor: Pat Jones

Castlepoint & Rayleigh Standard
01268 522792
www.thisisessex.co.uk
Weekly (Wed). Editor: Martin McNeil
News editor: Chris Hatton
Features editor: Sally King
Chief sub-editor: Neal Reeve
Chatteris Times
01354 652621
www.cambs-times.co.uk
Weekly (Thu). Editor: Brian Asplin
News editor: John Elworthy
Features editor: Maggie Gibson
Chelmsford Chronicle
01245 600700
www.thisisessex.co.uk
Weekly (Wed/Thu)
Editor: Stuart Rawlins
News editor: Matt Adams
Features editor: Darryl Webber
Chelmsford Weekly News
01245 493444
www.thisisessex.co.uk
Weekly (Thu). Editor: James Wills
News editor: Denise Rigby
Chelmsford Yellow Advertiser
01268 503400
www.trinitymirrorsouthern.co.uk
Weekly free (Thu).
Editor: Graham Allen
News editor: Paula Dady
Features editor: Pat Jones
Clacton & Frinton Gazette
01255 221221
www.thisisessex.co.uk
Weekly (Fri).
Editor: Neal Harrington
Chief sub-editor: Nigel Brown
Colchester Evening Gazette
01206 506000
www.nqe.info
Daily. Editor: Irene Kettle
News editor: Sally Tetheridge
Features editor: Iris Clapp
Chief sub-editor: Will Bramhill
Dereham & Fakenham Times
01603 628311
www.edp24.co.uk
Weekly (Thu). Editor: Terry Redhead
Diss Express
01379 642264
Weekly (Fri). Editor: Nicola Brown
Deputy editor: Fraser McKay
Diss Mercury
01603 628311
www.edp24.co.uk
Weekly (Fri). Editor: Terry Redhead

Dunmow & Stansted Chronicle
01245 600700
www.thisisessex.co.uk
Weekly (Wed/Thu)
Editor: Stuart Rawlins
News editor: Matt Adams
Features editor: Darryl Webber
Dunmow Broadcast and Recorder
01371 874537
www.dunmow-broadcast.co.uk
Weekly free (Thu)
Editor: Jenny Oliveira
Dunmow Observer
01279 866355
www.herts-essex-news.co.uk
Weekly (Thu). Editor: Val Brown
News editor: Sandra Perry
East Anglian Daily Star
01284 702588
www.eveningstar.co.uk
Daily. Editor: Nigel Pickover
News editor: Martin Davey
East Anglian Daily Times
01284 702588
www.eadt.co.uk
Daily. Editor: Terry Hunt
News editor: Aynsley Davidson
Features editor: Julian Ford
Chief sub-editor: Mike Crookwell
Eastern Daily Press
01603 628311
www.edp24.co.uk
Daily. Editor: Peter Franzen
Ely Standard
01353 667831
www.ely-standard.co.uk
Weekly (Thu). Editor: John Ison
News editor: Debbie Davies
Epping & Waltham Yellow Advertiser
01268 503400
www.trinitymirrorsouthern.co.uk
Weekly free (Fri).
Editor: Graham Allen
News editor: Paula Dady
Features editor: Pat Jones
Epping Guardian
01992 572285
Weekly (Thu).
Editor: David Jackman
Epping Independent
020 8498 3400
Weekly (Fri). Editor: David Jackman
Epping Star
01279 838111
www.thisisessex.co.uk
Weekly (Thu). Editor: Ken Morley
News editor: Beverley Rouse
Epworth Bells & Crowle Advertiser
01427 872202
Weekly (Thu).
Editor: Mandy McSorley

Essex Chronicle
01245 600700
www.thisisessex.co.uk
Weekly (Wed/Thu)
Editor: Stuart Rawlins
News editor: Matt Adams
Features editor: Darryl Webber
Essex County Standard
01206 506000
www.nqe.info
Weekly (Fri). Editor: Jo Robinson
News editor: David Grocott
Features editor: Iris Clapp
Chief sub-editor: Will Bramhill
Essex Enquirer
01277 627300
www.thisisessex.co.uk
Weekly (Thu). Editor: Carol Driver
Evening Echo
01268 522792
www.thisisessex.co.uk
Daily. Editor: Martin McNeil
News editor: Chris Hatton
Features editor: Sally King
Chief sub-editor: Neal Reeve
Evening News
01603 628311
www.eveningnews24.co.uk
Daily. Editor: David Bourn
Evening Star
01284 702588
www.eveningstar.co.uk
Daily. Editor: Nigel Pickover
News editor: Martin Davey
Features editor: Tracy Sparling
Fenland Citizen
01945 586100
Weekly (Wed). Editor: Keith Drayton
Gainsborough Standard
01427 615323
Weekly (Thu).
Editor: Mandy McSorley
Gainsborough Target
01427 810148
Weekly (Fri). Editor: Mike Sass
Goole Courier
01405 782400
www.gooletoday.co.uk/
Weekly (Thu). Editor: Janet Harrison
News editor: Stephanie Bateman
Goole Times/Selby Post
01405 720110
www.horshamonline.co.uk
Weekly (Thu). Editor: Peter Butler
Grantham Citizen
01476 562291
Weekly (Tue). Editor: Nick Woodhead
News editor: John Pinchbeck
Grantham Journal
01476 562291
Weekly (Fri). Editor: Nick Woodhead
News editor: John Pinchbeck

Great Yarmouth & Gorleston Advertiser
01493 601206
www.advertiser-online.co.uk
Weekly (Thu)
Senior reporter: Leanne Boast

Great Yarmouth Mercury
01603 628311
www.edp24.co.uk
Weekly (Tue). Editor: Terry Redhead

Grimsby Evening Telegraph
01472 360360
www.thisisgrimsby.co.uk
Daily. Editor: Michelle Lalor
News editor: Dave Atkin
Features editor: Lorraine Johnson

Grimsby Target
01472 360360
www.thisisgrimsby.co.uk
Weekly free (Wed)
Editor: Michelle Lalor
News editor: Dave Atkin
Features editor: Lorraine Johnson

Halstead Gazette
01376 343344
www.thisisessex.co.uk
Weekly (Fri). Editor: Neal Thomas
News editor: Veronica Balls

Harlow Herald
01279 624331
www.thisisessex.co.uk
Weekly (Thu). Editor: Peter Jeffery
News editor: Tracey Hubbard
Features editor: James Wilmore

Harlow Star
01279 866355
www.herts-essex-news.co.uk
Weekly (Thu). Editor: Val Brown
News editor: Sandra Perry

Harold Gazette
01277 219222
www.thisisessex.co.uk
Weekly (Wed). Editor: Roger Watkins
News editor: Sheelagh Bree
Features editor: Josie Stephenson

Harold Recorder
01708 771500
www.recorderonline.co.uk
Weekly (Fri).
Editor: Mark Sweetingham
News editor: Ross Hindley

Haverhill Echo
01440 703456
www.buryfreepress.co.uk
Weekly (Thu).
Editor: Heather Turner
News editor: David Hart

Haverhill Weekly News
01223 434434
www.cambridge-news.co.uk
Weekly (Thu). Editor: Nigel Brookes

Havering Herald
01603 628311
Weekly free (Fri)
Editor: Richard Thompson

Havering Yellow Advertiser
01268 503400
www.trinitymirrorsouthern.co.uk
Editor: Graham Allen
News editor: Paula Dady
Features editor: Pat Jones

Horncastle News
01507 353200
www.horncastletoday.co.uk
Weekly (Wed). Editor: Janet Richardson

Hornsea Gazette
01964 612777
Weekly (Thu)
News editor: Andrew Swales
Features editor: David McAughtrie

Huntingdon Town Crier
01480 402100
www.cambridge-news.co.uk
Weekly (Thu)
Editor: Anthony Hawkswell

Huntingdon Weekly News
01480 467670
www.cambridge-news.co.uk
Weekly (Wed). Editor: Colin Grant
News editor: John Deex

Hunts Post
01480 411481
www.huntspost.co.uk
Weekly (Wed).
Editor: Paul Richardson
Deputy editor: Angela Singer

Ilford & Redbridge Post
020 8491 2000
Weekly free (Wed).
Editor: Dave Russell
News editor: Scott Morrow
Chief sub-editor: Graham Whitmore

Ipswich Advertiser
01473 324700
www.advertiser-online.co.uk
Weekly (Thu). Editor: Paul Couch
News editor: Nicola Durrant

Island Times
01702 477666
www.thisisessex.co.uk
Monthly (Tue). Editor: Michael Guy

Leigh Times
01702 477666
www.thisisessex.co.uk
Fortnightly (Tue).
Editor: Michael Guy

Lincoln Target
01522 820000
www.thisislincolnshire.co.uk
Weekly (Wed). Editor: Mike Sassi

Lincolnshire Echo
01522 820000
www.thisislincolnshire.co.uk
Daily. Editor: Mike Sassi

Lincolnshire Free Press
01775 725021
www.spaldingtoday.co.uk
Weekly (Tue). Editor: Alan Salt
News editor: David Crossley
Features editor: Julie Williams
Chief sub-editor: Tracey Vale

The Local
01778 425876
Weekly (Fri). Editor: Lisa Bruen

Loughton & Epping Herald
01279 624331
www.thisisessex.co.uk
Weekly (Thu). Editor: Peter Jeffery
News editor: Tracey Hubbard
Features editor: James Wilmore

Loughton, Chigwell & Buckhurst Hill Guardian
01992 572285
Weekly (Thu).
Editor: David Jackman

Louth Citizen
01507 353200
www.louthtoday.co.uk
Weekly (Fri).
Editor: Charles Ladbrooke

Louth Leader
01507 353200
www.louthtoday.co.uk
Weekly (Wed)
Editor: Charles Ladbrooke

Lowestoft Journal
01603 628311
www.edp24.co.uk
Weekly (Fri). Editor: Terry Redheard

Lynn News
01553 761188
www.lynnnews.co.uk
Weekly (Tue, Fri)
Editor: Malcolm Powell
News editor: Donna Semmens

Maldon & Burnham Chronicle
01245 600700
www.thisisessex.co.uk
Weekly (Wed/Thu)
Editor: Stuart Rawlins
News editor: Matt Adams
Features editor: Darryl Webber

Maldon & Burnham Standard
01621 852233
Weekly (Thu). Editor: James Wills

Market Rasen Mail
01507 353200
www.marketrasentoday.co.uk
Weekly (Wed). Editor: Jason Hipsley

Newmarket Journal
01638 564104
Weekly (Thu). Editor: Colin Lucas

Newmarket Weekly News
01223 434434
www.cambridge-news.co.uk
Weekly (Thu). Editor: Nigel Brookes

Norfolk Citizen
01553 761188
Weekly (Fri). Editor: Chris Hornby
Norfolk North Advertiser
01603 740222
www.advertiser-online.co.uk
Weekly (Fri).
Editor: Sharon Richardson
Norfolk South Advertiser
01603 740222
www.advertiser-online.co.uk
Weekly (Fri). Editor: Sara Hardman
North Essex Advertiser
01473 324700
www.advertiser-online.co.uk
Weekly (Fri). Editor: Paul Couch
News editor: Nicola Durrant
North Norfolk & Broadland Town & Country News
01692 582287
Monthly (Fri nearest 1st)
Editor: Lawrence Watts
North Norfolk News
01603 628311
www.edp24.co.uk
Weekly (Thu). Editor: Terry Redhead
Norwich Advertiser
01603 740222
www.advertiser-online.co.uk
Weekly (Fri). Editor: Lisa Horton
Ongar and North Weald Gazette
01277 219222
www.thisisessex.co.uk
Weekly (Wed). Editor: Roger Watkins
News editor: Sheelagh Bree
Features editor: Josie Stephenson
Ongar Guardian
01992 572285
Weekly (Thu).
Editor: David Jackman
Peterborough Citizen
01733 555111
www.peterboroughnow.co.uk
Weekly (Wed).
Editor: Rebecca Stephens
News editor: James Kelly
Features editor: Rachael Gordon
Chief sub-editor: Tracey Crampton
Production editor: Brad Barnes
Peterborough Evening Telegraph
01733 555111
www.peterboroughnow.co.uk
Daily. Editor: Rebecca Stephens
News editor: James Kelly
Features editor: Rachael Gordon
Chief sub-editor: Tracey Crampton
Peterborough Herald & Post
01733 318600
www.peterborough.net
/heraldandpost
Weekly (Thu). Editor: Steve Rose
Features editor: Amanda Franklin

Ramsey Post
01480 411481
Weekly (Thu).
Editor: Paul Richardson
Deputy editor: Angela Singer
Rayleigh Times
01702 477666
www.thisisessex.co.uk
Monthly (Tue). Editor: Michael Guy
Redbridge Yellow Advertiser
01268 503400
www.trinitymirrorsouthern.co.uk
Editor: Graham Allen
News editor: Paula Dady
Features editor: Pat Jones
Redbridge, Waltham Forest & West Essex Guardian
020 8498 3400
Weekly (Thu). Editor: Pat Stannard
News editor: Matthew Finch
Romford & Havering Post
020 8491 2000
Weekly free (Wed).
Editor: Dave Russell
News editor: Scott Morrow
Chief sub-editor: Graham Whitmore
Romford Recorder
01708 771500
www.recorderonline.co.uk
Weekly (Fri).
Editor: Mark Sweetingham
Royston Weekly News
01223 434434
www.cambridge-news.co.uk
Weekly (Thu). Editor: Nigel Brookes
Rutland & Stamford Mercury & Citizen
01780 762255
www.stamfordmercury.co.uk
Weekly (Fri). Editor: Tor Clark
News editor: Suzanne Moon
St Ives Town Crier
01480 402100
www.cambridge-news.co.uk
Weekly (Thu)
Editor: Anthony Hawkswell
St Ives Weekly News
01223 434434
www.cambridge-news.co.uk
Weekly (Thu). Editor: Nigel Brookes
St Neots Town Crier
01480 402100
www.cambridge-news.co.uk
Weekly (Thu)
Editor: Anthony Hawkswell
St Neots Weekly News
01480 467670
www.cambridge-news.co.uk
Weekly (Wed). Editor: Nigel Brookes
Saffron Walden Observer
01279 866355
www.herts-essex-news.co.uk
Weekly (Thu). Editor: Val Brown
News editor: Sandra Perry

Saffron Walden, Stansted & Sawston Reporter
01763 245241
www.thisisessex.co.uk
Weekly (Thu). Editor: Les Baker
Saffron Walden Weekly News
01223 434434
www.cambridge-news.co.uk
Weekly (Thu). Editor: Nigel Brookes
Sawbridgeworth Star
01279 838111
www.thisisessex.co.uk
Weekly (Thu). Editor: Ken Morley
News editor: Beverley Rouse
Scunthorpe Target
01724 273273
www.thisisscunthorpe.co.uk
Weekly (Thu). Editor: John Grubb
News editor: Matthew Finch
Chief sub-editor: John Curtis
Scunthorpe Telegraph
01724 273273
www.thisisscunthorpe.co.uk
Daily. Editor: John Grubb
News editor: Matthew Finch
Chief sub-editor: John Curtis
Skegness Citizen
01507 353200
Weekly (Fri). Editor: John Calpe
Skegness Standard
01507 353200
www.skegnesstoday.co.uk
Weekly (Wed)
Editor: Charles Ladbrooke
Skegness Target
01205 315000
Weekly (Wed). Editor: Glyn Belsher
News editor: Katy Roberts
Sleaford Citizen
01529 413646
Weekly (Fri). Editor: John Lavery
News editor: Andy Hubbert
Sleaford Standard
01529 413646
Weekly (Wed). Editor: John Lavery
News editor: Andy Hubbert
Sleaford Target
01522 820000
www.thisislincolnshire.co.uk
Weekly (Wed). Editor: Glynn Belsher
Soham Standard
01353 667831
www.ely-standard.co.uk
Weekly (Thu). Editor: John Ison
News editor: Debbie Davies
South Woodham & Maldon Weekly News
01621 852233
www.thisisessex.co.uk
Weekly (Thu). Editor: James Wills

Southend Standard
01268 522792
www.thisisessex.co.uk
Weekly (Thu). Editor: Martin McNeil
News editor: Chris Hatton
Features editor: Sally King
Chief sub-editor: Neal Reeve
Southend Times
01702 477666
www.thisisessex.co.uk
Weekly (Tue). Editor: Michael Guy
Southend Yellow Advertiser
01268 503400
www.trinitymirrorsouthern.co.uk
Weekly free (Thu)
Editor: Graham Allen
News editor: Paula Dady
Features editor: Pat Jones
Spalding Guardian
01775 725021
www.spaldingtoday.co.uk
Weekly (Thu). Editor: Alan Salt
News editor: David Crossley
Features editor: Julie Williams
Chief sub-editor: Tracey Vale
Spalding Herald
01775 713723
www.spaldingtoday.co.uk
Monthly free (1st of month)
Editor: Natalie Ward
Spilsby Standard
01754 897120
Weekly (Wed). Editor: John Coupe
Spilsby Target
01205 315000
Weekly (Wed). Editor: Glyn Belsher
News editor: Katy Roberts
Stamford Citizen
01780 762255
www.stamfordmercury.co.uk
Weekly free (Tue). Editor: Tor Clark
News editor: Suzanne Moon
Stamford Herald & Post
01733 318600
Weekly (Thu). Editor: Steve Rose
Features editor: Amanda Franklin
Stansted Observer
01279 866355
www.herts-essex-news.co.uk
Weekly (Thu). Editor: Val Brown
News editor: Sandra Perry
Sudbury Mercury
01284 702588
www.edp24.co.uk
Weekly (Fri). Editor: Terry Hunt
News editor: Ainsley Davidson
Features editor: Julian Ford
Chief sub-editor: Mike Crookwell
Suffolk Advertiser
01473 324700
www.advertiser-online.co.uk
Weekly (Fri). Editor: Paul Couch
News editor: Nicola Durrant

Suffolk Free Press
01787 375271
www.sudburytoday.co.uk
Editor: Phil Minett
News editor: Nick Wells
Swaffham Mercury
01603 628311
www.edp24.co.uk
Monthly. Editor: Terry Redhead
Swaffham News
01553 761188
Weekly (Fri). Editor: Malcolm Powell
News editor: Donna Semmens
Tendring Weekly News
01206 506000
www.thisisessex.co.uk
Weekly free (Wed).
Editor: Irene Kettle
News editor: Sally Teatheredge
Thetford & Brandon Times
01603 628311
www.edp24.co.uk
Weekly (Wed). Editor: Terry Redhead
Thetford Citizen
01284 768911
www.johnstonpress.co.uk/anglia
Weekly. Editor: Barry Peters
News editor: Lesley Anslow
Features editor: Claire Brown
Thurrock Gazette
01375 411502
www.thisisessex.co.uk
Weekly free (Fri). Editor: Neil Speight
Thurrock Recorder
01708 771500
www.recorderonline.co.uk
Weekly (Fri).
Editor: Mark Sweetingham
News editor: Ross Hindley
Thurrock Yellow Advertiser
01268 503400
www.trinitymirrorsouthern.co.uk
Weekly free (Thu).
Editor: Graham Allen
News editor: Paula Dady
Features editor: Pat Jones
Thurrock, Lakeside & Grays Post
020 8491 2000
Weekly (Thu). Editor: Dave Russell
News editor: Scott Morrow
Chief sub-editor: Graham Whitmore
Walden Local
01799 516161
www.thisisessex.co.uk
Weekly (Wed). Editor: John Brooker
Waltham Forest Guardian
020 8498 3400
Weekly (Thu). Editor: Pat Stannard
Waltham Forest Independent
020 8498 3400
Weekly (Fri). Editor: Pat Stannard

Watton & Swaffham Times
01603 628311
www.edp24.co.uk
Weekly (Fri). Editor: Terry Redhead
Waveney Advertiser
01493 601206
www.advertiser-online.co.uk
Weekly (Fri)
Managing editor: Mike Almond
Whittlesey Times
01354 652621
www.cambs-times.co.uk
Weekly (Thu). Editor: Brian Asplin
News editor: John Elworthy
Features editor: Maggie Gibson
Wisbech Standard
01354 652621
www.wisbech-standard.co.uk
Weekly (Thu). Editor: Brian Asplin
News editor: John Elworthy
Features editor: Maggie Gibson
Witham Chronicle
01245 600700
www.thisisessex.co.uk
Weekly (Wed/Thu)
Editor: Stuart Rawlins
News editor: Matt Adams
Features editor: Darryl Webber
Woodham Chronicle
01245 600700
www.thisisessex.co.uk
Weekly (Wed/Thu)
Editor: Stuart Rawlins
News editor: Matt Adams
Features editor: Darryl Webber
Wymondham & Attleborough Mercury
01603 628311
www.edp24.co.uk
Weekly (Fri). Editor: Terry Redhead

Midlands

Derbyshire, Leicestershire,
Northamptonshire,
Nottinghamshire, Staffordshire

The Advertiser
01782 602525
Weekly free (Thu).
Editor: Sean Dooley
News editor: Robert Cotterill
Features editor:
Charlotte Little-Jones
Alfreton Chad
01623 456789
www.johnstonpress.co.uk
/yorkshire.asp
Weekly (Fri). Editor: Jeremy Plews
News editor: Joy Thompson
Chief sub-editor: Karen Robinson

Alfreton & Ripley Echo
01773 834731
Weekly (Fri).
Editor: David Hopkinson
Ashbourne News Telegraph
01283 512345
www.ashbournenewstelegraph.
co.uk
Weekly (Wed).
Editor: Paul Hazeldine
News editor: Steve Doohan
Features editor: Bill Pritchard
Chief sub-editor: Steve Davies
Production editor: Diane Finn
Ashfield Chad
01623 456789
www.ashfieldtoday.co.uk
Weekly (Wed). Editor: Jeremy Plews
News editor: Joy Thompson
Chief sub-editor: Karen Robinson
Ashby & Coalville Mail
0116 251 2512
www.thisisleicestershire.co.uk
Weekly (Tue). Editor: Nick Carter
News editor: Richard Bettsworth
Ashby Times
01530 813101
Weekly (Fri).
News editor: Mark Good
Features editor: Kay Moon
Chief sub-editor: Mark Good
Atherstone Herald
01827 848535
Weekly (Thu). Editor: Sam Holliday
Belper Express
01332 291111
Weekly free (Tue).
Editor: Andy Machin
Belper News
01629 582432
Weekly (Wed).
Editor: Amanda Hatfield
News editor: Helen Taylor
Biddulph Advertiser
01260 281012
Weekly (Thu). Editor: Harri Ashton
Biddulph Chronicle
01260 273737
Weekly (Fri).
Editor: Jeremy Condliffe
Birstall Post
0116 267 4213
www.birstallpost.co.uk
Monthly free (1st of month)
Editor: Jerry Jackson
News editor: Mrs E M Jackson
Brackley Post
01604 614600
Weekly (Fri).
Editor: Richard Howarth
Production editor: Julie Fisher
Burntwood Mercury
01827 848535
Weekly (Thu). Editor: Sam Holliday

Bolsover & District Advertiser
01246 202291
Fortnightly free (Wed)
Editor: Mike Wilson
Assistant editor: Phil Bramley
News editor: Tracy Mitchell
Entertainment editor: Gay Bolton
Assistant news editor: Sean Boyle
Burton Mail
01283 512345
www.burtonmail.co.uk
Daily. Editor: Paul Hazeldine
News editor: Steve Doohan
Features editor: Bill Pritchard
Chief sub-editor: Steve Davies
Production editor: Diane Finn
Burton & South Derbyshire Advertiser
01283 512345
www.uttoxeteradvertiser.co.uk
Weekly (Wed).
Editor: Paul Hazeldine
News editor: Steve Doohan
Features editor: Bill Pritchard
Chief sub-editor: Steve Davies
Production editor: Diane Finn
Burton Trader
01283 512200
Weekly (Wed). Editor: Paul Thomas
News editor: Paul Henshall
Chief sub-editor: Alan Payne
Buxton Advertiser
01298 22118
www.buxtontoday.co.uk
Weekly (Thu). Editor: John Phillips
News editor: Emma Downes
Buxton Times
01298 22118
www.buxtontoday.co.uk
Weekly free (Fri).
Editor: John Phillips
News editor: Emma Downes
Cannock & Rugeley Mercury
01827 848535
Weekly (Thu). Editor: Linda Young
Cannock & Rugeley Chronicle
01543 506311
Weekly (Fri). Editor: Susan Attwater
Cannock Chase & Burntwood Post
01543 501700
Weekly (Thu). Editor: Mike Lockley
Cheadle & Tean Times
01538 753162
Weekly (Wed). Editor: Nigel Titterton
Cheadle Post & Times
01538 750011
Weekly (Wed). Editor: Doug Pickford

Chesterfield Advertiser
01246 202291
Weekly free (Fri).
Editor: Mike Wilson
Assistant editor: Phil Bramley
News editor: Tracy Mitchell
Entertainment editor: Gay Bolton
Assistant news editor: Sean Boyle
Chesterfield Express
01246 504500
Weekly free (Wed).
Editor: Mike Wilson
Assistant editor: Phil Bramley
News editor: Tracy Mitchell
Entertainment editor: Gay Bolton
Assistant news editor: Sean Boyle
Chronicle and Echo (Northampton)
01604 467000
www.northantsnews.com
Daily. Editor: Mark Edwards
News editor: Richard Edmondson
Features editor: Sarah Freeman
Chief sub-editor: Joanne Cartwright
Production editor: Graham Tebbutt
Coalville & Ashby Echo
01509 635807
Weekly (Tue).
Editor: Pete Warrington
Coalville Times
01530 813101
Weekly (Fri).
News editor: Mark Good
Features editor: Kay Moon
Chief sub-editor: Mark Good
Coleshill Herald
01827 848535
Weekly (Thu). Editor: Sam Holliday
Corby Citizen
01536 506100
www.northantsnews.com
Weekly (Thu). Editor: David Penman
News editor: Nick Shaw
Features editor: Alistair Whitfield
Chief sub-editor: Andy Wynham
Production editor: Richard Yetman
Corby Herald & Post
01604 614600
Weekly (Thu).
Editor: Richard Howarth
Production editor: Julie Fisher
Daventry Express
01327 703383
www.daventryonline.co.uk
Weekly (Thu). Editor: Jason Gibbons
News editor: Adam Hollier
Derby Evening Telegraph
01332 291111
www.thisisderbyshire.co.uk
Daily. Editor: Mike Norton
News editor: Nicola Hodgson
Features editor: Cheryl Hague
Chief sub-editor: Peter Pheasant

Derby Express
01332 291111
Weekly free (Tue).
Editor: Andy Machin
Derby Trader
01332 253999
Weekly (Thu).
Editor: Patrick O'Connor
Features editor: Steve Eyley
Chief sub-editor: Richard Taylor
Derbyshire Guardian
01909 500500
Weekly (Fri).
Editor: George Robinson
News editor: Jackie Laver
Derbyshire Times
01246 504500
www.derbyshiretimes.co.uk
Weekly (Thu). Editor: Mike Wilson
Assistant editor: Phil Bramley
News editor: Tracy Mitchell
Entertainment editor: Gay Bolton
Assistant news editor: Sean Boyle
Dronfield Advertiser
01246 202291
Weekly free (Wed).
Editor: Mike Wilson
Assistant editor: Phil Bramley
News editor: Tracy Mitchell
Entertainment editor: Gay Bolton
Assistant news editor: Sean Boyle
Dukeries Advertiser
01636 681234
Weekly (Fri)
Editor: Harry Whitehouse
News editor: Lucy Millard
Chief sub-editor: Chris Prine
Eastwood & Kimberley Advertiser
01773 713563
www.eastwoodadvertiser.co.uk
Weekly (Fri). Editor: John Shawcroft
Eckington Leader
01246 434343
Weekly (Fri). Editor: Mike Wilson
Assistant editor: Phil Bramley
News editor: Tracy Mitchell
Entertainment editor: Gay Bolton
Assistant news editor: Sean Boyle
The Evening Telegraph
01536 506100
www.northantsnews.com
Daily. Editor: David Penman
News editor: Nick Shaw
Features editor: Alistair Whitfield
Chief sub-editor: Andy Wynham
Production editor: Richard Yetman
Glossop Chronicle
0161 304 7691
Weekly (Thu). Editor: Nigel Skinner

Harborough Mail
01858 462626
www.harboroughmail.co.uk
Weekly (Thu). Editor: Brian Dodds
News editor: Maria Thompson
High Peak Courier
01298 22118
www.buxtontoday.co.uk
Weekly free (Fri).
Editor: John Phillips
News editor: Emma Downes
Hinckley Herald & Journal
01455 891981
www.hinckley-times.co.uk
Weekly (Wed). Editor: Paul Webb
Hinckley Times
01455 891981
www.hinckley-times.co.uk
Weekly (Thu). Editor: Paul Webb
Hucknall & Bulwell Dispatch
01623 456789
www.hucknalltoday.co.uk
Weekly (Fri)
Editor: Richard Silverwood
Ilkeston & Ripley Trader
01332 253999
Weekly (Fri).
Editor: Patrick O'Connor
Features editor: Steve Eyley
Chief sub-editor: Richard Taylor
Ilkeston Advertiser
0115 944 4411
www.derbyshiretimes.co.uk
Weekly (Thu). Editor: David Horne
Ilkeston Express
01332 291111
Weekly free (Tue).
Editor: Andy Machin
Ilkeston Shopper
0115 944 4411
www.derbyshiretimes.co.uk
Weekly free (Tue).
Editor: David Horne
Kettering Citizen
01536 506100
www.northantsnews.com
Weekly (Thu). Editor: David Penman
News editor: Nick Shaw
Features editor: Alistair Whitfield
Chief sub-editor: Andy Wynham
Production editor: Richard Yetman
Kettering Evening Telegraph
01536 506100
www.northantsnews.com
Daily. Editor: David Penman
News editor: Nick Shaw
Features editor: Alistair Whitfield
Chief sub-editor: Andy Wynham
Production editor: Richard Yetman
Kettering Herald & Post
01604 614600
Weekly (Thu).
Editor: Richard Howarth
Production editor: Julie Fisher

Leek Post & Times
01538 399599
Weekly (Wed). Editor: Doug Pickford
News editor: Jane Griffiths
Leicester Mail
0116 251 2512
www.thisisleicestershire.co.uk
Weekly free (Tue). Editor: Nick Carter
News editor: Richard Bettsworth
Leicester Mercury
0116 251 2512
www.leicestermercury.co.uk
Daily. Editor: Nick Carter
News editor: Richard Bettsworth
Leicestershire Times Today
0115 982 7338
Weekly (Fri).
Editor: Matthew Palmer
Lichfield and Burntwood Edition Express and Star
01902 313131
www.expressandstar.com
Daily. Editor: Adrian Faber
Lichfield Mercury
01827 848535
Weekly (Thu). Editor: Sam Holliday
Lichfield Post
01543 258523
Weekly (Thu). Editor: Pam Thomas
Long Eaton Advertiser
0115 946 2837
Weekly (Wed). Editor: David Godsall
Long Eaton Recorder
0115 948 2000
www.thisisnottingham.co.uk
Weekly free (Thu).
Editor: Graham Glen
News editor: Claire Catlow
Features editor: Jeremy Lewis
Long Eaton Trader
0115 946 9909
Weekly (Thu).
Editor: Patrick O'Connor
Features editor: Steve Eyley
Chief sub-editor: Richard Taylor
Loughborough Echo
01509 232632
Weekly (Thu). Editor: John Ripon
News editor: John Brindley
Loughborough Mail
0116 251 2512
www.thisisleicestershire.co.uk
Weekly (Tue). Editor: Nick Carter
News editor: Richard Bettsworth
Lutterworth Mail
01858 462626
www.harboroughtoday.co.uk
Weekly (Thu). Editor: Brian Dodds
News editor: Maria Thompson
Mansfield & Ashfield Observer
01623 456789
Weekly free (Thu).
Editor: Tony Spittles

Mansfield & Ashfield Recorder
01623 420000
Weekly free (Wed)
Editor: Graham Glenn
Mansfield Chad
01623 456789
www.mansfieldtoday.co.uk
Weekly (Wed). Editor: Jeremy Plews
News editor: Joy Thompson
Chief sub-editor: Karen Robinson
**Market Harborough
Herald & Post**
01604 614600
Weekly (Fri).
Editor: Richard Howarth
Production editor: Julie Fisher
Matlock Mercury
01629 582432
www.matlockmercury.co.uk
Weekly (Thu).
Editor: Amanda Hatfield
News editor: Helen Taylor
Melton Citizen
01664 410041
www.meltontoday.co.uk/
Weekly free (Tue).
Editor: Andrew Plaice
Melton Times
01664 410041
www.meltontoday.co.uk/
Weekly (Thu). Editor: Andrew Plaice
**Mid Staffs Edition Express
and Star**
01543 506311
www.expressandstar.com
Daily. Editor: Adrian Faber
News editor: Mark Drew
Mountsorrel Post
0116 267 4213
4pa. Editor: Jerry Jackson
News editor: Mrs E M Jackson
Newark Advertiser
01636 681234
www.newarkadvertiser.co.uk
Weekly (Fri).
Editor: Harry Whitehouse
News editor: Lucy Millard
Newcastle Advertiser
01782 619830
Daily. Editor: Sean Dooley
News editor: Robert Cotterill
*Features editor: Charlotte Little-
Jones*
**North West Leics & South
Derbyshire Leader**
01530 813101
*Weekly (Wed). News editor: Mark
Good*
Features editor: Kay Moon
Chief sub-editor: Mark Good

Northampton Herald & Post
01604 614600
Weekly (Thu).
Editor: Richard Howarth
Production editor: Julie Fisher
Northampton Mercury
01604 467000
www.northantsnews.com
Weekly (Thu). Editor: Mark Edwards
News editor: Richard Edmondson
Features editor: Sarah Freeman
Chief sub-editor: Joanne Cartwright
Production editor: Graham Tebbutt
Northamptonshire Journal
0116 233 3635
Weekly (Tue). Editor: Paul Clark
Northants on Sunday
01536 467000
www.northantsnews.com
Sunday. Editor: Steve Scoles
**Nottingham & Trent Valley
Journal**
0115 982 7337
Weekly (Fri).
Editor: Matthew Palmer
**Nottingham & Long Eaton
Topper**
0115 969 6000
www.toppernewspapers.co.uk
Weekly free (Wed).
Editor: John Howarth
Nottingham Evening Post
0115 948 2000
www.thisisnottingham.co.uk
Daily. Editor: Graham Glen
News editor: Claire Catlow
Features editor: Jeremy Lewis
Nottingham Recorder
0115 948 2000
www.thisisnottingham.co.uk
Weekly free (Wed).
Editor: Graham Glen
News editor: Claire Catlow
Features editor: Jeremy Lewis
Oadby & Wigston Mail
0116 251 2512
www.thisisleicestershire.co.uk
Weekly (Tue). Editor: Nick Carter
News editor: Richard Bettsworth
Peak Advertiser
01629 812159
Fortnightly free (Thu)
Editor: Steve Wild
Peak Times
01629 582432
Weekly free (Fri)
Editor: Amanda Hatfield
News editor: Helen Taylor

Potteries Advertiser
01782 602525
Weekly free (Thu).
Editor: Sean Dooley
News editor: Robert Cotterill
*Features editor: Charlotte Little-
Jones*
Retford and Bawtry Guardian
01909 500500
www.retfordtoday.co.uk
Weekly (Thu)
Editor: George Robinson
News editor: Jackie Laver
Retford Trader
01909 500500
Weekly free (Thu)
Editor: George Robinson
News editor: Jackie Laver
**Retford, Gainsborough &
Worksop Times**
01777 702275
Weekly (Thu). Editor: Nick Purkiss
Ripley & Heanor News
01629 582432
Weekly (Thu).
Editor: Amanda Hatfield
News editor: Helen Taylor
Rothley Post
0117 267 4213
6pa. Editor: Jerry Jackson
News editor: Mrs E M Jackson
Rugeley Mercury
01543 414414
Weekly (Thu). Editor: Tim Hewitt
News editor: Andy Kerr
Rugeley Post
01543 258523
Weekly (Thu). Editor: Pam Thomas
Rutland Times
01572 757722
www.rutlandtimes.co.uk
Weekly (Thu). Editor: Brian Martin
The Sentinel (Stoke-On-Trent)
01782 602525
www.thesentinel.co.uk
Daily. Editor: Sean Dooley
News editor: Robert Cotterill
*Features editor:
Charlotte Little-Jones*
Sentinel Sunday
01782 602525
www.thesentinel.co.uk
Sunday. Editor: Sean Dooley
News editor: Robert Cotterill
*Features editor:
Charlotte Little-Jones*
Shepshed Echo
01509 232632
Weekly (Thu). Editor: John Ripon
News editor: John Brindley

Sherwood/Rainworth Chad
01623 456789
Weekly (Wed). Editor: Jeremy Plews
News editor: Joy Thompson
Chief sub-editor: Karen Robinson
Shirebrook & Bolsover Chad
01623 456789
Weekly (Wed). Editor: Jeremy Plews
News editor: Joy Thompson
Chief sub-editor: Karen Robinson
South Notts Advertiser
01636 681234
Weekly (Fri)
Editor: Harry Whitehouse
News editor: Lucy Millard
Stafford & Stone Chronicle
01785 247290
Daily. Editor: Klooran Wills
Stafford Post
01543 501700
Weekly (Thu). Editor: Mike Lockley
Staffordshire Newsletter
01785 257700
www.staffordshirenewsletter.co.uk
Weekly (Thu). Editor: Klooran Wills
Stapleford & Sandiacre News
0115 946 2837
Weekly (Wed). Editor: David Godsall
Stratford & Banbury Why
01527 588000
Weekly free (Fri).
Editor: Claire Smith
Swadlincote Times
01530 813101
Weekly (Fri).
News editor: Mark Good
Features editor: Kay Moon
Chief sub-editor: Mark Good
Tamworth Herald
01827 848535
www.tamworthherald.co.uk
Weekly (Thu). Editor: Sam Holiday
Tamworth Times
01827 308000
Weekly (Thu). Editor: Pam Thomas
Trader Pictorial
01636 681234
Weekly (Wed)
Editor: Harry Whitehouse
News editor: Lucy Millard
Towcester Post
01604 614600
Weekly (Fri).
Editor: Richard Howarth
Production editor: Julie Fisher
Uttoxeter Advertiser
01889 562050
www.uttoxeteradvertiser.co.uk
Weekly (Tue). Editor: Alan Harris
Uttoxeter Post & Times
01889 568999
Weekly (Thu). Editor: Alan Harris

Warsop Chad
01623 456789
Weekly (Wed). Editor: Jeremy Plews
News editor: Joy Thompson
Chief sub-editor: Karen Robinson
**Wellingborough & East
Northants Evening Telegraph**
01536 506100
www.northantsnews.com
Daily. Editor: David Penman
News editor: Nick Shaw
Features editor: Alistair Whitfield
Chief sub-editor: Andy Wynham
Production editor: Richard Yetman
**Wellingborough & Rushden
Citizen**
01536 506100
www.northantsnews.com
Weekly (Thu). Editor: David Penman
News editor: Nick Shaw
Features editor: Alistair Whitfield
Chief sub-editor: Andy Wynham
Production editor: Richard Yetman
**Wellingborough & Rushden
Herald & Post**
01604 614600
Weekly (Thu).
Editor: Richard Howarth
Production editor: Julie Fisher
Worksop Guardian
01909 500500
www.worksoptoday.co.uk
Weekly (Fri).
Editor: George Robinson
News editor: Jackie Laver
Worksop Trader
01909 500500
Weekly free (Wed)
Editor: George Robinson
News editor: Jackie Laver

West Midlands

West Midlands, Warwickshire

**Ad News – Willenhall,
Wednesbury & Darlaston**
01543 501700
Weekly (Wed). Editor: Mike Lockley
Bedworth Echo
024 7663 3633
www.iccoventry.co.uk
Weekly (Fri). Editor: Alan Kirby
News editor: John West
Features editor: Steven Chilton
Birmingham Evening Mail
0121 236 3366
www.icbirmingham.co.uk
Daily. Editor: Roger Borrell
News editor: Andy Richards
Features editor: Alison Handley

Birmingham News
0121 234 5073
www.icbirmingham.co.uk
Weekly (Thu). Editor: David Brook
News editor: Damien O'Laughlin
Birmingham Post
0121 236 3366
www.icbirmingham.co.uk
Daily. Editor: Fiona Alexander
News editor: Carole Cole
Features editor: Sid Langley
Black Country Bugle
01384 567678
www.blackcountrybugle.co.uk
Weekly (Thu). Editor: Robert Taylor
Coventry Citizen
024 7663 3633
www.iccoventry.co.uk
Weekly (Thu). Editor: Alan Kirby
News editor: John West
Features editor: Steven Chilton
Coventry Evening Telegraph
024 7663 3633
www.iccoventry.co.uk
Daily. Editor: Alan Kirby
News editor: John West
Features editor: Steven Chilton
Coventry Observer
024 7649 5900
www.coventryobserver.co.uk
Weekly free (Fri). Editor: Mike Green
Daventry Express
01788 535363
www.daventryonline.co.uk
Weekly (Thu). Editor: Jason Gibbons
Dudley Chronicle
01384 353211
www.expressandstar.com
Weekly (Fri).
Editor: Leon Burakowski
Features editor: Dave Pearce
Chief sub-editor: Jane Reynolds
Dudley Edition Express & Star
01384 355355
www.expressandstar.com
Daily. Editor: Adrian Faber
News editor: Mark Drew
Features editor: Dylan Evans
Chief sub-editor: Tony Reynolds
Dudley News
01384 358050
www.dudleynews.co.uk
Weekly (Fri). Editor: Jeff Gepheott
Features editor: Lynn Taylor
Express & Star
01902 313131
www.expressandstar.com
Daily. Editor: Adrian Faber
News editor: Mark Drew
Features editor: Dylan Evans
Chief sub-editor: Tony Reynolds
Express & Star (Stourbridge)
01384 399914

Express & Star (Walsall)
01922 444444
Great Barr and Erdington Chronicle
0121 553 7171
Weekly free (Wed).
Editor: Caroline Jones
Great Barr Observer
01827 848535
Weekly (Fri). Editor: Mark Eustace
Halesowen Chronicle
01384 353211
Weekly (Fri).
Editor: Leon Burakowski
Features editor: Dave Pearce
Chief sub-editor: Jane Reynolds
Halesowen News
01384 358050
www.halesowennews.co.uk
Weekly (Fri). Editor: Jeff Gepheott
Features editor: Lynn Taylor
Heartland Evening News
024 7635 3534
www.hen-news.com
Daily. Editor: Tony Parrott
News editor: Jack Linsted
Features editor: John Jevons
Production editor: Bob Clemens
Kenilworth Weekly News
01926 457777
www.kenilworthonline.co.uk
Weekly (Fri). Editor: Martin Lawson
News editor: Calista Lewis
Leamington Spa Courier
01926 457777
www.leamingtononline.co.uk
Weekly (Fri). Editor: Martin Lawson
News editor: Calista Lewis
Leamington Spa Observer
01926 451900
www.leamington-now.com
Weekly free (Thu).
Editor: Ian Hughes
Leamington Spa Review
01926 457777
www.leamingtonspatoday.co.uk
Weekly (Thu).
Editor: Martin Lawson
News editor: Calista Lewis
Metro Birmingham
020 7651 5200
www.metrobirmingham.co.uk
Daily. Editor: Kenny Campbell
News editor: Mark Dorman
Features editor: Kieran Meeke
Nuneaton Weekly Tribune
024 7663 3633
www.iccoverntry.co.uk
Weekly (Thu). Editor: Alan Kirby
News editor: John West
Features editor: Steven Chilton

Rugby Advertiser
01788 535363
www.rugbyadvertiser.co.uk
Weekly (Thu)
Editor: Peter Hengenheister
Rugby Observer
01788 535147
www.therugbyobserver.co.uk
Weekly free (Fri). Editor: Chris Smith
Rugby Review
01788 535363
www.rugbyreviewtoday.co.uk
Weekly (Thu)
Editor: Peter Hengenheister
Sandwell Chronicle
0121 553 7171
Weekly free (Wed).
Editor: Caroline Jones
Solihull News
0121 711 3993
www.midlandweeklymedia.co.uk
Weekly (Fri). Editor: Ross Crawford
Solihull Times
0121 711 3993
www.midlandweeklymedia.co.uk
Weekly (Fri). Editor: Roland Wilson
Stourbridge Chronicle
01384 399914
www.expressandstar.com
Weekly (Fri).
Editor: Leon Burakowski
Features editor: Dave Pearce
Chief sub-editor: Jane Reynolds
Stourbridge News
01384 358050
www.thisisstourbridge.co.uk
Weekly (Thu). Editor: Jeff Gepheott
Features editor: Lynn Taylor
Stratford-upon-Avon Herald
01789 266261
www.stratford-herald.co.uk
Weekly (Thu). Editor: Chris Turner
News editor: Dale Levack
Stratford-upon-Avon Journal
01442 386555
www.thisisstratford-upon-
avon.co.uk
Weekly (Thu). Editor: John Murphy
News editor: Pat Smith
Stratford-upon-Avon Midweek
01789 266261
www.stratford-herald.co.uk
Weekly (Tue). Editor: Chris Turner
News editor: Dale Levack
Stratford-upon-Avon Observer
01789 415717
www.stratfordstandard.co.uk
Weekly free (Thu).
Editor: Sarah Halford

Sunday Mercury
0121 236 3366
www.icbirmingham.co.uk
Sunday. Editor: David Brookes
News editor: Tony Larner
Features editor: Paul Cole
Sutton Coldfield News
0121 355 7070
Weekly (Fri). Editor: Pam Thomas
Sutton Coldfield Observer
01827 848535
Weekly (Fri). Editor: Gary Phelps
Walsall Advertiser
01827 848535
Weekly (Thu).
Editor: Natalie Missenden
Walsall Chronicle
01922 444444
Weekly (Thu). Editor: Mike Caldicott
Walsall Observer
01922 636666
www.thisiswalsall.co.uk
Weekly (Fri). Editor: Mike Lockley
Why Coventry, Nuneaton & Hinckley
01527 588000
Weekly free (Fri).
Editor: Claire Smith
Why Solihull & District
01527 588000
Weekly free (Fri).
Editor: Claire Smith
Why Warwick & Leamington
01527 588000
Weekly free (Fri).
Editor: Claire Smith
Wolverhampton Ad News
01543 501700
Weekly (Wed). Editor: Mike Lockley
Wolverhampton Chronicle
01902 313131
www.yourchronicle.com
Weekly free (Thu).
Editor: Adrian Faber
News editor: Mark Drew
Features editor: Dillion Evans
Chief sub-editor: Tony Reynolds

West of England

Gloucestershire, Herefordshire,
Shropshire, Worcestershire

Alcester Chronicle
01527 453500
www.thisisworcestershire.co.uk
Weekly (Wed). Editor: Paul Walker
News editor: Sarah Cross
Alcester Standard
01789 415717
Weekly (Fri). Editor: Sarah Halford

Berrow's Worcester Journal
01905 748200
www.berrowsjournal.co.uk
Weekly. Editor: Stewart Gilbert
News editor: Sala Lloyd
Chief sub-editor: Jim Collins
Bridgnorth Journal
01746 761411
www.bridgnorthjournal.co.uk
Weekly (Fri). Editor: Colin Northway
Bromsgrove Advertiser
01527 837000
www.thisisworcestershire.co.uk
Weekly (Wed). Editor: Alan Wallcroft
News editor: Peter Lammas
Bromsgrove Messenger
01527 837000
www.thisisworcestershire.co.uk
Weekly (Wed). Editor: Alan Wallcroft
News editor: Peter Lammas
Bromsgrove Standard
01527 574111
www.bromsgrovestandard.co.uk
Weekly free (Fri)
Editor: Charlotte Beavers
Cheltenham Independent
01453 762412
www.thisisstroud.com
Weekly (Wed). Editor: Skip Walker
News editor: Sue Smith
Cheltenham News
01452 424442
Weekly free (Thu).
Editor: Anita Syvrat
Cheltenham/Tewkesbury News
01452 420632
Weekly free (Thu). Editor: Chris Hill
Chipping Sodbury/Yate Gazette
01453 544000
Weekly (Fri).
Editor: David Cullimore
News editor: Carole Taylor
Cotswold Journal
01886 442555
www.thisistewkesbury.com
Weekly (Thu). Editor: John Murphy
News editor: Pat Smith
County Independent
01453 762412
www.thisisstroud.com
Weekly (Wed). Editor: Skip Walker
News editor: Sue Smith
Droitwich Spa Advertiser
01905 795097
www.thisisdroitwichspa.co.uk
Weekly (Wed). Editor: Alan Wallcroft
News editor: Peter Lammas
Droitwich Standard
01527 574111
Weekly (Fri).
Editor: Charlotte Beavers

Evesham Journal
01886 442555
www.thisisworcestershire.co.uk
Weekly (Thu). Editor: John Murphy
News editor: Pat Smith
Express and Star (Kidderminster)
01902 313131
www.expressandstar.com
Daily. Editor: Adrian Faber
News editor: Mark Drew
Features editor: Dylan Evans
Chief sub-editor: Tony Reynolds
Forest of Dean and Wye Valley Review
01594 841113
www.forest-and-wye-today.co.uk
Weekly free (Wed).
Editor: John Powell
The Forester
01594 820600
www.thisisgloucestershire.co.uk
Weekly (Thu).
Editor: Viv Hargreaves
Gloucester Citizen
01452 424442
www.thisisgloucestershire.co.uk
Daily. Editor: Ian Mean
Gloucester Independent
01453 762412
www.thisisstroud.com
Weekly (Wed). Editor: Skip Walker
News editor: Sue Smith
Gloucester News
01452 424442
Weekly free (Thu).
Editor: Anita Syvrat
Gloucestershire County Gazette
01453 544000
www.thisisthesouthcotswolds.co.uk
Weekly (Fri).
Editor: David Cullimore
News editor: Carole Taylor
Gloucestershire Echo
01242 271821
www.thisisgloucestershire.co.uk
Daily. Editor: Anita Syvret
News editor: Tanya Gledhill
Features editor: Ian Akerman
Chief sub-editor: Jason Clare
Hereford Admag
01432 376120
Weekly (Wed). Features editor: Clare Fry
Hereford Journal
01432 355353
www.herefordjournal.co.uk
Weekly free (Wed)
Editor: Mike Robinson
Assistant editor: Colin Osborne

Hereford Times
01432 274413
www.thisisherefordshire.co.uk
Weekly (Thu). Editor: Liz Griffin
News editor: Nigel Heins
Jobs Today – Cheltenham and Gloucester
01453 544000
Daily. Editor: David Cullimore
News editor: Carole Taylor
Kidderminster Chronicle
01562 829500
www.thisisworcestershire.co.uk
/worcestershire/kidderminster
Weekly (Wed). Editor: Brian Gough
Kidderminster Shuttle and Times and Stourport News
01562 633333
www.thisisworcestershire.co.uk
/worcestershire/kidderminster
Weekly (Thu). Editor: Clive Joyce
Ledbury Reporter
01684 892200
Weekly (Fri). Editor: Nick Howells
News editor: Ally Hardy
Leominster Journal
01432 355353
www.shropshirestar.co.uk
Weekly free (Wed)
Editor: Mike Robinson
Assistant editor: Colin Osborne
Ludlow Advertiser
01584 873796
www.thisisludlow.co.uk
Weekly (Wed). Editor: Jean Kingdon
News editor: Michael Baws
Features editor: Arun Marsh
Ludlow Journal
01743 248248
www.ludlowjournal.co.uk
Weekly free (Fri)
Editor: Mike Robinson
News editor: Vince Buston
Malvern Gazette
01684 892200
Weekly (Fri). Editor: Nick Howells
Market Drayton Advertiser
01630 698113
www.marketdraytonadvertiser.co.uk
Weekly (Fri). Editor: Sam Taylor
Newport Advertiser
01952 811500
www.newportadvertiser.co.uk
Weekly (Fri).
Editor: Samantha Taylor
News editor: Terry Morris
North Shropshire Chronicle
01743 248248
www.northshropshirechronicle.com
Weekly (Thu).
Editor: John Butterworth

Oswestry & Border Counties Advertiser
01691 655321
www.bordercountiesadvertiser.
co.uk
Weekly (Wed). Editor: Sue Perry
Redditch Advertiser
01527 453500
www.thisisworcestershire.co.uk
/worcestershire/redditch
Weekly (Wed). Editor: Paul Walker
News editor: Sarah Cross
Redditch Standard
01527 588688
www.redditchstandard.co.uk
Weekly free (Fri)
Editor: Andrew Powell
Ross Gazette
01989 562007
www.ross-today.co.uk
Weekly (Thu).
Editor: Chris Robertson
News editor: Pat Roberts
Ross-on-Wye Journal
01432 355353
www.shropshirestar.co.uk
Weekly free (Wed)
Editor: Mike Robinson
Assistant editor: Colin Osborne
Shrewsbury Admag
01743 241414
www.northshropshirechronicle.com
Weekly (Thu). Editor: Jan Edwards
Shrewsbury Chronicle
01743 248248
www.shrewsburychronicle.co.uk
Weekly (Thu).
Editor: John Butterworth
Shropshire Star
01952 242424
www.shropshirestar.com
Daily. Editor: Sarah Jane Smith
News editor: John Simcock
Features editor: Carl Jones
Chief sub-editor: Lisa Bailey
South Shropshire Journal
01584 876311
www.southshropshirejournal.co.uk
Weekly (Fri). Editor: Mike Robinson
News editor: Vince Buston
Stourport News
01562 633330
Weekly free (Thu). Editor: Clive Joyce
News editor: Peter McMillan
Chief sub-editor: Alison Grange
Stroud News & Journal
01453 762142
www.thisisstroud.com
Weekly (Wed). Editor: Skip Walker
News editor: Sue Smith

Telford Journal
01743 248248
www.telfordjournal.co.uk
Weekly free (Thu).
Editor: David Sharpe
Tenbury Wells Advertiser
01584 873796
www.thisistenbury-wells.co.uk
Weekly (Wed). Editor: Jen Green
Thornbury Gazette
01453 544000
www.thisissouthgloucestershire.
co.uk
Weekly (Fri).
Editor: David Cullimore
News editor: Carole Taylor
Why Evesham
01527 588000
Weekly free (Fri).
Editor: Claire Smith
Why Redditch & District
01527 588000
Weekly free (Fri).
Editor: Claire Smith
Why Worcester, Malvern & Kidderminster
01527 588000
Weekly free (Fri).
Editor: Claire Smith
Wilts & Gloucestershire Standard
01285 642642
www.thisiscirencester.com
Weekly (Thu). Editor: Peter Davidson
News editor: Charlotte White
Worcester Evening News
01905 748200
www.thisisworcestershire.co.uk
Daily. Editor: Stewart Gilbert
News editor: Sala Lloyd
Chief sub-editor: Jim Collins
Worcester Standard
01905 726200
www.worcesterstandard.co.uk
Weekly free (Thu). Editor: James Illes
News editor: David Dunham

North England

East, North, South & West
Yorkshire

Aire Valley Target
01274 729511
Weekly (Thu)
Editor: Perry Austin-Clarke
News editor: Martin Heminway
Features editor: David Barnett
Chief sub-editor: Neal Jones
Axholme Herald
01427 874417
Weekly (Fri). Editor: Ron Shipley

Barnsley Chronicle
01226 734734
www.barnsley-chronicle.co.uk
Weekly (Fri).
Editor: Robert Cockcroft
News editor: Andrew Harrod
Features editor: Maureen Middleton
Chief sub-editor: John Threlkeld
Barnsley Independent
01226 734734
www.barnsley-chronicle.co.uk
Weekly (Tue).
Editor: Robert Cockcroft
News editor: Andrew Harrod
Features editor: Maureen Middleton
Chief sub-editor: John Threlkeld
Batley News
01924 468282
www.dewsburytoday.co.uk
Weekly (Thu). Editor: John Wilson
News editor: Christine Littlewood
Beverley Advertiser
01482 327111
Weekly (Thu). Editor: Alex Leys
Production editor: Rosie Goodman
Beverley Guardian
01377 241122
www.beverleytoday.co.uk
Weekly free (Fri).
Editor: David Sissons
News editor: Steve Petch
Chief sub-editor: Gill Pick
Birstall News
01924 468282
www.dewsburytoday.co.uk
Weekly (Thu)
Editor: John Wilson
Bradford Target
01274 729511
Weekly (Tue)
Editor: Perry Austin-Clarke
News editor: Martin Heminway
Features editor: David Barnett
Chief sub-editor: Neal Jones
Bridlington Free Press
01262 606606
www.bridlingtontoday.co.uk
Weekly (Thu). Editor: Nick Procter
News editor: Simon Haldenbee
Features editor: Jenny Norton
Bridlington Gazette & Herald
01262 606606
www.bridlingtontoday.co.uk
Weekly free (Tue).
Editor: Nick Procter
News editor: Simon Haldenbee
Features editor: Jenny Norton
Brighouse Echo
01422 260200
www.brighousetoday.co.uk
Weekly (Fri). Editor: Stephen Firth

Calderdale News
01422 260200
www.halifaxtoday.co.uk
Weekly free (Wed)
Editor: John Furbisher
Production editor: Gordon Samson

Colne Valley Chronicle
01484 437747
www.ichuddersfield.co.uk
Weekly (Fri). Editor: Chris Burgess

Craven Herald & Pioneer
01756 794117
www.cravenherald.co.uk
Weekly (Fri). Editor: Ian Lockwood
News editor: Lindsey Moore

Dearne Valley Weekender
01709 571111
www.rotherhamadvertiser.com
Weekly (Fri). Editor: Doug Melloy

Dewsbury Reporter
01924 468282
www.dewsburytoday.co.uk
Weekly (Fri). Editor: John Wilson
News editor: Christine Littlewood

Dinnington & Maltby Guardian
01909 550500
www.dinningtontoday.co.uk
Weekly (Fri).
Editor: George Robinson
News editor: Jackie Laver

Dinnington & Maltby Trader News
01909 550500
Weekly (Thu).
Editor: George Robinson
News editor: Jackie Laver

Doncaster Advertiser
01302 564500
Weekly (Thu).
Editor: Martin Edmunds
News editor: John Hepperstall

Doncaster Free Press
01302 819111
www.doncastertoday.co.uk
Weekly (Thu).
Editor: Merrill Diplock
News editor: Keith Finlay
Features editor: Eddie Mardell
Production editor: David Crossland

Doncaster Star
01302 819111
www.doncastertoday.co.uk
Daily. Editor: Rob Hollingworth
News editor: David Kessen

Driffield Post
01377 241122
www.driffieldtoday.co.uk
Weekly (Fri). Editor: David Sissons
News editor: Steve Petch
Chief sub-editor: Gill Pick

Driffield Times
01377 241122
www.driffieldtoday.co.uk
Weekly (Wed). Editor: David Sissons
News editor: Steve Petch
Chief sub-editor: Gill Pick

Easingwold Advertiser & Weekly News
01347 821329
www.ghsmith.com/advertiser
Weekly (Thu).
Editor: Margery Smith

East Hull Advertiser
01482 327111
Weekly (Wed). Editor: Alex Leys
Production editor: Rosie Goodman

East Riding Advertiser
01482 327111
Weekly (Thu). Editor: Alex Leys
Production editor: Rosie Goodman

East Riding News
01482 887700
Monthly (1st week)
Editor: Andrew Milner

Elmsall & South Elmsall Express
01977 640107
www.wakefieldexpress.co.uk
Weekly free (Fri).
Editor: Delia Kitson

Epworth Bells & Crowle Advertiser
01427 615323
Weekly (Thu)
Editor: Amanda McForley
News editor: Stephanie Bateman

Filey & Hunmanby Mercury
01723 363636
www.scarboroughtoday.co.uk
Weekly (Sat). Editor: Ed Asquith
News editor: Neil Pickford
Chief sub-editor: Steve Banbridge
Production editor: Pete Hodgson

Gainsborough News
01427 872202
Weekly free (Fri)
Editor: Amanda McForley
News editor: Stephanie Bateman

Gainsborough Standard
01427 615323
Weekly (Thu)
Editor: Amanda McForley
News editor: Stephanie Bateman

Halifax Evening Courier
01422 260200
www.halifaxtoday.co.uk
Daily. Editor: John Furbisher

Harrogate Advertiser
01423 564321
www.harrogatetoday.co.uk
Weekly (Fri).
Editor: Jean Macquarrie
Assistant editor: Rita Sobot
Chief sub-editor: Michael Molsher

Harrogate Herald
01423 564321
www.harrogatetoday.co.uk
Weekly (Tue).
Editor: Jean Macquarrie
Assistant editor: Rita Sobot
Chief sub-editor: Michael Molsher

Hebden Bridge Times
01422 260200
www.halifaxtoday.co.uk
Weekly (Fri). Editor: Sheila Tordoff

Heckmondwike Herald
01924 468282
www.dewsburytoday.co.uk
Weekly (Fri). Editor: John Wilson

Holderness Advertiser
01482 327111
Weekly (Wed). Editor: Alex Leys
Production editor: Rosie Goodman

Holderness Gazette
01964 612777
holderness-online.com
Weekly (Thu)
News editor: Andrew Swales
Features editor: David McAughtrie

Huddersfield Daily Examiner
01484 437747
www.ichuddersfield.co.uk
Daily. Editor: Roy Wright
News editor: Neil Atkinson
Features editor: Andrew Flynn

Huddersfield District Chronicle
01484 437747
www.ichuddersfield.co.uk
Weekly (Fri). Editor: Chris Burgess

Huddersfield District News
01484 437747
www.ichuddersfield.co.uk
Weekly free (Tue).
Editor: Chris Burgess

Hull Daily Mail
01482 327111
www.hulldailymail.co.uk
Daily. Editor: John Meehan
News editor: Jeremy Deacon
Features editor: Paul Johnson
Chief sub-editor: Sarah Main-Prize

Ilkley Gazette
01943 607022
www.ilkleygazette.co.uk
Weekly (Thu). Editor: Mel Vasey
News editor: Paul Langan

The Journal
01482 327111
Monthly (24th).
Editor: Roy Woodcock

Keighley & Craven Target
01274 729511
Weekly (Tue)
Editor: Perry Austin-Clarke
News editor: Martin Heminway
Features editor: David Barnett
Chief sub-editor: Mel Jones

eighley News
01274 729511
www.keighleynews.co.uk
Weekly (Thu).
Editor: Malcolm Hoddy
News editor: Alistair Shand
Chief sub-editor: Ralph Badham
naresborough Post
01423 564321
www.knaresboroughtoday.co.uk
Weekly (Fri).
Editor: Jean Macquarrie
Assistant editor: Rita Sobot
Chief sub-editor: Michael Molsher
eeds and Yorkshire Times
01926 431601
Weekly (Fri). Editor: Dennis Draper
eeds Weekly News
0113 243 2701
Weekly (Thu). Editor: Sheila Holmes
ook Local
0114 283 1100
Weekly (Wed). Editor: Phil Dolby
Head of production: Adrian von
Werzbach
alton and Pickering Mercury
01723 363636
www.maltontoday.co.uk
Weekly (Wed). Editor: Ed Asquith
News editor: Neil Pickford
Chief sub-editor: Steve Banbridge
Production editor: Pete Hodgson
etro Yorkshire
020 7651 5200
www.metro.co.uk
Daily. Editor: Kenny Campbell
News editor: Mark Dorman
Features editor: Kieran Meeke
exborough & District Leader
01709 303030
www.doncastertoday.co.uk
Weekly (Fri). Editor: Linda Wasildge
News editor: Keilly Ball
Features editor: Kevin Rogers
irfield Reporter
01924 468282
www.dewsburytoday.co.uk
Weekly (Fri). Editor: John Wilson
orley Advertiser
0113 252 4020
www.wakefieldexpress.co.uk
Weekly (Wed). Editor: Robert Evans
News editor: Sarah Hall
orley Observer
01924 468282
www.dewsburytoday.co.uk
Weekly (Fri). Editor: John Wilson

North Yorkshire Advertiser
01325 381313
www.thisisdarlington.co.uk/the
_north_east/advertiser/ny
Weekly free (Tue).
Editor: Peter Barron
News editor: Nigel Burton
Features editor: Nick Morrison
Chief sub-editor: Ken Farrier
North Yorkshire Herald & Post
01642 245401
www.ncjmediainfo.co.uk
Weekly (Fri). Editor: Sue Giles
North Yorkshire News
01765 601248
Weekly (Wed).
Editor: Steve Barton
News editor: Stephen Pass
Northallerton, Thirsk & Bedale Times
01765 601248
Weekly (Fri). Editor: Steve Barton
News editor: Stephen Pass
Ossett Observer
01924 375111
www.wakefieldexpress.co.uk
Weekly (Fri).
Editor: Mark Bradley
News editor: Mark Lingard
Pateley Bridge & Nidderdale Herald
01423 564321
www.nidderdaletoday.co.uk
Weekly (Fri).
Editor: Jean Macquarrie
Assistant editor: Rita Sobot
Chief sub-editor: Michael Molsher
Pocklington Post
01723 363636
www.pocklingtontoday.co.uk
Weekly (Fri). Editor: Ed Asquith
News editor: Neil Pickford
Chief sub-editor: Steve Banbridge
Production editor: Pete Hodgson
Pontefract & Castleford Express
01977 737200
www.wakefieldexpress.co.uk
Weekly (Thu). Editor: David Ward
News editor: Julie Hawksworth
Pontefract & Castleford Extra
01977 737200
www.wakefieldexpress.co.uk
Weekly free (Fri).
Editor: David Ward
News editor: Julie Hawksworth
Pudsey Times
01943 466750
Weekly (Thu). Editor: Kate Evans

Ripon Gazette & Boroughbridge Herald
01423 564321
www.ripontoday.co.uk
Weekly (Fri).
Editor: Jean Macquarrie
Assistant editor: Rita Sobot
Chief sub-editor: Michael Molsher
Rotherham & South Yorkshire Advertiser
01709 364721
www.rotherhamadvertiser.com
Weekly (Fri). Editor: Doug Melloy
News editor: Ann Charlton
Rotherham Record
01709 364721
www.rotherhamadvertiser.com
Weekly (Wed). Editor: Doug Melloy
News editor: Ann Charlton
Scarborough Evening News
01723 363636
www.scarborougheveningnews.
co.uk
Daily. Editor: Ed Asquith
News editor: Neil Pickford
Chief sub-editor: Steve Banbridge
Production editor: Pete Hodgson
Scarborough Trader
01723 352269
www.scarboroughtoday.co.uk
Weekly free (Thu). Editor: Ed Asquith
Selby Chronicle
01757 702198
www.selbytoday.co.uk
Weekly free (Fri). Editor: Chris Page
News editor: Richard Parker
Selby Post
01405 720110
www.selbypost.co.uk
Weekly (Thu). Editor: Peter Butler
Selby Star
01904 653051
www.yorkandcountypress.co.uk
/york/ycp/star
Weekly free (Wed).
Editor: Lynne Martin
Selby Times
01757 702802
www.selbytoday.co.uk
Weekly (Thu). Editor: Chris Page
News editor: Richard Parker
Sheffield & South Yorkshire Times Today
0115 956 8858
Weekly free (Wed)
Editor: Matthew Palmer
Sheffield Journal
0114 276 7676
www.sheffieldtoday.net
Weekly free (Thu).
Editor: Peter Charlton
News editor: Bob Westerdale
Features editor: John Highfield
Head of content: Paul License

Sheffield Mercury
0114 274 6555
Weekly (Fri). Editor: David Hayes
Sheffield Telegraph
0114 276 7676
www.sheffieldtoday.net
Weekly (Fri). Editor: Alan Powell
News editor: Peter Kay
Head of content: Paul License
Sheffield Weekly Gazette
0114 276 7676
www.sheffieldtoday.net
Weekly (Fri). Editor: Peter Charlton
News editor: Peter Kay
Features editor: John Highfield
Head of content: Paul License
South Yorkshire Times
01709 303050
Weekly (Fri). Editor: Linda Waslidge
Spenborough Guardian
01924 468282
www.dewsburytoday.co.uk
Weekly (Fri). Editor: John Wilson
The Star (Sheffield)
0114 276 7676
www.sheffieldtoday.net
Daily. Editor: Peter Charlton
News editor: Bob Westerdale
Features editor: John Highfield
Head of content: Paul License
Telegraph and Argus (Bradford)
01274 729511
www.thisisbradford.co.uk
Daily. Editor: Perry Austin-Clarke
News editor: Martin Heminway
Features editor: David Barnett
Chief sub-editor: Neal Jones
The Town Crier
01274 729511
Weekly (Thu)
Editor: Perry Austin-Clarke
News editor: Martin Heminway
Features editor: David Barnett
Chief sub-editor: Mel Jones
Todmorden News & Advertiser
01422 260200
www.halifaxtoday.co.uk
Weekly (Fri). Editor: Sheila Tordoff
Wakefield Express
01924 375111
www.wakefieldexpress.co.uk
Weekly free (Fri).
Editor: Mark Bradley
News editor: Mark Lingard
Wakefield, Rothwell & Alton Extra
01924 375111
www.wakefieldexpress.co.uk
Weekly free (Thu).
Editor: Mark Bradley
News editor: Mark Lingard

Weekly Advertiser
01924 468282
www.dewsburytoday.co.uk
Weekly free (Fri).
Editor: John Wilson
West Hull Advertiser
01482 327111
Weekly (Wed). Editor: Alex Leys
Production editor: Rosie Goodman
Wetherby, Boston Spa & Tadcaster News
01423 564321
www.harrogatetoday.co.uk
Weekly (Fri).
Editor: Jean Macquarrie
Assistant editor: Rita Sobot
Chief sub-editor: Michael Molsher
Wharfe Valley Times
01943 466750
Weekly (Thu). Editor: Kate Evans
Wharfedale & Airedale Observer
01943 465555
www.wharfedaleobserver.co.uk
Weekly (Thu). Editor: Mel Vasey
News editor: Jim Jack
Whitby Gazette
01947 602836
www.whitbytoday.co.uk
Twice weekly (Tue, Fri)
Editor: Damien Holmes
Yorkshire Evening Post
0113 243 2701
www.leedstoday.net
Daily. Editor: Neil Hodgkinson
News editor: Gillian Howorth
Features editor: Anne Pickles
Production editor: Howard Corry
York Evening Press
01904 653051
www.yorkandcountypress.co.uk /york/ycp/ad
Daily. Editor: Kevin Booth
News editor: Francine Slee
Features editor: Chris Titley
Chief sub-editor: Steve Nelson
York Star
01904 653051
www.yorkandcountypress.co.uk /york/ycp/star
Weekly free (Wed).
Editor: Lynne Martin
Yorkshire Express
0115 956 8858
Weekly free (Wed)
Editor: Matthew Palmer
Yorkshire Gazette & Herald
01904 653051
www.thisisryedale.co.uk
Weekly (Wed). Editor: Bob McMillan

Yorkshire Post
0113 243 2701
www.yorkshireposttoday.co.uk
Daily. Editor: Rachael Campey
News editor: Hannah Start
Features editor: Catherine Scott
Head of production: Dick Porter

North-east England

Cleveland, Durham, Northumberland, Tyne & Wear

Berwick Advertiser
01289 306677
www.berwicktoday.co.uk
Weekly (Thu).
Editor: Janet Workershaw
News editor: Ian Smith
Features editor: Thomas Baldwin
Chief sub-editor: Keith Hamblin
Berwick Gazette
01289 306677
www.tweedalepress.co.uk
Weeekly free. Editor: Willie Mack
Chester-le-Street Advertiser
01325 381313
www.thisisthenortheast.co.uk
Weekly free (Thu).
Editor: Peter Barron
News editor: Nigel Burton
Features editor: Nick Morrison
Chief sub-editor: Ken Farrier
Citylife
0191 211 5093
www.newcastle.gov.uk/citylife
Monthly (last week of month)
Editor: Jane Byrne
Consett & Stanley Advertiser
01325 381313
www.thisisthenortheast.co.uk
Weekly free (Thu).
Editor: Peter Barron
News editor: Nigel Burton
Features editor: Nick Morrison
Chief sub-editor: Ken Farrier
Darlington & Stockton Times
01325 381313
www.thisisthenortheast.co.uk
Weekly (Fri). Editor: Peter Barron
News editor: Nigel Burton
Features editor: Nick Morrison
Chief sub-editor: Ken Farrier
Darlington Herald & Post
01325 262000
www.icteesside.co.uk
Weekly (Fri). Editor: Sue Giles

Darlington, Aycliffe & Sedgefield Advertiser
01325 381313
www.thisisthenortheast.co.uk
Weekly free (Wed).
Editor: Peter Barron
News editor: Nigel Burton
Features editor: Nick Morrison
Chief sub-editor: Ken Farrier
Durham Advertiser
01325 381313
www.thisisthenortheast.co.uk
Weekly free (Thu).
Editor: Peter Barron
News editor: Nigel Burton
Features editor: Nick Morrison
Chief sub-editor: Ken Farrier
East Cleveland Advertiser
01325 381313
www.theclarion.co.uk
Weekly free (Fri).
Editor: Peter Barron
News editor: Nigel Burton
Features editor: Nick Morrison
Chief sub-editor: Ken Farrier
East Cleveland Herald & Post
01642 245401
www.icteesside.co.uk
Weekly (Wed). Editor: Sue Giles
Evening Chronicle
0191 232 7500
www.icnewcastle.co.uk
Daily (Mon–Fri)
Editor: Paul Robertson
News editor: Mick Smith
Features editor: Richard Ord
Chief sub-editor: Adrian Hogg
Evening Gazette
01642 245401
www.icteesside.co.uk
Daily. Editor: Steve Dyson
News editor: Jim Horsley
Features editor: Kathryn Armstrong
Gateshead Herald and Post
0191 201 6405
Weekly (Wed).
Editor: Catherine Welford
News editor: Roger Woodcock
Hartlepool Mail
01429 239333
www.hartlepoolmail.co.uk
Daily. Editor: Paul Napier
News editor: Brian Nuttley
Hartlepool Star
01429 239333
www.hartlepoolmail.co.uk
Weekly free (Thu).
Editor: Paul Napier
News editor: Brian Nuttley
Hexham Courant
01434 602351
www.hexham-courant.co.uk
Weekly (Fri). Editor: Eve Fuller
News editor: Brian Tilley

Houghton Star
0191 501 5800
Weekly free (Thu). Editor: Betty Long
**The Journal
(Newcastle Upon Tyne)**
0191 201 6230
www.icnewcastle.co.uk
Daily. Editor: Brian Aitken
News editor: Stephen Rouse
Features editor: Jane Hall
Chief sub-editor: Roger Brown
Metro North East
0191 477 8200
www.metronortheast.co.uk
Daily. Editor: Deane Hodgson
Middlesbrough Herald & Post
01642 245401
www.icteesside.co.uk
Weekly (Wed). Editor: Sue Giles
Morpeth Herald
01670 510522
www.morpethtoday.co.uk
Weekly (Thu). Editor: Terry Hackett
Newcastle Herald & Post
0191 201 6405
www.icnewcastle.co.uk
Weekly (Wed).
Editor: Catherine Welford
News editor: Roger Woodcock
Newcastle Times
01332 205900
Weekly (Thu). Editor: Ruth Dhanda
News editor: Simon Howorth
Features editor: Emily Clarke
Chief sub-editor: Fatt Basra
Production editor: Sonia Watters
News Post Leader
0191 251 8484
www.blyth-wansbecktoday.co.uk
Weekly. Editor: Ross Weeks
North Tyneside Herald & Post
0191 201 6405
www.icnewcastle.co.uk
Weekly (Wed).
Editor: Catherine Welford
News editor: Roger Woodcock
Northern Echo
01325 381313
www.thisisthenortheast.co.uk
Daily. Editor: Peter Barron
News editor: Nigel Burton
Features editor: Nick Morrison
Chief sub-editor: Ken Farrier
Northumberland Gazette
01665 602234
www.northumberlandtoday.co.uk
Weekly (Thu). Editor: Andrew Smith
**Northumberland Herald
and Post**
0191 201 6405
Weekly (Wed).
Editor: Catherine Welford
News editor: Roger Woodcock

Peterlee Star
0191 501 5800
Weekly free (Thu). Editor: Betty Long
Seaham Star
0191 501 5800
Weekly free (Thu). Editor: Betty Long
South Durham Herald & Post
01642 245401
www.icteesside.co.uk
Weekly (Fri). Editor: Sue Giles
South Shields Gazette
0191 455 4661
www.southtynesidetoday.co.uk
Daily. Editor: John Syzmanski
South Tyne Star
0191 455 4661
Weekly free (Thu)
Editor: John Syzmanski
South Tyneside Herald & Post
0191 201 6405
www.icnewcastle.co.uk
Weekly (Wed).
Editor: Catherine Welford
News editor: Roger Woodcock
**Stockton & Billingham
Herald & Post**
01642 245401
www.icteesside.co.uk
Weekly (Wed). Editor: Sue Giles
Sunday Sun (Newcastle)
0191 232 7500
www.icnewcastle.co.uk
Sunday. Editor: Peter Montellier
News editor: Mike Kelly
Chief sub-editor: Lesley Oldfield
Production editor: Colin Patterson
Sunderland Echo
0191 501 7208
www.sunderland-today.co.uk
Daily. Editor: Rob Lawson
News editor: Patrick Lavelle
Features editor: Paul Taylor
Chief sub-editor: Paul Woods
Production editor: Paul Larkin
Sunderland Star
0191 501 5800
Weekly free (Thu). Editor: Betty Long
Teesside Focus
01332 365811
Weekly free (Mon).
Editor: Sean Peaty
News editor: Fiona Smith
Teesside Herald & Post
01642 245401
www.icteesside.co.uk
Weekly (Wed). Editor: Sue Giles
Wallsend News Guardian
01670 517171
www.northtynesidetoday.co.uk
Weekly free (Thu).
Editor: Terry Hackett
Washington Star
0191 501 5800
Weekly free (Thu). Editor: Betty Long

Whitley Bay News Guardian
0191 251 8566
www.northtynesidetoday.co.uk
Weekly free (Thu). Editor: Ross Weeks

North-west England

Cheshire, Cumbria, Lancashire,
Manchester, Merseyside

Accrington Observer
01254 871444
www.accringtonobserver.co.uk
Weekly (Fri). Editor: Mervyn Kay
News editor: Michells McKenna
Anfield and Walton Star
0151 236 2000
Weekly (Thu)
News editor: Kevin Mathews
Ashton-under-Lyne Reporter
0161 303 1910
Weekly (Thu). Editor: Nigel Skinner
Asian News
01706 354321
www.theasiannews.co.uk
Monthly (4th Fri)
Editor: Steve Hammond
Barnoldswick & Earby Times
01282 426161
www.eastlancashireonline.co.uk
Weekly (Fri). Editor: Roy Penton
News editor: Peter Dewhurst
Features editor: Barry Bradshaw
Chief sub-editor: Rebecca Smith
Production editor: Paul Watson
Barrow Advertiser
01229 840150
www.cumbria-online.co.uk
Weekly free (Thu).
Editor: Steve Brauner
News editor: Steve Hartley
Features editor: Peter Leach
Chief sub-editor: Sarah Farrell
Production editor: Bill Myers
Bentham Guardian
01524 32525
Weekly (Fri). Editor: Sue Riley
News editor: Louise Bryning
Features editor: Paul Collins
Chief sub-editor: Bryan Carter
Birkenhead News
0151 647 7111
Weekly (Wed). Editor: Sue McCann
News editor: Louise Powney
Blackburn Citizen
01254 678678
www.thisislancashire.co.uk
Weekly (Thu)
Editor-in-chief: Kevin Young
News editor: Andrew Turner
Features editor: John Anson

Blackpool & Fylde Citizen
01253 292005
www.thisislancashire.co.uk
Weekly (Thu). Editor: Greg Morgan
News editor: Steve Dunthorne
Features editor: Nikki Smith
Blackpool Gazette & Herald
01253 400888
www.blackpoolonline.co.uk
Daily. Editor: David Halliwell
News editor: Adrian Derbyshire
Features editor: Paul McKenzie
Chief Sub-editor: Linda Chatburn
Blackpool Reporter
01253 400800
www.blackpoolonline.co.uk
Daily. Editor: David Halliwell
News editor: Adrian Derbyshire
Chief sub-editor: Linda Chatburn
Bolton Evening News
01204 522345
www.thisisbolton.co.uk
Daily. Editor: Steve Hughes
News editor: John Horn
Features editor: Andrew Mosley
Production editor: John Bird
Bolton Journal
01204 522345
www.thisisbolton.co.uk
Weekly (Thu). Editor: Steve Hughes
News editor: John Horn
Features editor: Andrew Mosley
Production editor: John Bird
Bootle Times
0151 932 1000
Weekly (Thu). Editor: Peter Harvey
News editor: Peter Elliott
Bromborough & Bebington News
0151 647 7111
Weekly (Wed). Editor: Sue McCann
News editor: Louise Powney
Burnley Citizen
01254 678678
www.thisislancashire.co.uk
Weekly (Thu)
Editor-in-chief: Kevin Young
News editor: Andrew Turner
Features editor: John Anson
Burnley Express
01282 426161
www.burnleytoday.co.uk
Weekly (Tue & Fri)
Editor: Chris Daggett
News editor: Margaret Parsons
Features editor: Barry Bradshaw
Chief sub-editor: Rebecca Smith
Production editor: Paul Watson
Bury Journal
0161 764 9421
www.thisisbury.co.uk
Weekly (Wed). Editor: Bill Allen
News editor: Steve Orrell
Chief sub-editor: John Ellavy

Bury Times
0161 764 9421
www.thisisbury.co.uk
Weekly (Tue, Fri). Editor: Bill Allen
News editor: Steve Orrell
Chief sub-editor: John Ellavy
Buy Sell Cheshire
01928 736200
www.cheshirenews.co.uk
Weekly (Thu). No editorial
Carlisle News & Star
01228 612600
www.news-and-star.co.uk
Daily (Mon–Thu).
Editor: Keith Sutton
News editor: Sue Crawford
Features editor: Kath Smart
Chief sub-editor: Phil Taylor
Production editor: Richard Eccles
Carnforth Guardian
01524 32525
Weekly (Fri). Editor: Sue Riley
News editor: Louise Bryning
Features editor: Paul Collins
Chief sub-editor: Bryan Carter
Chester & District Standard
01244 304500
Weekly (Thu).
Editor: Jonathan White
Chester Chronicle
01244 340151
www.cheshirenews.co.uk
Weekly (Fri). Editor: Barry Elans
Chester Mail
01244 340151
www.cheshirenews.co.uk
Weekly (Fri). Editor: Barry Elans
Chorley Citizen
01257 269313
www.thisislancashire.co.uk
/lancashire/chorley
Weekly (Wed)
Editor-in-chief: Kevin Young
Chorley Guardian
01257 264911
www.chorleytoday.co.uk
Weekly (Wed). Editor: Tracy Bruce
News editor: Vanessa Taylor
Chief sub-editor: Mal Morris
Chronicle Weekend (Oldham)
0161 633 2121
www.oldham-chronicle.co.uk
Daily. Editor: Jim Williams
News editor: Mike Attelborough
Chief sub-editor: Jim Austin
Clitheroe Advertiser & Times
01282 426161
www.clitheroe.co.uk
Weekly (Thu). Editor: Vivien Meath
News editor: Duncan Smith

Clitheroe Express
01200 422324
Weekly (Fri). Editor: Vivien Heath
News editor: Margaret Parsons
Features editor: Barry Bradshaw
Chief sub-editor: Rebecca Smith
Production editor: Paul Watson
Colne Times
01282 612561
www.eastlancashireonline.co.uk
Weekly (Fri). Editor: Roy Preston
News editor: Peter Dewhurst
Features editor: Barry Bradshaw
Chief sub-editor: Rebecca Smith
Production editor: Paul Watson
Community News
01625 503322
Weekly (Thu). Editor: Jean Ellis
Congleton Advertiser
01782 602525
Weekly free (Thu).
Editor: Sean Dooley
News editor: Robert Cotterill
Features editor:
Charlotte Little-Jones
Congleton Chronicle
01260 273737
www.beartown.co.uk
Weekly (Fri).
Editor: Jeremy Condliffe
Congleton Guardian
01260 280686
www.thisischeshire.co.uk
Weekly (Fri). Editor: Paul Smith
News editor: Ian Ross
Crewe & Nantwich Guardian
01925 434000
www.thisischeshire.co.uk
Weekly (Thu). Editor: Jan Lever
Crewe Chronicle
01270 256631
www.cheshirenews.co.uk
Weekly (Wed). Editor: Dave Fox
News editor: Jan Roberts
Chief sub-editor: Neil Avery
Crewe Mail
01270 211767
www.cheshirenews.co.uk
Weekly (Fri). Editor: Dave Fox
News editor: Jan Roberts
Chief sub-editor: Neil Avery
Crosby Herald
0151 932 1000
Weekly (Thu). Editor: Peter Harvey
News editor: Peter Elliott
Cumberland and Westmorland Herald
01768 862313
www.cwherald.com
Weekly (Sat). Editor: Colin Maughan
News editor: Liz Stannard
Features editor: Helen Phillips

Cumberland News
01228 612600
www.cumberland-news.co.uk
Weekly (Fri). Editor: Keith Sutton
News editor: Sue Crawford
Features editor: Kath Smart
Chief sub-editor: Phil Taylor
Production editor: Richard Eccles
Deeside Chronicle
01244 340151
www.cheshirenews.co.uk
Weekly (Fri). Editor: Paul Cook
East Cumbrian Gazette
01228 612600
www.cumbria-online.co.uk
Weekly free (Thu).
Editor: Keith Sutton
News editor: Sue Crawford
Features editor: Kath Smart
Chief sub-editor: Phil Taylor
Production editor: Richard Eccles
Ellesmere Port Pioneer
0151 355 5181
www.cheshirenews.co.uk
Weekly (Wed). Editor: Phil Robinson
Ellesmere Port Standard
01244 304500
www.ellesmereportstandard.co.uk
Weekly (Thu).
Editor: Jonathan White
Evening Leader – Chester
01352 707707
Daily. Editor: Richard Williams
Features editor: Joanne Shone
Chief sub-editor: Joanne Shone
Production editor: Karen Perry
Fleetwood Weekly News and Chronicle
01253 772950
Weekly (Wed). Editor: Gary Miller
News editor: Karen Evans
Chief sub-editor: Linda Chatburn
Flint and Holywell Chronicle
01244 821911
www.cheshirenews.co.uk
Weekly (Fri). Editor: Paul Cook
News editor: Kevin Hughes
Formby Champion
01704 392392
www.championonline.net
Weekly (Wed).
Editor: Martin Horden
Formby Times
01704 872237
Weekly (Thu). Editor: Hazel Shaw
Freestyle
01704 392392
Monthly (Fri). Editor: Erica Dillon
Frodsham & Helsby Chronicle
01244 340151
www.cheshirenews.co.uk
Weekly (Fri). Editor: Paul Cook

Garstang Courier
01995 602494
Weekly (Fri).
Editor: Richard Machin
News editor: Tony Coppin
Garstang Guardian
01524 32525
www.prestontoday.net/
Weekly (Fri). Editor: Sue Riley
News editor: Louise Bryning
Features editor: Paul Collins
Chief sub-editor: Bryan Carter
Heswall News
0151 647 7111
Weekly (Wed). Editor: Sue McCann
News editor: Louise Powney
Heywood Advertiser
01706 360626
www.heywoodadvertiser.co.uk
Weekly (Wed)
Editor: Margaret Cheesebrough
Hoylake & West Kirby News
0151 647 7111
Weekly (Wed). Editor: Sue McCann
News editor: Louise Powney
Huyton & Roby Star
0151 236 2000
Weekly (Thu)
News editor: Kevin Mathews
Keswick Reminder
01768 772140
www.keswickreminder.co.uk
Weekly (Fri). Editor: Jane Grave
Kirkby Extra
07831 090566
Monthly (1st Wed).
Editor: Chris O'Shea
Kirkham Express
01253 724236
Weekly (Thu). Editor: Gary Miller
News editor: Chris Dixon
Knowsley Challenge
0151 236 2426
www.knowsleychallenge.co.uk
Monthly (15th). Editor: Alan Birkett
Knutsford Guardian
01925 434000
www.thisischeshire.co.uk
Weekly (Wed). Editor: Jan Lever
Lakeland Echo
01524 833111
www.lakelandtoday.co.uk
Weekly (Fri).
Editor: David Waddington
Lancashire Evening Post
01772 838103
www.lep.co.uk
Daily. Editor: Simon Reynolds
News editor: Suzanne Ellsworth

Lancashire Evening Telegraph
01254 298220
www.thisislancashire.co.uk
Daily. Editor-in-chief: Kevin Young
News editor: Andrew Turner
Features editor: John Anson
Lancaster & Morecambe Citizen
01524 382121
www.thisislancashire.co.uk
Weekly (Thu). Editor: Phil Fleming
Lancaster Guardian
01524 32525
www.lancastertoday.co.uk
Weekly (Fri). Editor: Sue Riley
News editor: Louise Bryning
Features editor: Paul Collins
Chief sub-editor: Bryan Carter
Leigh Journal
01942 672241
www.thisislancashire.co.uk
Weekly (Thu). Editor: Mike Hulme
Leigh Reporter
01942 603334
www.leightoday.co.uk
Weekly free (Thu).
Editor: Wendy Moss
Leyland Guardian
01257 264911
www.leylandtoday.co.uk
Weekly (Wed). Editor: Tracy Bruce
News editor: Vanessa Taylor
Chief sub-editor: Mal Morris
Liverpool Post & Echo
0151 227 2000
www.icliverpool.co.uk
Daily. Editor: Mark Dickinson
News editor: Alison Gow
Longridge News
01772 783265
www.thisislancashire.co.uk
Weekly (Thu).
Editor: Richard Machin
Lytham St Annes & Fylde Express
01253 724236
Weekly (Thu). Editor: Gary Miller
News editor: Chris Dixon
Macclesfield Express
01625 424445
www.macclesfield-express.co.uk
Weekly (Wed). Editor: Mike Quilley
News editor: Pat Hills
Macclesfield Times
01625 424445
www.manchesteronline.co.uk/new
spapers/macctimes.html
Weekly (Thu). Editor: Mike Quilley
News editor: Pat Hills
Maghull & Aintree Star
0151 236 2000
Weekly (Thu)
News editor: Kevin Mathews

Maghull Champion
01704 392392
www.championline.net
Weekly (Wed).
Editor: Martin Horden
Manchester Evening News
0161 832 7200
www.manchesteronline.co.uk
Daily. Editor: Paul Horrocks
News editor: Ian Woods
Chief sub-editor: John Whittaker
Marketplace
0151 906 3000
Weekly (Thu). Editor: Leigh Marles
Metro North West
0161 832 7200
www.metronorthwest.co.uk
Weekly free (Fri).
Editor: Richard Butt
Middleton & North Manchester Guardian
0161 643 3615
www.middletonguardian.co.uk
Weekly (Thu).
Editor: Gerry Sammon
Middlewich Chronicle
01244 340151
www.cheshirenews.co.uk
Weekly (Fri). Editor: Paul Brown
Middlewich Guardian
01925 434000
www.thisischeshire.co.uk
Weekly (Wed). Editor: Jan Lever
Midweek Advertiser
01695 572501
Weekly (Thu). Editor: Rob Hopkins
News editor: Clifford Birchall
Mold & Buckley Chronicle
01244 340151
www.cheshirenews.co.uk
Weekly (Fri). Editor: Paul Cook
Morecambe Guardian
01524 32525
Weekly (Fri). Editor: Sue Riley
News editor: Louise Bryning
Features editor: Paul Collins
Chief sub-editor: Bryan Carter
Morecambe Visitor
01524 833111
www.morecambetoday.co.uk
Weekly (Wed). Editor: Glen Cooper
News editor: Ingrid Kent
Nantwich Chronicle
01244 340151
www.cheshirenews.co.uk
Weekly (Fri). Editor: Alan Jarvis
Nelson Leader
01282 612561
www.burnleytoday.co.uk
Weekly (Fri). Editor: Roy Preston
News editor: Peter Dewhurst
Features editor: Barry Bradshaw
Chief sub-editor: Rebecca Smith
Production editor: Paul Watson

Neston News
0151 647 7111
Weekly (Wed). Editor: Sue McCann
News editor: Louise Powney
Newton & Golborne Guardian
01925 434000
www.thisischeshire.co.uk
Weekly (Thu). Editor: Jan Lever
Northwest Evening Mail (Barrow)
01229 821835
www.nwemail.co.uk
Daily. Editor: Steve Brauner
News editor: Steve Hartley
Features editor: Peter Leach
Chief sub-editor: Sarah Farrell
Production editor: Bill Myers
Northwich & District Guardian
01925 434000
www.thisischeshire.co.uk
Weekly (Wed). Editor: Jan Lever
Northwich Chronicle
01244 340151
www.cheshirenews.co.uk
Weekly (Fri). Editor: Paul Brown
Northwich Herald & Post
01244 340151
www.cheshirenews.co.uk
Weekly (Fri). Editor: Paul Brown
Northwich Mail
01606 42272
Weekly (Thu). Editor: Paul Brown
Oldham Evening Chronicle
0161 633 2121
www.oldham-chronicle.co.uk
Daily. Editor: Jim Williams
News editor: Mike Attelborough
Chief sub-editor: Jim Austin
Ormskirk Advertiser
01695 572501
Weekly (Thu). Editor: Rob Hopkins
News editor: Clifford Birchall
Ormskirk Champion
01704 392392
www.championline.net
Weekly (Wed).
Editor: Malcolm Hindle
Padiham Express
01282 426161
Weekly (Tue & Fri)
Editor: Chris Daggett
News editor: Margaret Parsons
Pendle Express
01282 426161
Weekly (Tue & Fri).
Editor: Roy Preston
News editor: Peter Dewhurst
Features editor: Barry Bradshaw
Chief sub-editor: Rebecca Smith
Production editor: Paul Watson

Pendle View
01282 612561
Weekly free (Fri). Editor: Roy Preston
News editor: Peter Dewhurst
Features editor: Barry Bradshaw
Chief sub-editor: Rebecca Smith
Production editor: Paul Watson

Poynton Times
01625 424445
Weekly (Wed). Editor: Mike Quilley
News editor: Pat Hills

Preston & Leyland Reporter
01772 838103
Weekly free (Thu)
Editor: Simon Reynolds
News editor: Suzanne Ellsworth

Preston and Leyland Citizen
01772 824631
www.thisislancashire.co.uk
Weekly (Thu). Editor: Jill Ellis
News editor: Jill Willis

Prestwich Advertiser
0161 789 5015
www.manchesteronline.co.uk
/newspapers/prestwich.html
Weekly (Fri). Editor: Vince Hale

Prestwich & Whitefield Guide
0161 764 9421
www.thisisbury.co.uk
Weekly (Fri). Editor: Bill Allen
News editor: Steve Orrell
Chief sub-editor: John Ellavy

Radcliffe Times
0161 764 9421
www.thisisbury.co.uk
Weekly (Thu). Editor: Bill Allen
News editor: Steve Orrell
Chief sub-editor: John Ellavy

Rochdale Express
01706 354321
www.manchesteronline.co.uk/new
spapers/rochdaleexpress.html
Weekly free (Fri).
Editor: Claire Mooney

Rochdale Observer
01706 354321
www.rochdaleobserver.co.uk
Weekly (Wed, Sat)
Editor: Claire Mooney

Rossendale Free Press
01706 213311
www.therossendalefreepress.co.uk
Weekly (Thu).
Editor: Adrian Purslow

Runcorn and Widnes Herald & Post
0151 424 5921
Weekly (Fri). Editor: Ian Douglas
News editor: Simon Drury

Runcorn Weekly News
0151 424 5921
www.cheshireonline.icnetwork.
co.uk
Weekly (Thu). Editor: Ian Douglas
News editor: Simon Drury

Runcorn World
0151 907 8525
Weekly (Wed). Editor: Carla Flynn
News editor: Barbara Jordan
Chief sub-editor: Graham Bailey

St Helens Star
01925 434000
www.thisisst-helens.co.uk
Weekly (Thu). Editor: Jan Lever

St Helens, Prescot & Knowsley Reporter
01744 22285
Weekly (Wed).
Editor: Julie McCormick

Sale & Altrincham Messenger
0161 908 3360
www.thisistrafford.co.uk/trafford
/sale__altrincham
Weekly (Thu). Editor: Lyn Hughes

Salford Advertiser
0161 789 5015
www.manchesteronline.co.uk
/newspapers/salford.html
Weekly (Fri). Editor: Vince Hale

Skelmersdale Advertiser
01695 572501
Weekly (Thu). Editor: Rob Hopkins
News editor: Clifford Birchall

Skelmersdale Champion
01704 392392
www.championline.net
Weekly (Wed)
Editor: Malcolm Hindle

South Cheshire Advertiser
01782 602525
Weekly free (Thu).
Editor: Sean Dooley
News editor: Robert Cotterill
Features editor: Charlotte Little-Jones

South Cheshire Guardian
01925 434000
www.thisischeshire.co.uk
Weekly (Wed). Editor: Jan Lever
News editor: Richard Babbington

South Cheshire Mail
01270 256631
www.cheshirenews.co.uk
Weekly (Wed). Editor: Dave Fox
News editor: Jan Roberts
Chief sub-editor: Neil Avery

South Lakes Citizen
01539 720555
www.thisisthelakedistrict.co.uk
Weekly free (Wed).
Editor: Mike Glover
News editor: Mike Addison
Chief sub-editor: Richard Belk

South Liverpool Merseymart
0151 734 4000
Weekly (Thu)
News editor: Kevin Mathews

South Manchester Reporter
0161 446 2213
www.southmanchesterreporter.
co.uk
Weekly (Thu)
Editor: Laurence Matheson
News editor: Andy Cranshaw

South Wirral News
0151 355 5181
Weekly free. Editor: Phil Robinson

Southport Champion
01704 392392
www.championline.net
Weekly (Wed).
Editor: Martin Horden

Stockport Citizen
0161 491 5700
www.thisislancashire.co.uk
Fortnightly (Thu).
Editor: Mike Shields

Stockport Express
0161 480 4491
Weekly (Wed). Editor: Mike Quilley
News editor: Craig Archer
Features editor: Clare Sheridan

Stockport Times
0161 480 4491
www.manchesteronline.co.uk/
newspapers/stockporttimeseast.
html
Weekly free (Thu).
Editor: Mandy Leigh
News editor: Craig Archer
Features editor: Clare Sheridan

Stockport Times East
0161 475 4834
Weekly (Thu). Editor: Mandy Leigh
News editor: Duncan Porter
Features editor: Clare Sheridan

Stockport Times West
0161 475 4834
Weekly (Thu). Editor: Mandy Leigh
News editor: Duncan Porter
Features editor: Clare Sheridan

Stretford & Urmston Messenger
0161 908 3360
www.thisistrafford.co.uk/trafford
/stretford__urmston
Weekly (Thu). Editor: Ian Probert

Tameside Advertiser
0161 339 7611
www.tamesideadvertiser.co.uk
Weekly free (Thu).
Editor: David Porter

Tameside Reporter
0161 304 7691
Weekly (Thu). Editor: Nigel Skinner

**Thornton, Cleveleys
& Poulton Citizen**
01253 292005
www.thisislancashire.co.uk
Weekly (Thu). Editor: Greg Morgan
News editor: Steve Dunthorne
Features editor: Nikki Smith
Village Visiter
01695 572501
Weekly (Thu). Editor: Rob Hopkins
News editor: Clifford Birchall
Wallasey News
0151 647 7111
Weekly (Wed). Editor: Sue McCann
News editor: Louise Powney
Warrington Guardian
01925 434000
www.thisischeshire.co.uk
Weekly (Thu). Editor: Jan Lever
News editor: Gareth Dunning
Warrington Guardian Midweek
01925 434000
www.thisischeshire.co.uk
Weekly free (Tue). Editor: Jan Lever
Warrington Mercury
01925 434000
www.thisischeshire.co.uk
Weekly free (Fri). Editor: Jan Lever
**West Cumberland Times
and Star**
01900 607600
www.times-and-star.co.uk
Weekly (Fri).
Editor: Stephen Johnson
Deputy editor: Ian Brogden
West Cumbrian Gazette
01228 612600
www.cumbria-online.co.uk
Weekly free (Thu).
Editor: Keith Sutton
News editor: Sue Crawford
Features editor: Kath Smart
Chief sub-editor: Phil Taylor
Production editor: Richard Eccles
West Derby and Tuebrook Star
0151 236 2000
Weekly (Thu)
News editor: Kevin Mathews
Westmorland Gazette
01539 720555
www.thisisthelakedistrict.co.uk
Weekly (Fri). Editor: Mike Glover
News editor: Mike Addison
Chief sub-editor: Richard Belk
Westmorland Messenger
01539 720555
www.thisisthelakedistrict.co.uk
Weekly (Wed). Editor: Mike Glover
News editor: Mike Addison
Chief sub-editor: Richard Belk
Whitchurch Herald
01948 662332
Weekly (Thu). Editor: Andrew Bowan

Whitehaven News
01946 595100
www.whitehaven-news.co.uk
Weekly (Thu). Editor: Colin Edgar
News editor: Christine Peacock
Widnes Weekly News
0151 424 5921
Weekly (Thu). Editor: Ian Douglas
News editor: Adrian Short
Widnes World
0151 907 8525
Weekly (Wed). Editor: Carla Flynn
News editor: Barbara Jordan
Chief sub-editor: Graham Bailey
Wigan Courier
01257 400026
Monthly (last Fri).
Editor: Mark Ashley
Wigan Evening Post
01772 838103
www.wigantoday.net
Daily. Editor: Simon Reynolds
News editor: Gillian Gray
Wigan Observer
01772 838103
www.wigantoday.net
Weekly (Tue). Editor: Gillian Gray
Wigan Reporter
01772 838103
www.wigantoday.net
Weekly (Thu). Editor: Gillian Gray
Wilmslow Citizen
0161 491 5700
Fortnightly (Thu).
Editor: Mike Shields
Wilmslow Express
01625 529333
www.thewilmslowexpress.co.uk
Weekly (Wed). Editor: Mike Quilley
News editor: Betty Anderson
Winsford Chronicle
01244 340151
www.cheshirenews.co.uk
Weekly (Fri). Editor: Richard Ault
Winsford Guardian
01925 434000
www.thisischeshire.co.uk
Weekly (Wed). Editor: Jan Lever
Wirral Chronicle
01244 340151
www.cheshirenews.co.uk
Weekly (Fri). Editor: Richard Ault
Wirral Globe
0151 906 3000
www.thisiswirral.co.uk
Weekly (Wed). Editor: Leigh Marles
Wirral Target
0151 906 3000
www.thisiswirral.co.uk
Fortnightly free (Wed)
Editor: Leigh Marles

Wythenshawe World
0161 998 4786
Fortnightly free (Fri)
Editor: John Oatway

Isle of Man

Isle of Man Courier
01624 695695
www.iomonline.co.im
Weekly (Thu). Editor: Lionel Cowin
News editor: Jo Overty
Chief sub-editor: Dave Corbett
Isle of Man Examiner
01624 695695
www.iomonline.co.im
Weekly (Tue). Editor: Lionel Cowin
News editor: Jo Overty
Chief sub-editor: Dave Corbett
The Manx Independent
01624 695695
www.iomonline.co.im
Weekly (Fri). Editor: Lionel Cowin
News editor: Jo Overty
Chief sub-editor: Dave Corbett

Regional newspapers – Wales

Wales on Sunday
Thomson House, Havelock St
Cardiff CF10 1XR
029 2058 3583
www.icwales.co.uk
Sunday. Editor: Tim Gordon
News editor: Laura Kemp

Western Mail
Thomson House, Havelock St
Cardiff CF10 1XR
029 2058 3583
www.icwales.co.uk
Daily. Editor: Allan Edmunds
News editor: Duncan Higgitt

North Wales

Abergele Visitor
01492 584321
www.icnorthwales.co.uk
Weekly (Thu). Editor: Alan Davies

Bangor Chronicle
01248 387400
www.northwaleschronicle.co.uk
Weekly (Thu). Editor: Emlyn Roberts
News editor: Helen Speddy
Features editor: Tony Coates

Bangor Spectator
028 9127 0270
Weekly (Thu). Editor: Paul Flowers

Bangor/Anglesey Mail
01286 671111
www.icnorthwales.co.uk
Weekly (Wed). Editor: Jeff Eames
News editor: Lindi Roberts
Production editor: Mark Jones

Buy Sell (Flintshire Edition)
01978 290400
Weekly (Wed). No editorial

Caernarfon & Denbigh Herald
01286 671111
www.icnorthwales.co.uk
Weekly (Thu). Editor: Jeff Eames
News editor: Lindi Roberts
Production editor: Mark Jones

Daily Post
01492 574455
www.icnorthwales.co.uk
Daily. Editor: Alastair Macrae

Denbighshire Free Press
01745 813535
www.denbighshirefreepress.co.uk
Weekly (Thu). Editor: Alistair Syme

Flintshire Chronicle
01244 821911
www.icnorthwales.co.uk
Weekly (Fri). Editor: Paul Cook
News editor: Kevin Hughes

Flintshire Leader
01244 304500
www.chesterstandard.co.uk
Weekly (Thu).
Editor: Jonathan White

Flintshire Leader & Standard
01352 707707
www.flintshirestandard.co.uk
Weekly (Thu).
Editor: Richard Williams
Features editor: Joanne Shone
Chief sub-editor: Joanne Shone
Production editor: Karen Perry

Gwynedd Chronicle
01248 387400
www.chroniclenow.co.uk
Weekly (Thu). Editor: Emlyn Roberts
News editor: Helen Speddy
Features editor: Tony Coates

Holyhead and Anglesey Mail
01286 671111
www.icnorthwales.co.uk
Weekly (Wed). Editor: Jeff Eames
News editor: Lindi Roberts
Production editor: Mark Jones

North Wales Chronicle
01248 387400
www.chroniclenow.co.uk
Weekly (Thu). Editor: Emlyn Roberts
News editor: Helen Speddy
Features editor: Tony Coates

North Wales Pioneer
01492 531188
www.northwalespioneer.co.uk
Weekly (Thu). Editor: Steve Rogers

North Wales Weekly News
01492 584321
www.icnorthwales.co.uk
Weekly (Thu). Editor: Alan Davies

Rhyl & Prestatyn Visitor
01745 334144
www.icnorthwales.co.uk
Weekly free (Wed).
Editor: Alan Davies
News editor: Dave Jones

Rhyl Prestatyn & Abergele Journal
01745 357500
Weekly (Thu). Editor: Steve Rogers
Deputy editor: Diane Ashton

Vale Advertiser
01492 584321
icnorthwales.icnetwork.co.uk
/news/valeadvertiser
Weekly (Fri). Editor: Alan Davies

Wrexham Evening Leader
01978 355151
www.eveningleader.co.uk
Daily. Editor: Richard Williams

Wrexham Leader
01978 355151
www.bigleader.co.uk
Weekly free (Fri)
Editor: Richard Williams

Wrexham Mail
01978 351515
www.icnorthwales.co.uk
Weekly (Thu). Editor: Paul Cook
News editor: Kevin Hughes

Y Cymro
01970 615000
www.y-cymro.co.uk
Weekly (Mon). Editor: Rob Jones

Ynys Mon Chronicle
01248 387400
www.chroniclenow.co.uk
Weekly (Thu). Editor: Emlyn Roberts
News editor: Helen Speddy
Features editor: Tony Coates

Yr Herald
01286 671111
www.icnorthwales.co.uk
Weekly (Sat). Editor: Jeff Eames
News editor: Lindi Roberts
Production editor: Mark Jones

South Wales

South Wales Echo
Thomson House, Havelock St
Cardiff CF10 1XR
029 2058 3583
www.icwales.co.uk
Daily. Editor: Alistair Milburn
News editor: Nick Machin

South Wales Evening Post
PO Box 14, Adelaide St
Swansea SA1 1QT
01792 510000
www.swep.co.uk
Daily. Editor: Spencer Feeney
News editor: Peter Lee
Features editor: Catherine Ings
Chief sub-editor: Lynne Fernquest

Abergavenny Chronicle
01873 852187
www.abergavenny.co.uk
Weekly (Thu). Editor: Liz Davies

Abergavenny Free Press
01873 857497
www.thisismonmouthshire.co.uk
Weekly (Wed). Editor: Carl Difford
News editor: Lesley Flynn

Barry & District News
01446 704981
www.thisisbarry.co.uk
Weekly (Thu). Editor: Carl Difford
News editor: Sue Vincent-Jones

Barry Gem
01446 774484
www.barry-today.co.uk
Weekly (Thu). Editor: Don John

Brecon & Radnor Express
01874 610111
www.brecon-radnor.co.uk
Weekly (Wed). Editor: Dave Meechan

125

Bridgend & District Recorder
01446 774484
Weekly (Tue). Editor: Don John
Cambrian News
01970 611611
www.aberystwyth-today.co.uk
Weekly (Wed). Editor: Beverley Davis
News editor: Simon Middlehurst
Campaign Blackwood
01633 777212
www.thisisgwent.co.uk
Weekly (Fri). Editor: Carl Difford
News editor: Andy Sambridge
Campaign Caerphilly
01633 777212
www.thisisgwent.co.uk
Weekly (Fri). Editor: Carl Difford
News editor: Andy Sambridge
Campaign North Gwent
01633 777212
www.thisisgwent.co.uk
Weekly (Fri). Editor: Carl Difford
News editor: Andy Sambridge
Campaign Pontypridd
01633 777212
www.thisisgwent.co.uk
Weekly (Fri). Editor: Carl Difford
News editor: Andy Sambridge
Cardiff Advertiser & Property Times
029 2030 3900
www.icwales.co.uk
Weekly (Fri). Editor: David Hynes
Cardigan & Tivyside Advertiser
01239 614343
www.thisistivyside.net
Weekly (Wed). Editor: Areurin Evans
News editor: Sue Lewis
Carmarthen Herald
01267 227222
www.carmarthenjournal.co.uk
Weekly free (Fri).
Editor: David Hardy
News editor: Diane Williams
Carmarthen Journal
01267 227222
www.carmarthenjournal.co.uk
Weekly (Wed). Editor: David Hardy
News editor: Diane Williams
Chepstow Free Press
01291 621882
www.thisismonmouthshire.co.uk
Weekly (Wed). Editor: Carl Difford
News editor: Jacqui Carole
County Echo
01348 874445
www.newport-today.co.uk
Weekly (Fri). Editor: Chris Taylor
County Times & Gazette
01938 553354
www.countytimes.co.uk
Weekly (Thu). Editor: Martin Wright

Courier
01792 510000
Weekly (Tue). Editor: Paul Turner
Cowbridge Gem
01446 774484
www.cowbridge-today.co.uk
Weekly (Thu). Editor: Don John
Cynon Valley Leader
01685 873136
Weekly (Wed). Editor: Gary Marsh
Glamorgan Gazette
01656 304924
Weekly (Thu). Editor: Paul Jones
Gwent Gazette
01495 304589
www.buckinghamtoday.co.uk
Weekly (Tue). Editor: Sarah Harris
Heart of Wales Chronicle
01874 610111
Weekly (Mon). Editor: Dave Meechan
Llanelli Star
01554 745300
www.thisissouthwales.co.uk
Weekly (Wed, Thu)
Editor: Andy Pearson
News editor: Laura Grime
Llantwit Major Gem
01446 774484
www.llantwit-major-today.co.uk
Weekly (Thu). Editor: Don John
Merthyr Express
01685 856500
Weekly (Fri).
Editor: Gordon Caldicott
Mid Wales Journal
01597 828060
www.midwalesjournal.co.uk
Weekly (Fri). Editor: Mike Robinson
News editor: Karen Evans
Milford & West Wales Mercury
01646 698971
Weekly (Thu)
News editor: Richard Harris
Monmouth Free Press
01600 713631
www.thisismonmouthshire.co.uk
Weekly (Wed). Editor: Carl Difford
News editor: Sarah Wood
Monmouthshire Beacon
01600 712142
www.monmouth-today.co.uk
Weekly (Thu).
Editor: Robert Williams
Narbeth & Whitland Observer
01834 843262
Weekly (Fri). Editor: Neil Dickinson
Neath & Port Talbot Guardian
01639 778885
Weekly (Thu). Editor: Fay Harris
Neath & Port Talbot Tribune
01792 510000
Monthly (2nd Fri).
Editor: Paul Turner

Penarth Times
029 2070 7234
www.thisispenarth.co.uk
Weekly (Thu)
News editor: Susan Vincent Jones
Chief reporter: Jessica Hinton
Pontypool Free Press
01495 751133
www.thisismonmouthshire.co.uk
Weekly (Wed). Editor: Carl Difford
News editor: Adrian Osmond
Pontypridd Observer
01443 665161
www.icwales.com
Weekly (Wed). Editor: Dean Powell
Rhondda Leader
01443 665151
Weekly (Thu). Editor: Kiyrin Davis
News editor: Dave Edwards
South Wales Argus
01633 810000
www.thisisgwent.co.uk
Daily. Editor: Gerry Keightley
News editor: Mark Templeton
Chief sub-editor: Caroline Woolard
South Wales Echo
029 2058 3583
www.icwales.co.uk
Daily. Editor: Alistair Milburn
News editor: Nick Machin
South Wales Evening Post
01792 510000
www.swep.co.uk
Daily. Editor: Spencer Feeney
News editor: Peter Lee
Features editor: Catherine Ings
Chief sub-editor: Lynne Fernquest
South Wales Guardian
01269 592781
www.thisisammanford.co.uk
Weekly (Wed). Editor: Steve Robbin
News editor: Emma Evans
Features editor: Richard Sharpe
Swansea Herald
01792 514630
Weekly (Thu). Editor: David Robbi
Tenby Observer
01834 843262
Weekly (Fri). Editor: Neil Dickinso
Tenby Times
01834 843262
Monthly free (first Wed)
Editor: Neil Dickinson
Weekly Argus
01633 810000
www.thisisgwent.co.uk
Weekly (Thu).
Editor: Gerry Keightley
News editor: Mark Templeton
Chief sub-editor: Caroline Woolard
Western Telegraph
01437 763133
www.thisispembrokeshire.net
Weekly (Wed). Editor: Fiona Phipp

Main papers

Aberdeen Press and Journal
Aberdeen Journals
Lang Stracht, Mastrick
Aberdeen AB15 6DF
01224 690222
www.pressandjournal.co.uk
Daily. Editor: Derek Tucker
News editor: Fiona McWair
Features editor: Richard Neville
Chief sub-editor: Jim Urquart

Courier and Advertiser
DC Thomson & Co,
2 Albert Square
Dundee DD1 9QJ
01382 223131
www.thecourier.co.uk
Daily. Editor: Bill Hutcheon
News editor: Arliss Rhind
Features editor: Catriona Macinnes
Production editor: Brian Clarkson

Daily Record
One Central Quay,
Glasgow
G3 8DA
0141 309 3000
www.dailyrecord.co.uk
Daily. Editor: Bruce Waddell
News editor: Tom Hamilton
Features editor: Melanie Harvey

Edinburgh Evening News
Barclay House,
108 Holyrood Rd
Edinburgh EH8 8AS
0131 620 8620
www.edinburghnews.com
Daily. Editor: Ian Stewart
News editor: Ewan McGrory
Features editor: Jeanne Davidson
Chief sub-editor: Howard Dorman
Production editor: Mark Endie

Glasgow Evening Times
200 Renfield St,
Glasgow
G2 3QB
0141 302 7000
www.eveningtimes.co.uk
Daily. Editor: Charles McGhee
News editor: Hugh Boag

Glasgow Herald
200 Renfield St,
Glasgow
G2 3QB
0141 302 7000
www.theherald.co.uk
Daily. Editor: Mark Douglas-Home

Scotland On Sunday
Barclay House, 108 Holyrood Rd
Edinburgh EH8 8AS
0131 620 8620
www.scotlandonsunday.com
Sunday. Editor: John McLellan
News editor: Peter Laing
Chief sub-editor: Martin Allen
Production editor: Chris Dry

The Scotsman
Barclay House,
108 Holyrood Rd
Edinburgh EH8 8AS
0131 620 8620
www.scotsman.com
Daily. Editor: Ian Martin
News editor: Nick Drainey

Sunday Herald
200 Renfield St,
Glasgow G2 3QB
0141 302 7800
www.sundayherald.com
Sunday. Editor: Andrew Jaspan
News editor: David Milne
Features editor: Charlene Sweeney

Sunday Mail
One Central Quay,
Glasgow G3 8DA
0141 309 3230
www.sundaymail.co.uk
Sunday. Editor: Allan Rennie
News editor: Brendan McGinty
Features editor: Susie Cormack
Chief sub-editor: George Welsh

Sunday Post
DC Thomson & Co,
2 Albert Square
Dundee DD1 9QJ
01382 223131
www.thesundaypost.co.uk
Sunday. Editor: David Pollington
News editor: Tom McKay
Features editor: Brian Wilson
Chief sub-editor: Alastair Bennett

Other Scottish newspapers

Aberdeen & District Independent
01224 618300
www.aberdeen-indy.co.uk
Weekly (Thu). Editor: Derek Piper
News editor: Donna Morrison

Aberdeen Citizen
01224 690222
Weekly (Wed).
Editor: Donald Martin

Aberdeen Evening Express
01224 690222
Daily. Editor: Donald Martin
News editor: Richard Prest
Chief sub-editor: James Donaldson

The Advertiser
0131 561 6600
Weekly (Wed). Editor: Roy Scott
News editor: Alex Hogg

Airdrie & Coatbridge Advertiser
01236 748648
www.icScotland.co.uk
Weekly (Wed). Editor: John Murdoch

Alloa & Hillfoots Advertiser
01259 214416
Weekly (Thu).
Editor: Kevin McRoberts
News editor: Karen Payton

Annandale Herald
01461 202078
www.thisisthewestcountry.co.uk
Weekly (Thu).
Editor: Bryan Armstrong
News editor: Alan Hall

Annandale Observer
01461 202078
www.thisisthewestcountry.co.uk
Weekly (Fri).
Editor: Bryan Armstrong
News editor: Alan Hall

Arbroath Herald
01241 872274
Weekly (Fri). Editor: Craig Nisbet
News editor: Brian Forsythe

Ardrossan & Saltcoats Herald
01294 464321
www.threetowners.com/Herald
/herald_files.htm
Weekly (Fri). Editor: Alex Clarke
News editor: Craig Nisbet

Argyllshire Advertiser
01631 563058
www.argyllshireadvertiser.co.uk
Weekly (Fri).
Editor: Stewart Mackenzie
News editor: Joanne Simms

Arran Banner
01631 568000
www.obantimes.co.uk
Weekly (Sat).
Editor: Stewart Mackenzie

Ayr Advertiser
01292 267631
Weekly (Wed). Editor: Alex Clarke
News editor: Caroline Paterson

Ayrshire Extra
01292 611666
Weekly (Thu). Editor: Scott Back

Ayrshire Post
01292 261111
www.icScotland.co.uk
Weekly (Wed).
Editor: Cheryl McEvoy
Features editor: Yonnie McInnes

Ayrshire Weekly Press
01294 464321
Weekly (Fri). Editor: Alex Clarke
News editor: Craig Nisbet

Ayrshire World
01294 272233
www.icScotland.co.uk
Weekly free (Wed)
Editor: Alan Woodison
News editor: Lex Brown
Chief sub-editor: Murray Stevenson
Banff Gazette
01224 618300
www.aberdeen-indy.co.uk
Weekly (Fri). Editor: Derek Piper
News editor: Donna Morrison
Banffshire Herald
01542 886262
www.bannfshireherald.com
Weekly (Fri).
Editor: Morven Macneil
Barrhead News
0141 887 7055
Weekly (Wed).
Editor: Tom McConigley
Bearsden, Milngavie and Glasgow Extra
0141 427 7878
www.icscotland.co.uk
Weekly (Thu). Editor: Allan Hodge
News editor: Colin Macdonald
Chief sub-editor: John Mathews
Bellshill Speaker
01698 264611
Weekly (Thu). Editor: Archie Fleming
Berwick Gazette
01289 306677
www.berwicktoday.co.uk
Weekly (Thu).
Editor: David Johnstone
News editor: Sandy Brydon
Features editor: Janice Gillie
Chief sub-editor: Diane Welsh
Berwickshire News
01289 306677
www.berwickshiretoday.co.uk
Weekly (Fri).
Editor: David Johnstone
News editor: Sandy Brydon
Features editor: Janice Gillie
Chief sub-editor: Diane Welsh
Blairgowrie Advertiser
01250 872854
www.icScotland.co.uk
Weekly (Tue, Fri).
Editor: Alison Lowson
Border Telegraph
01896 758395
www.bordertelegraph.com
Weekly (Tue). Editor: Atholl Innes
Brechin Advertiser
01356 622767
www.brechinadvertiser.com
Weekly (Thu). Editor: Alan Ducat
News editor: Gregor Wilson
Features editor: Jenny Hill

Buchan Observer
01779 472017
www.buchanie.co.uk
Weekly (Tue). Editor: Ken Duncan
The Buteman
01700 502503
www.icScotland.co.uk
Weekly (Fri). Editor: Craig Borland
Caithness Courier
01955 602424
www.caithness-courier.co.uk
Weekly (Wed). Editor: Alan Henry
News editor: Karen Macdonald
Campbell Times Courier
01631 563058
Weekly (Sat).
Editor: Stewart Mackenzie
News editor: Joanne Simms
Campbeltown Courier & Argyllshire Advertiser
01586 554646
www.campbeltowncourier.co.uk
Weekly (Fri). Editor: Ronald Watson
Carrick Gazette
01671 402503
Weekly (Thu). Editor: Peter Jeal
Central Fife Times & Advertiser
01383 728201
Weekly (Wed). Editor: Jim Stark
Chief sub-editor: Susan Dryburgh
Clyde Post
01475 726511
Weekly free (Wed)
Editor: David Carndess
News editor: Wilma Riley
Clyde Weekly News
01294 273421
www.icScotland.co.uk
Weekly (Wed). Editor: Alex Clarke
Clydebank Post
0141 952 0565
Weekly (Thu). Editor: James Walsh
Craigmillar Chronicle
0131 661 0791
www.craignet.org.uk/chronicle
Monthly free (1st of month)
Cumbernauld News & Advertiser
01236 725578
www.falkirktoday.co.uk
Weekly free (Fri)
Editor: Archie Fleming
Chief sub-editor: Neil Smith
Cumbernauld News & Kilsyth Chronicle
01236 725578
www.falkirktoday.co.uk
Weekly (Wed).
Editor: Archie Fleming
Chief sub-editor: Neil Smith

Cumnock Chronicle
01290 421633
Weekly (Wed).
Editor: Douglas Skelton
News editor: Amanda Smith
Deeside Piper
01330 824955
www.deesidepiper.com
Weekly (Fri). Editor: Phil Allan
Donside Piper & Herald
01330 824955
www.donsidepiper.com
Weekly (Fri). Editor: Phil Allan
Dumbarton & Vale Of Leven Reporter
01436 673434
Weekly (Tue). Editor: Julian Calver
News editor: Steve MacIlroy
Dumfries & Galloway Standard
01387 240342
www.icScotland.co.uk
Weekly (Wed)
Editor: Adrian Barnfather
News editor: Ian Pollock
Dumfries and Galloway Today
01387 240342
www.icScotland.co.uk
Weekly (Wed)
Editor: Adrian Barnfather
News editor: Ian Pollock
Dumfries Courier
01461 202078
www.thisisthewestcountry.co.uk
Weekly free (Fri)
Editor: Bryan Armstrong
News editor: Alan Hall
Dunfermline Press & West of Fife Advertiser
01383 728201
www.snpa.org.uk
Weekly (Thu). Editor: Tom Davidso[?]
News editor: Simon Harris
Dunoon Observer & Argyllshire Standard
01369 703218
www.dunoon-observer.co.uk
Weekly (Fri). Editor: Bill Jardin
Features editor: Michelle Robertson
Chief sub-editor: Gerald Deveney
Production editor: Michelle Robertson
East End Independent
0141 647 6156
www.iclanarkshire.icnetwork.co.u[?]
Weekly free (Wed).
Editor: Gordon Bury
Features editor: Gary Thomas
East Fife Mail
01592 261451
www.fifenow.co.uk
Weekly free (Wed)
Editor: Ian Muirhead

East Kilbride News
01355 265000
www.berwickshire-news.co.uk
Weekly (Wed). Editor: Gordon Bury
News editor: Lynda Nichol
East Kilbride World
01698 283200
Weekly free (Fri).
Editor: Joseph Kelly
East Lothian Courier
01620 822451
www.eastlothiancourier.com
Weekly (Fri). Editor: Elaine Reid
East Lothian Herald
01289 306677
www.berwickshire-news.co.uk
Weekly (Thu).
Editor: David Johnstone
News editor: Sandy Brydon
Features editor: Janice Gillie
Chief sub-editor: Diane Welsh
East Lothian News
0131 561 6600
Weekly (Thu). Editor: Roy Scott
News editor: Alex Hogg
East Lothian Times
0131 561 6600
Weekly free (Fri). Editor: Roy Scott
News editor: Alex Hogg
Ellon Advertiser
01888 563589
Weekly (Fri). Editor: Joyce Summers
Ellon Times &
East Gordon Advertiser
01779 472017
Weekly (Thu).
Editor: Anne Robertson
Eskdale and Liddesdale
Advertiser
01387 380012
Weekly (Thu). Editor: Rachael Norris
Evening Telegraph
01382 223131
Daily. Editor: Alan Proctor
News editor: Elaine Harrison
Features editor: Phillip Smith
The Extra
01292 611666
Weekly (Thu). Editor: Scott Back
Falkirk Herald
01324 624959
www.falkirktoday.co.uk
Weekly (Thu). Editor: Colin Hume
News editor: Duncan McCullum
Features editor: Alan Muir
Falkirk, Grangemouth &
Linlithgow Advertiser
01324 638314
Weekly (Wed). Editor: Colin Hume
News editor: Duncan McCullum
Features editor: Alan Muir

Fife & Kinross Extra
01383 728201
Weekly free (Fri). Editor: Andrew
Cowie
Fife Free Press
01592 261451
www.fifenow.co.uk
Weekly free (Thu). Editor: Allen Crow
Fife Herald
01592 261451
www.fifenow.co.uk
Weekly free (Fri).
Editor: Graham Scott
Fife Leader
01592 261451
www.fifenow.co.uk
Weekly free (Tue).
Editor: Jack Snedden
Forfar Dispatch
01307 464899
www.forfardispatch.com
Weekly (Tue). Editor: Alan Ducat
Forres Gazette
01309 672615
www.forres-gazette.co.uk
Weekly (Wed). Editor: Ken Smith
Fraserburgh Herald
01779 472017
Weekly (Fri). Editor: Alex Shand
Galloway Gazette
01671 402503
www.gallowaygazette.com
Weekly (Thu). Editor: Peter Jeal
Galloway News
01556 504141
www.icScotland.co.uk
Weekly (Thu).
Editor: Elizabeth Martin
Chief sub-editor: Chris McIntyre
The Gazette
0141 887 7055
Weekly (Wed).
Editor: Tom McConigley
Glasgow East News
0141 573 5060
Weekly free (Fri)
Editor: Christine McPherson
News editor: Jim Holland
Glasgow South & Eastwood
Extra
0141 427 7878
www.icscotland.co.uk
Weekly (Thu). Editor: Allan Hodge
News editor: Colin Macdonald
Chief sub-editor: John Mathews
Glasgow West Extra
0141 427 7878
www.icscotland.co.uk
Weekly (Thu). Editor: Allan Hodge
News editor: Colin Macdonald
Chief sub-editor: John Mathews
The Glaswegian
0141 309 3132
Weekly free. Editor: Trevor Walls

Glenrothes Gazette
01592 261451
www.fifenow.co.uk
Weekly free (Wed)
Editor: Brian Stormont
Gorgie Dalry Gazette
0131 337 2457
Monthly (Fri)
Editor: Brian Montgomery
Greenock Telegraph
01475 726511
www.greenocktelegraph.co.uk
Weekly (Wed).
Editor: David Carndess
News editor: Wilma Riley
Hamilton Advertiser
01698 283200
www.icScotland.co.uk
Weekly (Thu). Editor: Joseph Kelly
Hamilton Extra People
01698 261321
Weekly (Fri). Editor: Martin Clark
Hawick News
01750 21581
www.hawicktoday.co.uk
Weekly (Fri). Editor: Willie Mack
Helensburgh Advertiser
01436 673434
Weekly (Thu). Editor: Julian Calvert
News editor: Steve MacIlroy
Herald & Post Edinburgh
0131 620 8620
Weekly free (Thu)
Editor: Stuart Farquhar
News editor: Adrian Mather
Highland News
01463 732222
www.highland-news.co.uk
Weekly (Thu). Editor: Helen Macrae
Huntly Express
01466 793622
Weekly (Fri). Editor: Helen Macrae
Ileach (Islay)
01496 810355
www.ileach.co.uk
Weekly (Sat). Editor: Stuart Todd
Inverness & Nairnshire Herald
01463 732222
Weekly (Thu). Editor: Helen Macrae
Inverness Courier
01463 233059
www.inverness-courier.co.uk
Weekly (Tue, Fri). Editor: Jim Love
Inverurie Advertiser
01888 563589
Weekly (Fri). Editor: Joyce Summers
Inverurie Herald
01467 625150
www.inverurieherald.com
Weekly (Thu). Editor: David Duncan
Irvine and North Ayrshire Extra
01292 611666
Weekly (Thu). Editor: Scott Back

Irvine Herald
01294 222288
www.icScotland.co.uk
Weekly (Wed).
Editor: Alan Woodison
News editor: Lex Brown
Chief sub-editor: Murray Stevenson
Irvine Times
01294 273421
Weekly (Wed). Editor: Alex Clarke
John O'Groat Journal
01955 602424
www.johnogroat-journal.co.uk
Weekly (Fri). Editor: Alan Henry
News editor: Karen Macdonald
Kilmarnock & District Extra
01292 611666
Weekly (Thu). Editor: Scott Back
Kilmarnock Standard
01563 525115
www.icScotland.co.uk
Weekly (Wed).
Editor: Alan Woodison
News editor: Lex Brown
Kincardineshire Observer
01561 377283
Weekly (Fri). Editor: Charles Wallace
Kirkintilloch Herald
0141 775 0040
www.kirkintillochtoday.co.uk
Weekly (Wed)
Editor: Christie McPherson
Chief sub-editor: Jim Holland
Kirriemuir Herald
01307 464899
www.kirriemuirherald.com
Weekly (Wed). Editor: Alan Ducat
Lanark Gazette
01555 663937
Weekly (Thu).
Editor: Aileen McCulloch
Lanarkshire Extra
01698 261321
www.icscotland.co.uk
Weekly (Thu). Editor: Martin Clark
Lanarkshire World
01698 283200
www.icScotland.co.uk
Weekly (Wed). Editor: Joseph Kelly
Largs & Millport Weekly News
01475 689009
Weekly (Wed)
Editor: Andrew Cochrane
Lennox Herald
01389 742299
www.icScotland.co.uk
Weekly (Wed)
Editor: Graham Crawford
Linlithgowshire Journal & Gazette
01506 844592
www.icScotland.co.uk
Weekly (Fri). Editor: Jack Shennan
Features editor: Julie Currie

Lochaber News
01463 732222
www.lochaber-news.co.uk
Weekly (Thu). Editor: Helen Macrae
Lothian Times East
0131 561 6600
Weekly free (Fri). Editor: Roy Scott
News editor: Alex Hogg
Mearns Leader
01569 762139
www.mearnsleader.com
Weekly (Fri). Editor: John McIntosh
Metro Scotland
020 7651 5200
www.metroscot.co.uk
Daily. Editor: Kenny Campbell
News editor: Mark Dorman
Features editor: Kieran Meeke
Mid Lothian Times
0131 561 6600
Weekly free (Fri). Editor: Roy Scott
News editor: Alex Hogg
Midlothian Advertiser
0131 561 6600
Weekly (Wed). Editor: Roy Scott
News editor: Alex Hogg
Milngavie and Bearsden Herald
0141 956 3533
Weekly (Fri). Editor: Alistair Blyth
News editor: Rena O'Neill
Moffat News
01461 202078
www.thisisthewestcountry.co.uk
Weekly (Thu).
Editor: Bryan Armstrong
News editor: Alan Hall
Montrose Review
01674 672605
www.montrosereview.net
Weekly (Thu). Editor: Douglas Hill
Motherwell Extra
01698 261321
Weekly (Fri). Editor: Martin Clark
Motherwell Times
01698 264611
Weekly (Thu). Editor: Archie Fleming
Musselburgh News
0131 561 6600
Weekly (Thu). Editor: Roy Scott
News editor: Alex Hogg
North Ayrshire World
01294 272233
www.icScotland.co.uk
Weekly (Wed).
Editor: Alan Woodison
News editor: Lex Brown
Chief sub-editor: Murray Stevenson
North Edinburgh News
0131 467 3972
www.northedinburghnews.co.uk
Monthly free (2nd Wed)
Editor: Mary Burnside

North Star
01463 732222
www.highland-news.co.uk
Weekly (Thu). Editor: Helen Macrae
North West Highlands Bratach
01641 521227
www.bratach.co.uk
Monthly (1st Thu)
Editor: Donald McCloud
Northern Scot
01343 548777
www.northern-scot.co.uk
Weekly (Fri). Editor: Pauline Taylor
Northern Times
01408 633993
www.northern-times.co.uk
Weekly (Thu). Editor: Duncan Ross
Oban Times
01631 563058
www.obantimes.co.uk
Weekly (Thu).
Editor: Stewart Mackenzie
News editor: Joanne Simms
The Orcadian
01856 879000
www.orcadian.co.uk
Weekly (Thu). Editor: Stuart Laurd
Paisley & District People
0141 887 7055
Weekly free (Fri)
Editor: Tom McConigley
Paisley & Renfrewshire Extra
0141 427 7878
www.icscotland.co.uk
Weekly (Thu). Editor: Allan Hodge
News editor: Colin Macdonald
Chief sub-editor: John Mathews
Paisley Daily Express
0141 887 7911
www.icScotland.co.uk
Daily. Editor: Jonathan Russell
News editor: Anne Dalrymple
Chief sub-editor: Wendy Slavin
Peebles Times
0131 561 6600
Weekly free (Fri). Editor: Roy Scott
News editor: Alex Hogg
Peeblesshire News
01896 758395
www.peeblesshirenews.com
Weekly (Fri). Editor: Atholl Innes
Perth Shopper
01738 626211
www.northshropshirechronicle.com
Weekly (Fri). Editor: Alison Lowson
Perthshire Advertiser
01738 626211
www.northshropshirechronicle.com
Weekly (Tue/Fri).
Editor: Alison Lowson
Ross-shire Herald
01463 732222
Weekly (Thu). Editor: Helen Macrae

Ross-shire Journal
01349 863436
www.rsjournal.co.uk
Weekly (Fri). Editor: Caroline Bham
Features editor: Jacqui McKenzie

Rutherglen Reformer
0141 647 2271
www.icscotland.co.uk
Weekly (Thu). Editor: Louise Reilly

Selkirk Advertiser
01750 21581
www.selkirktoday.co.uk
Weekly (Fri). Editor: Willie Mack

Shetland Life
01595 693622
www.shetlandtoday.co.uk
Monthly (1st Fri)
Editor: Andrew Morrison

Shetland News
01806 577332
www.shetland-news.co.uk
Daily, online. Editor: John Daly

Shetland Times
01595 693622
www.shetlandtoday.co.uk
Weekly. Editor: Viala Wishart

South West News & Star
01228 612300
www.news-and-star.co.uk
Daily. Editor: Keith Sutton
News editor: Sue Crawford
Features editor: Kath Smart
Chief sub-editor: Phil Taylor
Production editor: Richard Eccles

Southern Reporter
01750 21581
www.borderstoday.co.uk
Weekly (Fri). Editor: Willie Mack

St Andrews Citizen
01592 261451
www.fifenow.co.uk
Weekly free (Fri)
Editor: Mike Rankin

Stirling News
01259 214416
Weekly free (Wed)
Editor: Andrew Cowie

Stirling Observer
01786 451110
Twice-weekly free (Wed, Fri)
Editor: Alan Rennie
News editor: Donald Morton

Stirling/Alloa & Hillfoots Shopper
01786 451110
Weekly free (Fri).
Editor: Alan Rennie
News editor: Donald Morton

Stornoway Gazette & West Coast Advertiser
01851 702687
www.stornowaygazette.co.uk
Weekly (Thu).
Editor: Juliette Conway

Stranraer & Wigtownshire Free Press
01776 702551
www.stranraer.org/freepress
Weekly (Wed). Editor: John Neil

Strathearn Herald
01738 626211
www.northshropshirechronicle.com
Weekly (Fri). Editor: Alison Lowson

Strathkelvin Advertiser
0141 775 0040
Weekly (Sat)
Editor: Christie McPherson
Chief sub-editor: Jim Holland

Strathspey Herald
01479 872102
Weekly (Wed).
Editor: Gavin Musgrove

Turriff Advertiser
01888 563589
Weekly (Fri). Editor: Joyce Summers

Wee County News
01259 724724
www.wee-county-news.co.uk
Weekly (Thu). Editor: Joan McCann
Chief sub-editor: Susan Carden
Production editor: Bryan Watson

West Highland Free Press
01471 822464
www.whfp.co.uk
Weekly (Thu).
Editor: Ian McCormack

West Lothian Courier
01506 633544
www.icScotland.co.uk
Weekly (Thu). Editor: Mike Barr

West Lothian Herald & Post
0131 620 8620
Weekly free (Thu)
Editor: Stuart Farquhar

Wishaw Press
01698 373111
www.icScotland.co.uk
Weekly (Wed). Editor: John Murdoch

Wishaw World
01698 283200
www.icScotland.co.uk
Weekly (Fri). Editor: Joseph Kelly

Main papers

Belfast Telegraph
124–144 Royal Avenue
Belfast BT1 1EB
028 9026 4000
www.belfasttelegraph.co.uk
Daily. Editor: Edmund Curran
News editor: Paul Connolly
Features editor: John Caruth

Sunday Life
124–144 Royal Avenue
Belfast BT1 1EB
028 9026 4000
www.sundaylife.co.uk
Sunday. Editor: Martin Lyndsey
News editor: Martin Hill
Features editor: Audrey Watson

Belfast

Belfast News
028 9068 0000
www.icnorthernireland.co.uk
Weekly (Thu). Editor: Julie McClay
News editor: Rick Clarke
Features editor: Jeff Hill

The Daily Mirror (NI)
028 9056 8000
Daily. Editor: Jerry Miller
News editor: Morris Fitzmaurice
Features editor: Jilly Beattie

Derry Journal
028 7127 2200
www.icnorthernireland.co.uk
Weekly (Tue & Fri).
Editor: Pat Meart
News editor: Sioban McEleney

Farming Life
028 9068 0000
www.farminglife.com
Weekly (Wed, Sat)
Editor: David McCoy
News editor: Rick Clarke
Features editor: Jeff Hill

Irish News
028 9032 2226
www.irishnews.com
Daily. Editor: Noel Doran
News editor: Steven O'Reilly
Features editor: Joanna Braniff

News Letter
028 9068 0000
www.icnorthernireland.co.uk
Daily. Editor: Austin Hunter
News editor: Rick Clarke
Features editor: Jeff Hill

North Belfast News
028 9058 4444
www.irelandclick.com
Weekly (Fri). Editor: John Ferris
News editor: Andrea McKernon
Features editor: Aine Mcentee
The People (Northern Ireland editions)
028 9056 8000
Sunday. Editor: Greg Harkin
News editor: Jason Johnson
South Belfast News
028 9024 2411
www.irelandclick.com
Weekly (Fri). Editor: Maria McCourt
Sunday Mirror
028 9056 8000
www.sundaymirror.co.uk
Sunday. Editor: Christian McCashin
Assistant editor: Donna Carton
Sunday World (Northern Ireland edition)
00 353 1 406 3500
www.sundayworld.com
Sunday. Editor: Colm McGinty
News editor: John Donlon
Features editor: John Sheils

Other newspapers

Andersonstown News
028 9061 9000
www.irelandclick.com
Weekly (Mon /Thu)
Editor: Robin Livingstone
Antrim Guardian
028 9446 2624
www.ulster-ni.co.uk
Weekly (Wed). Editor: Liam Hesfron
Antrim Times
028 3839 3939
www.mortonnewspapers.com
Weekly (Wed).
Editor: David Armstrong
Assistant editor: Dessie Blackadder
Armagh-Down Observer
028 8772 2557
Weekly (Thu).
Editor: Desmond Mallon
News editor: Desmond Mallon Jr
Armagh Observer
028 8772 2557
Weekly (Wed). Editor: Desmond Mallon
News editor: Desmond Mallon Jr
Ballycastle Chronicle
028 7034 3344
www.ulsternet-ni.co.uk/chronicle
/pages/ballycastle.htm
Weekly (Wed). Editor: John Fillis
Ballyclare Advertiser
028 9336 3651
www.ulster-ni.co.uk
Weekly (Wed). Editor: Raymond Hughes

Ballymena Chronicle
028 8772 2557
Weekly (Wed).
Editor: Desmond Mallon
News editor: Desmond Mallon Jr
Ballymena Guardian
028 2564 1221
www.macunlimited.net
Weekly (Wed). Editor: Maurice O'Neil
Assistant editor: Shaun O'Neil
Ballymena Times
028 2565 3300
www.mortonnewspapers.com
Weekly (Wed).
Editor: David Armstrong
Assistant editor: Dessie Blackadder
Ballymoney & Coleraine Chronicle
028 7034 3344
www.ulsternet-ni.co.uk/chronicle
/pages/ballymoney.htm
Weekly (Wed). Editor: John Fillis
Ballymoney Times
028 2766 6216
www.mortonnewspapers.com
Weekly (Wed).
Editor: David Armstrong
Assistant editor: Lyle McMullen
Banbridge Chronicle
028 4066 2322
Weekly (Wed). Editor: Bryan Hooks
Banbridge Leader
028 4066 2745
www.bambridgeleader.com
Weekly (Wed). Editor: Damien Wilson
Features editor: Cathy Wilson
Carrick Gazette
028 9336 3651
www.ulster-ni.co.uk
Weekly (Wed).
Editor: Raymond Hughes
Carrick Times
028 3839 3939
www.mortonnewspapers.com
Weekly (Thu).
Editor: David Armstrong
Assistant editor: Lyle McMullen
Carrickfergus Advertiser
028 8772 2274
www.ulsternet-ni.co.uk/carrick
/CPAGES/CMAIN.htm
Weekly (Wed). Editor: Raymond Hughes
City News
028 7127 2200
Weekly (Wed). Editor: Pat McArt
Deputy editor: Siobhan McEleney
Coleraine Times
028 7035 5260
www.mortonnewspapers.com
Weekly (Wed). Editor: David Armstrong
Assistant editor: David Rankin
County Down Spectator
028 9127 0270
Weekly (Thu). Editor: Paul Flowers

Craigavon Echo
028 3839 3939
www.mortonnewspapers.com
Weekly free (Wed)
Editor: David Armstrong
Assistant editor: Hugh Vance
Derry Journal
028 7127 2200
Twice-weekly (Tues/Fri)
Editor: Pat McArt
Deputy editor: Siobhan McEleney
Derry Journal (Sunday)
028 7127 2200
Weekly (Sunday). Editor: Pat McArt
Deputy editor: Siobhan McEleney
Derry News
028 7129 6600
Twice-weekly (Thu/Sat)
Editor: Joanne McCool
Down Democrat
028 4461 4400
www.downdemocrat.com
Weekly (Tue).
Editor: Terry McLaughlin
Down Recorder
028 4461 3711
www.thedownrecorder.com
Weekly (Wed).
Editor: Paul Symington
Dromore Leader
028 3839 3939
www.mortonnewspapers.com
Weekly (Wed).
Editor: David Armstrong
Dungannon News & Tyrone Courier
028 8772 2271
www.ulsternet-ni.co.uk/courier
/cpages/CMAIN.htm
Weekly (Wed). Editor: Ian Grear
Dungannon Observer
028 8772 2557
Weekly (Fri).
Editor: Desmond Mallon
News editor: Desmond Mallon Jr
East Antrim Advertiser
028 2827 2303
www.mortonnewspapers.com
Monthly. Editor: David Armstrong
Assistant editor: High Vance
East Antrim Guardian
028 2564 1221
www.macunlimited.net
Weekly (Wed). Editor: Maurice O'Ne
Assistant editor: Shaun O'Neil
Fermanagh Herald
028 8224 3444
www.fermanaghherald.com
Weekly (Wed). Editor: Pauline Lear
Fermanagh News
028 8772 2557
Weekly (Fri).
Editor: Desmond Mallon
News editor: Desmond Mallon Jr

Foyle News
028 7127 2200
www.icderry.icnetwork.co.uk
/ournewspapers/foylenews/
Weekly (Wed). Editor: Pat McArt
Deputy editor: Siobhan McEleney
The Guardian
028 7034 3344
Weekly (Wed). Editor: John Fillis
Impartial Reporter
028 6632 4422
www.impartialreporter.com
Weekly (Thu).
Editor: Denzil McDaniel
Lakeland Extra
028 6632 4422
www.impartialreporter.com
Monthly free (3rd Mon)
Editor: Denzil McDaniel
Larne Gazette
028 9336 3651
www.ulster-ni.co.uk
Weekly (Wed).
Editor: Raymond Hughes
Larne Times
028 3839 3939
www.mortonnewspapers.com
Weekly (Thu).
Editor: David Armstrong
Assistant editor: Hugh Vance
The Leader
028 2827 2303
www.mortonnewspapers.com
Weekly (Wed).
Editor: David Armstrong
Assistant editor: Damien Wilson
The Leader (Coleraine)
028 7034 3344
www.ulsternet-ni.co.uk/leader
/pages/leader.htm
Weekly (Mon). Editor: John Fillis
Limavady Chronicle
028 7034 3344
www.ulsternet-ni.co.uk/chronicle
/pages/limavady.htm
Weekly (Wed). Editor: John Fillis
Lisburn Echo
028 3839 3939
www.mortonnewspapers.com
Weekly free (Wed)
Editor: David Armstrong
Assistant editor: Hugh Vance
Londonderry Sentinel
028 7134 8889
www.mortonnewspapers.com
Weekly (Wed).
Editor: David Armstrong
Assistant editor: Chris McNabb
Lurgan & Portadown Examiner
028 8772 2557
Weekly (Wed).
Editor: Desmond Mallon
News editor: Desmond Mallon Jr

Lurgan Mail
028 3832 7777
www.mortonnewspapers.com
Weekly (Thu).
Editor: David Armstrong
Assistant editor: Richard Elliott
Magherafelt & Limavady Constitution
028 7034 3344
www.ulsternet-ni.co.uk/ncon
/pages/limavady.htm
Weekly (Wed). Editor: John Fillis
Mid-Ulster Echo
028 8676 2288
www.mortonnewspapers.com
Weekly free (Wed)
Editor: David Armstrong
Assistant editor: John Fillis
Mid-Ulster Mail
028 8676 2288
www.mortonnewspapers.com
Weekly (Thu).
Editor: David Armstrong
Assistant editor: John Fillis
Mid-Ulster Observer
028 8772 2557
Weekly (Wed).
Editor: Desmond Mallon
News editor: Desmond Mallon Jr
Mourne Observer & County Down News
028 4372 2666
www.mourneobserver.com
Weekly (Wed).
Editor: Terrance Bowman
Newry Advertiser
028 8772 2557
Monthly free. Editor: Desmond Mallon
News editor: Desmond Mallon Jr
Newry Democrat
028 3025 1250
www.newrydemocrat.com
Weekly (Tue).
Editor: Caroline McEvoy
News editor: John Grant
Features editor: Patrick Ryan
Newtownabbey Times
028 3839 3939
www.mortonnewspapers.com
Weekly (Thu).
Editor: David Armstrong
Assistant editor: Hugh Vance
Newtownards Chronicle
028 9127 0270
Weekly (Thu). Editor: Paul Flowers
Newtownards Spectator
028 9127 0270
Weekly (Thu). Editor: Paul Flowers
North West Echo
028 3839 3939
www.mortonnewspapers.com
Weekly free (Wed)
Editor: David Armstrong
Assistant editor: John Fillis

Northern Constitution
028 7034 3344
www.ulsternet-ni.co.uk/ncon
/pages/coleraine.htm
Weekly (Wed). Editor: John Fillis
The Outlook
028 4063 0202
www.ulsternet-ni.co.uk/outlook
/outpages/OMAIN.htm
Weekly (Wed). Editor: Ruth Rogers
Portadown Times
028 3833 6111
www.mortonnewspapers.com
Weekly (Fri).
Editor: David Armstrong
Roe Valley Sentinel
028 3839 3939
www.mortonnewspapers.com
Weekly (Wed).
Editor: David Armstrong
Assistant editor: John Fillis
Strabane Chronicle
028 8224 3444
www.strabanechronicle.com
Weekly (Thu).
Editor: Michelle Canning
Strabane Weekly News
028 8224 2721
www.ulsternet-ni.co.uk/strabane
/spages/SMAIN.htm
Weekly (Thu).
Editor: Wesley Atchison
Features editor: Geraldine Wilson
Tyrone Constitution
028 8224 2721
www.ulsternet-ni.co.uk/tcon
/conpages/CMAIN.htm
Weekly (Thu).
Editor: Wesley Atchison
Features editor: Geraldine Wilson
Tyrone Times
028 8775 2801
www.mortonnewspapers.com
Weekly (Fri).
Editor: David Armstrong
Assistant editor: Paul McCready
Ulster Gazette & Armagh Standard
028 3752 2639
www.ulsternet-ni.co.uk
Weekly (Thu).
Editor: Richard Stewart
Ulster Herald
028 8224 3444
www.ulsterherald.com
Weekly (Thu).
Editor: Darach McDonald
Ulster Star
028 9267 9111
www.mortonnewspapers.com
Weekly (Fri).
Editor: David Armstrong

Irish newspapers

Irish Times
00 353 1 675 8000
www.ireland.com
Daily

Irish Independent
00 353 1 705 5333
www.independent.ie
Daily

Connacht Tribune
00 353 91 536222
www.connacht-tribune.ie
Weekly

Cork Evening Echo
00 353 21 480 2142
www.eveningecho.ie
Daily

Evening Herald (Dublin)
Try 00 353 1 705 5333
Daily

Irish Daily Star
00 353 1 490 1228
www.thedailystar.ie
Daily

Ireland on Sunday
00 353 1 637 5800
Sunday

Irish Examiner
00 353 21 427 2722
www.examiner.ie
Daily

Kerryman
00 353 66 71 45500
www.kerryman.ie
Weekly

Leinster Leader
00 353 45 897302
www.leinsterleader.ie
Weekly

Limerick Leader
00 353 61 214503/6
www.limerick-leader.ie
Weekly

Limerick Post
00 353 61 413322
www.limerickpost.ie
Weekly

Sunday Business Post
00 353 1 602 6000
www.sbpost.ie
Sunday

Sunday Independent
00 353 1 705 5333
www.independent.ie
Sunday

Sunday Tribune
00 353 1 631 4300
www.tribune.ie
Sunday

Sunday World
00 353 1 490 2177
www.sundayworld.com
Sunday

Magazines Contacts

Main magazine & contract magazine publishers

Brooklands Group
Medway House,
Lower Rd
Forest Row, East Sussex
RH18 5HE
01342 828700
www.brooklandsgroup.com

BBC Worldwide
Woodlands,
80 Wood Lane
London W12 0TT
020 8433 2000
www.bbcworldwide.com

Cedar
Pegasus House,
37–43 Sackville St
London W15 3EH
020 7534 2400
info@cedarcom.co.uk
www.cedarcom.co.uk
Managing director: Jules Rastelli;
editorial director: Mark Jones

Centaur
50 Poland St, London
W1F 7AX
020 7970 4000
www.centaur.co.uk
Publishing directors: Robin Coates,
Roger Beckett

CMP Information
Ludgate House,
245 Blackfriars Rd
London SE1 9UY
020 7921 5000
nmain@cmpinformation.com
www.cmpinformation.com
Part of United Business Media

Condé Nast
Vogue House,
Hanover Square
London W1S 1JU
020 7499 9080
www.condenast.co.uk

DC Thomson
185 Fleet St, London
EC4A 2HS
020 7400 1030
www.dcthomson.co.uk

Dennis Publishing
30 Cleveland St,
London W1T 4JD
020 7907 6000
www.dennis.co.uk

Emap
40 Bernard St, London
WC1N 1LW
020 7278 1452
www.emap.com
Emap Communications
Scriptor Court, 155 Farringdon Rd
London EC1R 3AD
020 7841 6600
Emap Consumer Media
Endeavour House
189 Shaftesbury Avenue
London WC2H 8JG
020 7437 9011
Emap Performance
Mappin House, 4 Winsley St
London W1W 9HF
020 7436 1515

Future
Beauford Court,
30 Monmouth St
Bath BA1 2BW
01225 442244
www.futurenet.com
London office
99 Baker Street
London W1M 1FB
020 7317 2600

H Bauer
Academic House,
24–28 Oval Rd
London NW1 7DT
020 7241 8000
www.bauer.co.uk

Hachette Filipacchi
64 North Row, London
W1K 7LL
020 7150 7000
www.hachettefilipacchiuk.co.uk

Haymarket
174 Hammersmith Rd
London W6 7JP
020 8267 5000
hpg@haymarketgroup.com
www.haymarketgroup.co.uk
Haymarket Customer Publishing
38–42 Hampton Rd
Teddington
Middlesex TW11 0JE
haycustpub@haynet.com
www.haycustpub.com

Highbury House
Communications
1–3 Highbury Station Road
Islington, London N1 1SE
020 7226 2222
www.hhc.co.uk
Highbury Entertainment
53–79 Highgate Road
London NW5 1TW
020 7331 1000
Highbury Leisure
8–10 Knoll Rise
Orpington, Kent BR6 0PS
01689 887200

IPC Media
King's Reach Tower
Stamford St
London SE1 9LS
0870 444 5000
www.ipc.co.uk

John Brown Citrus
The New Boathouse
136–142 Bramley Rd
London W10 6SR
020 7565 3000
www.jbcp.co.uk
Managing director: Dean Fitzpatrick
020 7565 3202; editorial director:
Paul Colbert

Mediamark
11 Kingsway
London WC2B 6PH
020 7212 9000
info@mediamark.co.uk
www.mediamark.co.uk

National Magazine Company
National Magazine House
72 Broadwick St
London W1F 9EP
020 7439 5000
www.natmags.co.uk

New Crane Publishing
20 Upper Ground
London SE1 9PD
020 7633 0266
enquiries@newcrane.co.uk
www.newcrane.com

Publicis Blueprint
Whitfield House
83–89 Whitfield Street
London W1A 4XA
020 7462 7777
www.publicis-blueprint.com

135

Quantum Business Media
Quantum House, 19 Scarbrook Rd
Croydon, Surrey CR9 1LX
020 8565 4200
enquiries@
  quantumbusinessmedia.com
www.quantumbusinessmedia.com
Rare Publishing
102 Sydney Street
London SW3 6NJ
020 7368 9600
Bristol office 0117 929 7680
www.rarecontent.co.uk
Formerly AMD Brass Tacks. Part of Chime Communications. Editorial director: Maureen Rice; editor-in-chief: Matthew Cowen
Redwood
7 St Martin's Place
London WC2N 4HA
020 7747 0700
infohub@redwoodgroup.net
www.redwoodgroup.net
Reed Business Information
Quadrant House, The Quadrant
Sutton SM2 5AS
020 8652 3500
www.reedbusiness.co.uk
River Group
Victory House, Leicester Square
London WC2H 7QH
020 7306 0304
info@riverltd.co.uk
www.therivergroup.co.uk
Swan Publishing
4–5 Greenwich Quay, Clarence Rd
London SE8 3EY
020 8469 9700
info@swanpublishing.co.uk
www.swanpublishing.co.uk
VNU Business
VNU House, 32–34 Broadwick St
London W1A 2HG
020 7316 9000
www.vnunet.com

Adult

Asian Babes
020 7308 5092
Monthly. Editor: Phil Brock
Escort
020 7292 8000
Monthly. Editor: James Hundleby
Fiesta
01376 534500
13pa. Editor: Ross Gilfillan
For Women
020 7308 5363
Editor: Liz Beresford
Forum
020 7308 5363
13pa. Editor: Elizabeth Coldwell

Knave
01376 534500
13pa. Editor: Ross Gilfillan
Mayfair
020 7292 8000
Monthly. Editor: David Rider
Men Only
020 7292 8000
Monthly. Editor: David Rider
Skin Two
020 7498 5533
4pa. Editor: Tony Mitchell
Viz
020 7907 6000
www.viz.co.uk
Monthly

Children and teenage

2000 AD
01865 200603
www.2000adonline.com
Weekly. Editor: Matt Smith
Action Man
01892 500100
www.paninicomics.co.uk
17pa. Editor: Rob Jones
Angel Magazine
020 7250 0750
Monthly. Editor: Mark Kebble
Animal Action
0870 754 0145
www.rspca.org.uk
Bi-monthly. Editor: Simon Corrall
Animals and You
01382 223131
www.dcthomson.co.uk
Monthly. Editor: Margaret Monaghan
Aquila Children's Magazine
01323 431313
www.aquila.co.uk
Monthly. Editor: Jackie Berry
Art Attack
01892 500100
www.paninicomics.co.uk
17pa. Editor: Karen Brown
Barbie
020 7380 6430
www.egmontmagazines.co.uk
Every 3 weeks. Editor: Beckie Brookes
BBC Toybox
020 8433 3442
www.bbcmagazines.com/toybox
Monthly. Editor: Coralie Noakes
Beano
01382 223131
www.beanotown.com
Weekly. Editor: Euan Kerr
Bliss
020 7208 3791
www.blissmag.co.uk
Monthly. Editor: Helen Johnston

Breakout
01235 553444
www.couriergroup.com
6pa. Editor: Lawrence Webb
Chill Out
01908 651270
2pa. Editor: Liz Slee
CosmoGirl!
020 7439 5000
www.cosmogirl.co.uk
Monthly. Editor: Celia Duncan
Dandy
01382 223131
www.dandy.com
Weekly. Editor: Morris Heggie
Digimon
01892 500100
www.paninicomics.co.uk
13pa. Editor: Ed Hammond
Disney & Me
020 7380 6430
www.egmontmagazines.co.uk
Fortnightly. Editor: Jeanette Ryall
Elle Girl
020 7150 7000
www.hf-uk.com
Monthly. Editor: Claire Irvin
Fresh Magazine
01392 677321
Monthly. Editor: Joanne Trump
Girl
01392 664141
Monthly. Editor: Joanne Trump
Girl Talk
020 8433 2758
www.bbcmagazines.com/girltalk
Fortnightly.
Editor: Samantha McEvoy
Go Girl
020 7380 6430
www.egmontmagazines.co.uk
13pa. Editor: Sarah Delmege
Guiding
020 7592 1821
www.girlguiding.org.uk
Monthly. Editor: Wendy Kewley
Mizz
020 7261 7358
Weekly. Editor: Sharon Christal
Plus/Eagles' Wings
01903 824174
10pa. Editor: Donald Banks
Pokemon World
01202 299900
www.paragon.co.uk
10pa. Editor: Charlotte Martyn
Pony
01428 601020
www.horseandridermagazine.co.uk
Monthly. Editor: Janet Rising
Rugrats
0161 624 0414
13pa. Editor: Patris Gordan

Scouting Magazine
020 8433 7100
www.scoutingmagazine.org
Bi-monthly. Editor: Anna Sorensen
Shout Magazine
01382 223131
www.dcthomson.co.uk
Fortnightly. Editor: Ria Welch
Simpsons Comic
020 7620 0200
www.titanmagazines.com
Monthly. Editor: Paul Terry
Sindy
01892 500100
www.paninicomics.co.uk
13pa. Editor: Jan Comley
Sneak
020 7312 8932
www.sneakmagazine.com
Weekly. Editor: Michelle Garnett
Spectacular Spiderman
01892 500100
www.paninicomics.co.uk
17pa. Editor: Tom O'Malley
Sugar
020 7150 7000
www.sugarmagazine.co.uk
Monthly. Editor: Nick Chalmers
Young Scot
0131 313 2488
www.youngscot.org
Monthly. Editor: Fiona McIntyre

Computing

.net
01225 442244
www.netmag.co.uk
13pa. Editor: Paul Douglas
Computer & Video Games
020 7907 6000
www.dennis.co.uk
Monthly. Editor: Alex Simmons
Computer Arts
01225 442244
www.computerarts.co.uk
13pa. Editor: Gillian Carson
Computer Buyer
020 7907 6000
www.computerbuyer.co.uk
Monthly. Editor: James Nixon
Computer Music
01225 442244
www.computermusic.co.uk
13pa. Editor: Ronan MacDonald
Computer Shopper
020 7907 6000
www.computershopper.co.uk
Monthly. Editor: Paul Sanders
Computeractive
01858 438881
www.computeractive.co.uk
Fortnightly. Editor: Dylan Armbrust

Computing Which?
0845 301 8000
www.computingwhich.co.uk
Bi-monthly. Editor: Jessica Ross
Cube
01202 299900
www.totalgames.net
13pa. Editor: Miles Guttery
Digital Creative Arts
01202 299900
www.paragon.co.uk
9pa. Editor: Paul Newman
Edge
01225 442244
www.edge-online.co.uk
13pa. Editor: Tony Mott
Games Domain
0121 326 0900
www.gamesdomain.com
Website, updated daily
Games TM
01202 299900
www.totalgames.net
13pa. Editor: Simon Philips
GamesMaster
01225 442244
www.futurenet.com/gamesmaster
13pa. Editor: Robin Alway
iCreate
01202 299900
www.paragon.co.uk
9pa. Editor: Paul Newman
Internet and Broadband Advisor
01225 442244
www.netadvisor.co.uk
13pa. Editor: Graham Barlow
Internet User
01202 299900
www.paragon.co.uk
13pa. Editor: Dominic Brookman
Internet World
020 8232 1600
www.internetworld.co.uk
Monthly. Editor: Janine Milne
It's On The Net
01689 887200
www.iotn.co.uk
4pa. Editor: Annette Connor
Login Magazine
01702 582895
Monthly. Editor: Rick Haynes
MacFormat
01225 442244
www.macformat.co.uk
13pa. Editor: Rachel Spooner
MacUser
020 7907 6000
www.macuser.co.uk
Fortnightly. Editor: Nick Rawlinson
Macworld
020 7831 9252
www.macworld.co.uk
13pa. Editor: David Fanning

Max
01225 442244
www.futurenet.com/macmagazine
13pa. Editor: Adam Waring
Micro Mart
0121 233 8712
www.micromart.co.uk
Weekly. Editor: Simon Brew
Official Playstation 2 Magazine
01225 442244
www.playstation.co.uk
13pa. Editor: Richard Keith
Official Xbox Magazine
020 7317 2471
www.officialxboxmagazine.co.uk
Monthly
P2
01202 299900
www.totalgames.net
13pa. Editor: Roy Kimber
PC Advisor
020 7291 5939
www.pcadvisor.co.uk
Monthly. Editor: Guy Dixon
PC Answers
01225 442244
www.pcanswers.co.uk
13pa. Editor: Simon Pickstock
PC Basics
01202 299900
www.paragon.co.uk
13pa. Editor: Geoff Spick
PC Essentials
01202 299900
www.paragon.co.uk
9pa. Editor: Geoff Spick
PC Format
01225 442244
www.pcformat.co.uk
13pa. Editor: Adam Oxford
PC Gamer
01225 442244
www.pcgamer.co.uk
13pa. Editor: Mark Donald
PC Home
01202 299900
www.paragon.co.uk
13pa. Editor: Paul Lester
PC Plus
01225 442244
www.pcplus.co.uk
13pa. Editor: Ian Robson
PC Pro
020 7907 6000
www.pcpro.co.uk
Monthly. Editor: Tim Danton
PC Utilities
01625 855086
www.pc-utilities.co.uk
13pa. Editor: Gavin Burrell
PC Zone
020 7907 6000
www.pczone.co.uk
Monthly. Editor: David Woods

PDA Essentials
01202 299900
www.paragon.co.uk
9pa. Editor: David Harfield
Personal Computer World
01858 438881
www.pcw.co.uk
Monthly. Editor: Rob Jones
Play
01202 299900
www.totalgames.net
13pa. Editor: Nick Jones
Pokemon World
01202 299900
www.paragon.co.uk
10pa. Editor: Charlotte Martyn
Powerstation
01202 299900
www.totalgames.net
13pa. Editor: Mike O'Sullivan
Practical Web Projects
01202 299900
www.paragon.co.uk
10pa. Editor: James Thornton
PSM2
01225 442244
www.futurenet.com/psm2
13pa. Editor: Daniel Griffith
Solutions
01202 299900
www.totalgames.net
13pa. Editor: Phil King
Web Designer
01202 299900
www.paragon.co.uk
13pa. Editor: Thomas Watson
Web Pages Made Easy
01202 299900
www.paragon.co.uk
9pa. Editor: Rob Clymo
WebUser
020 7261 7376
www.web-user.co.uk/
Fortnightly. Editor: Richard Clark
What Laptop & Handheld PC
020 8334 1600
www.whatlaptop.co.uk
Monthly. Editor: Michael Browne
Windows XP Made Easy
01202 299900
www.paragon.co.uk
13pa. Editor: Stuart Tarrant
Windows XP: The Official Magazine
01225 442244
www.windowsxpmagazine.co.uk
13pa. Editor: David Bradley
XBM
01202 299900
www.totalgames.net
13pa. Editor: Ian Dean

XP First Aid
01202 299900
www.paragon.co.uk
4pa. Editor: Geoff Spick

Current affairs

AFF Families Journal
01980 615517
www.aff.org.uk
4pa. Editor: Sue Bonney
The American
01297 561147
www.the-american.co.uk
Monthly. Editor: Catherine Russell
Big Issue
020 7526 3200
www.bigissue.com
Weekly. Editor: Matt Ford
Big Issue in Scotland
0141 418 7000
www.bigissuescotland.com
Weekly. Editor: Claire Black
Big Issue in the North
0161 834 6300
www.bigissueinthenorth.com
Weekly. Editor: Ato Erzan
Challenge Newsline
0800 195 7969
Monthly. Editor: Debbie Bunn
Connect Magazine (Greenpeace)
020 7865 8100
www.greenpeace.org.uk
4pa. Editor: Stokeley Webster
EarthMatters (Friends of the Earth)
020 7490 1555
www.foe.co.uk
3pa. Editor: Adam Bradbury/ Nicola Baird
Ecologist
020 7351 3578
www.theecologist.org
10pa. Editor: Zac Goldsmith
Economist
020 7830 7000
www.economist.com
Weekly. Editor: Bill Emmott
Glasgow Magazine
0141 287 0901
Bi-monthly. Editor: Jim Clark
Granta
020 7704 9776
www.granta.com
4pa. Editor: Ian Jack
Green Futures
020 7324 3660
www.greenfutures.org.uk
Bi-monthly. Editor: Martin Wright

The House Magazine
020 7878 1520
www.epolitix.com
Weekly. Editor: Sir Patrick Cormack
Impact International
020 7263 1417
Monthly. Editor: Ahmad Irfan
Index on Censorship
020 7278 2313
www.indexoncensorship.org
4pa. Editor: Judith Bidal-Hall
Liberty
020 7403 3888
www.liberty-human-rights.org.uk
4pa. Editor: Lincoln E Steed
Middle East Expatriate
020 8943 3630
www.middleeastexpatonline.com
10pa. Editor: Babu Kalyanpur
New African
020 7713 7711
www.africasia.com
Monthly. Editor: Baffour Ankomah
New Internationalist
01865 728181
www.newint.org
Monthly. Editor: Adam Ma'anit
New Statesman
020 7730 3444
www.newstatesman.com
Weekly. Editor: Peter Wilby
News Africa
020 7713 8135
www.newsafrica.net
Monthly. Editor: Moffat Ekoriko
Newsweek
020 7851 9799
www.newsweek.com
Weekly. Editor: Fareed Zakaria
Nexus
01342 322854
www.nexus.com
Bi-monthly. Editor: Duncan Roads
Outrage – magazine of Animal Aid
01732 364546
www.animalaid.co.uk
4pa. Editor: Mark Gold
Party Politics
020 7324 8500
www.sagepub.co.uk
6pa. Editor: Lucy Robinson
Private Eye
020 7437 4017
www.private-eye.co.uk
Fortnightly. Editor: Ian Hislop
Prospect
020 7255 1281
www.prospect-magazine.co.uk
Monthly. Editor: David Goodhart
Red Pepper
020 7281 7024
www.redpepper.org.uk
Monthly. Editor: Hilary Wainwright

Report
020 7930 6441
www.askatl.org.uk
10pa. Editor: Heather Pinnell
SchNews
01273 685913
www.schnewsatbrighton.co.uk
Weekly. Editor: Jo Makepeace
Socialism Today
020 8988 8782
www.socialistparty.org.uk
Monthly. Editor: Lynn Walsh
The Socialist
020 8988 8782
www.socialistparty.org.uk
Weekly. Editor: Ken Smith
Socialist Review
020 7538 3308
www.socialistreview.org.uk
11pa. Editor: Peter Morgan
Socialist Worker
020 7538 0828
www.socialistworker.co.uk
Weekly. Editor: Chris Harman
Spectator
020 7405 1706
www.spectator.co.uk
Weekly. Editor: Boris Johnson
The Sticks Magazine
01462 486810
www.the-sticks.com
Monthly. Editor: John Boston
Time
020 7499 4080
www.time.com
Weekly. Editor: Eric Pooley
Tribune
020 7433 6410
www.tribuneweb.co.uk
Weekly. Editor: Mark Seddon
The Week
020 7907 6000
www.theweek.co.uk
Weekly. Editor: Jeremy O'Grady
The World Today
020 7957 5712
www.theworldtoday.org
Monthly. Editor: Graham Walker
WWF News
01483 426444
www.wwf.org.uk
Quarterly. Editor: Guy Jowett

Arts & entertainment

All About Soap
020 7150 7000
www.allaboutsoap.co.uk
Fortnightly. Editor: Lorna Cowan
Amateur Photographer
020 7261 5100
www.amateurphotographer.com
Weekly. Editor: Garry Coward-Williams
AN Magazine
0191 241 8000
www.a-n.co.uk
Monthly. Editor: Gillian Nicol
The Art Book
01323 811759
4pa. Editor: Sue Ward
The Art Newspaper
020 7735 3331
www.theartnewspaper.com
Monthly. Editor: Cristina Ruiz
Art Quarterly
020 7225 4818
www.artfund.org
4pa. Editor: Caroline Bugler
Art Review
020 7246 3350
www.art-review.com
Monthly. Editor: Rebecca Wilson
The Artist
01580 763315
www.theartistmagazine.co.uk
Monthly. Editor: Sally Bulgin
Artists & Illustrators
020 7700 8500
www.aimag.co.uk
Monthly. Editor: James Hobbs
Arts East
01284 701190
www.acornmagazines.co.uk
Monthly. Editor: Unity Norwak
BBC Music Magazine
020 8433 3283
www.bbcmagazines.com/music
Monthly. Editor: Harriet Smith
The Big Cheese
020 7607 0303
www.bigcheesemagazine.com
Monthly. Editor: Eugene Butcher
Billboard
020 7420 6000
www.billboard.com
Weekly. Editor: Emmanuel Legrand
Blues & Soul
020 7402 6869
www.bluesandsoul.com
Fortnightly. Editor: Bob Killbourn
The Brighton Source
01273 561617
Monthly. Editor: Marcus O'Dair

Buzz Magazine
029 2025 6883
Monthly. Editor: Emma Clark
Camcorder User
020 7331 1000
www.camuser.co.uk
13pa. Editor: Robert Hull
Cineworld
01225 737300
Bi-monthly. Editor: Sally Thomson
Classic FM – The Magazine
020 8267 5000
www.haymarketpublishing.co.uk
Monthly. Editor: Emma Baker
Classic Rock
020 7317 2654
www.classicrockmagazine.com
13pa. Editor: Mick Wall
Classical Music
020 7333 1742
www.rhinegold.co.uk
Fortnightly. Editor: Keith Clarke
Country Music People
020 8854 7217
www.countrymusicpeople.com
Monthly. Editor: Craig Baguley
Country Music Round-up
01472 821707
www.cmru.co.uk
Monthly. Editor: John Emptage
The Crack
0191 2303038
www.thecrackmagazine.com
Monthly. Editor: Robert Meddes
Cult Times
020 8875 1520
www.visimag.com
Monthly. Editor: Paul Spragg
Dance Europe
020 8985 7767
www.danceeurope.net
Monthly. Editor: Emma Manning
Dance Gazette
020 7326 8000
www.rad.org.uk
3pa. Editor: Olivia Swift
Desi
020 8571 7700
www.snooplife.com
Monthly. Editor: Raj Kaushal
Digital Camera Buyer
01202 299900
www.paragon.co.uk
13pa. Editor: James Broomfield
Digital Camera Magazine
01225 442244
www.dcmag.co.uk
13pa. Editor: Adam Evans
Digital Music Maker
01202 299900
www.paragon.co.uk
Monthly. Editor: Karl Foster

Digital Photo
01733 282748
www.greatmagazines.co.uk
Monthly. Editor: Jon Adams

Digital Photographer
01202 299900
www.paragon.co.uk
13pa. Editor: Michael Roscoe

Digital Photography Made Easy
01202 299900
Monthly. Editor: Jo Cole

Digital Video Made Easy
01202 299900
www.paragon.co.uk
13pa. Editor: Mark Hattersley

DJ
020 7331 1000
www.djmag.com
Fortnightly. Editor: David Eserin

DMC Update
020 7262 6777
www.dmcworld.com/update
Weekly. Editor: Nick Darby

DVD Monthly
01392 434477
www.predatorpublishing.co.uk
Monthly. Editor: Tim Isaac

DVD Review
01202 299900
www.dvdreview.net
13pa. Editor: Paul Morgan

DVD World
020 7331 1000
www.highburywv.com
13pa. Editor: Richard Marshall

Early Music Today
020 7333 1744
www.rhinegold.co.uk
Bi-monthly. Editor: Lucien Jenkins

Edge
01225 442244
www.edge-online.co.uk
13pa. Editor: Tony Mott

Empire
020 7182 8000
www.empireonline.co.uk
Monthly. Editor: Colin Kennedy

Entertainer
01302 819555
www.doncastertoday.co.uk
Weekly. Editor: Martin Edmonds

EP Magazine
0118 958 1878
10pa. Editor: Jon Ewing

Essential Hi-fi and Home Cinema
020 7331 1000
www.highburywv.com
13pa. Editor: Adrian Justins

Film Review
020 8875 1520
www.visimag.com
Monthly. Editor: David Richardson

First on Video
020 7608 6789
www.firstonvideo.co.uk
Monthly. Editor: Sharon Lacey

The Fly
020 7691 4555
Monthly. Editor: Will Kinsman

Freetime
01252 621513
www.freetimemag.co.uk
4pa. Editor: Vic Robbie

fRoots
020 8340 9651
www.frootsmag.com
Monthly. Editor: Ian Anderson

Future Music
01225 442244
www.futuremusic.co.uk
13pa. Editor: Andy Jones

Gramophone
020 8267 5000
www.gramophone.co.uk
Monthly. Editor: James Jolly

Granta
020 7704 9776
www.granta.com
4pa. Editor: Ian Jack

Guitar Buyer
01954 252983
Monthly. Editor: Mick Taylor

Guitar Techniques
01225 442244
www.futurenet.com/
guitartechniques
13pa. Editor: Cliff Douse

Guitarist
01225 442244
www.guitarist.co.uk
13pa. Editor: Michael Leonard

Hi-Fi Choice
020 7317 2495
www.hifichoice.co.uk
13pa. Editor: Tim Bowern

Hi-Fi News
020 8774 0850
www.hifinews.com
Monthly. Editor: Steve Harris

Hi-Fi World
01275 371386
www.hi-fiworld.co.uk
Monthly. Editor: David Price

Hip Hop Connection
01223 210536
www.hiphop.co.uk
Monthly. Editor: Andy Cowan

Hollywood Reporter
020 7420 6000
www.hollywoodreporter.com
Weekly. Editor: Stuart Kemp

Home Cinema Choice
020 7331 1000
www.homecinemachoice.com
Monthly. Editor: Steve May

Hotdog
01202 299900
www.paragon.co.uk
13pa. Editor: Andy McDermott

Impact
01484 435011
www.martialartsltd.co.uk
Monthly. Editor: John Mosby

Inside Soap
020 7150 7000
www.insidesoap.co.uk
Weekly. Editor: Steven Murphy

It's Hot
020 8433 1432
www.bbcmagazines.com/hot
Monthly. Editor: Peter Hart

Jazz at Ronnie Scott's
020 7485 9803
www.ronniescotts.co.uk
Bi-monthly. Editor: God Bolt

Jazz Guide
01908 312392
Monthly. Editor: Bernie Tyrrell

Jazz UK
029 2066 5161
www.jazzservices.org.uk
Bi-monthly. Editor: John Fordham

Kerrang!
020 7436 1515
www.kerrang.com
Weekly. Editor: Ashley Bird

Knowledge
020 8533 9300
www.knowledgemag.co.uk
10pa. Editor: Colin Steven

Leisure Gazette
01782 860800
Monthly. Editor: Terry Winter

Leisure Painter
01580 763315
www.leisurepainter.co.uk
Monthly. Editor: Ingrid Lyon

The List
0131 550 3050
www.list.co.uk
Fortnightly; extra festival issues in August. Editor: Nick Barley

London Review of Books
020 7209 1101
www.lrb.co.uk
Fortnightly. Editor: Mary-Kay Wilmers

London Theatre Guide
020 7557 6700
www.officiallondontheatre.co.uk
Fortnightly. Editor: Richard Embra

M8
0141 840 5980
www.m8magazine.com
Monthly. Editor: Kevin McFarlane

Magpie
0870 071 1611
www.magpiedirect.com
Bi-monthly. Editor: Mark Rye

Metal Hammer
020 7317 2691
www.metalhammer.co.uk
13pa. Editor: Alex Burrows
Mixmag
020 7182 8000
www.mixmag.net
Monthly. Editor: Viv Craske
Mojo
020 7312 8716
www.mojo4music.com
Monthly. Editor: Phil Alexander
Movie Mag International
020 8574 2222
www.movie-mag.net
Monthly. Editor: Bharathi Pradhan
Musician
020 7840 5531
www.musiciansunion.org.uk
Quarterly. Editor: Keith Ames
National Gallery Season Guide
020 7747 2836
www.nationalgallery.org.uk
3pa. Editor: Andrea Easey
Night & Day – The Essential Visitor Guide
0121 212 4141
www.icbirmingham.co.uk
Yearly. Editor: Stacey Barnfield
NME
020 7261 5564
www.nme.com/
Weekly. Editor: Conor McNicholas
NW
020 7792 2626
www.hhc.co.uk
Monthly. Editor: Cathy Levy
Official Elvis Presley Fan Club Magazine
0116 253 7271
www.elvisweb.co.uk
Bi-monthly. Editor: Todd Slaughter
Opera
020 8563 8893
www.opera.co.uk
Monthly. Editor: John Allison
Opera Now
020 7333 1740
www.rhinegold.co.uk
6pa. Editor: Ashutosh Khandekar
Piano
020 7333 1724
www.rhinegold.co.uk
Bi-monthly. Editor: Jeremy Siepmann
Practical Photography
01733 282736
www.greatmagazines.co.uk
Monthly. Editor: Andrew James
Q
020 7312 8182
www.q4music.com
Monthly. Editor: Paul Rees

RA Magazine
020 7300 5820
www.ramagazine.org.uk
4pa. Editor: Sarah Greenberg
Radio Times
020 8433 2235
www.radiotimes.com
Weekly. Editor: Gill Hudson
Record Buyer
01522 511265
Monthly. Editor: Paul Rigby
Rock Sound
020 7278 5559
www.rock-sound.net
Monthly. Editor: Darren Taylor
Rolling Stone
001 212 484 1616
www.rollingstone.com
26pa. Editor: Jann S Wenner
Satellite and Digital Choice
020 7331 1000
www.bettersat.com
8pa. Editor: Grant Rennell
Satellite TV Monthly
020 7226 2222
www.satellitetvtoday.com
Monthly. Editor: Paul Hirons
Screen International
020 7505 8080
www.screendaily.com
Weekly. Editor: Tim McLoughlin
SFX
01225 442244
www.sfx.co.uk
13pa. Editor: Dave Golder
Shivers
020 8875 1520
www.visimag.com
Monthly. Editor: David Miller
Sight & Sound
020 7255 1444
www.bfi.org.uk/sightandsound
Monthly. Editor: Nick James
Sky Customer Magazine
020 7565 3000
www.jbcp.co.uk
Monthly. Editor: Liz Murphy
Smash Hits
020 7436 1515
www.smashhits.com
Fortnightly. Editor: Lisa Smosarski
Soaplife
020 7261 7568
www.soaplife.co.uk/
Fortnightly. Editor: Hellen Gardner
Songlines
01753 865342
www.songlines.co.uk
Bi-monthly. Editor: Simon Broughton
Sound on Sound
01954 789888
www.soundonsound.com
Monthly. Editor: Ian Gilby

The Stage
020 7403 1818
www.thestage.co.uk
Weekly. Editor: Brian Attwood
Starburst
020 8875 1520
www.visimag.com
Monthly. Editor: Stephen Payne
Stardust International
020 8795 5318
www.stardustindia.com
Monthly. Editor: Ashwin Warde
The Strad
020 7203 6731
www.thestrad.com
Monthly. Editor: Naomi Sadler
Straight No Chaser
020 8533 9999
www.straightnochaser.co.uk
Bi-monthly. Editor: Paul Bradshaw
Theatregoer
020 7684 7111
www.theatregoer.net
Monthly. Editor: Deirdre Vine
This is London Magazine
020 7434 1281
www.thisislondon.com
Weekly. Editor: Julie Jones
Time Out
020 7813 3000
www.timeout.com
Weekly. Editor: Laura Lee Davies
Time Out Student Guide
020 7813 3000
www.timeout.com
Annually. Editor: Sharon Lougher
Times Literary Supplement
020 7782 3000
www.the-tls.co.uk
Weekly. Editor: Peter Stothard
Top of the Pops Magazine
020 8433 3701
www.bbcmagazines.com/totp
Monthly. Editor: Corinna Shaffer
Total DVD
020 7331 1000
www.totaldvd.net
13pa. Editor: Chris Jenkins
Total Film
020 7317 2449
www.totalfilm.co.uk
13pa. Editor: Matt Mueller
Total Guitar
01225 442244
www.totalguitar.co.uk
13pa. Editor: Scott Rowley
TV & Satellite Week
020 7261 7534
www.tvandsatelliteweek.com/
Weekly. Editor: Jonathan Bowman
TV Choice
020 7241 8000
www.bauer.co.uk
Weekly. Editor: Lori Miles

TV Hits!
020 7150 7000
www.tvhits.co.uk
Monthly. Editor: Helen Lamont
TV Quick
020 7241 8000
www.bauer.co.uk
Weekly. Editor: Lori Miles
TV Times
020 7261 7740
Weekly. Editor: Mike Hollingsworth
TV Zone
020 8875 1520
www.visimag.com
Monthly. Editor: Jan Vincent-Rudzki
Twenty 4-seven
01752 294130
www.twenty4-seven.co.uk
Monthly. Editor: Lucy Griffiths
Ultimate DVD
020 8875 1520
www.visimag.com
Monthly. Editor: David Richardson
Uncut
020 7261 6992
www.uncut.net
Monthly. Editor: Allan Jones
Unlimited
0117 927 9009
www.originpublishing.co.uk
Monthly. Editor: Pat Reed
Unreel
01225 737300
www.unreelmovies.co.uk
Bi-monthly. Editor: Sally Thomson
V&A Magazine
020 7942 2505
4pa. Editor: Charlotte Mullins
Variety
020 7611 4580
www.variety.com
Daily and weekly. Editor: Steven Gaydos
What Camcorder
020 7331 1000
www.whatcamcorder.net
Monthly. Editor: Jake Williams
What Camera?
020 7261 5266
4pa. Editor: Joel Lacey
What Digital Camcorder
020 7331 1000
www.whatcamcorder.net
13pa. Editor: Ali Upham
What Digital Camera
020 7261 7284
www.whatdigitalcamera.com/
Monthly. Editor: Nigel Atherton
What Guitar?
01225 442244
www.whatguitar.co.uk
13pa. Editor: Stephen Lawson

What Hi-Fi? Sound and Vision
020 8267 5000
www.whathifi.com
Monthly, plus awards issue
Editor: Clare Newsome
What Home Cinema
020 7331 1000
www.whathomecinemamag.com
Monthly. Editor: Rob Lane
What Satellite and Digital TV
020 7331 1000
www.wotsat.com
Monthly. Editor: Alex Lane
What Satellite TV
020 7331 1000
www.wotsat.com
Monthly. Editor: Grant Rennell
What Video and Widescreen TV
020 7331 1000
www.whatvideomag.com
Monthly. Editor: Danny Phillips
What's on in London
020 7278 4393
www.whatsoninlondon.co.uk
Weekly. Editor: Michael Darvell
What's on TV
020 7261 7535
Weekly. Editor: Colin Tough
Where London
020 7242 5222
Monthly. Editor: Mary-Anne Evans
The Wire
020 7422 5010
www.thewire.co.uk
Monthly. Editor: Chris Bohn
Word
020 7520 8625
www.wordmagazine.co.uk
Monthly. Editor: Mark Ellen
Writers' News
0113 200 2929
www.writersnews.co.uk
Monthly. Editor: Derek Hudson
The X Files
020 7620 0200
Monthly. Editor: Martin Eden
X-pose
020 8875 1520
www.visimag.com
Bi-monthly. Editor: Anthony Brown
The Zone
mail@zone-sf.com
www.zone-sf.com
Website. Editor: Tony Lee

Food & drink

BBC Good Food
020 8433 3781
www.bbcmagazines.com/
goodfood
Monthly. Editor: Gillian Carter

Decanter
020 7261 3929
www.decanter.com/
Monthly. Editor: Amy Wislocki
Food & Travel
020 8332 9090
www.fox-publishing.com
Monthly. Editor: Nicky Symington
Food Chain
01603 274130
www.foodchain-magazine.com
Bi-monthly. Editor: Libbie Hammond
Foodie Magazine
01202 535666
www.foodiemag.com
Monthly. Editor: Karleh Light
Italian Wines & Spirits
020 8458 4860
www.iwines.it
Website updated monthly
Editor: Bruno Roncarati
M&S Magazine
020 7747 0871
www.redwoodgroup.net
4pa. Editor: Diane Kenwood
Sainsbury's Magazine
020 7633 0266
www.sainsburysmagazine.co.uk
Monthly. Editor: Sue Robinson
Somerfield Magazine
0117 989 7800
www.somerfield.co.uk
13pa. Editor: Hannah Smith
The Vegetarian
0161 925 2000
www.vegsoc.org
4pa. Editor: Jane Bowler
Waitrose Food Illustrated
020 7565 3000
www.jbcp.co.uk
Monthly. Editor: William Sitwell
What's Brewing
01727 867201
www.camra.org.uk
Monthly. Editor: Ted Bruning
Whisky Magazine
01603 633808
www.whiskymag.com
8pa. Editor: Dominic Roskrow
Wine
020 7549 2567
www.wineint.com
Monthly. Editor: Catharine Lowe

Gay and lesbian

▶▶ see **Diversity**, page 187

General interest

American in Britain
020 8661 0186
www.americaninbritain.com
4pa. Editor: Helen Elliott
Another Magazine
020 7336 0766
www.anothermag.com
2pa. Editor: Jefferson Hack
Asian Image
01254 298263
www.asianimage.co.uk
Monthly. Editor: Shuiab Khan
Astronomy Now
01903 266165
www.astronomynow.com
Monthly. Editor: Steven Young
BBC History Magazine
020 8433 3289
www.bbchistorymagazine.com
Monthly. Editor: Greg Neale
Choice
01733 555123
Monthly. Editor: Norman Wright
Contemporary
020 7740 1704
www.contemporary-
magazine.com
Monthly. Editor: Roger Tatley
Der Spiegel
020 8605 3893
www.spiegel.de
Weekly. Editor: Matthias Matussek
DV8
01202 388388
www.dv8online.co.uk
Monthly. Editor: Nina Tsang
Epicurean Life
020 7376 5959
www.epicureanlife.co.uk
4pa. Editor: Azzy Asghar
Expression
01392 263052
www.exeter.ac.uk/alumni
2pa. Editor: Karen Lippoldt
Focus Magazine
0117 927 9009
www.originpublishing.co.uk
Monthly. Editor: Paul Parsons
Folio
0117 942 8491
Monthly. Editor: Rebecca Dean
Forward
0118 983 8243
www.guidedogs.org.uk
4pa. Editor: Tracey Gurr
Freemasonry Today
01284 754155
www.freemasonrytoday.co.uk
4pa. Editor: Michael Baigent

Fresh Direction
020 7424 0400
www.freshdirection.co.uk
3pa. Editor: Paul Russell
The Green
020 7792 2626
www.hhc.co.uk/thegreen
Monthly. Editor: Hugh Fasken
Guide Magazine
020 7792 2626
www.hhc.co.uk
Monthly. Editor: Ed Ewing
H&E Naturist
01405 769712
www.henaturist.co.uk
Monthly. Editor: Mark Nisbet
Harrods
020 7152 3842
2pa. Editor: Darius Sanai
Harvey Nichols Magazine
020 7747 0700
www.redwoodgroup.net
4pa. Editor: Deborah Bee
The Hill
020 7792 2626
www.hhc.co.uk/thehill
Monthly. Editor: Jane Turney
History Today
020 7534 8000
www.historytoday.com
Monthly. Editor: Peter Furtado
Hot Press
00 353 1 241 1500
www.hotpress.com
Fortnightly. Editor: Niall Stokes
Hotline (Virgin Trains)
020 7306 0304
www.riverltd.co.uk
Quarterly. Editor: Rod Stanley
i-D
020 7490 9710
www.i-dmagazine.com
Monthly. Editor: Avril Mair
Illustrated London News
020 7805 5555
www.ilng.co.uk
Bi-annual. Editor: Alison Booth
The Insight
01273 245956
www.theinsight.co.uk
Monthly. Editor: Nic Compton
Kindred Spirit
01803 866686
www.kindredspirit.co.uk
6pa. Editor: Richard Beaumont
The Lifeboat
01202 663188
www.rnli.org.uk
4pa. Editor: Liz Cook
Limited Edition
01689 885661
www.thisislimitededition.co.uk
Monthly. Editor: Andrew Parkes

Living South
020 7223 0022
www.hhc.co.uk/livingsouth
Monthly. Editor: Pendle Harte
**Magnet – The Village
Communicator**
01825 732796
www.magnetpublications.com
Monthly. Editor: Mary Hillyar
Majesty
020 7436 4006
www.majestymagazine.com
Monthly. Editor: Joe Little
Mayfair and St James's Life
020 7344 9121
www.mayfairlife.co.uk
Monthly. Editor: Stephen Goringe
New Humanist
020 7436 1151
www.newhumanist.org.uk
Bi-monthly. Editor: Frank Jordans
North Magazine
020 7250 0750
Monthly. Editor: Mark Kebble
O Magazine
020 7565 3000
www.jbcp.co.uk
Monthly. Editor: Dan Linstead
Occasions
020 7650 2000
www.occasions-mag.com
4pa. Editor: Raza Sharma
The Oldie
020 7436 8801
www.theoldie.co.uk
Monthly. Editor: Richard Ingrams
Password
020 7261 9878
Bi-monthly. Editor: Alistair Gordon
Perth Life
01738 567700
Monthly. Editor: Steven Lavery
Platform
0115 848 1510
www.su.ntu.ac.uk/platform
Fortnightly. Editor: Loay El Hady
Quicksilver Magazine
020 7747 9390
www.quicksilvermagazine.co.uk
Bi-monthly. Editor: Alex Johnson
Reader's Digest
020 7715 8000
www.readersdigest.co.uk
Monthly. Editor: Katherine Walker
Reform
020 7916 8630
www.urc.org.uk
11pa. Editor: David Lawrence
The Resident
020 7384 9124
www.theresident.co.uk
Monthly. Editor: Amanda Constance

Ritz Magazine
020 7269 7416
www.electricink.net
2pa. Editor: Giles Morgan
Royalty
020 8201 9978
www.royalty-magazine.com
Monthly. Editor: M Houston
Saga Magazine
01303 771523
www.saga.co.uk
Monthly. Editor: Emma Soames
Salvationist
020 7367 4897
www.salvationarmy.org.uk/
salvationist
Weekly. Editor: Dean Pallant
Scots Magazine
01382 223131
www.scotsmagazine.com
Monthly. Editor: John Methven
Select
01484 437737
www.ichuddersfield.co.uk
Bi-monthly. Editor: Julian Pratt
Sixer
0114 267 9686
www.northernlifestyle.com
Monthly. Editor: Chris Wilson
Snoop Magazine
020 8571 7700
www.snooplife.com
Monthly. Editor: Raj Kaushal
The Spark
0117 914 3434
www.thespark.co.uk
4pa. Editor: John Dawson
Tank
020 7434 0110
www.tankmagazine.com
Quarterly. Editor: Masoud Golsorkhi
Toni & Guy
020 7462 7777
www.publicis-blueprint.co.uk
4pa. Editor: Scarlett Brady
Town & Country News
01692 582287
Monthly. Editor: Laurence Watts
Trafford Magazine
020 7387 9888
www.babersmith.co.uk
2pa. Editor: Debbie Hyams
The Visitor
01963 351256
Monthly. Editor: Helen Dunion
Vivid
020 7307 8620
www.vivid-magazine.com
*Quarterly. Editor: Anna
Westermann*
Vivid Magazine
020 7307 8620
*Quarterly. Editor: Anna
Westermann*

Wavelength
01637 878629
Monthly. Editor: Steve Bough
Weekly News
01382 223131
www.dcthomson.co.uk
Weekly. Editor: Dave Burness
Which?
0845 307 4000
www.which.co.uk
Monthly. Editor: Malcolm Coles
**The World of Yachts & Boats
(pan-Arab)**
020 7625 8030
www.worldofyachts.com
Bi-monthly. Editor: Nabil Farhat
You Can! Magazine
01242 544873
3pa. Editor: Anthony McClaran
Your Family Tree
01225 442244
www.yourfamilytreemag.co.uk
13pa. Editor: Garrick Webster
Yours
01733 264666
www.emap.com
Monthly. Editor: Valerie McConnell

Home and garden

25 Beautiful Homes
020 7261 5718
www.25beautifulhomes.co.uk
Monthly. Editor: Rhoda Parry
Amateur Gardening
01202 440840
Weekly. Editor: Tim Rumball
BBC Gardeners' World
020 8433 3593
www.gardenersworld.com
Monthly. Editor: Adam Pasco
BBC Good Homes
020 8433 2337
www.bbcmagazines.com/
goodhomes
Monthly. Editor: Lisa Allen
BBC Homes & Antiques
020 8433 3483
www.bbcmagazines.com
/homesandantiques
Monthly. Editor: Mary Carroll
Country Homes & Interiors
020 7261 6451
www.countryhomesandinteriors.
co.uk
Monthly. Editor: Deborah Barker
Country House & Home
01689 887200
Monthly. Editor: Jennifer Morgan
Country Living
020 7439 5000
www.countryliving.co.uk/
Monthly. Editor: Susy Smith

Country Market
01273 837703
www.country-mkt.co.uk
Monthly. Editor: David Somerville
Elle Decoration
020 7150 7000
www.hf-uk.com
*Monthly. Editor: Michelle
Ogunadehin*
The English Garden
020 7751 4800
www.theenglishgarden.co.uk
Monthly. Editor: Janine Wookey
The English Home
020 7751 4800
www.theenglishhome.co.uk
*Monthly.
Editor: Charlotte Coward-Williams*
**The Essential Kitchen,
Bathroom & Bedroom Magazine**
01206 851117
www.essentialpublishing.co.uk
Monthly. Editor: Gail Major
Essential Water Garden
01206 505900
www.essentialwatergarden.co.uk
10pa. Editor: Georgina Wroe
Fabric
020 7747 0700
www.redwoodgroup.net
Monthly. Editor: Steven Short
The Garden
01733 775775
www.rhs.org.uk
Monthly. Editor: Ian Hodgson
Garden Answers
01733 282683
www.greatmagazines.co.uk
Monthly. Editor: Nicola Dela-Croix
Garden News
01733 282680
www.greatmagazines.co.uk
Weekly. Editor: Sarah Page
The Gardeners' Atlas
01603 633808
www.gardenersatlas.co.uk
Website. Editor: Matthew Page
Gardening Which?
0845 903 7000
www.which.co.uk/gardeningwhich
10pa. Editor: Julia Bolton
Gardens Illustrated
020 8433 1354
www.bbcmagazines.com
/gardensillustrated
10pa. Editor: Clare Foster
Gardens Monthly
01689 887200
Monthly. Editor: Helen Griffin
Good Housekeeping
020 7439 5000
www.goodhousekeeping.co.uk
Monthly. Editor: Lindsay Nicholson

Home
01689 887200
Monthly. Editor: Jocelyn Garside
Home & Country
020 7731 5777
www.womens-institute.co.uk
Monthly. Editor: Susan Seager
Home Building & Renovating
01527 834400
www.homebuilding.co.uk
Monthly. Editor: Michael Holmes
Home DIY
01689 886677
www.highburyleisure.co.uk
Monthly. Editor: John McGowen
Home Efficiency
01753 884216
www.4ecotips.com
Bi-monthly. Editor: Andrew Leech
Home Furnishing News (HFN)
020 7240 0420
www.hfnmag.com
Weekly. Editor: Warren Shoulberg
Home Life Magazine
028 3832 4006
Monthly. Editor: M Kinsella
Home View
01277 366134
www.homeviewpropertymagazine
.com
Bi-monthly. Editor: Garry Clarke
Homebase Magazine
020 7462 7777
www.publicis-blueprint.co.uk
Quarterly. Editor: Ward Hellewell
Homebuilding & Renovating
020 7970 4000
www.centaur.co.uk
Monthly. Editor: Michael Holmes
Homes & Gardens
020 7261 5678
www.homesandgardens.com/
Monthly. Editor: Isobel McKenzie-Price
Homes & Interiors Scotland
0141 331 2221
www.homesandinteriorsscotland.
com
Bi-monthly. Editor: Sandra Colamartino
Homes Overseas
020 7939 8888
www.homesoverseas.co.uk
Monthly. Editor: Mike Hayes
Homes Review
01206 506250
Monthly
HomeStyle
01206 851117
www.essentialpublishing.co.uk
Monthly. Editor: Sally Narraway

House & Garden
020 7499 9080
www.houseandgarden.co.uk
Monthly. Editor: Susan Crewe
House Beautiful
020 7439 5000
www.housebeautiful.co.uk
Monthly. Editor: Kerryn Harper
Housing Association Magazine
0121 682 8881
Bi-monthly. Editor: Bruce Meecham
Ideal Home
020 7261 6474
www.idealhomemagazine.co.uk
Monthly. Editor: Susan Rose
Inside Readers Homes
01689 887200
Monthly. Editor: Karen Bray
Inspirations for your Home
01689 887200
Monthly. Editor: André Frieze
International Homes
01245 358877
www.international-homes.com
9pa. Editor: Jill Keene
International Relocation
01295 255177
www.intrel.co.uk
Yearly. Editor: Martin Coomber
Ireland's Homes Interiors & Living
028 9147 3979
Monthly. Editor: Mike Keenan
KBB – Kitchens, Bedrooms & Bathrooms Magazine
020 8515 2000
www.dmgworldmedia.com
Monthly. Editor: Rosalind Anderson
Key
020 7494 3155
2pa. Editor: Clare Weatherall
Livingetc
020 7261 6603
www.livingetc.com
Monthly. Editor: Suzanne Imre
Perfect Home
01342 828700
www.brooklandsgroup.com
Monthly. Editor: Sarah Giles
Period House
01206 851117
www.essentialpublishing.co.uk
Monthly. Editor: Sarah Wiltshire
Period Ideas
01206 505900
www.periodideas.com
Monthly. Editor: Jeannine McAndrew
Period Living & Traditional Homes
020 7182 8775
Monthly. Editor: Sharon Parsons

Real Homes Magazine
020 7226 2222
www.hhc.co.uk
Monthly. Editor: Karen Williams
Renovations
020 7384 1985
4pa. Editor: Liz Cowley
Rooms, Rooms, Rooms
01206 851117
www.essentialpublishing.co.uk
Monthly. Editor: Sarah Gallaher
Traditional Homes & Interiors
01795 599191
www.cplmedia.co.uk
10pa. Editor: Lisa Perry
What House?
020 7939 9888
www.whathouse.co.uk
Monthly. Editor: Lisa Isaacs
World of Interiors
020 7499 9080
www.worldofinteriors.co.uk
Monthly. Editor: Rupert Thomas
Your New Home
020 8349 1380
www.yournewhome.co.uk
Bi-monthly. Editor: Karen Keeman

Leisure

Absolute Horse
01473 461515
www.ahmagazine.com
Monthly. Editor: Sandy Lee
Adrenalin (International Edition)
020 7345 5066
www.adrenalin.com
4pa. Editor: Mike Fordham
Aeroplane
020 7261 5849
www.aeroplanemonthly.com/
Monthly. Editor: Michael Oakey
Air Enthusiast
01780 755131
www.airenthusiast.com
Bi-monthly. Editor: Ken Ellis
Air Transport World
01628 477775
www.atwonline.com
Monthly. Editor: Perry Flint
Aircraft Illustrated
01932 266600
www.aircraftillustrated.com
Monthly. Editor: Alan Burney
Airliner World
01780 755131
www.airlinerworld.com
Monthly. Editor: Tony Dixon
Allotment & Leisure Gardener
01425 616459
4pa. Editor: David Gibbs

Animal Life
0870 010 1181
www.rspca.org.uk
Quarterly. Editor: Amanda Bailey

Antique Collecting
01394 389950
www.antique-acc.com
Monthly. Editor: Susan Wilson

Antique Dealer & Collectors Guide
020 8691 4820
www.antiquecollectorsguide.co.uk
Bi-monthly. Editor: Philip Bartlam

Argos
01732 848499
www.prodogs.org
2pa. Editor: Mike Findlay

Asda Magazine
020 7462 7777
www.publicis-blueprint.co.uk
Monthly. Editor: Amanda Morgan

At Home in Cardiff Bay
029 2045 0532
4pa. Editor: Andy Meredith

Aviation News
01424 720477
www.aviation-news.co.uk
Monthly. Editor: Barry Wheeler

Aviation Week & Space Technology
020 7409 1482
www.aviationnow.com/
Weekly. Editor: Anthony L Velocci Jr

Award Journal
01753 727470
www.theaward.org
3pa. Editor: Dave Wood

BBC Wildlife Magazine
0117 973 8402
www.bbc.co.uk/nature/animals/
Monthly. Editor: Sophie Stafford

Bird Life
01767 680551
www.rspb.org.uk
Bi-monthly. Editor: Derek Niemann

Bird Watching
01733 465972
www.greatmagazines.co.uk
Monthly. Editor: David Cromack

Birds
01767 680551
www.rspb.org.uk
4pa. Editor: Rob Hume

Birdwatch
020 8881 0550
www.birdwatch.co.uk
Monthly. Editor: Dominic Mitchell

Black Beauty & Hair
020 7720 2108
www.blackbeautyandhair.com
Bi-monthly. Editor: Irene Shelley

BMFA News
0116 244 0028
www.bmfa.org/news
Bi-monthly. Editor: Eric Clark

Boat International
020 8547 2662
www.boatinternational.co.uk/
Monthly. Editor: Amanda McCracken

Boats & Yachts for Sale
01243 533394
www.boats-for-sale.com
Monthly. Editor: Sue Milne

Book & Magazine Collector
0870 732 8080
13pa. Editor: Jonathan Scott

Bridge Magazine
020 7388 2404
www.bridgemagazine.co.uk
Bi-monthly. Editor: Mark Horton

British Birds
01580 882039
www.britishbirds.co.uk
Monthly. Editor: Roger Riddington

British Horse
0870 120 8880
www.bhs.org.uk
Bi-monthly. Editor: David Prince

British Naturism
01604 620361
www.british-naturism.org.uk
4pa. Editor: Tracey Major

Budgerigar World
01678 520262
Monthly. Editor: G Evans

Buy a Boat (for under £20,000)
01243 533394
www.boats-for-sale.com
Monthly. Editor: Sue Milne

Cage & Aviary Birds
020 7261 6201
www.cageandaviarybirds.com
Weekly. Editor: Donald Taylor

Cakes & Sugarcraft
0845 225 5671/2
www.squires-shop.com
4pa. Editor: Beverley Dutton

Camping & Caravanning
024 7669 4995
www.campingandcaravanningclub.co.uk
Monthly. Editor: Nick Harding

Camping Magazine
01778 391000
www.campingmagazine.co.uk
Monthly. Editor: Darren Webb

Canal & Riverboat
01603 708930
www.canalandriverboat.com
Monthly. Editor: Chris Cattrall

Canal Boat & Inland Waterways
0118 977 1677
www.canalboatmagazine.com
Monthly. Editor: Emrhys Barrell

Caravan Club Magazine
01342 336804
www.caravanclub.co.uk
Monthly. Editor: Barry Williams

Caravan Life
01778 391000
www.caravanlife.co.uk
Monthly. Editor: Michael Le Caplain

Caravan Magazine
020 8774 0737
Monthly. Editor: Steve Rowe

The Cat
01403 221936
www.cats.org.uk
Bi-monthly. Editor: Clare Jeater

Cat World
01403 711511
www.catworld.co.uk
Monthly. Editor: Jo Rothery

Chess
020 7388 2404
www.chess.co.uk
Bi-monthly. Editor: Jimmy Adams

Christmas Cakes – A Design Source
0845 225 5671/2
www.squires-shop.com
Yearly. Editor: Beverley Dutton

Church Music Quarterly
01306 872800
www.rscm.com
4pa. Editor: Esther Jones

Club News
020 8469 9700
www.swanpublishing.co.uk
6pa. Editor: David Tickner

Coast
020 7287 0035
www.coastmagazine.co.uk
Monthly. Editor: Jo Denbury

Coin News
01404 46972
www.tokenpublishing.com/
Monthly. Editor: John Mussell

Coin Yearbook
01404 46972
www.tokenpublishing.com/
Yearly. Editor: John Mussell

Collect it!
01206 851117
www.collectit.info
Monthly. Editor: Charlotte Barber

Collections
020 7870 9000
www.bostonhannah.co.uk
3pa. Editor: Charles Ford

Collector
020 8740 7020
www.artefact.co.uk
Bi-monthly. Editor: Paul Hooper

Collectors Gazette
01778 391124
Monthly. Editor: Denise Burrows

Companions Magazine
01952 290999
www.pdsa.org.uk
4pa. Editor: Clare Evans
Continental Modeller
01297 20580
www.peco-uk.com
Monthly. Editor: Andrew Burnham
Country Illustrated
020 7255 3330
www.countryclubuk.com
Monthly. Editor: Julie Spencer
Country Life
020 7261 6969
www.countrylife.co.uk/
Weekly. Editor: Clive Aslet
Country Market
01273 837703
www.country-mkt.co.uk
Monthly. Editor: David Somerville
Country Smallholding
01392 888475
www.countrysmallholding.com
Monthly. Editor: Diane Cowgill
Country Walking
01733 282614
www.greatmagazines.co.uk
Monthly. Editor: Jonathan Manning
The Countryman
01756 701033
www.countrymanmagazine.co.uk
Monthly. Editor: Bill Taylor
The Countryman's Weekly
01822 855281
www.countrymansweekly.co.uk
Weekly. Editor: David Venner
Countryside La Vie
0116 212 2555
www.countryside-lavie.com
Bi-monthly. Editor: Marlene Bowley
Crafts
020 7806 2500
www.craftscouncil.org.uk
Bi-monthly. Editor: Geraldine Rudge
Crafts Beautiful
01206 505900
www.crafts-beautiful.com
Monthly. Editor: Lynn Martin
Crafty Carper
0114 258 0812
www.anglingpublications.com
Monthly. Editor: Simon Crow
Cross Stitch Collection
01225 442244
www.crossstitchcollection.co.uk
13pa. Editor: Debora Bradley
Cross Stitch Gallery
01227 750215
Bi-monthly. Editor: Mary Hickmott
Cross Stitcher
01225 442244
www.cross-
stitchermagazine.co.uk
13pa. Editor: Cathy Lewis

Cumbria
01756 701033
www.dalesman.co.uk
Monthly. Editor: Terry Fletcher
Dalesman
01756 701033
www.dalesman.co.uk
Monthly. Editor: Terry Fletcher
Dartmoor Magazine
01822 614899
www.dartmoormagazine.co.uk
4pa. Editor: Elisabeth Stanbrook
Dog World
01233 621877
www.dogworld.co.uk
Weekly. Editor: Stuart Baillie
Dogs Today
01276 858880
Monthly. Editor: Beverley Cuddy
Doll Magazine
01403 711511
www.dollmagazine.com
Monthly. Editor: Emma Brown
Dollond & Aitchison Magazine
020 7747 0700
www.redwoodgroup.net
2pa. Editor: Laurence Weinberger
Dolls House World
01403 711511
www.dollshouseworld.com
Monthly. Editor: Laura Quiggan
Engineering in Miniature
01926 614101
www.engineeringinminiature.co.uk
Monthly. Editor: CL Deith
EOS Magazine
01869 331741
www.eos-magazine.com
4pa. Editor: Angela August
EQ
01986 782368
www.feedmark.com
4pa. Editor: Clare Macleod
Erotic Review
020 7907 6404
www.theeroticreview.co.uk
Monthly. Editor: Rowan Pelling
ESP Magazine
01733 253477
www.espmag.co.uk
Monthly. Editor: Sharon McAllister
Evergreen
01242 537900
www.thisengland.co.uk
4pa. Editor: Roy Faiers
Everyday Practical Electronics
01202 873872
www.epemag.co.uk
Monthly. Editor: Mike Kenward
Families East
020 8694 8694
www.familiesonline.co.uk
Bi-monthly. Editor: Mewe Mechese

Families Edinburgh
0131 552 6005
www.familiesonline.co.uk
Bi-monthly. Editor: Louise Armour
Families Liverpool
0151 522 9361
www.familiesonline.co.uk
Bi-monthly. Editor: Jennifer-Paige Deenihan
Families North
020 7794 5690
www.familiesonline.co.uk
Bi-monthly. Editor: Cathy Youd
Families Together
01903 821082
www.cfnetwork.co.uk
3pa. Editor: Clive Price
Families Upon Thames
01932 254584
www.familiesonline.co.uk
Bi-monthly. Editor: Francis Loates
The Flower Arranger
020 7247 5567
www.theflowerarrangermagazine
.co.uk
4pa. Editor: Judith Blacklock
Flyer
01225 481440
www.flyer.co.uk
Monthly. Editor: Nick Wall
FlyPast
01780 755131
www.flypast.com
Monthly. Editor: Ken Ellis
Fortean Times
020 7907 6000
www.forteantimes.com
Monthly. Editor: David Sutton
Galleries
020 8740 7020
www.artefact.co.uk
Monthly. Editor: Andrew Aitken
Gardens of England & Wales Open for Charity
01483 211795
www.ngs.org.uk
Yearly. Editor: Julia Grant
Gibbons Stamp Monthly
01425 472363
www.gibbonsstampmonthly.com
Monthly. Editor: Hugh Jefferies
Goodtimes
020 7431 2259
www.arp050.org.uk
6pa. Editor: Susi Rogol
Goodwood Magazine
01243 755000
www.goodwood.co.uk
Yearly. Editor: Kathryn Bellamy
The Great Outdoors
0141 302 7700
Monthly. Editor: Cameron McNaish

Gulliver's World
01228 404350
www.lilliputlane.co.uk
4pa. Editor: Jean Mounsey
Gun Mart
01206 505900
www.gunmart.net
Monthly. Editor: Pat Farey
Heritage Magazine
020 7751 4800
www.heritagemagazine.co.uk
Bi-monthly. Editor: Penelope Rance
Home DIY
01689 887200
Monthly. Editor: John McGowan
Hoofprint
01565 872107
www.hoofprint.co.uk
Monthly. Editor: Barry Hook
Horoscope
01202 873872
www.horoscope.co.uk
Monthly. Editor: Mike Kenward
Horse
020 7261 7969
www.horsemagazine.co.uk
Monthly. Editor: Jaki Bell
Horse & Hound
020 7261 6453
www.horseandhound.co.uk
Weekly. Editor: Lucy Higginson
Horse & Rider
01428 601020
www.horseandridermagazine.co.uk
Monthly. Editor: Alison Bridge
Jane Greenoff's Cross Stitch
01225 442244
www.futurenet
.com/janegreenoffscrossstitch
Bi-monthly. Editor: Faye Dixon
K9 Magazine
0870 011 4115
www.k9magazine.com
Quarterly. Editor: Ryan O'Meara
Kew
020 8332 5906
www.rbgkew.org.uk
4pa. Editor: Sue Seddon
Koi Carp
01202 735090
www.koi-carp.com
Monthly. Editor: Louise Harper
Lakeland Walker
01778 391000
www.lakelandwalker.co.uk
Bi-monthly. Editor: Michael Cowton
Legion – Royal British Legion
020 7296 4200
Bi-monthly. Editor: Claire Townley-Jones
Leisure Painter
01580 763315
www.leisurepainter.co.uk
Monthly. Editor: Ingrid Lyon

Leisure Scene
01494 888433
www.cssc.co.uk
3pa. Editor: Gemma Thomson
Lifewatch Magazine
020 7449 6241
www.zsl.org
3pa. Editor: Debbie Curtis
Machine Knitting News
01273 400425
www.machineknittingnews.co.uk
Monthly. Editor: Christine Richardson
Marine Modelling International
01684 588604
www.traplet.com
Monthly. Editor: Chris Jackson
Microlight Flying
01524 841010
www.bmaa.org
6pa. Editor: David Bremner
Military Illustrated Past & Present
0870 870 2345
www.publishingnews.co.uk
Monthly. Editor: Tim Newark
Military Model Craft International
01494 799982
www.modelactivitypress.com
Monthly. Editor: Tony Little
Military Modelling
01689 887200
www.militarymodelling.com
15pa. Editor: Ken Jones
Miniature Wargames
01202 297344
www.miniwargames.com
Monthly. Editor: Iain Dickie
Model & Collectors Mart
0121 233 8712
www.modelmart.co.uk
Monthly. Editor: Dean Shepherd
Model Boats
01689 887200
www.modelboats.co.uk
Monthly. Editor: John Cundell
Model Collector
020 8774 0600
Monthly. Editor: Lindsey Amrani
Model Engineer
01689 887200
26pa. Editor: Mike Chrisp
Model Engineers' Works
01689 887200
8pa. Editor: David Fenner
Model Helicopter World
01684 588612
www.traplet.com
Monthly. Editor: Jon Tanner
Motor Boat & Yachting
020 7261 5308
www.ybw.com/
Monthly. Editor: Tom Isitt

Motor Boats Monthly
020 7261 7257
www.motorboatsmonthly.com/
Monthly. Editor: Hugo Andreae
Motor Caravanner
01480 496130
www.motorcaravanners.org.uk
Monthly. Editor: Susan Lomax
Motorcaravan & Camping Mart
01778 391000
www.caravanmart.co.uk
11pa. Editor: Peter Sharpe
Motorhome Monthly
020 8302 6150
www.stoneleisure.com
Monthly. Editor: R Griffiths
National Trust Magazine
020 7222 9251
www.nationaltrust.org.uk
3pa. Editor: Gaynor Aaltonen
New Stitches
01227 750215
www.newstitches.com
Monthly. Editor: Mary Hickmott
Our Dogs
0870 731 6500
www.ourdogs.co.uk
Weekly. Editor: William Moores
Paddles
01202 735090
www.freestyle-group.com
Monthly. Editor: Richard Parkin
Patchwork & Quilting
01684 588601
www.traplet.com
Monthly. Editor: Dianne Huck
Paws
020 7627 9293
www.dogshome.org
4pa. Editor: Helen Tennant
The Peak
01756 701033
www.dalesman.co.uk
Monthly. Editor: Terry Fletcher
The People's Friend
01382 223131
www.dcthomson.co.uk
Weekly. Editor: Margaret McCoi
Pet Patter
020 7212 9000
www.mediamark.co.uk
Quarterly. Editor: Emily Bamber
Pilot
01799 544200
www.pilotweb.co.uk
Monthly. Editor: Dave Calderwood
Popular Crafts
01689 887200
www.popularcrafts.com
13pa. Editor: Dawn Frosdick-Hople
Popular Patchwork
01689 887200
13pa. Editor: Stacey Kerr

Practical Boat Owner
01202 680593
www.pbo.co.uk
Monthly. Editor: Sarah Norbury

Practical Caravan
020 8267 5000
www.practicalcaravan.com
Monthly. Editor: Alex Newby

Practical Fishkeeping
01733 282764
www.greatmagazines.co.uk
Monthly. Editor: Karen Youngs

Practical Wireless
01202 659910
www.pwpublishing.ltd.uk/pw
Monthly. Editor: Rob Mannion

Practical Woodworking
01689 887200
www.getwoodworking.com
Monthly. Editor: Mark Chisholm

Prediction
020 8774 0600
www.predictionmagazine.co.uk
Monthly. Editor: Tania Ahsan

Quick & Easy Cross Stitch
01225 442244
www.futurenet.com
/quickandeasycrossstitch
13pa. Editor: Jenny Dixon

RA Magazine
020 7300 5820
www.ramagazine.org.uk
4pa. Editor: Sarah Greenberg

RadCom
01707 659015
www.rsgb.org
Monthly. Editor: Steve Telenius-Lowe

Radio Control Jet International
01684 594505
www.traplet.com
Bi-monthly. Editor: Simon Delaney

Radio Control Model Flyer
01525 222573
Monthly. Editor: Ken Shepherd

Radio Control Model World
01684 588500
www.traplet.com
Monthly. Editor: Peter Dawson

Radio Race Car International
01684 588605
www.traplet.com
Monthly. Editor: Chris Deakin

Rail Express
01780 470086
www.railexpress.co.uk
Monthly. Editor: Philip Sutton

Railway Modeller
01297 20580
www.peco-uk.com
Monthly. Editor: John Brewer

Raw Vision
01923 856644
www.rawvision.com
4pa. Editor: John Maizels

RC Scale International
01684 588606
www.traplet.com
Bi-monthly. Editor: Simon Delaney

RCM & E
01689 887200
www.modelflying.co.uk
Monthly. Editor: Graham Ashby

RIB International
01884 266100
www.ribmagazine.com
Bi-monthly. Editor: Hugo Montgomery-Swan

Routing
01689 887200
www.getwoodworking.com
6pa. Editor: Neil Mead

RYA Magazine
023 8060 4100
www.rya.org.uk
Quarterly. Editor: Deborah Cornick

Sailing Today
01489 585225
www.sailingtoday.co.uk
Monthly. Editor: John Goode

Scale Aviation Modeller
0870 733 3373
www.sampublications.com
Monthly. Editor: Richard Franks

Scamp's Diary
01628 771232
www.scampsdiary.co.uk
2pa. Editor: Phillip Sheahan

Sew Bridal
0870 777 9955 x105
www.sewbridal.co.uk
Annually. Editor: Rosemary Sellers

Sewing With Butterick
0870 777 9955 x105
www.sewdirect.com
4pa. Editor: Rosemary Sellers

Sewing World
01684 588608
www.traplet.com
Monthly. Editor: Wendy Gardiner

Ships Monthly
01283 542721
www.shipsmonthly.co.uk
Monthly. Editor: Iain Wakefield

Short Wave Magazine
01202 659910
www.pwpublishing.ltd.uk/swm
Monthly. Editor: Kevin Nice

Stamp Magazine
020 8774 0600
www.stampmagazine.co.uk/
Monthly. Editor: Steve Fairclough

Steam Days
01202 304849
www.steamdaysmag.co.uk
Monthly. Editor: Douglas Kennedy

Steam Railway
01733 282719
www.greatmagazines.co.uk
Monthly. Editor: Tony Streeter

Surrey Nature Line
01483 488055
www.surreywildlifetrust.co.uk
3pa. Editor: Christine Reeves

The Teddy Bear Club International
01206 505979
www.planet-teddybear.com
12pa. Editor: Lorna Floyde

Time Out Shopping Guide
020 7813 3000
www.timeout.com
Annually. Editor: Janice Fuscoe

Today's Fishkeeper
01234 714644
Monthly. Editor: Christina Guthrie

Toy Soldier & Model Figure
01403 711511
www.toy-soldier.com
Monthly. Editor: Stuart Hessney

Treasure Hunting
01376 521900
www.greenlightpublishing.co.uk
Monthly. Editor: Gregg Payne

Trends
020 8340 6868
www.independentregionals.com
4pa. Editor: Ollie Lane

Used Bike Guide
01507 525771
www.usedbikeguide.com
Monthly. Editor: Brian Tarbox

Vogue Patterns
0870 777 9955 x105
www.sewdirect.com
Bi-monthly. Editor: Rosemary Sellers

Wag
020 7837 0006
www.dogstrust.org.uk
3pa. Editor: Joanna Bould

Walk
020 7339 8500
Quarterly. Editor: Christopher Sparrow

Waterways
01283 790447
www.waterways.org.uk
Quarterly. Editor: Harry Arnold

Waterways World
01283 742970
Monthly. Editor: Hugh Potter

Wild Times
01767 680551
www.rspb.org.uk
6pa. Editor: Derek Niemann

Wildfowl & Wetlands
01453 891900
www.wwt.org.uk
4pa. Editor: Mike Daw

Wolverine & Gambit
01892 500100
www.paninicomics.co.uk
13pa. Editor: Scott Gray
Woodcarving
01273 477374
Bi-monthly. Editor: Stuart Lawson
The Woodturner
01689 887200
www.getwoodworking.com
6pa. Editor: Nick Hunton
Woodturning
01273 477374
13pa. Editor: Mark Baker
The Woodworker
01689 887200
www.getwoodworking.com
Monthly. Editor: Mark Ramuz
Workbox
01579 340100
www.ebony.co.uk/workbox
Bi-monthly. Editor: Victor Briggs
The Yorkshire Journal
01756 701033
www.dalesman.co.uk
Quarterly. Editor: Mark Whiteley
You & Your Vet
020 7636 6541
www.bva-awf.org.uk
4pa. Editor: Martin Alder
Your Cat
01780 766199
www.yourcat.co.uk
Monthly. Editor: Sue Parslow
Your Dog
01780 766199
www.yourdog.co.uk
Monthly. Editor: Sarah Wright
Your Horse
01733 282750
www.greatmagazines.co.uk
Monthly. Editor: Natasha Simmonds

Men's interest

Arena
020 7520 6518
www.emap.com
Monthly. Editor: Anthony Noguera
Arena Homme Plus
020 7520 6571
www.emap.com
2pa. Editor: Ashley Heath
Bizarre
020 7907 6000
www.bizarremag.com
Monthly. Editor: Alex Godfrey
Boys Toys
01202 735090
www.boystoys.co.uk
Monthly. Editor: Mark Nuttall

Dazed & Confused
020 7336 0766
www.confused.co.uk
Monthly. Editor: Callum McGeoch
Details
020 7240 0420
www.details.com
10pa. Editor: Daniel Peres
DNR
020 7240 0420
www.dnrnews.com
Weekly. Editor: Jon Birmingham
Esquire
020 7439 5000
www.esquire.co.uk
Monthly. Editor: Simon Tiffin
FHM
020 7436 1515
www.fhm.com
Monthly. Editor: David Davies
FHM Collections
020 7436 1515
www.fhm.com
Monthly. Editor: Gary Kingsnorth
Front
020 7288 7500
www.hhc.co.uk
Monthly. Editor: Ioin McSorley
GQ
020 7499 9080
www.gq.com
Monthly. Editor: Dylan Jones
Jack
020 7907 6000
www.jackmagazine.co.uk
Monthly. Editor: Michael Hodges
Loaded
020 7261 5562
www.uploaded.com
Monthly. Editor: Martin Daubney
Maxim
020 7907 6000
www.maxim-magazine.co.uk
Monthly. Editor: Greg Gutfeld
Men's Fitness
020 7907 6000
www.mensfitnessmagazine.co.uk
Monthly. Editor: Peter Muir
Men's Health
020 7439 5000
www.menshealth.co.uk
11pa. Editor: Morgan Rees
Menz
029 2039 6600
www.hilspublications.com
4pa. Editor: Hilary Ferda
Muscle & Fitness
01423 504516
www.muscle-fitness-europe.com
Monthly. Editor: Geoff Evans

Musclemag International
0121 327 7525
www.tropicanahealthandfitness.
com
Monthly. Editor: Gary Hill
Nuts
020 7261 5661
www.nutsmag.co.uk
Weekly. Editor: Phil Hilton
Stuff
020 8267 5000
www.stuffmagazine.co.uk
Monthly. Editor: Tom Dunmore
T3
020 7317 2433
www.t3.co.uk
13pa. Editor: James Beechinor-Collins
The Veteran
01582 663880
www.pensioneronline.com
8pa. Editor: Lee Wilson
Wallpaper
020 7322 1592
www.wallpaper.com
Monthly. Editor: Jeremy Langmead
Zoo Weekly
020 7208 3797
www.zooweekly.co.uk
Weekly. Editor: Paul Merrill

Money and property

Bloomberg Money
020 7484 9771
www.bloomberg.com
Monthly. Editor: Julian Marr
Business Week
020 7176 6060
www.businessweek.com
Weekly. Editor: Stanley Reed
Complete Guide to Homebuying
020 7827 5454
www.homebuying.co.uk
Monthly. Editor: Nia Williams
Country Land & Business Magazine
020 7235 0511
www.cla.org.uk
Monthly. Editor: Tom Quinn
Euroslot
01622 687031
www.datateam.co.uk
Monthly. Editor: Alan Campbell
Forbes
020 7534 3900
www.forbes.com
Fortnightly. Editor: Tim Ferguson
Fortune
020 7322 1074
www.fortune.com
Fortnightly. Editor: Nelson Schwart (European editor of Fortune Europe

Investment International
020 7827 5454
www.investmentinternational.com
Monthly. Editor: James Featherstone
Investors Chronicle
020 7382 8000
www.investorschronicle.co.uk
Weekly. Editor: Matthew Vincent
ISA Direct
020 7409 1111
www.alanbridge.co.uk
2pa. Editor: Anthony Yadgaroff
London Property News
01933 271611
www.londonpropertynews.co.uk
Monthly. Editor: Julia Read
The MBA Career Guide
020 7554 3350
www.mba.com
2pa. Editor: Nunzio Quacquarelli
Money Observer
020 7713 4188
www.moneyobserver.com
Monthly. Editor: Andrew Pitts
Moneywise
020 7715 8303
www.moneywise.co.uk
Monthly. Editor: Ben Livesey
Mortgage Advisor & Home Buyer
020 8334 1600
www.mortgageadvisormag.co.uk
Monthly. Editor: Ruth Bell
The Mortgage Edge
020 7404 3123
www.mortgageedge.co.uk
Monthly. Editor: Andy Stuart
Mortgage Finance Gazette
020 7827 5454
www.mfgonline.co.uk
Monthly. Editor: John Murray
Mortgage Introducer
020 7827 5454
www.mortgageintroducer.com
Fortnightly. Editor: Rob Griffiths
Negotiator
020 7772 8300
www.negotiator-magazine.co.uk
Fortnightly. Editor: Rosalind Renshaw
Optima
020 8420 4488
www.optimamagazine.co.uk
Fortnightly. Editor: Kathryn Michaels
Personal Finance Confidential
020 7447 4000
www.fleetstreetpublications.co.uk
Monthly. Editor: tbc
Personal Finance Magazine
020 7827 5454
www.pfmagazine.co.uk
Monthly. Editor: Martin Fagan

Post Magazine
020 7484 9700
www.postmagazine.co.uk
Weekly. Editor: Jonathan Swift
The Property Magazine
01480 494944
www.property-platform.com
Monthly. Editor: Malcolm Lindley
What House?
020 7939 9888
www.whathouse.co.uk
Monthly. Editor: Lisa Isaacs
What Investment
020 7827 5454
www.what-investment-mag.co.uk
Monthly. Editor: Sally Wright
What Investment Trust
020 7827 5454
www.charterhouse-communications.co.uk
3pa. Editor: Kieran Root
What ISA
020 7827 5454
www.charterhouse-communications.co.uk
3pa. Editor: Amanda Jarvis
What Mortgage
020 7827 5454
www.what-mortgage-mag.co.uk
Monthly. Editor: Hilary Osborne
Your Money: Savings & Investments
020 7404 3123
www.yourmoney.com
Quarterly. Editor: Mike Collins
Your Mortgage
020 7404 3123
www.yourmortgage.co.uk
Monthly. Editor: Paula John
Your New Home
020 8301 9311
www.yournewhome.co.uk
Bi-monthly. Editor: Jon Wadeson

Motoring

100% Biker
01244 663400
www.100-biker.co.uk
Monthly. Editor: Pat Ringwood
4x4
020 8774 0600
www.offroad4wd.co.uk/
Monthly. Editor: John Carroll
911 & Porsche World Magazine
01844 260959
www.chpltd.com
Monthly. Editor: Chris Horton
Advanced Driving
01483 230323
3pa. Editor: Ian Webb

American Motorcycle Dealer
01892 511516
www.dealer-world.com
Monthly. Editor: Fraser Addecott
Audi Driver
01525 750500
www.autometrix.co.uk
Monthly. Editor: Paul Harris
The Audi Magazine
01590 683222
2pa. Editor: Clive Richardson
Auto Express
020 7907 6000
www.autoexpress.co.uk
Weekly. Editor: David Johns
Auto Italia
01707 273999
www.auto-italia.co.uk
Monthly. Editor: Philip Ward
Auto Weekly
01392 442211
www.autoweekly.co.uk
Weekly. Editor: Steve Hall
Autocar
020 8267 5000
www.autocarmagazine.co.uk
Weekly. Editor: Steve Sutcliffe
The Automobile
01483 268818
www.oldcar-discoveries.com
Monthly. Editor: Michael Bowler
AutoTrader
020 8544 7000
www.autotrader.co.uk
Weekly. Editor: Graham Luff
Back Street Heroes
020 7772 8300
Monthly. Editor: Stu Garland
Banzai
01732 748000
www.banzaimagazine.com
Monthly. Editor: Joe Clifford
BBC Top Gear
020 8433 3710
www.topgear.com
Monthly. Editor: Michael Harvey
Bike
01733 468000
www.emap.com
12pa. Editor: Tim Thompson
BMW Car
01732 748000
www.bmwcarmagazine.com
Monthly. Editor: Bob Harper
BMW Magazine
020 7534 2400
www.cedarcom.co.uk
Quarterly. Editor: Jason Barlow
Car
01733 468000
www.car-magazine.co.uk
12pa. Editor: tbc

Car Mechanics
01959 541444
www.carmechanicsmag.co.uk
Monthly. Editor: Peter Simpson

Carbuyer
01689 887200
www.highburyleisure.co.uk
Monthly. Editor: Carlin Gerbick

CarSport Magazine
028 9078 3200
www.carsportmag.net
Monthly. Editor: Pat Burns

Classic & Sports Car
020 8267 5000
www.classicandsportscar.com/
Monthly. Editor: James Elliott

Classic American
0161 836 4457
www.classic-american.com
Monthly. Editor: Ben Klemenzson

Classic Bike
01733 468000
www.emap.com
12pa. Editor: Hugo Wilson

The Classic Bike Guide
01507 524004
www.classicbikeguide.com
Monthly. Editor: Tim Britton

Classic Car
01733 468000
www.classiccarsmagazine.com
12pa. Editor: Martyn Moore

Classic Car Mart
0121 233 8712
www.classic-car-mart.co.uk
Monthly. Editor: Frank Westworth

Classic Car Weekly
01733 347559
www.classic-car-weekly.co.uk
Weekly. Editor: Russ Smith

Classic Ford
01452 317765
www.classicfordmag.co.uk
Monthly. Editor: Marc Stretton

Classic Military Vehicle
01959 541444
www.kelsey.co.uk
Monthly. Editor: Pat Ware

Classic Motor Monthly
01204 657212
www.classicmotor.co.uk
Monthly. Editor: John Hodson

Classic Motorcycle
01507 525771
www.classicmotorcycle.co.uk
Monthly. Editor: James Robinson

Classic Racer
01507 525771
www.classicracer.com
Bi-monthly. Editor: Nigel Clark

Classics
01689 887200
13pa. Editor: Dan Harris

Custom Car
01959 541444
www.kelsey.co.uk
Monthly. Editor: Kev Elliott

Dirt Bike Rider
01524 834077
www.dirtbikerider.co.uk
Monthly. Editor: Sean Lawless

Enjoying MG
01954 231125
www.mgcars.org.uk
Monthly. Editor: Richard Ladds

Evo
020 7907 6000
www.evo.co.uk
Monthly. Editor: Peter Tomalin

Fast Bikes
01689 887200
www.fastbikesmag.com
13pa. Editor: Dan Harris

Fast Car
01689 887200
www.fastcar.co.uk
13pa. Editor: Gez Jones

Fast Ford
01452 307181
www.fastfordmag.co.uk
Monthly. Editor: Paul Wager

Good Motoring
01342 825676
www.motoringassist.com
Quarterly. Editor: Derek Hainge

Ignition
020 8420 1210
www.ignitionmotoringfor
women.co.uk
Quarterly. Editor: Claire Bowen

Intersection
020 7608 1166
www.intersectionmagazine.com
Bi-monthly. Editor: Emma E Forrest

Jaguar Driver
01582 419332
www.jaguardriver.co.uk
Monthly. Editor: Steve Fermore

Jaguar World Monthly
01959 541444
www.jaguar-world.com
Monthly. Editor: Phil Weeden

Kit Car
01924 469410
www.kit-cars.com
Monthly. Editor: Ian Hyne

Land Rover Enthusiast
01379 890056
www.landroverenthusiast.com
Monthly. Editor: James Taylor

Land Rover Owner International
01733 468000
www.lro.com
13pa. Editor: John Pearson

Land Rover World
020 8774 0976
www.landroverworld.co.uk
Monthly. Editor: Luke Evans

Lexus Magazine
020 7837 8337
www.justcomm.net
4pa. Editor: Lucy Reid

LRM – Land Rover Monthly
01359 240066
www.lrm.co.uk
Monthly. Editor: Richard Howell-Thomas

Max Power
01733 468000
www.maxpower.co.uk
13pa. Editor: Roger Payne

Mercedes
01789 490530
3pa. Editor: Eric Lafone

Mercedes Enthusiast
020 8639 4400
www.mercedesenthusiast.co.uk
Monthly. Editor: Dan Trent

MG Enthusiast Magazine
01924 499261
www.mgcars.org.uk/mgmag
10pa. Editor: Martyn Wise

MiniWorld
020 8774 0600
www.miniworld.co.uk
Monthly. Editor: Monty Watkins

Motor Cycle News (MCN)
01733 468000
www.motorcyclenews.com
53pa. Editor: Marc Potter

Motor Sport
020 8267 5000
www.haymarketpublishing.co.uk
Monthly. Editor: Paul Fearnley

Motorcycle Mechanics
01507 523456
www.classicmechanics.com
Monthly. Editor: Rod Gibson

Motorcycle Racer
01353 616000
www.motorcycleracer.net
Monthly. Editor: Tony Carter

Motorcycle Rider
01652 680060
www.rbp-ltd.co.uk
4pa. Editor: Andy Dukes

Motorcycle Sport & Leisure
01353 616000
www.motorcyclemag.co.uk
Monthly. Editor: Rod Chapman

Motoring & Leisure
01273 744759
www.csma.uk.com
10pa. Editor: David Arnold

The Motorist
020 8994 3239
Weekly. Editor: BJ Charig

Performance Bikes
01733 468000
www.emap.com
12pa. Editor: Simon Hargreaves
Performance VW
01732 748000
www.performancevwmag.com
Monthly. Editor: Elliot Roberts
Peugeot Rapport
0117 925 1696
www.specialist.co.uk
3pa. Editor: Karen Ellison
Porsche Post
01608 652911
www.porscheclubgb.com
Monthly. Editor: Stephen Mummery
Post Office Motoring
0191 418 3970
4pa. Editor: Alan Fairbairn
Practical Classics
01733 468000
www.emap.com
13pa. Editor: Martyn Moore
Rally XS
020 8267 5000
www.haymarketpublishing.co.uk
Bi-monthly. Editor: Oliver Peagam
Redline
01225 442244
www.redlinemag.co.uk
13pa. Editor: Dan Lewis
The Renault Magazine
01342 828700
4pa. Editor: Ann Wallace
Revs
01733 468000
www.revs.co.uk
13pa. Editor: Nigel Grimshaw
Ride
01733 468000
www.emap.com
13pa. Editor: Stefan Bartlett
Saab Magazine
01603 664242
www.archantdialogue.co.uk
2pa. Editor: Charlie Watson
Safety Fast!
01235 555552
www.mgcc.co.uk
Monthly. Editor: Peter Browning
Scootering
01507 525771
www.scootering.com
Monthly. Editor: Andy Gillard
Street Fighters
020 7772 8300
Monthly. Editor: Stu Garland
SuperBike
020 8774 0670
www.superbikemagazine.co.uk
Monthly. Editor: Kenny Pryde

Torque
01455 891515
www.triumph.co.uk
Quarterly. Editor: Neil Webster
Total Car Audio
01452 317773
www.totalcaraudio.co.uk
Bi-monthly. Editor: Chris Anderson
Toyota's In Front
020 7837 8337
www.justcomm.net
4pa. Editor: Oliver Parsons
Twist & Go Scooter Magazine
01507 524004
www.twistngo.com
Monthly. Editor: Mau Spencer
TWO – Two Wheels Only
020 8267 5000
www.haymarketpublishing.co.uk
Monthly. Editor: Bertie Simmonds
The Used Bike Guide
01507 524004
www.usedbikeguide.com
Monthly. Editor: Brian Tarbox
VM – Vauxhall
020 7212 9000
www.mediamark.co.uk
Quarterly. Editor: Zeta Eldridge
Volks World
020 8774 0600
www.volksworld.com
Monthly. Editor: Ivan McCutcheon
Volkswagen Driver
01525 750500
www.autometrix.co.uk
Monthly. Editor: Neil Birkitt
The Volvo Magazine
020 7747 0700
www.redwoodgroup.net
4pa. Editor: Zac Assemakis
VW Magazine
01778 391000
www.warners.co.uk
Monthly. Editor: Peter Rosenthal
What Car?
020 8267 5000
www.whatcar.co.uk
Monthly. Editor: Rob Aherne
Which Kit?
01737 222030
www.which-kit.com
Monthly. Editor: Peter Filby

Puzzles

100 Crosswords
01737 378700
www.puzzler.co.uk
13pa. Editor: Debbie Hardy
Cross Reference
01737 378700
www.puzzler.co.uk
13pa. Editor: Charles Sloan

Kriss Kross
01737 378700
www.puzzler.co.uk
13pa. Editor: Jo MacLeod
Logic Problems
01737 378700
www.puzzler.co.uk
13pa. Editor: Steve Bull/Catherine Bygrave
Pocket Puzzler Crosswords
01737 378700
www.puzzler.co.uk
13pa. Editor: Maggie Ayres
Puzzle Compendium
01737 378700
www.puzzler.co.uk
10pa. Editor: Birgitta Bingham
Puzzle Corner Special
01737 378700
www.puzzler.co.uk
10pa. Editor: Debbie Hardy
Puzzler
01737 378700
www.puzzler.co.uk
13pa. Editor: Catherine Filby
Puzzler Quiz Kids
01737 378700
www.puzzler.co.uk
11pa. Editor: Jenny Anstruther
Take a Break
020 7241 8000
www.bauer.co.uk
Weekly. Editor: John Dale

Sport

Ace
020 7381 7000
Monthly. Editor: Nigel Billen
Air Gunner
0118 977 1677
www.romseypublishing.net
Monthly. Editor: Nigel Allen
Airgun World
0118 977 1677
www.romseypublishing.net
Monthly. Editor: Adam Smith
Angler's Mail
020 7261 5829
Weekly. Editor: Tim Knight
Angling Times
01733 465520
www.greatmagazines.co.uk
Weekly. Editor: Richard Lee
Angling Times Advanced
01733 465705
Monthly. Editor: Steve Cole
The Arsenal Magazine
020 7704 4010
www.arsenal.com
Monthly. Editor: Andy Exley

Athletics Weekly
01733 898440
www.athletics-weekly.com
Weekly. Editor: Jason Henderson

Autosport
020 8267 5000
www.autosport.com
Weekly. Editor: Lawrence Foster

Badminton Magazine
020 8866 6517
Monthly. Editor: William Kings

Bogey
020 7987 6166
www.bogeymag.com
Quarterly. Editor: Richard Redmond

Boxing Monthly
020 8986 4141
www.boxing-monthly.co.uk
Monthly. Editor: Glyn Leach

Boxing News
020 7618 3456
www.boxingnewsonline.net
Weekly. Editor: Claude Abrams

British Homing World
01938 552360
www.pigeonracing.com
Weekly. Editor: Cameron Stansfield

British Waterski & Wakeboard
01932 570885
www.britishwaterski.org.uk
5pa. Editor: Gill Hill

Bunkered
0141 950 2216
www.bunkered.co.uk
8pa. Editor: Martin Dempster

Calcio Italia
020 7005 2000
www.independent.co.uk
Monthly. Editor: Bill Williamson

Canoe Focus
01480 465081
www.canoefocus.demon.co.uk
Bi-monthly. Editor: Peter Tranter

Carpworld
0114 258 0812
www.anglingpublications.com
Monthly. Editor: Simon Crow

Carve Surfing Magazine
01637 878074
www.orcasurf.co.uk
8pa. Editor: Chris Power

Celtic View
0141 551 4218
www.celticfc.com
Weekly. Editor: Paul Cuddihy

Clay Shooting
01264 889533
www.clay-shooting.com
Monthly. Editor: Keith Fisher

Climber
01778 391000
www.climber.co.uk
Monthly. Editor: Jo Cooke

Coarse Fisherman
07971 241484
www.coarse-fisherman.co.uk
Website, updated daily
Editor: Phil Runciman

Combat
0121 344 3737
www.martialartsinprint.com
Monthly. Editor: Paul Clifton

Combat & Survival
01484 435011
www.combatandsurvival.com
Monthly. Editor: Bob Morrison

Corporate Golf Magazine
01273 777994
www.golfnews.co.uk
4pa. Editor: Nick Bayly

Country Walking
01733 282614
www.greatmagazines.co.uk
Monthly. Editor: Jonathan Manning

Cricket World Magazine
01476 561944
www.cricketworld.com
Quarterly. Editor: Alistair Symondson

Cycle
0870 873 0060
www.ctc.org.uk
Bi-monthly. Editor: Dan Joyce

Cycle Sport
020 8774 0703
Monthly. Editor: Robert Garbult

Cycling Plus
01225 442244
www.cyclingplus.co.uk
13pa. Editor: Tony Farrelly

Cycling Weekly
020 8774 0703
www.cyclingweekly.co.uk/
Weekly. Editor: Robert Garbult

Daily Mail Ski & Snowboard Magazine
020 8515 2000
www.skiingmail.com
6pa Sep–Mar. Editor: Henry Druce

Darts World
020 8650 6580
www.dartsworld.com
Monthly. Editor: Tony Wood

Direct Hit
020 7953 7473
www.surreycricket.com
5pa. Editor: Matt Thacker

Dirt MTB Magazine
01305 251263
www.dirtmag.co.uk
Bi-monthly. Editor: Mike Rose

Distance Running
0141 810 9000
www.inpositionmedia.co.uk
/publishing/drun.html
3pa. Editor: Hugh Jones

DIVE Magazine
020 8940 3333
www.divemagazine.co.uk
Monthly. Editor: Simon Rogerson

Diver
020 8943 4288
www.divernet.com
Monthly. Editor: Nigel Eaton

Document Skateboard
01305 251263
www.documentskateboard.com
9pa. Editor: Percy Dean

Document Snowboard
dickie@fall-line.co.uk
www.thesnowboardmag.co.uk
Bi-annual. Editor: Ian Samson

Dog Training Weekly
01348 875011
www.dogtrainingweekly.co.uk
Weekly. Editor: Angela Barrah

England Rugby
01707 273999
www.trmg.co.uk
Quarterly. Editor: Howard Johnson

Equi-Ads
01738 567700
www.equiads.net
Monthly. Editor: Mary Moore

Evening Times Wee Red Book
0141 302 6606
Yearly. Editor: Philip Joyce

Eventing
020 7261 5388
www.eventing.com
Monthly. Editor: Amanda Gee

The Evertonian
0151 227 2000
Monthly. Editor: Steve Hanrahan

F1 Racing
020 8267 5000
www.haymarketpublishing.co.uk
Monthly. Editor: Anthony Rowlinson

The Fairway Golfing News
01633 666700
www.fairway.org.uk
Monthly. Editor: John Doherty

Fall Line (skiing)
dickie@fall-line.co.uk
www.fall-line.co.uk
Bi-annual. Editor: Ian Samson

The Field
020 7261 5198
www.thefield.co.uk/
Monthly. Editor: Jonathan Young

First Down
020 7005 2000
www.first-down.co.uk
Weekly. Editor: Keith Webster

Fitness First
01932 841450
www.fitnessfirst.com
Quarterly. Editor: Iain Mackie

FitPro
0870 513 3434
www.fitpro.com
Bi-monthly. Editor: Gemma Carr

Flex
01423 504516
www.flex-europe.com
Monthly. Editor: Geoff Evans

Football First
020 7878 1007
www.sportfirst.com
Sunday. Editorial director: Chris Mann

Football Insider
020 7937 3759
www.sportservicesgroup.com
Quarterly mag, daily email Editor: Jay Stuart

Football Italia
01494 564564
www.channel4.co.uk/sport /football_italia
Monthly. Editor: John D Taylor

FourFourTwo
020 8267 5000
www.haymarketpublishing.co.uk
Monthly. Editor: Mat Snow

Glory Glory Man United
020 7317 2614
www.futurenet.com
13pa. Editor: Sarah Shaddick

Go Tenpin
01502 560445
Monthly. Editor: Eric Hayton

Going for Golf
01268 554100
www.goingforgolf.com
Quarterly. Editor: Neil Webber

The Golf Guide: Where to Play/Where to Stay
0141 887 0428
www.holidayguides.com
Yearly. Editor: Anne Cuthbertson

Golf International
020 7828 3003
www.golfinternationalmag.co.uk
9pa. Editor: Robert Green

Golf Monthly
020 7261 7237
www.golf-monthly.co.uk
Monthly. Editor: Jane Carter

Golf News
01273 777994
www.golfnews.co.uk
Monthly. Editor: Nick Bayly

Golf Weekly
01733 288035
www.greatmagazines.co.uk
Weekly. Editor: Peter Masters

Golf World
01733 288011
www.greatmagazines.co.uk
Monthly. Editor: Andy Carlton

Good Ski Guide
020 7332 2000
www.goodskiguide.com
4 issues in the winter. Editor: Kate Langmuir

Greenside
0870 900 6415
www.foremostonline.com
Quarterly. Editor: Jenni O'Connor

The Gymnast
0116 247 8766
www.british-gymnastics.org
Bi-monthly. Editor: Trevor Low

High Mountain Sports
0114 236 9296
www.planetfear.com/climbing /highmountainmag
Monthly. Editor: Geoff Birtles

Improve Your Coarse Fishing
01733 465822
www.greatmagazines.co.uk
Monthly. Editor: Kevin Wilmot

In The Know
0870 513 3345
www.itkonline.com
Monthly. Editor: Darren Croft

The Informer
01923 821909
www.middlesexrugby.com
4pa. Editor: John King

International Rugby News
020 7005 2000
www.independent.co.uk
Monthly. Editor: Graeme Gillespie

Ireland's Equestrian Magazine
028 3833 4272
www.equestrian.co.ni
Bi-monthly. Editor: Diane Wray

Irish Golf Review
00 353 1 662 2266
www.worldsfair.co.uk
Quarterly. Editor: Robert Heuston

Karting
01689 897123
www.kartingmagazine.com
Monthly. Editor: Mark Burgess

The Kop
0151 285 8412
Monthly. Editor: Chris McLoughlin

Lady Golfer
01274 851323
Monthly. Editor: Mickey Walker

LFC
0845 143 0001
Weekly. Editor: Steve Hanrahan

Liverpool Monthly
01392 664141
Monthly. Editor: Joanne Trump

London Cyclist
020 7928 7220
www.lcc.org.uk
Bi-monthly. Editors: Jonathan Hewett, Rebecca Lack

Manchester United Magazine
020 7317 2614
www.manunited.com/magazine
13pa. Editor: Sarah Shaddick

Martial Arts Illustrated
01484 435011
www.martialartsltd.co.uk
Monthly. Editor: Bob Sykes

Match
01733 288138
www.greatmagazines.co.uk
Weekly. Editor: Simon Caney

Match Fishing Magazine
01327 311999
www.total-fishing.com
Monthly. Editor: Dave Harrell

Moto
01305 251263
www.motomagazine.co.uk
Bi-monthly. Editor: Rob Walters

Motor Sport
020 8267 5000
www.haymarketpublishing.co.uk
Monthly. Editor: Paul Fearnley

Motorsport News
020 8267 5385
Weekly. Editor: Tim Bowdler

Motorsports Now!
01753 765000
www.msauk.org
Quarterly. Editor: Dave Hancock

Mountain Bike Rider
020 8774 0600
Monthly. Editor: John Kitchiner

Mountain Biking UK
01225 442244
www.mbuk.com
13pa. Editor: Mat Brett

Muscle & Fitness
01423 504516
www.muscle-fitness-europe.com
Monthly. Editor: Geoff Evans

Muscle & Fitness Hers
01423 504516
www.muscle-fitness-europe.com
Bi-monthly. Editor: Geoff Evans

Musclemag International
0121 327 7525
www.tropicanahealthand fitness.com
Monthly. Editor: Gary Hill

National Club Golfer
01274 851323
www.nationalclubgolfer.com
Monthly. Editor: Chris Bertram

The Non-League Paper
020 8971 4333
www.thenon-leaguepaper.com
Twice weekly (Aug–May), weekly (May–Aug). Editor: David Emery

The Official Tour de France Guide
020 7331 1000
www.procycling.com
Yearly. Editor: Jeremy Whittle

On The Edge
01298 72801
www.ontheedgemag.co.uk
10pa. Editor: Neil Pearsons

Pool Industry
01420 563602
www.spata.co.uk
Quarterly. Editor: Stephen Delany

PQ International
020 7924 2550
www.poloworld.co.uk
4pa. Editor: Roger Chatterton-Newman

Procycling
020 7331 1000
www.procycling.com
Monthly. Editor: Jeremy Whittle

Pull!
01780 754900
www.countrypursuits.co.uk
10pa. Editor: Mike Barnes

Raceform Update
020 7293 3000
www.racingpost.co.uk
Weekly. Editor: Bernie Ford

Racing Calendar
0870 871 2000
www.britishcycling.org.uk
Quarterly. Editor: Phil Ingham

Racing Pigeon Weekly
01689 600006
www.racingpigeon.co.uk
Weekly. Editor: Steve Dunn

Racing Post
020 7293 3000
www.racingpost.co.uk
Daily. Editor: Chris Smith

Rally XS
020 8267 5000
www.haymarketpublishing.co.uk
Bi-monthly. Editor: Oliver Peagam

Ride BMX
01305 251263
www.ridebmxmag.co.uk
9pa. Editor: Mark Noble

Rugby League World
01484 401895
www.totalrl.com
Monthly. Editor: Tim Butcher

Rugby Leaguer & League Express
01484 401895
www.totalrl.com
Weekly. Editor: Martyn Sadler

Rugby Times
01484 401895
www.rugbytimes.com
Weekly. Editor: Jon Newcombe

Rugby World
020 7261 6810
www.rugbyworld.com
Monthly. Editor: Paul Morgan

Runner's World
020 7439 5000
www.runnersworld.co.uk
Monthly. Editor: Steven Seaton

Running Fitness
01733 347559
www.running-fitness.co.uk
Monthly. Editor: Paul Larkins

Salmon & Trout Association Newsletter
020 7283 5838
www.salmon-trout.org
2pa. Editor: Carmel Jorgensen

Scottish Rugby
0141 309 1400
Bi-monthly. Editor: Scott Monroe

Scuba World
01202 735090
www.freestyle-group.com
Monthly. Editor: Frank Raines

Sea Angler
01733 465702
www.greatmagazines.co.uk
Monthly. Editor: Mel Russ

Seahorse
01590 671899
www.seahorsemagazine.com
Monthly. Editor: Andrew Hurst

Shoot Monthly
020 7261 7452
www.shootmonthly.co.uk
Monthly. Editor: Colin Mitchell

Shooting Gazette
01780 754900
www.countrypursuits.co.uk
Monthly. Editor: Will Hetherington

Shooting Sports
01206 505900
www.shooting-sports.net
Monthly. Editor: Peter Moore

Shooting Times and Country Magazine
020 7261 7659
www.shootingtimes.co.uk
Weekly. Editor: Robert Gray

Sidewalk Skateboarding Magazine
01235 536229
www.sidewalkmag.com
Monthly. Editor: Ben Powell

The Skier and Snowboarder Magazine
0845 310 8303
5pa. Editor: Frank Baldwin

Snooker Scene
0870 220 2125
Monthly. Editor: Clive Everton

Speedway Star
020 8335 1100
www.speedwaystar.net
Weekly. Editor: Richard Clark

Sport Cities and Venues
020 7937 3759
www.sportservicesgroup.com
*Quarterly. Also a weekly email
Editor: Jay Stuart*

Sport Diver
01799 544200
www.sportdiver.co.uk
*Monthly. Editors: Mark Evans,
Rebecca Corbally*

Sporting Gun
020 7261 7199
www.sportinggun.co.uk
Monthly. Editor: Robin Scott

Sportsbetting Update
020 7937 3759
www.sportservicesgroup.com
*Quarterly. Also a weekly email
Editor: Jay Stuart*

Sportsmedia
020 7937 3759
www.sportservicesgroup.com
*Quarterly. Also a daily email
Editor: Jay Stuart*

Sportsmedia Report
020 7937 3759
www.sportservicesgroup.com
Monthly. Editor: Jay Stuart

Spurs Monthly
01708 379877
Monthly. Editor: Tony McDonald

The Squash Player
01753 775511
www.squashplayer.co.uk
10pa. Editor: Ian McKenzie

Summit
0161 438 3308
www.thebmc.co.uk
Quarterly. Editor: Alex Messenger

Super Reds
01392 664141
Monthly. Editor: Joanne Trump

Surf News
01637 876474
www.britsurf.co.uk
4pa. Editor: Chris Power

The Surfer's Path
01235 536229
www.surferspath.com
Bi-monthly. Editor: Alex Dick-Rea

Swimming
01509 632230
www.britishswimming.org
Monthly. Editor: Peter Hassall

Swimming Pool News
01353 777656
www.swimmingpoolnews.co.uk
*Bi-monthly. Editor: Christina
Connor*

Taekwondo & Korean Martial Arts Magazine
0121 344 3737
www.martialartsinprint.com
Monthly. Editor: Paul Clifton

Target Sports
01905 795564
www.targetsportsmag.com
Monthly. Editor: Richard Atkins

Thoroughbred Owner and Breeder
020 7408 0903
www.racehorseowners.net
Monthly. Editor: Michael Harris

Today's Golfer
01733 288016
www.greatmagazines.co.uk
Monthly. Editor: Paul Hamblin

Today's Pilot
01780 755131
www.todayspilot.co.uk
Monthly. Editor: Dave Unwin

Total Carp
01327 311999
www.total-fishing.com
Monthly. Editor: Mark Coulson

Traditional Karate
0121 344 3737
www.martialartsinprint.com
Monthly. Editor: Paul Clifton

Trail
01733 282620
www.greatmagazines.co.uk
Monthly. Editor: Guy Procter

Trials & Motorcross News
01524 834029
www.tmxnews.co.uk
Weekly. Editor: John Dickinson

Trout & Salmon
01733 465821
www.greatmagazines.co.uk
Monthly. Editor: Sandy Leventon

Ultra-Fit
01736 350204
www.ultra-fitmagazine.com
pa. Editor: Charles Mays

Unity
01993 811181
www.unitymag.co.uk
pa. Editor: Steve Glidewell

Warren Miller's Impact
020 7240 4071
www.blackdiamond.co.uk/tour
early. Editor: Guy Chambers

What Mountain Bike
1225 442244
www.whatmtb.co.uk
3pa. Editor: Jane Bentley

When Saturday Comes
20 7729 1110
www.wsc.co.uk
Monthly. Editor: Andy Lyons

White Lines Snowboarding Magazine
01235 536229
www.whitelines.com
6pa (Oct–Mar). Editor: Matt Barr

Windsurf Magazine
01993 811181
www.windsurf.co.uk
10pa. Editor: Mark Kasprowicz

Women & Golf
020 7261 7237
Monthly. Editor: Jane Carter

World Soccer
020 7261 5714
www.worldsoccer.com
Monthly. Editor: Gavin Hamilton

Yachting World
020 7261 6800
www.ybw.com
Monthly. Editor: Andrew Bray

Yachts & Yachting
01702 582245
www.yachtsandyachting.com
Fortnightly. Editor: Gael Pawson

Travel

Activity Wales
01437 766888
www.activitywales.com
Yearly. Editor: Matthew Evans

Adventure Travel
01789 450000
www.atmagazine.co.uk
Bi-monthly. Editor: Alun Davies

Arab Traveller
01621 842745
Bi-monthly. Editor: Jeremy Wright

Australian News
01323 726040
www.australian-news.co.uk
Monthly. Editor: Paul Beasley

BA Impressions
020 7269 7480
www.impressions-ba.com
Quarterly. Editor: Charlotte Methven

Best of Britain
020 8740 2040
www.morriseurope.com
Yearly. Editor: Leonora Peralta

Big City
020 7212 9000
www.mediamark.co.uk
Bi-monthly. Editor: Zeta Eldridge

Bradmans Business Travel Guides
020 7269 7416
www.bradmans.com
Yearly. Editor: Giles Morgan

Canada News
01323 726040
www.canadanews.co.uk
Monthly. Editor: Paul Beasley

City to Cities
020 8469 9700
www.swanpublishing.co.uk
Bi-monthly. Editor: David Tickner

CN Traveller (Condé Nast Traveller)
020 7499 9080
www.cntraveller.com
Monthly. Editor: Sarah Miller

Destination New Zealand
01323 726040
www.destination-newzealand.com
Monthly. Editor: Paul Beasley

Easyjet Magazine
020 7269 7480
www.easyjetinflight.com
Monthly. Editor: Michael Keating

Edinburgh Shopping & Tourist Guide
01506 508001
2pa. Editor: Roger Sadler

Education Travel Magazine
020 7440 4025
www.hothousemedia.com
Bi-monthly. Editor: Amy Baker

Enjoy Dorset & Hampshire Magazine
01202 737678
www.enjoydorset.co.uk
Yearly. Editor: Zoe Wilson

Ensign
01202 414200
Yearly. Editor: Karen Portnall

Essentially America
020 7243 6954
www.phoenixip.com
Quarterly. Editor: Mary Moore Mason

Essex Life & Countryside
01206 571348
www.archant.co.uk
Monthly. Editor: Robin Bechelet

Everything France Magazine
01342 828700
www.efmag.co.uk
Monthly. Editor: Ann Wallace

Flybe. Uncovered
020 8649 7233
www.bmipublications.com
Bi-monthly. Editor: Alan Orbell

Food & Travel
020 8332 9090
Monthly

France
01242 216050
www.francemag.com
Monthly. Editor: Kate McNally

French Property News
020 8543 3113
www.french-property-news.com
Monthly. Editor: Karen Tate

Gap Year
0870 241 6704
www.gapyear.com
Website. Editor: Tom Griffiths
Geographical
020 8960 6400
www.geographical.co.uk
Monthly. Editor: Nick Smith
Going USA
01323 726040
www.goingusa.com
Bi-monthly. Editor: Paul Beasley
Greece
01225 786800
www.merricksmedia.co.uk
Bi-monthly. Editor: Diana Cambridge
High Life
020 7534 2400
www.cedarcom.co.uk
Monthly. Editor: Alex Finer
Holiday & Events Guide
0870 444 2702
www.nealsyardagency.com
4pa. Editor: Ulriche Speyer
Holiday Which?
0845 309 4000
4pa. Editor: Patricia Yates
Holiday, The RCI Magazine
01536 310101
3pa. Editor: Simon McGrath
Homes Overseas
020 7939 9888
www.homesoverseas.co.uk
Monthly. Editor: Mike Hayes
In Britain
020 7751 4800
www.romseypublishing.net
Bi-monthly. Editor: Andrea Spain
In London
020 8740 2040
www.morriseurope.com
Bi-monthly. Editor: Chris Johnson
Italy
01305 266360
www.italymag.co.uk
Monthly. Editor: Fiona Tankard
Kuoni World Magazine
01306 744247
www.kuoni.co.uk
4pa. Editor: Mary Donovan
LAM – Living Abroad Magazine
020 7005 5000
www.lam-online.co.uk
Monthly. Editor: Bill Williamson
The London Guide
020 8740 2040
www.morriseurope.com
Monthly. Editor: Leonora Peralta
London Hotel Magazine
020 7373 7282
Bi-monthly. Editor: E R Spence

London Planner
020 7751 4800
www.londonplanner.co.uk
Monthly. Editor: Nick Buglione
Mediterranean Life
020 7415 7020
Quarterly. Editor: Glyn Wilmshurst
Msafiri-Kenya Airways
01442 875431
www.dfadesign.com
4pa. Editor: Dennis Fairey
My Travel Recline & Life Magazines
020 7269 7480
www.electricink.net
Quarterly. Editor: Chloe Wilson
National Geographic
01483 522068
www.nationalgeographic.com
Monthly. Editor: Bill Allen
Orient-Express Magazine
020 7805 5555
www.ilng.co.uk
4pa. Editor: Alison Booth
Overseas
020 7016 6905
4pa. Editor: Pat Treasure
Pride of Britain
020 7739 1434
www.prideofbritainhotels.com
2pa. Editor: Sophie MacKenzie
The Railway Magazine
020 7261 5821
www.railwaymagazine.co.uk
Monthly. Editor: Nick Pigott
Redhot Magazine
020 7269 7480
www.ontoeurope.com
Quarterly. Editor: Charlotte Methven
South Africa News
01323 726040
www.southafricanews.co.uk
Bi-monthly. Editor: Paul Beasley
Spain
0131 226 7766
www.spainmagazine.info
Monthly. Editor: Nicola McCormack
Sunday Times Travel
020 7306 0304
www.sundaytimestravel.co.uk
Bi-monthly. Editor: Jane Knight
TNT Magazine
020 7373 3377
www.tntmagazine.com
Twice weekly. Editor: Lyn Eyb
Travel & Leisure
020 8554 4456
4pa. Editor: Terry Stafford
Travel Australia
01424 223111
www.consylpublishing.co.uk
2pa. Editor: Bill Deacon

Travel GBI
020 7729 4337
Monthly. Editor: Richard Cawthorn
Traveller
020 7589 3315
www.travelleronline.com
Quarterly. Editor: Jonathan Lorie
Travelmag
01672 810202
www.travelmag.co.uk
Online magazine. Editor: Jack Barker
Wanderlust
01753 620426
www.wanderlust.co.uk
Bi-monthly. Editor: Lyn Hughes
Welcome to London
020 8297 4444
www.welcometolondon.com
Bi-monthly. Editor: Melanie Armstrong

Women and health

Accent Magazine
0191 284 9994
Monthly. Editor: Kevin Wright
Al Jamila
020 7831 8181
www.alkhaleejiahadv.com.sa/srp/jamila
Weekly. Editor: Sanaa Elhadethee
Allergy Magazine
020 7269 7416
www.allergymagazine.com
Bi-monthly. Editor: Charmaine Yabsley
Asian Woman
0870 755 5501
Quarterly. Editor: Beena Nadeem
Asthma News
020 7226 2260
www.asthma.org.uk
4pa. Editor: Jenny Cockin
A–Z of Calories
01984 623014
Bi-monthly. Editor: Gertude Pertl
B
020 7150 7000
www.bmagazine.co.uk
Monthly. Editor: Frances Sheen
Baby & You
020 7226 2222
www.hhc.co.uk
Monthly. Editor: Amanda Burney
Balance
020 7424 1000
www.diabetes.org.uk
Bi-monthly. Editor: Martin Cullen
Be Slim
01984 623014
4pa. Editor: Gertude Pertl

Beautiful Brides
0117 934 3742
www.thisisbristol.co.uk
/beautifulbrides
4pa. Editor: Harry Mottram

Bella
020 7241 8000
www.bauer.co.uk
Weekly. Editor: Jayne Marsden

Best
020 7439 5000
www.natmags.co.uk
Weekly. Editor: Louise Court

Blackhair
01376 534500
Bi-monthly. Editor: Jane MacArthur

Bliss for Brides
01376 534500
Bi-monthly. Editor: Abbey Marjoram

Boots Health and Beauty
020 7747 0960
www.redwoodgroup.net
5pa. Editor: Jan Boxshall

Bride & Groom
020 8477 3771
www.recorderonline.co.uk
2pa. Editor: Emma Rice

Brides
020 7499 9080
www.bridesuk.net
Bi-monthly. Editor: Liz Savage

Caduceus Journal
01926 451897
www.caduceus.info
4pa. Editor: Sarida Brown

Candis
0151 632 3232
www.candis.co.uk
Monthly. Editor: Jenny Campbell

Chat
020 7261 6559
Weekly. Editor: June Smith-Sheppard

Closer
020 7859 8463
www.emap.com
Weekly. Editor: Jane Johnson

Company
020 7439 5000
www.company.co.uk
Monthly. Editor: Victoria White

Cosmopolitan
020 7439 5000
www.cosmopolitan.co.uk
Monthly
acting editor: Nina Ahmad

Cosmopolitan Hair & Beauty
020 7439 5000
www.cosmohairandbeauty.co.uk
Monthly. Editor: Melanie Goose

Ele
020 7150 7000
www.hf-uk.com
Monthly. Editor: Lorraine Candy

Essentials
020 7261 6970
www.essentialsmagazine.com
Monthly. Editor: Karen Livermore

Eve
020 8433 2041
www.bbcmagazines.com/eve
Monthly. Editor: Jane Bruton

Executive Woman
020 8420 1210
www.execwoman.com
Bi-monthly. Editor: Angela Giveon

Family Circle
020 7261 6195
www.familycircle.co.uk
Monthly. Editor: Julie Barton-Breck

Family Magazine
01200 453000
Bi-monthly. Editor: Jeremy Nicholls

For the Bride
01376 534500
Bi-monthly. Editor: Abbey Marjoram

For Women
020 7308 5363
9pa. Editor: Liz Beresford

Glamour
020 7499 9080
www.glamour.com
Monthly. Editor: Jo Elvin

Good Health Magazine
01376 534500
www.gh-online.co.uk
Monthly. Editor: Jane MacArthur

Hair
020 7261 6974
www.hairmagazine.co.uk
Bi-monthly. Editor: Zoe Richards

Hair & Beauty
020 7436 9766
Bi-monthly. Editor: Laura Curtis

Hair Now
020 7436 9766
Bi-monthly. Editor: Tim Frisby

Hairflair
01376 534500
Bi-monthly. Editor: Ruth Page

Hairstyles Only
01376 534500
Bi-monthly. Editor: Ruth Page

Harpers & Queen
020 7439 5000
www.harpersandqueen.co.uk
Monthly. Editor: Lucy Yeomans

Health & Fitness
020 7226 2222
www.hfonline.co.uk
Monthly. Editor: Mary Comber

The Health Store Magazine
0115 955 5259
www.thehealthstore.co.uk
Bi-monthly. Editor: Jane Garton

Healthy
020 7306 0304
www.riverltd.co.uk
Bi-monthly. Editor: Annabel Meggeson

Healthy Times
020 7819 1111
www.squareonegroup.co.uk
Quarterly. Editor: Sharon Gray

Heat
020 7437 9011
www.emap.com
Weekly. Editor: Mark Frith

Hello!
020 7667 8901
www.hellomagazine.com
Weekly; website updated daily
Editor: Ronnie Whelan;
website editor: Tree Elven

Hia
020 7539 2270
Monthly. Editor: Mai Badr

Holistic London Guide
020 8672 7111
www.healthyinfo.co.uk
3pa. Editor: Samantha Stent

In Style
020 7261 4747
Monthly. Editor: Louise Chunn

Jane
020 7240 0420
www.janemag.com
Monthly. Editor: Jane Pratt

Junior
020 7761 8900
www.juniormagazine.co.uk
Monthly. Editor: Catherine O'Dolan

Junior Pregnancy & Baby
020 7761 8900
www.juniormagazine.co.uk
Bi-monthly. Editor: Debora Stottor

Ladies First
029 2039 6600
www.hilspublications.com
4pa. Editor: Hilary Ferda

The Lady
020 7379 4717
www.thelady.co.uk
Weekly. Editor: Arline Usden

Marie Claire
020 7261 5177
Monthly. Editor: Marie O'Riordan

Memsahib
020 8571 7700
www.snooplife.com
Quarterly. Editor: Jay Kumar

More!
020 7208 3165
www.moremagazine.co.uk
Fortnightly. Editor: Ali Hall

Mother & Baby
020 7347 1869
www.emapmagazines.co.uk
Monthly. Editor: Eleanor Dalrymple

Ms London
020 7005 2000
www.independent.co.uk
Daily. Editor: Bill Williamson

MS Matters
020 8438 0700
www.mssociety.org.uk
Bi-monthly. Editor: Debbie Reeves

My Weekly
01382 223131
www.dcthomson.co.uk
Weekly. Editor: Harrison Watson

New Woman
020 7437 9011
www.newwoman.co.uk
Monthly. Editor: Claire Baylis

Now
020 7261 6274
www.nowmagazine.co.uk
Weekly. Editor: Jane Ennis

Now Star Diet & Fitness
020 7261 7366
www.ipcmedia.com
3pa. Editor: Jane Ennis

Now Star Style
020 7261 7366
www.ipcmedia.com
3pa. Editor: Jane Ennis

Number Ten
020 7439 9100
www.numberten.co.uk
Bi-annual. Editor: Laura Sheed

OK!
020 7928 8000
Weekly. Editor: Nic McCarthy

Parent News UK
020 8337 6337
www.parents-news.co.uk
Monthly. Editor: Penny McCarthy

Parent Talk
020 7450 9073
www.parentalk.co.uk
Website updated weekly
Editor: Maggie Doherty

People
020 7322 1134
www.people.com
Weekly. Editor: Bryan Alexander

Practical Parenting
020 7261 5058
www.practicalparenting.co.uk
Monthly. Editor: Sara Pates

Pregnancy and Birth
020 7347 1885
www.emapmagazines.co.uk
Monthly. Editor: Charlotte Coleman

Pregnancy Magazine
020 7226 2222
www.hhc.co.uk
Monthly. Editor: Amanda Hemmings

Pride Magazine
020 7228 3110
www.pridemagazine.com
Monthly. Editor: Amina J Taylor

Prima
020 7439 5000
www.primamagazine.co.uk
Monthly. Editor: Maire Fahey

Prima Baby
020 7439 5000
www.primababy.co.uk
Monthly. Editor: Julia Goodwin

Real
020 7241 8000
www.bauer.co.uk
Fortnightly. Editor: Sian Rees

Real Health & Fitness
020 7306 0304
www.riverltd.co.uk
Bi-monthly.
Editor: Andrea Hammett

Red
020 7150 7000
www.redmagazine.co.uk
Monthly. Editor: Trish Halpin

Rosemary Conley Diet & Fitness Magazine
01509 620444
www.conley.co.uk/magazine
Bi-monthly. Editor: Gerri Hosier

Sayidaty
020 7539 2242
www.sayidaty.net
Weekly. Editor: Hani Nakshabandi

Sayidaty Fashion
020 7539 2242
www.sayidaty.net
4pa. Editor: Lucy Habib

Scottish Home & Country
0131 225 1724
www.swri.org.uk
Monthly. Editor: Liz Ferguson

Select Magazine
0121 212 4141
www.icbirmingham.co.uk
Monthly. Editor: Ann Roberts

Shape
020 7907 6531
Monthly. Editor: Liz Jarvis

She
020 7439 5000
www.she.co.uk
Monthly. Editor: Terry Tavner

Slimmer, Healthier, Fitter
01206 505900
www.slimmerrecipes.co.uk
10pa. Editor: Helen Mulley

Slimming Magazine
020 7347 1854
www.emapmagazines.co.uk
Monthly. Editor: Marie Farqharson

Slimming World
01773 546360
www.slimming-world.com
7pa. Editor: Christine Michael

Spirit of Superdrug
020 7306 0304
www.riverltd.co.uk
Bi-monthly. Editor: Brigid Moss

Take a Break
020 7241 8000
www.bauer.co.uk
Weekly. Editor: John Dale

Tatler
020 7499 9080
www.tatler.co.uk
Monthly. Editor: Geordie Greig

That's Life!
020 7241 8000
www.bauer.co.uk
Weekly. Editor: Jo Checkley

Tiara
029 2039 6600
www.hilspublications.com
3pa. Editor: Hilary Ferda

Top Santé Health & Beauty
020 7208 3772
www.emap.com
Monthly. Editor: Marina Gask

Twins, Triplets & More Magazine
01909 500874
3pa. Editor: Sheila Payne

Ulster Bride
028 9068 1371
www.ulstertatler.com
Bi-monthly. Editor: Christopher Sherry

Ulster Tatler
028 9068 1371
www.ulstertatler.com
Monthly. Editor: Richard Sherry

Ultra-Fit
01736 350204
www.ultra-fitmagazine.com
8pa. Editor: Charles Mays

Vanity Fair
020 7499 9080
www.vanityfair.co.uk
Monthly. Editor: Henry Porter

Vogue
020 7499 9080
www.vogue.com
Monthly.
Editor: Alexandra Shulman

W
020 7240 0420
www.wmagazine.com
Monthly. Editor: John B Fairchild

Wave
01273 818160
www.wavemagazine.co.uk
Monthly. Editor: Emma Amyatt-L

Wedding & Home
020 7261 7470
www.weddingandhome.co.uk
Monthly. Editor: Kate Barlow
Wedding Cakes – A Design Source
0845 225 5671/2
www.squires-shop.com
4pa. Editor: Beverley Dutton
Wedding Day
020 7761 8980
www.beachpublishing.co.uk
Bi-monthly. Editor: Alice Kodell
Wedding Journal
028 9045 7457
www.weddingjournalonline.com
Quarterly. Editor: Tara Craig
Weight Watchers
020 8882 2555
www.weight-watchers.co.uk
8pa. Editor: Barbara Raine-Allen
WM
029 2058 3592
www.icwales.co.uk
Quarterly. Editor: Nina Rabaiotti
Woman & Home
020 7261 5176
www.womanandhome.co.uk/
Monthly. Editor: Sue James
Woman Alive
01903 821082
www.womanalive.co.uk
Monthly. Editor: Jackie Stead
Woman's Own
020 7261 5500
Weekly. Editor: Elsa McAlonan
Woman's Weekly
020 7261 6131
Weekly. Editor: Gilly Sinclair
Women's Health
020 7226 2222
www.hhc.co.uk
Monthly. Editor: Tracey Smith
Women's Wear Daily (WWD)
020 7240 0420
www.wwd.com
Daily. Editor: James Fallon
Yoga and Health
020 7480 5456
www.yogaandhealthmag.co.uk
Monthly. Editor: Jane Sill
You & Your Wedding
020 7439 5000
www.youandyourwedding.co.uk
5pa. Editor: Carole Hamilton
Zest
020 7439 5000
www.zest.co.uk
Monthly. Editor: Alison Pylkkanen

Business and trade

Business

Accountancy
020 8247 1387
www.accountancymagazine.com
Monthly. Editor: Chris Quick
Accountancy Age
020 8606 7505
www.accountancyage.com
Weekly. Editor: Damian Wild
Accounting & Business
020 7396 5966
www.accaglobal.com
10pa. Editor: John Prosser
Accounting Technician
020 7880 6200
www.accountingtechnician.co.uk
Monthly. Editor: Martin Allen-Smith
Assessment
020 7801 2884
www.pcs.org.uk/revenue
Monthly. Editor: Dennis Calnan
Bradmans Business Travel Guides
020 7269 7416
www.bradmans.com
Yearly. Editor: Giles Morgan
Brand Strategy
020 7970 4000
www.mad.co.uk
Monthly. Editor: Elen Lewis
Business Informer
0191 518 4281
Bi-monthly. Editor: Alan Roxborough
Business Traveller
020 7778 0000
www.businesstraveller.com
10pa. Editor: Tom Otley
CFO Europe
020 7830 7000
www.cfoeurope.com
11pa. Editor: Janet Kersnar
CIMA Insider
020 8849 2313
www.cimaglobal.com
Monthly. Editor: Ruth Prickett
Creative Review
020 7970 4000
www.mad.co.uk
Monthly. Editor: Patrick Burgoyne
Design Week
020 7970 4000
www.mad.co.uk
Weekly. Editor: Lynda Relph-Knight
Director
020 7766 8950
www.iod.com
Monthly. Editor: Joanna Higgins

Euromoney
020 7779 8888
www.euromoneyplc.com
Monthly. Editor: Peter Lee
European Business
020 7269 7416
www.electricink.net
Monthly. Editor: John Lawless
Financial Advisor
020 7382 8000
www.ftadvisor.com
Weekly. Editor: Hal Austin
Financial Management
020 8849 2313
www.cimaglobal.com
Monthly. Editor: Ruth Prickett
Financial News
020 7426 3333
www.efinancialnews.com
Weekly. Editor: William Wright
Financial World
01227 818609
www.financialworld.co.uk
Monthly. Editor: Denise Smith
First Voice of Business
01223 477411
www.campublishers.com
Bi-monthly. Editor: Warren Clark
Growing Business
020 8334 1600
www.gbmag.co.uk
Monthly. Editor: Marcus Austin
Human Resources
020 8267 5000
www.humanresources
magazine.com
11pa. Editor: Trevor Merriden
Industrial Focus
020 7014 0300
www.industrialfocus.co.uk
Bi-monthly. Editor: Mike Wearing
Institutional Investor International Edition
020 7779 8888
www.iilondon.com
Monthly. Editor: Andrew Capon
In-Store
020 7970 4000
www.mad.co.uk
Monthly. Editor: Matthew Valentine
Insurance Age
020 7484 9700
www.insuranceage.com
Monthly. Editor: Michelle Worvell
Investor Relations
020 7637 3579
www.ironthenet.com
Monthly. Editor: Claire Hunte
The Journal
020 7534 2400
www.cedarcom.co.uk
Bi-monthly. Editor: Martin Baker

**Landscape and Amenity
Product Update**
01952 200809
www.landscapespecification.com
6pa. Editor: David Stiles
Management Today
020 8267 5000
www.mtmagazine.co.uk
Monthly. Editor: Matthew Gwyther
Marketing Week
020 7970 4000
www.marketing-week.co.uk/
Weekly. Editor: Stuart Smith
MiD
020 7612 9300
www.infoconomy.com
Bi-monthly. Editor: Graeme Burton
Money Marketing
020 7970 4000
www.moneymarketing.co.uk
Weekly. Editor: John Lappin
New Business
020 7407 9800
www.newbusiness.co.uk
Quarterly. Editor: Chris Head
New Media Age
020 7970 4000
www.nma.co.uk/
Weekly. Editor: Michael Nutley
OS Magazine
0141 567 6000
www.peeblesmedia.com
Bi-monthly. Editor: Clare Bodel
Overseas Trade
020 7368 9600
www.overseas-trade.co.uk
Monthly. Editor: Janet Tibble
Pensions & Investments
020 7457 1430
www.pionline.com
Fortnightly. Editor: Nancy Webman
Pensions Age
020 7426 0101
www.pensions-age.com
Monthly. Editor: Francesca Fabrizi
People Management
020 7880 6200
www.peoplemanagement.co.uk
Fortnightly. Editor: Steve Crabb
Personnel Today
020 8652 3705
www.personneltoday.com
Weekly. Editor: Jane King
Professional Manager
020 7421 2705
www.managers.org.uk
Bi-monthly. Editor: Sue Mann
Real Business
020 7828 0733
www.realbusiness.co.uk
Monthly. Editor: Adam Leyland

Recruiter Magazine
020 7296 4200
www.recruiter.co.uk
Fortnightly. Editor: Karen Dempsey
StartUps.co.uk
20 8334 1600
www.startups.co.uk
*Website, updated hourly
Editor: Matthew Thomas*
Supply Management
020 7880 6200
www.supplymanagement.co.uk
Fortnightly. Editor: Geraint John
What's New In Industry
020 7970 4000
www.centaur.co.uk
Monthly. Editor: David Keighly

Construction and engineering

ABC&D
01527 834451
www.abc-d.co.uk
Monthly. Editor: Barry Cook
Architecture Today
020 7837 0143
www.architecturetoday.co.uk
*10pa. Editors: Ian Latham, Mark
Swenarton*
Builder & Engineer
0161 236 2782
www.excelpublishing.co.uk
Monthly. Editor: Alex Kearns
Building
020 7560 4000
www.building.co.uk
Weekly. Editor: Denise Chevin
Building Design
01732 364422
www.cmpinformation.com
Weekly. Editor: Robert Booth
Building Products
020 8565 4387
www.buildingproducts.co.uk
Monthly. Editor: Phil Stronach
Civil Engineering
020 7665 2448
www.ice.org.uk
6pa. Editor: Simon Fuller-Love
Construction Manager
020 7560 4000
www.construction-manager.co.uk
10pa. Editor: Rod Sweet
Construction News
020 7505 6600
www.cnplus.co.uk
Weekly. Editor: Aaron Morby
Construction Products
020 7505 6868
www.cnplus.co.uk
Bi-monthly. Editor: Julian Birch

Contract Journal
020 8652 4756
www.contractjournal.com
Weekly. Editor: Rob Willock
Electronics
01474 565625
www.connectingindustry.com
11pa. Editor: Jo Bennett
Electronics Weekly
020 8652 3650
www.electronicsweekly.com
Weekly. Editor: Richard Wilson
Gas Installer
020 7401 4101
Monthly. Editor: Ian McManus
IEE Review
01438 313311
www.iee.org/review
Monthly. Editor: Svetlana Josifovsko
New Civil Engineer
020 7505 6600
www.nceplus.co.uk
Weekly. Editor: Antony Oliver
Offshore
020 8946 7783
www.offshore-mag.com
Monthly. Editor: Eldon Ball
Offshore Engineer
020 8956 2835
www.offshore-engineer.com
Monthly. Editor: David Morgan
Pipeline World
01245 496321
www.pipemag.com
Bi-monthly. Editor: John Tiratsoo
PIR Construction
01234 348878
www.pirnet.co.uk
6pa. Editor: Derek Cooper
**Professional Electrician &
Installer**
01923 237799
www.hamerville.co.uk
11pa. Editor: Richard Pagett
Professional Engineering
020 7973 1299
www.profeng.com
Fortnightly. Editor: John Pullin
**Professional Heating &
Plumbing Installer**
01923 237799
www.hamerville.co.uk
11pa. Editor: Stuart Hamilton
Public Sector Building
020 7970 4000
www.centaur.co.uk
6pa. Editor: Derek Rogers
RIBA Journal
020 7921 8000
www.ribajournal.com
Monthly. Editor: Amanda Baillieu

The Engineer
020 7970 4000
www.e4engineering.com
Fortnightly. Editor: George Coupe
What's New In Building
01732 364422
www.cmpinformation.com
Monthly. Editor: Mark Pennington

Defence

Airforces Monthly
01780 755131
www.airforcesmonthly.com
Monthly. Editor: Alan Warnes
Jane's Defence Weekly
020 8700 3700
www.janes.com
Weekly. Editor: Peter Felstead
Navy News
023 9272 4194
www.navynews.co.uk
Monthly. Editor: Jim Allaway
Soldier
01252 347356
www.soldiermagazine.co.uk
Monthly. Editor: John Elliott

Education

Child Education
01926 887799
www.scholastic.co.uk
Monthly. Editor: Michael Ward
Education Today
020 7947 9536
www.collegeofteachers.ac.uk
Quarterly. Editor: Brychan Thomas
Education Travel Magazine
020 7440 4025
www.hothousemedia.com
Bi-monthly. Editor: Amy Baker
FE Now
01458 830033
www.feonline.net
4pa. Editor: Sara Clay
Gair Rhydd
029 2078 1400
www.cardiffstudents.com
Weekly. Editor: Sally Strachan
Governors' News
0121 643 5787
www.nagm.org.uk
5pa. Editor: Gillian Stunell
Higher Education Review
020 8341 1366
www.highereducationreview.com
3pa. Editor: John Pratt
ICT for Education
020 8334 1600
www.ictforeducation.co.uk
Monthly. Editor: Ian Delaney

The Lecturer
020 7837 3636
www.natfhe.org.uk
5pa. Editor: Midge Purcell
London Student
020 7664 2054
Fortnightly during term
Editor: Alexi Duggins
LSE Magazine
020 7955 7582
www.lse.ac.uk
2pa. Editor: Judith Higgin
The Magic Key
020 8433 2883
Monthly. Editor: Stephanie Cooper
Nursery Education
01926 887799
www.scholastic.co.uk
Monthly. Editor: Sarah Sodhi
Nursery World
020 7782 3120
www.nurseryworld.co.uk
Weekly. Editor: Liz Roberts
Open Learner
01223 400359
www.nec.ac.uk
Website. Editor: Jo McGowan
Oxford Today
01865 280545
www.oxfordtoday.ox.ac.uk
3pa. Editor: Georgina Ferry
Report
020 7930 6441
www.askatl.org.uk
10pa. Editor: Heather Pinnell
Right Start
020 7878 2338
www.rightstartmagazine.co.uk
Bi-monthly. Editor: Lynette Lowthian
Scottish Educational Journal
0131 225 6244
www.eis.org.uk
5pa. Editor: Simon MacAulay
Sesame
01908 652451
www.open.ac.uk/sesame
6pa. Editor: Debbie Dixon
Special Schools Guide
020 7970 4000
www.centaur.co.uk
Annual. Editor: Derek Rogers
Student Direct
0161 275 2943
www.student-direct.co.uk
Weekly during term
Editor: Alexa Gainsbury
The Teacher
020 7380 4708
www.teachers.org.uk
8pa. Editor: Mitch Howard

Teaching Today
0121 453 6150
www.teachersunion.org.uk
5pa. Editor: Joe Devo
Times Educational Supplement
020 7782 3000
www.tes.co.uk
Weekly. Editor: Bob Doe
Times Higher Education Supplement
020 7782 3000
www.thes.co.uk
Weekly. Editor: John O'Leary

Farming

Arable Farming
01728 687970
18pa. Editor: Dominic Kilburn
British Dairying
01438 716220
Monthly. Editor: Judie Allen
Crop Production Magazine
01743 235594
www.cpm.gb.net
Monthly Feb–Oct
Editor: Angus McKirdy
Crops
020 8652 3500
www.reedbusiness.co.uk
Fortnightly. Editor: Charles Able
Dairy Farmer
01732 377273
16pa. Editor: Peter Hollinshead
Farmers Guardian
01772 799411
Weekly. Editor: Liz Falkingham
Farmers Weekly
020 8652 4911
www.fwi.co.uk
Weekly. Editor: Stephen Howe
Feed International
01730 261951
www.wattnet.com
Monthly. Editor: Clay Gill
Living Earth
0117 914 2434
www.soilassociation.org
3pa. Editor: Elisabeth Winkler
NFU Horticulture
020 7331 7359
www.nfuonline.com
3pa. Editor: Martin Stanhope
Poultry International
01730 261951
www.wattnet.com
Monthly. Editor: Jackie Linden
Scottish Farmer
0141 302 7700
Weekly. Editor: Alistair Fletcher

Tractor & Machinery
01959 541444
www.kelsey.co.uk
Monthly. Editor: Peter Love

Health and social care

Ambulance Today
0151 708 8864
www.eclipsepublishing.co.uk
Quarterly. Editor: Declan Heneghan
Arthritis News
020 7380 6500
www.arthritiscare.org.uk
Bi-monthly. Editor: Kate Llewelyn
BMJ
020 7387 4499
www.bmj.com
Weekly. Editor: Richard Smith
CareandHealth
0870 907 7773
www.careandhealth.com
Weekly
Managing editor: Marcia White
Community Care
020 8652 3500
www.communitycare.co.uk
Weekly. Editor: Polly Neate
Doctor
020 8652 3500
www.doctorupdate.net
Weekly. Editor: Charles Creswell
GP
020 8267 5000
www.gponline.com
Weekly. Editor: Colin Cooper
Health Service Journal
020 7874 0253
www.hsj.co.uk
Weekly. Editor: Alastair McLellan
Hospital Doctor
020 8652 3500
www.hospital-doctor.net
Weekly. Editor: Mike Broad
The Lancet
020 7611 4100
www.lancet.com
Weekly. Editor: Richard Horton
Medeconomics
020 8267 5000
www.gponline.com
Monthly. Editor: Julian Tyndale-Biscoe
MIMS
020 8267 5000
www.gponline.com
Monthly. Editor: Colin Duncan
NHS Magazine
0113 306 0000
www.nhs.uk/nhsmagazine
10pa. Editor: Richard Spencer

Nursing Standard
020 8423 1066
www.nursing-standard.co.uk
Weekly. Editor: Jean Gray
Nursing Times
020 7874 0500
www.nursingtimes.net
Weekly. Editor: Rachel Downey
The Pharmaceutical Journal
020 7572 2420
www.pjonline.com
Weekly. Editor: Olivia Timbs
The Practitioner
020 7921 8113
www.practitioner-i.co.uk
Monthly. Editor: Gavin Atkin
The Psychologist
0116 252 9573
www.bps.org.uk/publications
/thepsychologist.cfm
Monthly. Editor: John Sutton
Pulse
020 7921 8102
www.pulse-i.co.uk
Weekly. Editor: Phil Johnson
RCN Bulletin
020 8423 1066
www.nursing-standard.co.uk
Weekly. Editor: Ken Edwards
Update
020 8652 8878
www.doctorupdate.net
Fortnightly. Editor: Andrew Baxter

►► see also **disability**, page 188

Law

Law Society Gazette
020 7320 5820
www.lawgazette.co.uk
Weekly. Editor: Jonathan Ames
The Lawyer
020 7970 4000
www.centaur.co.uk
Weekly. Editor: Catrin Griffiths
Legal Week
020 7566 5600
www.legalweek.com
Weekly. Editor: John Malpas
Media Lawyer
01229 716622
www.medialawyer.press.net
Bi-monthly. Editor: Tom Welsh

Police

Constabulary Magazine
01932 820123
Monthly. Editor: Chris Lock

Police Magazine
020 8335 1000
www.polfed.org
Monthly. Editor: Metin Enver
Police Review
020 8276 4701
www.policereview.com
Weekly. Editor: Katriona Marchant

Property

The Estate Agent
01926 496800
www.naea.co.uk
10pa. Editor: June Warner
Estates Gazette
020 7411 2540
www.reedbusiness.co.uk
Weekly. Editor: Peter Bill
Facilities Management Journal
020 8771 3614
www.fmarena.com
Monthly. Editor: Mark Povey
Facilities Management UK
0161 683 8032
www.worldsfair.co.uk
Bi-monthly. Editor: Mike Appleton
Scotland's New Home Buyer
0131 556 9702
4pa. Editor: Anna Baird

Retail and catering

Asian Trader
020 7928 1234
www.gg2.net
Fortnightly. Editor: R Solanki
Caterer and Hotelkeeper
020 8652 3500
www.caterer-online.com
Weekly. Editor: Mark Lewis
Caterer and Licensee News
01202 552333
Monthly. Editor: Peter Adams
Catering Update
020 8652 3500
www.reedbusiness.co.uk
Monthly. Editor: Kathy Bowry
Class
01293 610442
www.william-reed.co.uk
Monthly. Editor: Paul Wootton
Convenience Store
01293 610277
www.william-reed.co.uk
Fortnightly. Editor: Sonia Young
DNR
020 7240 0420
www.dnrnews.com
Weekly. Editor: Jon Birmingham

Drapers
020 7391 3300
Weekly. Editor: Eric Musgrave

Food Manufacture
01293 610231
www.foodmanufacture.co.uk
Monthly. Editor: Rick Pendrous

Footwear News (FN)
020 7240 0420
www.footwearnews.com
Weekly. Editor: Michel Atmore

Forecourt Trader
01293 610219
www.william-reed.co.uk
Monthly. Editor: Merrill Boulton

The Franchise Magazine
01603 620301
www.franchise-group.com
8pa. Editor: Stuart Anderson

The Grocer
01293 610259
www.grocertoday.co.uk
Weekly. Editor: Julian Hunt

Hospitality
0161 236 2782
www.excelpublishing.co.uk
Monthly. Editor: Lucy Bryson

Independent Retail News
01322 660070
www.irn-talkingshop.co.uk
Fortnightly. Editor: Richard Siddle

Leisure Report
01293 846569
www.martin-info.com
Monthly. Editor: Mel Flaherty

MA Scotland
0131 247 7542
www.william-reed.co.uk
Fortnightly. Editor: Mairi Clarke

MBR
01293 610268
www.william-reed.co.uk
Monthly. Editor: Mary Carmichael

Morning Advertiser
01293 610344
www.william-reed.co.uk
Weekly. Editor: Andrew Pring

Off Licence News
01293 610344
www.william-reed.co.uk
Weekly. Editor: Graham Holter

Party Times
020 7819 1200
www.partytimes.biz
Bi-monthly. Editor: Andrew Maiden

The Pub Business
01474 574435
www.dewberry-boyes.co.uk
Monthly. Editor: Tim Palmer

PubChef
01293 610487
www.william-reed.co.uk
Monthly. Editor: Jo Bruce

Publican
020 8565 4200
www.thepublican.com
42pa. Editor: Lorna Harrison

The Restaurant Business
01474 574436
www.dewberry-boyes.co.uk
Monthly. Editor: David Foad

Shopping Centre
01293 610294
www.william-reed.co.uk
Monthly. Editor: Pat Morgan

Supermarket News
020 7240 0420
www.supermarketnews.com
Weekly. Editor: David Orgel

The Trader
01202 445320
www.thetrader.co.uk
Monthly. Editor: Angela Boyer

Women's Wear Daily (WWD)
020 7240 0420
www.wwd.com
Daily. Editor: James Fallon

WWDBeautyBiz
020 7240 0420
www.wwd.com
9pa. Editor: Peter Born

Science

Clinical Laboratory International
01442 877777
www.cli-online.com
8pa. Editor: Alan Barclay

Nature
020 7833 4000
www.nature.com
Weekly. Editor: Phil Campbell

New Scientist
020 7331 2735
www.newscientist.com
Weekly. Editor: Jeremy Webb

Science
01223 326500
www.sciencemag.org
Weekly. Editor: Andrew Sugden

Technology

Computer Bulletin
01793 417474
www.bcs.org
Bi-monthly. Editor: John Cavanagh

Computer Business Review
020 7919 5000
www.cbronline.com
Monthly. Editor: Jason Stamper

Computer Weekly
020 8652 8979
www.reedbusinessinformation.
co.uk
Weekly. Editor: Karl Schneider

Computing
020 8606 7505
www.computing.co.uk
Weekly. Editor: Mike Gubbins

Developer Network Journal
0117 930 0255
www.dnjonline.com
Website. Editor: Matt Nicholson

Information Age
020 7612 9300
www.infoconomy.com
Monthly. Editor: Kenny MacIver

IT Week
020 8606 7505
www.itweek.co.uk
Weekly. Editor: Toby Wolpe

Scientific Computing World
01223 477411
www.europascience.com
Bi-monthly. Editor: Tom Wilkie

Travel trade

Travel Trade Gazette
020 7921 8029
www.ttglive.com
Weekly. Editor: John Welsh

Travel Weekly
020 8652 8230
www.travelweekly.co.uk
Weekly. Editor: Martin Lane

Transport

Aerospace International
020 7670 4300
www.aerosociety.com
Monthly. Editor: Richard Gardner

Air International
01780 755131
www.airinternational.com
Monthly. Editor: Malcolm English

Automotive Engineer
020 7304 6809
www.pepublishing.com
Monthly. Editor: William Kimberley

Autowired
01565 872107
www.autowired.co.uk
Daily. Editor: Barry Hook

Commercial Motor
020 8652 3252
Weekly. Editor: Andy Salter

Flight International
020 8652 3842
www.flightinternational.com
Weekly. Editor: Kate Sarsfield

Helicopter International
01934 822524
www.helidata.rotor.com
Bi-monthly. Editor: Elfan ap Rees

Motor Trader
01322 660070
www.motortrader.co.uk
Weekly. Editor: Curtis Hutchinson

Motor Transport
020 8652 3284
www.reedbusinessinformation.
co.uk
Weekly. Editor: Andrew Brown

Professional Motor Mechanic
01923 237799
www.hamerville.co.uk
11pa. Editor: Nick Holt

Rail
01733 282718
www.greatmagazines.co.uk
Fortnightly. Editor: Nigel Harris

Railnews
020 7278 6100
www.railnews.co.uk
Monthly. Editor: David Harding

Truck
020 8652 3251
Monthly. Editor: Peter Shakespeare

Truck & Driver
020 8652 3251
Monthly. Editor: Dave Young

Trucking
01452 317753
www.truckingmag.co.uk
Monthly. Editor: Richard Simpson

Journalism trade press

Best Sellers
Newtrade Publishing
11 Angel Gate, City Road
London EC1V 2SD
020 7689 3357
robin.parker@newtrade.co.uk
www.newtrade.co.uk
2pa. Consumer magazine data and ABC results. Editor: Robin Parker

CPU News
Commonwealth Press Union
17 Fleet Street
London EC4Y 1AA
020 7583 7733
cpu@cpu.org.uk
www.cpu.org.uk
6pa. In-house newspaper of the Association of Commonwealth Newspapers.
Editorial contact: Rosie Vlasto

The Journal
The Chartered Institute of Journalists
2 Dock Offices
Surrey Quays Road
London SE16 2XU
020 7252 1187
memberservices@ioj.co.uk
www.ioj.co.uk
Quarterly. reports the activities of the Institute and industry developments
Editor: Andy Smith

The Journalist
National Union of Journalists
Acorn House
308–312 Gray's Inn Rd
London WC1X 8DP
020 7278 7916
timg@nuj.org.uk
www.nuj.org.uk
10pa. free to union members
Editor: Tim Gopsill

Magazine Retailer
Newtrade Publishing
11 Angel Gate, City Road
London EC1V 2SD
020 7689 3357
robin.parker@newtrade.co.uk
www.newtrade.co.uk
2pa. Information on magazine sales in all sectors. Editor: Robin Parker

Magazine World
FIPP
Queens House
55–56 Lincoln's Inn Field
London WC2A 3LJ
020 7404 4169
info@fipp.com
www.fipp.com
Quarterly. International consumer and b2b publishing trends.
Editor: Arif Durrani

Media Moves
Quantum Business Media
Quantum House
19 Scarbrook Road
Croydon CR9 1LX
020 8565 4333
www.mediamoves.co.uk
Website. Online selection of jobs in the media industry.
Editorial contact: Kevin May

News from NewstrAid
Newstraid Benevolent Society
PO Box 306, Great Dunmow
Essex CM6 1HY
01371 874198
oldben@newstraid.demon.co.uk
www.newstraid.org.uk
Annual. Charity for the newspaper industry.
Editorial contact: Tansey Davis

Press Gazette
Quantum Business Media
Quantum House
19 Scarbrook Road
Croydon CR9 1LX
020 8565 4448
pged@pressgazette.co.uk
www.pressgazette.co.uk
Weekly. Editor: Ian Reeves

Ulrich's Periodical Directory
Bowker
3rd Floor, Farringdon House
Wood Street, East Grinstead
West Sussex RH19 1UZ
01342 310450
sales@bowker.co.uk
www.ulrichsweb.com
Updated annually in print, quarterly on cd, monthly on website International directory

TV trade press

Advance Production News
Crimson Communications
211a Station House
Greenwich Communication Centre
Greenwich High Road
London SE10 8JL
020 8305 6905
www.crimson.uk.com
Monthly. Listings for production companies. Editor: Alan Williams

BFI Film and Television Handbook
The British Film Institute
21 Stephen Street
London W1T 1LN
020 7255 1444
eddie.dyja@bfi.org.uk
www.bfi.org.uk/handbook
Annual. Editor: Eddie Dyja

Broadband TV News
3 Jansen Walk, Hope Street
London SW11 2AZ
020 7585 3849
office@broadbandtvnews.com
www.broadbandtvnews.com
Free weekly emails & subscription newsletters. Editor: Julian Clover

Broadcast
Emap Media
33–39 Bowling Green Lane
London EC1R 0DA
020 7505 8000
bcletters@emap.com
www.broadcastnow.co.uk
Weekly. Trade magazine for TV & radio. Editor: Conor Dignam

Broadcast Hardware International
Hardware Creations
48 The Broadway, Maidenhead
Berks SL6 1PW
01628 773935
cathy@hardwarecreations.tv
www.hardwarecreations.tv
10 pa. Editor: Dick Hobbs

Cable & Satellite Europe
Informa Media and Telecoms
Mortimer House
37–41 Mortimer Street
London W1T 3JH
020 7017 5533
media.enquiries@informa.com
www.informamedia.com
10 pa. Editor: Stuart Thomson

Cable & Satellite International
Perspective Publishing
402 The Fruit and Wool Exchange
Brushfield Street, London E1 6EP
020 7426 0101
justin@cable-satellite.com
www.cable-satellite.com
6pa. Editor: John Moulding

Channel 21 International magazine
C21 Media
Top Floor, 25 Phipp Street
London EC2A 4NP
020 7729 7460
press@c21media.net
www.c21media.net
10pa. Editor: David Jenkins

Commonwealth Broadcaster
Commonwealth Broadcasting Association
17 Fleet Street
London EC4Y 1AA
020 7583 5550
cba@cba.org.uk
www.cba.org.uk
Quarterly. Editor: Elizabeth Smith

Contacts
The Spotlight, 7 Leicester Place
London WC2H 7RJ
020 7437 7631
info@spotlightcd.com
www.spotlightcd.com
Annual. Contacts for stage, film, TV and radio. Editor: Kate Poynton

Crewfinder
Adleader Publications
15 Chartwell Park
Belfast BT8 6NG
028 9079 7902
mail@adleader.co.uk
www.crewfinderwales.co.uk
Annual. Wales' film, TV and video directory. Proprietor: Stan Mairs

Digilook
7 Burgess Green, Deal
Kent CT14 0AU
07709 118854
andi@digilook.net
www.digilook.net
*Web. Digital TV & radio
Editors: Andi Gasking, Alex Oughton*

Digital Spy
6 Queen's Elm Square
London SW3 6ED
07814 776894
nwilkes@digitalspy.co.uk
www.digitalspy.co.uk
Web. Digital TV. Editor: Neil Wilkes

FilmBang
Marianne Mellin
43 Hyndland Road
Glasgow G12 9UX
0141 334 2456
info@filmbang.com
www.filmbang.com
Annual. Scotland's film and video directory. Editor: Marianne Mellin

IBE
DMG Business Media
Queensway House, 2 Queens Way
Redhill, Surrey RH1 1QS
01737 855224
info@ibeweb.com
www.ibeweb.com
12pa. International broadcast engineering. Editor: Neil Nixon

Kemps Film, TV, Video Handbook (UK edition)
Reed Business Information
Windsor Court, East Grinstead
House East Grinstead
West Sussex RH19 1XA
01342 332073
kemps@reedinfo.co.uk
www.kftb.com
Annual. Guide to international production. Editor: Pat Huwson

The Knowledge
CMP Information
Riverbank House, Angel Lane
Tonbridge, Kent TN9 1SE
01732 377591
knowledge@cmpinformation.com
www.theknowledgeonline.com
Annual. Production directory

Line Up
Line Up Publications
The Hawthornes
4 Conference Grove
Crowle WR7 4SF
01905 381725
editor@lineup.biz
www.ibs.org.uk
*6pa. Journal of the Institute of Broadcast Sound.
Editor: Hugh Robjohns*

Multichannel News
Chilton Company, 37 The Towers
Lower Mortlake Road
Richmond TW9 2JR
020 8948 8561
chrisforrester@compuserve.com
www.multichannel.com
Weekly. Editor: Chris Forester

Pact Directory of Independent Producers

Producers Alliance for Cinema and Television (PACT)
45 Mortimer Street
London W1W 8HJ
020 7331 6000
enquiries@pact.co.uk
www.pact.co.uk
Annual. Directory of independent producers. Editor: Louise Bateman

Pro Sound News

CMP Information, Ludgate House
245 Blackfriars Road
London SE1 9UR
020 7921 8319
info@cmpinformation.com
www.cmpinformation.com
12pa. Audio industry
Editor: David Robinson

The Production Guide

Emap Information
33–39 Bowling Green Lane
London EC1R 0DA
020 7505 8000
theproductionguide@Emap.com
www.productionguideonline.com
Annual. Information on production
Editor: Mei Mei Rogers

Satellite Finance

Thompson Stanley Publishers
1–3 Leonard Street
London EC2A 4AQ
020 7251 2967
oliver.cann@satellitefinance.com
www.telecomfinance.com
11pa. Finance journal for executives
Editor: Oliver Cann

Screen Digest

Screen Digest
Lymehouse Studios
38 Georgiana Street
London NW1 0EB
020 7424 2820
editorial@screendigest.com
www.screendigest.com
Monthly. Editor: David Fisher

Screen International

Emap Media
33–39 Bowling Green Lane
London EC1R 0DA
020 7505 8080
screeninternational@hotmail.com
www.screendaily.com
Weekly. News service for global film industry. Editor: Colin Brown

Sports TV Yearbook

Perspective Media, PO Box 22499
London W6 9YS
020 7937 3636
pnicholson@sportsvisionnews.com
www.sportscentric.com
Annual. Editor: Jay Stuart

Stage Screen and Radio

Bectu, 373–377 Clapham Road
London SW9 9BT
020 7346 0900
janice@stagescreenandradio.org.uk
www.bectu.org.uk
10pa. Broadcasting union
Editor: Janice Turner

Televisual

Centaur Communications
50 Poland Street
London W1F 7AX
020 7970 4000
mundy.ellis@centaur.co.uk
www.mad.co.uk
Monthly. Trade magazine for TV
Editor: Mundy Ellis

TV International

Informa Media and Telecoms
Mortimer House
37–41 Mortimer Street
London W1T 3JH
020 7017 4269
toby.scott@informa.com
www.informamedia.com
Daily. International TV listings
Editor: Stewart Clarke

TBI (Television Business International)

Informa Media and Telecoms
Mortimer House
37–41 Mortimer Street
London W1T 3JH
020 7453 2300
kevin.scott@informa.com
www.informamedia.com
Annual. Directory to businesses
Editor: Kevin Scott

TV Technology and Production

IMAS Publishing UK
Atlantica House, 11 Station Road
St Ives, Cambs PE27 5BH
01480 461555
tvteurope@aol.com
www.imaspub.com
6pa. Broadcasting and production technology. Editor: Mark Hallinger

TVB Europe

CMP Information, Prospect House
1 Prospect Road, Dublin 9
00 353 1 882 4444
sgrice@cmpinformation.com
www.tvbeurope.com
Monthly. Broadcasting innovation and technology.
Editor: Fergal Ringrose

VLV Bulletin

Voice of the Listener and Viewer
101 Kings Drive
Gravesend DA12 5BQ
01474 352835
vlv@btinternet.com
www.vlv.org.uk
Quarterly. Consumer campaigning body. Editor: Jocelyn Hay

Zerb

The Deeson Group
Ewell House, Gravney Road
Faversham, Kent ME13 8UP
01795 535468
alichap@mac.com
www.gtc.org.uk
2pa. For camera operators
Editor: Alison Chapman

Radio trade press

Advance Production News
Crimson Communications
211a Station House, Greenwich
Communication Centre
Greenwich High Road
London SE10 8JL
020 8305 6905
www.crimson.uk.com
*Monthly. Listings for production
companies. Editor: Alan Williams*

Audio Media
IMAS Publishing UK
Atlantica House, 11 Station Road
St Ives, Cambs PE27 5BH
01480 461555
pr@audiomedia.com
www.audiomedia.com
*Monthly. Professional audio.
Editor: Paul Mac*

Broadcast
Emap Media
33–39 Bowling Green Lane
London EC1R 0DA
020 7505 8000
bcletters@emap.com
www.broadcastnow.co.uk
*Weekly. TV & radio industry.
Editor: Conor Dignam*

Broadcast Hardware
International
Hardware Creations
48 The Broadway
Maidenhead, Berks SL6 1PW
01628 773935
cathy@hardwarecreations.tv
www.hardwarecreations.tv
10pa. Editor: Dick Hobbs

Commonwealth Broadcaster
Commonwealth Broadcasting
Association, 17 Fleet Street
London EC4Y 1AA
020 7583 5550
cba@cba.org.uk
www.cba.org.uk
Quarterly. Editor: Elizabeth Smith

Contacts
The Spotlight, 7 Leicester Place
London WC2H 7RJ
020 7437 7631
info@spotlightcd.com
www.spotlightcd.com
*Annual. Contacts for stage, film, TV
and radio. Editor: Kate Poynton*

Line Up
Line Up Publications
The Hawthornes
4 Conference Grove
Crowle WR7 4SF
01905 381725
editor@lineup.biz
www.ibs.org.uk
*6pa. Journal of the Institute of
Broadcast Sound. Editor: Hugh
Robjohns*

Pro Sound News
CMP Information, Ludgate House
245 Blackfriars Road
London SE1 9UR
020 7921 8319
info@cmpinformation.com
www.cmpinformation.com
*12pa. Audio industry. Editor: David
Robinson*

QSheet
10 Northburgh Street
London EC1V 0AT
020 7253 8888
*Monthly. Support material for
presenters and producers.
Contact: Nik Harta*

Radcom
Radio Society of Great Britain
Lambda House
Cranbourne Road
Potters Bar EN6 3JE
01707 659015
radcom@rsgb.org.uk
www.rsgb.org
*Monthly. Radio enthusiasts.
Editor: Steve Telenius-Lowe*

Radio Magazine
Radio Magazine
Crown House, 25 High Street
Rothwell, Northants NN14 6AD
01536 418558
info@theradiomagazine.co.uk
www.theradiomagazine.co.uk
*Weekly. Radio news for industry.
Editor: Paul Boon*

Stage Screen and Radio
Bectu, 373–377 Clapham Road
London SW9 9BT
020 7346 0900
janice@stagescreenandradio.org.uk
www.bectu.org.uk
*10pa. Broadcasting union.
Editor: Janice Turner*

VLV Bulletin
Voice of the Listener and Viewer
101 Kings Drive
Gravesend DA12 5BQ
01474 352835
vlv@btinternet.com
www.vlv.org.uk
*Quarterly. Consumer campaigning
body. Editor: Jocelyn Hay*

New media trade press

3G Mobile (informa UK)
Informa Telecoms Group
Mortimer House
37–41 Mortimer Street
London W1T 3JH
Press: 020 7017 5000
press@informa.com
www.telecoms.com
23pa

Computer Weekly
Quadrant House, The Quadrant
Sutton, Surrey SM2 5AS
020 8652 3500
editorial@computerweekly.com
www.computerweekly.co.uk
Weekly

Computing
VNU Business Publications
VNU House
32–34 Broadwick Street
London W1A 2HG
Switchboard: 020 7316 9000
www.computing.co.uk
Weekly

Content Management Focus
Ark Publishing
86–88 Upper Richmond Road
Putney, London SW15 2UR
020 8785 2700
cmfocus@ark-group.com
www.cmfocus.com
10pa

IT Europa
656 The Crescent
Colchester Business Park
Colchester CO4 9YQ
01206 224400
contact@iteuropa.com
www.iteuropa.com
20pa

New Media Age
Centaur Communications
St Giles House, 50 Poland Street
London W1F 7AX
020 7970 4000
michael.nutley@centaur.co.uk
www.newmediazero.com
Weekly

The Online Reporter
Information Express
PO Box 2077, Verney Park
Buckingham MK18 1WQ
01280 820560
simon@g2news.com
www.g2news.com
Weekly

The Register
www.theregister.co.uk
Website

Revolution
Haymarket Business Publications
174 Hammersmith Road
London W6 7JP
020 8267 4947
donlawrencejones@haynet.com
www.revolutionmagazine.com
Monthly

VNUnet.com
VDU House
32–34 Broadwick Street
London W1A 2HG
020 7316 9725
www.vnunet.com
Website

World Telemedia
Network for Online
    Commerce Services
Tulip House
70 Borough High Street
London SE1 1XF
0870 7327327
info@noconline.org
www.noconline.org
Quarterly

ZDNet UK and Silicon.com
International House
1 St Katherines Way
London E1W 1UN
020 7903 6800
silicon.marketing@silicon.com
www.silicon.com
www.zdnet.co.uk
Website

Books trade press

Annual Bibliography of English Language and Literature
Modern Humanities Research
    Association
c/o Cambridge University Library
West Road, Cambridge CB3 9DF
01223 333058
abell@bibl.org
www.mhra.org.uk
/Publication/Journals/abell.html
Annual

Books
Publishing News, 7 John Street
London WC1N 2ES
0870 870 2345
info@publishingnews.co.uk
www.publishingnews.co.uk
Weekly

Books in the Media
VNU Entertainment Media
Fifth Floor, Endeavour House
189 Shaftesbury Avenue
London WC2H 8TJ
020 7420 6006
webeditor@bookseller.co.uk
www.thebookseller.com
Weekly

The Bookseller
VNU Entertainment Media
5th Floor Endeavour House
189 Shaftesbury Avenue
London WC2H 8TJ
020 7420 6006
joel.rickett@bookseller.co.uk
www.thebookseller.com
Weekly

Booksellers Association Directory of Members
The Booksellers Association of
    the UK and Ireland
272 Vauxhall Bridge Road
London SW1V 1BA
020 7802 0802
mail@booksellers.org.uk
www.booksellers.org.uk
Annual

BookWorld Magazine
Christchurch Publishers
2 Caversham Street
London SW3 4AH
020 7351 4995
leonard.holdsworth@
    btopenworld.com
Monthly

Digital Demand – The Journal of Printing and Publishing Technology
PIRA International, Randalls Road
Leatherhead KT22 7RU
01372 802080
publications@pira.co.uk
www.piranet.com
6pa

London Review of Books
Nicholas Spice
28 Little Russell Street
London WC1A 2HN
020 7209 1141
edit@lrb.co.uk
www.lrb.co.uk
Fortnightly

Publishing News
Publishing News
39 Store Street
London WC1E 7DS
0870 870 2345
mailbox@publishingnews.co.uk
www.publishingnews.co.uk
Weekly

Writers Forum
Writers International
PO Box 3229
Bournemouth BH1 1ZS
01202 589828
editorial@writers-forum.com
www.writers-forum.com
12pa

Writers News/ Writing Magazine
Warner Group Publications
1st Floor, Victoria House
143–145 The Headrow
Leeds LS1 5RL
0113 200 2929
derek.hudson@writersnews.co.uk
www.writersnews.co.uk
Monthly

Global media trade press

Advertising Age Global
711 Third Ave, New York
NY 10017-4036, USA
00 1 212 210 0100
editor@adage.com
www.adageglobal.com
Website

The Fourth Estate
Suite 3, 79 Roscoe Street
Bondi Beach, Sydney NSW 2026
Australia
00 61 416 178 908
michael@walsh.net
www.fourth-estate.com
Website & newsletter. Editor: Mike Walsh. Digital techology & media

MediaChannel
575 8th Avenue, #2200
New York, NY 10018, USA
00 1 212 246 0202
editor@mediachannel.org
www.mediachannel.org
Website. Executive director: Timothy Karr; executive editor: Danny Schechter

Middle East Media Guide
PO Box 74375
Dubai, UAE
00 971 50 553 0209
editor@
  middleeastmediaguide.com
www.middleeastmediaguide.com
Annual. Editor: Ben Smalley

Online Journalism Review
3502 Watt Way, Los Angeles
CA 90089-0281, USA
00 1 213 821 1285
editor@ojr.org
www.ojr.org
Website. Editor: Larry Pryor

PR Week
Haymarket Professional
Publications
174 Hammersmith Road
London W6 7JP
020 8267 4429
prweek@haynet.com
www.prweek.com
Weekly. Editor-in-chief: Kate Nicholas; news editor: Ravi Chandiramani

World Press Freedom Review
IPI Headquarters, Spiegelgasse 2
A-1010 Vienna, Austria
00 43 1 512 90 11
ipi@freemedia.at
www.freemedia.at/wpfr/world.html
Website. Director: Johann P Fritz

Advertising trade press

Advertising Age Global
711 Third Ave, New York
NY 10017-4036, USA
00 1 212 210 0414
editor@adage.com
www.adageglobal.com
Website. Editor: Hoag Levins

Brand Strategy
Centaur Communications
St Giles House, 50 Poland Street
London W1F 7AX
020 7943 8160
elen.lewis@centaur.co.uk
www.mad.co.uk/bs
Monthly. Editor: Elen Lewis

Campaign
Haymarket Business Publications
174 Hammersmith Road
London W6 7JP
020 8267 4683
campaign@haynet.com
www.brandrepublic.com
Weekly. Editor: Caroline Marshall

Creative Review
Centaur Communications
St Giles House, 50 Poland Street
London W1F 7AX
020 7970 4000
patrick.burgoyne@centaur.co.uk
www.creativereview.co.uk
Monthly. Editor: Patrick Burgoyne

Design Week
Centaur Communications
St Giles House, 50 Poland Street
London W1F 7AX
020 7970 4000
lyndark@centaur.co.uk
www.designweek.co.uk
Weekly. Editor: Lynda Relph-Knight

Marketing
Haymarket Business Publications
174 Hammersmith Road
London W6 7JP
020 8267 5000
marketing@haynet.com
www.marketingmagazine.co.uk
Weekly. Editor: Craig Smith

Marketing Direct
Haymarket Business Publications
174 Hammersmith Road
London W6 7JP
020 8267 5000
bill.britt@haynet.com
www.mxdirect.co.uk
Monthly. Editor: Bill Britt

Marketing Week
Centaur Communications
St Giles House, 50 Poland Street
London W1F 7AX
020 7970 4000
mw.editorial@centaur.co.uk
www.marketing-week.co.uk
Weekly. Editor: Stuart Smith

Media Week
Quantum Business Media
Quantum House, 19 Scarbrook
Road
Croydon CR9 1LX
020 8565 4326
editorial@mediaweek.co.uk
www.mediaweek.co.uk
Weekly. Editor: Tim Burrowes.
Covers media agencies, media sales
and marketers

Shots
Emap Information
33–39 Bowling Green Lane
London EC1R 0DA
020 7505 8000
lyndy.stout@shots.net
www.shots.net
International advertising, 6pa.
Editor: Lyndy Stout

PR trade press

Hollis UK PR Annual
Hollis Publishing, Harlequin House
7 High Street
Teddington TW11 8EL
020 8977 7711
prannual@hollis-pr.co.uk
www.hollis-pr.com
Press and PR contacts. Annual.
Editor: Sarah Hughes

PR Week
Haymarket Business Publications
174 Hammersmith Road
London W6 7JP
020 8267 4429
prweek@haynet.com
www.prweek.com
Weekly. Editor-in-Chief: Kate
Nicholas

Contact (PRWeek Black Book)
Haymarket Business Publications
174 Hammersmith Road
London W6 7JP
020 8267 4496
sales@haynet.com
www.prweek.co.uk
Press and PR contacts. Annual

Media law journals

Entertainment and Media Law Reports
Sweet and Maxwell
100 Avenue Road
London NW3 3PF
020 7393 7000
marketinginformation@
sweetandmaxwell.co.uk
www.sweetandmaxwell.co.uk
6pa

Entertainment Law Review
Sweet and Maxwell
100 Avenue Road
London NW3 3PF
020 7393 7000
marketinginformation@
sweetandmaxwell.co.uk
www.sweetandmaxwell.co.uk
8pa

International Journal of Communications Law and Policy
Offentlich-rechtliche Abteilung
Universitatsstrasse 14–15
48143 Munster, Germany
00 49 251 832 8411
www.digital-law.net/IJCLP
2pa, Jan & July

IP Law and Business
International Publications
020 7936 9401
rmenzies@
amlaw-international.com
www.ipww.com
12pa & annual digest issue

Media Law and Policy
New York Law School
57 Worth Street, New York
NY 10013-2960, USA
001 212 431 2899 x4305
aabrigo@nyls.edu
www.nyls.edu/pages/1572.asp

Media Lawyer
01229 716622
Media_lawyer@pa.press.net
www.medialawyer.press.net
Bi-monthly

Association of American Correspondents in London
c/o Time Life International
Brettenham House,
Lancaster Place
London WC2E 7TL
020 7499 4080
elizabeth_lea@timemagazine.com

Association of British Science Writers (ABSW)
Wellcome Wolfson Building
165 Queen's Gate
London SW7 5HE
870 770 3361
absw@absw.org.uk
www.absw.org.uk

Association of Freelance Writers
Sevendale House,
7 Dale Street
Manchester M1 1JB
0161 228 2362
nn@writersbureau.com
www.writersbureau.com
/resources.htm

Audit Bureau of Circulations (ABC)
Saxon House,
211 High Street
Berkhamsted
Hertfordshire HP4 1AD
1442 870800
marketing@abc.org.uk
www.abc.org.uk

Authors' Club
40 Dover Street,
London W1S 4NP
020 7499 8581
circles@author.co.uk
www.author.co.uk

British Copyright Council
29–33 Berners Street
London W1T 3AB
01986 788122
secretary@britishcopyright.org
www.britishcopyright.org

British Guild of Beer Writers
83B Elmwood Rd
London SE24 9NR
020 8853 8585
peterhaydon@onetel.net.uk
www.beerguild.com

British Guild of Travel Writers
51B Askew Crescent
London W12 9DN
020 8749 1128
charlotte.c@virtualnecessities.com
www.bgtw.org

British Newspaper Library
The British Library
Newspaper Library, Colindale
Avenue
London NW9 5HE
020 7412 7353
newspaper@bl.uk
www.bl.uk/catalogues
/newspapers.html

British Society of Magazine Editors (BSME)
137 Hale Lane, Edgware
Middlesex HA8 9QP
020 8906 4664
admin@bsme.com
www.bsme.com

Broadcasting Press Guild
Tiverton, The Ridge, Woking
Surrey GU22 7EQ
01483 764895
torin.douglas@bbc.co.uk

Bureau of Freelance Photographers
Focus House, 497 Green Lanes
London N13 4BP
020 8882 3315
info@thebfp.com
www.thebfp.com

Campaign for Freedom of Information
Suite 102, 16 Baldwins Gardens
London EC1N 7RJ
020 7831 7477
admin@cfoi.demon.co.uk
www.cfoi.org.uk

Campaign for Press and Broadcasting Freedom
2nd Floor, Vi and Garner Smith
House, 23 Orford Road
Walthamstow, London E17 9NL
020 8521 5932
freepress@cpbf.org.uk
www.cpbf.org.uk

Chartered Institute of Journalists
2 Dock Offices, Surrey Quays
Road
London SE16 2XU
020 7252 1187
memberservices@ioj.co.uk
www.ioj.co.uk

The Critics' Circle
51 Vartry Road, London N15 6PS
info@criticscircle.org.uk
www.criticscircle.org.uk

Foreign Press Association in London
11 Carlton House Terrace
London SW1Y 5AJ
020 7930 0445
secretariat@foreign-press.org.uk
www.foreign-press.org.uk

Garden Writers' Guild
c/o Institute of Horticulture
14/15 Belgrave Square
London SW1X 8PS
020 7245 6943
gwg@horticulture.org.uk
www.gardenwriters.co.uk

Guild of Agricultural Journalists
Charmwood,
47 Court Meadow
Rotherfield, East Sussex
TN6 3LQ
01892 853187
don.gomery@farmingline.com
www.gaj.org.uk

Guild of Food Writers
020 7610 1180
guild@gfw.co.uk
www.gfw.co.uk

Guild of Motoring Writers
39 Beswick Avenue
Bournemouth BH10 4EY
01202 518808
gensec@gomw.co.uk
www.guildofmotoringwriters.co.uk

International Newspaper Marketing Association
10300 North Central Expressway
Suite 467, Texas 75231
USA
00 1 214 373 9111
inma@inma.org
www.inma.org

Medical Writers' Group
The Society of Authors
84 Drayton Gardens
London SW10 9SB
020 7373 6642
info@societyofauthors.org
www.societyofauthors.org

National Union of Journalists
Acorn House,
308–312 Gray's Inn Rd
London WC1X 8DP
020 7278 7916
info@nuj.org.uk
www.nuj.org.uk

Newspaper Marketing Agency
Berkeley Square House
Berkeley Square,
London W1J 6BD
020 7887 6112
enquiries@nmauk.co.uk
www.nmauk.co.uk

Newspaper Society
Bloomsbury House
74–77 Great Russell St
London WC1B 3DA
020 7636 7014
ns@newspapersoc.org.uk
www.newspapersoc.org.uk

Outdoor Writers' Guild
PO Box 118,
Twickenham TW1 2LR
info@owg.org.uk
www.owg.org.uk

Periodical Publishers Association (PPA)
Queens House,
28 Kingsway
London WC2B 6JR
020 7404 4166
info1@ppa.co.uk
www.ppa.co.uk

The Picture Research Association
c/o 1 Willow Court,
off Willow Street
London EC2A 4QB
chair@picture-research.org.uk
www.picture-research.org.uk

Press Complaints Commission
1 Salisbury Square
London EC4Y 8JB
020 7353 1248
complaints@pcc.org.uk
www.pcc.org.uk

Scottish Newspaper Publishers Association
48 Palmerston Place
Edinburgh EH12 5DE
0131 220 4353
info@snpa.org.uk
www.snpa.org.uk

Scottish Print Employers Federation and Scottish Daily Newspaper Society
48 Palmerston Place
Edinburgh EH12 5DE
0131 220 4353
info@spef.org.uk
www.spef.org.uk

Society of Editors
University Centre,
Granta Place
Mill Lane, Cambridge
CB2 1RU
01223 304080
info@societyofeditors.org
www.societyofeditors.org

Society of Women Writers & Journalists
swwriters@aol.com
www.swwj.co.uk

The Sports Journalists' Association of Great Britain
c/o Victoria House
Bloomsbury Square
London WC1B 4SE
020 7273 1589
petta.naylor@sportengland.org
www.sportsjournalists.co.uk

News and picture agencies Contacts

National Association of Press Agencies
41 Lansdowne Crescent
Leamington Spa
Warwickshire CV32 4PR
01926 424181
secretariat@napa.org.uk
www.napa.org.uk

4/7 Media (Photography)
200 St Andrews Road
Bordesley Village,
Birmingham
West Midlands B9 4JG
0121 753 1329
Photographer covering news, sports, features, PR and commercial

7 Day Press
32 West Nile Street
Glasgow G1 2RQ
0141 572 0060
7daypress@aol.com
www.7daypress.co.uk
Scottish sport

AFX News
Finsbury Tower
103–105 Bunhill Row
London EC1Y 8TN
020 7422 4870
john.manley@afxnews.com
www.afxpress.com
Financial news, pan-European

Agence France-Presse, UK
78 Fleet Street, London
EC4Y 1NB
020 7353 7461
london.bureau@afp.com
www.afp.com
Major agency

Airtime Television News
PO Box 258,
Maidenhead SL6 9YR
01628 482763
info@airtimetv.co.uk
www.airtimetv.co.uk
Heathrow airport

Alscot News Agency
PO Box 6, Haddington
EH41 3NQ
01620 822578
allscotnewsuk@compuserve.com
Scottish news

Anglia Press Agency
17A Whiting Street
Bury St Edmunds,
Suffolk IP33 1NR
01284 702421
East Anglia, words and pictures

ANSA News Agency
Essex House, 12–13 Essex Street
London WC2R 3AA
020 7240 5514
ansalondra@yahoo.com
www.ansa.it
News worldwide

Apex News and Picture Agency
Priests Court, Main Road
Exminster, Exeter EX6 8AP
01392 824024
apex@apexnewspix.com
www.apexnewspix.com
South-west. All news

APTN
The Interchange, Oval Road
Camden Lock, London NW1 7DZ
020 7482 7400
aptninfo@ap.org
www.aptn.com
International newsgathering

Associated Press News Agency
12 Norwich Street
London EC4A 1BP
020 7353 1515
www.ap.org
Worldwide all news

Associated Sports Photography
21 Green Walk,
Leicester LE3 6SE
0116 232 0310
asp@sports-photos.co.uk
www.sporting-heroes.net
Worldwide sports, politics, travel

Australian Associated Press
Associated Press Building
12 Norwich Street
London EC4A 1QJ
020 7353 0153
news.london@aap.com.au
www.aap.com.au
Overseas news to London & New York

Bellis News Agency
14B Kenelm Road
Rhos on Sea, Colwyn Bay
North Wales LL28 4ED
01492 549503
bellisd@aol.com
North Wales (excluding Deeside)

Big Picture Press Agency
50–54 Clerkenwell Road
London EC1M 5PS
020 7250 3555
picturedesk@bigpictures.com
www.bigpicturesphoto.com
Celebrities

Bloomberg LP
City Gate House
39–45 Finsbury Square
London EC2A 1PQ
020 7330 7500
newsdesk@bloomberg.net
www.bloomberg.com
Worldwide financial

Bournemouth News & Picture Service
1st Floor Offices
5–7 Southcote Road
Bournemouth BH1 3LR
01202 558833
news@bnps.co.uk
www.bnps.co.uk
News and features

Calyx Multimedia
41 Churchward Avenue
Swindon SN2 1NJ
01793 520131
richard@calyxpix.com
www.calyxpix.com
Stills, news and freelance cameraman

Canadian Press
Associated Press House
12 Norwich Street
London EC4 1QE
020 7353 6355
www.cp.org

Capital Press Agency
14 Canongate Venture
New Street,
Edinburgh
EH8 8BH
0131 652 3999
capitalnews@hemedia.co.uk;
capitalpix@hemedia.co.uk
www.hemedia.co.uk
Edinburgh, Lothians and Borders

Capital Pictures
85 Randolph Avenue
London W9 1DL
020 7286 2212
sales@capitalpictures.com
www.capitalpictures.com
International celebrities

Cassidy & Leigh Southern News Service
Exchange House, Hindhead Road
Hindhead GU26 6AA
01428 607330
denis@cassidyandleigh.com
News and pictures

Caters News Agency
Queens Gate, Suite 40
121 Suffolk Street Queensway
Birmingham B1 1LX
0121 616 1100
news@catersnews.com;
features@catersnews.com;
pix@catersnews.com
West Midlands news, featuring pictures and sport

Cavendish Press and CPMedia
3rd Floor, Albert House
17 Bloom Street
Manchester M1 3HZ
0161 237 1066
newsdesk@cavendish-
    press.co.uk
www.cavendish-press.co.uk;
www.cpmedia.co.uk
News & pictures

Celtic News
PO Box 26, Llangadog
Carmarthenshire SA19 9YR
01550 740 209
features@celticnews.co.uk
www.celticnews.co.uk
UK-wide features for nationals and magazines

Central News Network
Suite 7, 350 Main Street
Canelon, Falkirk FK1 4EG
01324 630505
jimdavisofcnn@aol.com
Central Scotland news features

Central Press Features
5th Floor, BEP Building
Temple Way, Bristol BS99 7HD
0117 934 3600
mail@central-press.co.uk
www.central-press.co.uk
Worldwide editorial syndication

Centre Press Agency
2 Clairmont Gardens
Glasgow G3 7LW
0141 332 8888
centrenews@hemedia.co.uk;
centrepix@hemedia.co.uk
www.hemedia.co.uk
Central and southern Scotland

Chapman & Page
Dengate House, Amber Hill
Boston PE20 3RL
01205 290477
chapmanpage@
    internett.demon.co.uk

Chester News Service
Linen Hall House,
Stanley Street
Chester CH1 2LR
01244 345562
news@chesterstandard.co.uk
www.chesterstandardnow.co.uk
North Wales area

Chester Press Bureaux
Riverside House
Brymau 3 Trading Estate
River Lane Saltney
Chester CH4 8RQ
01244 678575
ron@chesterpb.freeserve.co.uk
Chester area

Computer Wire
Charles House
108–110 Finchley Road
London NW3 5JJ
020 7675 7000
kevin.white@computerwire.co.uk
www.computerwire.com
Worldwide IT index links

Copyline Scotland
Second Floor,
17 Queensgate
Inverness IV1 1DF
copylinescotland@aol.com
Scottish Highlands

Cotswold & Swindon News Service
Oxford House,
101 Bath Road
Swindon SN1 4AX
01793 485461
cotswin@stares.co.uk
www.stares.co.uk
Swindon area

Coventry News Service
7 Queen Victoria Road
Coventry CV1 3JS
024 7663 3777
adent@
    advent-communications.co.uk
www.advent-
    communications.co.uk
Coventry area

David Hoffman Photo Library
c/o BAPLA, 18 Vine Hill
London EC1R 5DZ
020 8981 5041
lib@hoffmanphotos.com
www.hoffmanphotos.com
Social issues in UK & Europe

DBSP
112 Cornwall Street South
Glasgow G41 1AA
0141 427 5344
stewart.mcdougall@btclick.com
Worldwide sport

DobsonAgency.co.uk
20 Seafield Avenue, Osgodby
Scarborough YO11 3QG
01723 585141
pix@dobsonagency.co.uk
www.dobsonagency.co.uk
Press and PR, around UK

Double Red Photographic
The Old School
Thorn Lane, Goxhill
Barrow upon Humber DN19 7JE
01469 531416
doublered@atlas.co.uk
www.doublered.co.uk
Motorsport photography

Dow Jones Newswires
10 Fleet Place, Limeburner Lane
London EC4M 7QN
020 7842 9900
djequitiesnews.london@
    dowjones.com
www.djnewswires.com
International financial news

DPA (German Press Agency)
30 Old Queen Street
St James's Park
London SW1H 9HP
020 7233 2888
london@dpa.com
www.dpa.com
Global media services

Dragon News & Picture Agency
21 Walter Road
Swansea SA1 5NQ
01792 464800
mail@dragon-pictures.com
www.dragon-pictures.com
All news & PR

Edittech International (IT News Agency)
5 Exeter Close
Chippenham SN14 0YG
01249 444416
elspethwales@aol.com
www.edittech.com
Articles and publications from US t Australia

Emirates News Agency
The Studio, 143 Lavender Hill
London SW11 5QJ
020 7228 1060
mia@mia.gb.com
www.mia.gb.com
News from Arab emirates

Empics Sports Photo Agency
Pavilion House, 16 Castle Boulevard
Nottingham NG7 1FL
0115 844 7447
info@empics.com
www.empics.com
Sports worldwide

Entertainment News
Dragon Court
27–29 Mackin Street
London WC2B 5LX
020 7190 7795
info@entnews.co.uk
www.entnews.co.uk

Essex News Service
121 High Street
Witham CM8 1BE
01206 211413
perfect@
   essexnews.freeserve.co.uk
Essex area news

Evertons News Agency
Cavalier House
202 Hagley Road, Edgbaston
Birmingham B16 9PQ
0121 454 2931
clive.everton@talk21.com
News and pictures

Feature Story News
The Interchange, Oval Road
London NW1 7DZ
020 7485 0303
drewc@featurestory.com
www.featurestory.com
*Domestic & international radio &
TV stories*

Ferrari Press Agency
7 Summerhill Road, Dartford
Kent DA1 2LP
01322 628444
news@ferraripress.com
www.ferraripress.com
*Kent, south London, south Essex,
East Sussex, Calais and Boulogne etc*

Fleetline News Service
Southern House
1a Bedford Road, East Finchley
London N2 9DB
020 8444 9183
fleetlinenews@hotmail.com
*Law courts, magistrates courts,
appeals. Employment tribunals
throughout London*

Foresightnews
Dragon Court,
27–29 Mackin Street
London WC2B 5LX
020 7190 7799
info@foresightnews.co.uk
www.foresightnews.co.uk

Frank Ryan News Service
Cargenriggs, Islesteps
Dumfries DG2 8ES
1387 253700
meddum@btinternet.com
*South-west Scotland, general news
and features*

Freemans Press Agency
Raleigh House, 1 Mill Road
Barnstable EX31 1JQ
01271 324000
tonyfreemanpressagency@bp.com
www.bipp.com
All news, north Devon

Front Page News Agency
The Whitehouse
24 the Ridgeway, Astwood Bank
Worcestershire B96 6HT
01527 892123
saralain@btopenworld.com
www.frontpagenewsagency.co.uk
True life, human interest stories UK

Future Events News Service
FENS House, 8–10 Wiseton Road
London SW17 7EE
020 8672 3191
uk@fens.demon.co.uk
www.fens.com
*Diary news service,
UK/international. Entertainment
and business*

Getty Images
116 Bayham Street
London NW1 1OG
0800 376 7981
allsportlondon@gettyimages.com
www.gettyimages.com

Gloucestershire News Service
Maverdine Chambers
26 Westgate Street
Gloucester GL1 2NG
01452 522270
john.hawkins@glosnews.com
www.glosnews.com
Gloucester general news

Gosnay's Sports Agency
Park House, 356 Broadway
Horsforth, Leeds LS18 4RE
0113 258 5864
gosnays@aol.com

Government News Network
London
River Wall House
157–161 Millbank
London SW1P 4RR
020 7217 3091
london@gnn.gsi.gov.uk
www.gnn.gov.uk
Government press office
West Midlands
Five Ways House
Islington Row Middleway
Birmingham B15 1SL
0121 626 2033
birmingham@gsi.gov.uk
www.gnn.gov.uk

East Midlands
Belgrave Centre,
Stanley Place
Talbot Street, Nottingham
NG1 5GG
0115 971 2780
nottingham@gnn.gov.uk
www.gnn.gov.uk
North-west
27th Floor, Sunley Tower
Picadilly Plaza, Manchester
M1 4BD
0161 952 4500
manchester@gnn.gov.uk
www.gnn.gov.uk
All North-west, Carlisle to Stoke
North-east
Wellbar House, Gallowgate
Newcastle upon Tyne
NE1 4TB
0191 202 3600
newcastle@gsi.gov.uk
www.gnn.gov.uk
Yorkshire & Humber
1st Floor, City House
New Station Street
Leeds LS1 4JG
0113 283 6599
leeds@gnn.gsi.gov.uk
www.gnn.gov.uk

Harrison Photography
37/39 Great Northern Street
Belfast BT9 7FJ
028 9066 3100
mail@harrisonphotography.co.uk
www.harrisonphotography.co.uk
*All Northern Ireland. Business, PR,
photography*

Hayters Teamwork
Image House, Station Road
London N17 9LR
020 8808 3300
sport@haytersteamwork.com
www.haytersteamwork.com
Home and international sports

IPS Photo Agency
21 Delisle Road
London SE28 0JD
020 8855 1008
info@ips-net.co.uk
*Agents in Japan, Italy, Germany,
Spain, France, Scandinavia*

Independent Radio News (IRN)
ITN Radio, 200 Gray's Inn Road
London WC1X 8XZ
020 7430 4814
irn@itn.co.uk
www.irn.co.uk
National and international news

Independent Sports Network
London Television Centre
Upper Ground, London SE1 9LT
020 7827 7700
jane.tatnall@isntv.co.uk
www.lsntv.co.uk
UK sport transmissions

Islamic Republic News Agency (IRNA)
3rd Floor, Imperial Life House
390–400 High Road
Wembley, Middlesex HA9 6AS
020 8903 5531
irna@irna.com
www.irna.com
Islamic Republic news agency

Information Telegraph Agency of Russia (ITAR-TASS)
Suite 12–20, 2nd Floor
Morley House
314–320 Regent Street
London W1B 3BD
020 7580 5543
iborisenko@yahoo.co.uk
www.itar-tass.com
Russian business news agency

Jarrold's Press Agency
68 High Street, Ipswich IP1 3QJ
01473 219193
jarroldspress@cix.compulink.co.uk
Suffolk, north Essex, south Norfolk, East Anglia and football coverage

Jenkins Group
Berkeley House, 186 High Street
Rochester ME1 1EY
01634 830888
nickand marion@hotmail.com
PR worldwide

Jewish Chronicle News Agency
25 Furnival Street
London EC4A 1JT
020 7415 1500
marketing@thejc.com
www.thejc.com
Worldwide all news

JIJI Press
4th Floor
International Press Centre
76 Shoe Lane, London
EC4A 3JB
020 7936 2847
edit@jiji.co.uk
www.jiji.co.jp
London economic news

John Connor Press Associates
57a High Street, Lewes BN7 1XE
01273 486851
news@jcpa.co.uk
News and features in Sussex

John Fairfax (UK)
1 Bath Street, London
EC1V 9LB
020 7688 2777
linda@fairfaxbn.com
www.f2.com
Worldwide news

John Wardle Agency
Trafalgar House,
5 High Lane
Manchester M21 9DJ
0161 861 8015
iwhittell@aol.com
Sports agency nationwide

Kuwait News Agency (KUNA)
6th Floor, New Premier House
150 Southampton Row
London WC1B 5AL
020 7278 5445
kuwait@btclick.com
www.kuwait-info.com
News around the world

Kyodo News
5th Floor,
20 Orange Street
London WC2H 7EF
020 7766 4400
london@kyodonews.jp
www.kyodo.co.jp
Japan news, worldwide news

Lakeland Press Agency
16 Stonecroft, Ambleside
Lancashire LA22 0AU
01539 431749
craigwilson23@yahoo.co.uk
Cumbria/Lake District. All news and features

Lappas of Exeter
IVA House,
13 South Grange
Clyst Heath, Exeter
Devon EX2 7EY
01392 446670
lappas@freeuk.com
Devon, Cornwall, Somerset, Dorset

M&Y News Agency
65 Osborne Road, Southsea
Portsmouth PO5 3LS
023 9282 0311
mynews@dircon.co.uk
www.mynewsagency.co.uk
News, sports & pictures. Hants, Sussex, Dorset

M2 Communications
PO Box 475, Coventry
CV1 1ZB
024 7623 8200
m2pw@m2.com
www.m2.com
Global all news

Maghreb Arabe Press
35 Westminster Bridge Road
London SE1 7JB
020 7401 8146
mapldn@aol.com
www.map.co.ma
North Africa, Middle East & Mediterranean. All news

Market News International
Ocean House
10–12 Little Trinity Lane
London EC4V 2AR
020 7634 1655
ukeditorial@marketnews.com
www.marketnews.com
International economics, politics an financial markets

Marshall's Sports Service
2 Newfield Drive
Kingswinford DY6 8HY
01384 274877
marshall@bham-sport.demon.co.uk
West Midlands sports

Masons News Service
Unit 2, Clare Hall, Parsons Green
St Ives, Cambs PE27 4WY
01480 302302
newsdesk@masons-news.co.uk
www.campix.co.uk
General news from East Anglia

Media Features
36 Holcroft Court
Carburton Street
London W1W 5DJ
020 7436 3678
leozanelli@aol.com
Worldwide press syndication

Mercury Press Agency
7th Floor, Cotton Exchange
Old Hall Street
Liverpool L3 9LQ
0151 236 6707
reporters@mercurypress.co.uk
Merseyside, Lancashire, Cheshire, parts of North Wales

National News Agency
4–5 Academy Buildings
Fanshaw Street
London N1 6LQ
020 7684 3000
news@nationalnews.co.uk
www.nationalpictures.co.uk
General news. London and South-east

News of Australia
1 Virginia Street
London E98 1NL
020 7702 1355
anne.wall@newsint.co.uk
www.news.com.au

News Team International
41–43 Commercial Street
Birmingham B1 1RS
0121 246 5511
commercial@newsteam.co.uk
www.newsteam.co.uk
Midlands, London news

Newsflash Scotland
1st Floor, Viewfield Chambers
Viewfield Place, Stirling
FK8 1NQ
01786 477310
news@nflash.co.uk
www.newsflashscotland.com
Scotland

North News and Pictures
The Newgate Centre
59 Grainger Street
Newcastle upon Tyne NE1 5JE
0191 233 0223
pictures@northnews.co.uk;
news@northnews.co.uk
North-east England, Cumbria and borders

Northscot Press Agency
18 Adelphi, Aberdeen AB11 5BL
01224 212141
northnews@hemedia.co.uk;
northpix@hemedia.co.uk
www.hemedia.co.uk
Grampian and Highlands

Nunn Syndication
3a Shade Thames,
Butlers Wharf
London SE1 2PU
020 7407 4666
production@nunn-
syndication.com
www.nunn-syndication.com
London Press agency

Press Association (PA)
292 Vauxhall Bridge Road
London SW1V 1AE
020 7963 7000
information@pa.press.net
www.pa.press.net
National news agency of UK and Ireland; provider of real-time news and sports information and images

PA News Birmingham
312–313 The Custard Factory
Gibb Street, Digbeth
Birmingham B9 4AA
0121 224 7686
pa_birmingham@hotmail.com
www.pa.press.net

PA News Liverpool
PO Box 48, Old Hall Street
Liverpool L69 3EB
0151 472 2548
paliverpool@pa.press.net
www.pa.press.net

PA News Scotland
1 Central Quay
Glasgow G3 8DA
0870 830 6725
pascotland@pa.press.net
www.pa.press.net

Pacemaker Press International
787 Lisburn Road
Belfast BT9 7GX
028 9066 3191
david@pacemakerpressintl.com
www.pacemakerpressintl.com
Northern Ireland, Republic of Ireland

Parliamentary & EU News Service
19 Douglas Street, Westminster
London SW1P 4PA
020 7233 8283
info@parliamentary-
monitoring.co.uk
www.parliamentary-
monitoring.co.uk
Parliamentary news service

PPP News Service
109 Conway Road,
London N14 7BH
020 8886 2721
wkastor@compuserve.com
Germany and its politics

Press Agency (Gatwick)
1a Sunview Avenue
Peacehaven BN10 8PJ
01273 583103
Gatwick & south coast, national press

Press Team Scotland
22 St John's Street,
Coatbridge
Lanarkshire ML5 3EJ
01236 440077
news@pressteam.co.uk
Lanarkshire, Glasgow and West of Scotland

Press Trust of India
Suite 303, Radnor House
93–97 Regent Street
London W1B 4ET
020 7494 0602
ptilondon@aol.com
www.ptinews.com
Worldwide news and photos

Profile Group (UK)
Dragon Court
27–29 Macklin Street
London WC2B 5LX
020 7190 7777
info@profilegroup.co.uk
www.profilegroup.co.uk
Future events info and business leads

Racenews
85 Blackstock Road
London N4 2JW
020 7704 0326
racenews@compuserve.com
www.racenews.co.uk
Worldwide horse racing

Raymonds Press Agency
3rd Floor Abbots Hill Chambers
Gower Street, Derby DE1 1SD
01332 340404
news@raymondspress.com
Sports, news and photography

Reuters
85 Fleet Street, London
EC4P 4AJ
020 7250 1122
robert.woodward@reuters.com
www.reuters.com
Worldwide news and features

Rex Features
18 Vine Hill, London
EC1R 5DZ
020 7278 7294
rex@rexfeatures.com
www.rexfeatures.com
International & USA picture agency

Richard Harris News
Woody Glen, How Mill
Branton CA8 9JY
01228 670381
richardwjharris@aol.com
News in north Cumbria

Ross Parry Agency
40 Back Town Street
Farsley, Leeds LS28 5LD
0113 236 1842
newsdesk@rossparry.co.uk
www.rossparry.co.uk
Yorkshire, news features and photos

Russian Information Agency – Novosti (RIA-Novosti)
3 Rosary Gardens
London SW7 4NW
020 7370 3002
ria@novosti.co.uk
www.rian.ru
Russia

Scottish News Agency
Avian House, 4 Lindsay Court
Dundee Technology Park
Dundee DD2 1SW
01382 427035
g.ogilvy@scottishnews.com
East and central Scotland, Perthshire, Fife, Edinburgh, Lothians and Borders

Scottish News & Sport
15 Fitzroy Place,
Glasgow
G3 7RW
0141 221 3602
info@snspix.com
www.snspix.com
Scotland sport

Smith Davis Press
Queens Chambers
8 Westport Road,
Burslem
Stoke on Trent
ST6 4AW
01782 829850
smith-davis@smith-davis.co.uk
www.smith-davis.co.uk
*Photography, graphic design and
freelance journalists*

Snowmedia Consultancy
Unit G4, Broadway Studio
28 Tooting High Street
London SW17 0RG
020 8672 9800
info@snowmedia.net
www.snowmedia.net
*Nationwide lifestyle profiles on
health and sport*

Solent News and Photo Agency
23 Mitchell Point
Ensign Way, Hamble
Southampton SO31 4RF
023 8045 8800
news@solentnews.biz
www.solentnews.biz
*Hants, Wilts, Isle of Wight news
features for all media*

Somerset News Service
3 Lewis Road, Taunton
Somerset TA2 6DU
01823 331856
somersetnews@boltblue.com
Contact: Richard Briers

Somerset Photo News
12 Jellalabad Court
The Mount, Taunton
Somerset TA1 3RZ
01823 282053, 07860 207333
somersetnews@boltblue.com
somersetphotonews@boltblue.com
Somerset

South Beds News Agency
Bramingham Park Business
Centre
Enterprise Way, Bramingham Park
Luton, Beds LU3 4BU
01582 572222
south.b@virgin.net;
southbedsnews@btconnect.com
Herts, Beds, Bucks, Northants

South West News & Picture Service
Media Centre
Emma-Chris Way,
Abbeywood Park
Bristol BS34 7JU
0117 906 6500
news@swns.com
www.swns.com
*South-west general news, features
and photos*

Space Press News and Pictures
Bridge House, Blackden Lane
Goostrey, Cheshire CW4 8PZ
01477 533403
scoop2001@aol.com
*Knutsford, Macclesfield, Crewe,
Nantwich, Wilmslow, Alderley Edge,
Northwich, Cheshire, Shropshire and
North-west*

Specialist News Services
27 Newton Street
London WC2B 5EL
020 7831 3267
desk@snsnews.co.uk
*National. Consumer, media, city,
travel and motor industry,
advertising and marketing, new
products, science and nature*

Speed Media One
3 Kings Court, Horsham
RH13 5UR
01403 259661
info@speedmediaone.co.uk
www.speedmediaone.co.uk
*General news and features. Sport,
sport development, education, local
government*

Sport & General Press Agency
63 Gee Street, London
EC1V 3RS
020 7253 7705
info@alphapress.com
www.alphapress.com

Sportsphoto
20 Clifton Street
Scarborough YO12 7SR
01723 367264
library@sportsphoto.co.uk
www.sportsphoto.co.uk
*All sport and entertainment,
national and international*

Tim Wood Agency
Press Room
Central Criminal Courts
London EC4M 7EH
020 7248 6858
*Court cover at Old Bailey and
Southwark and Knightsbridge crown
courts*

Tony Scase News Service
Little Congham House
Congham, Kings Lynn
PE32 1DR
01485 600650
news@scase.co.uk
www.scase.co.uk
East Anglia news

TV News
Feature Story News
The Interchange
Oval Road, London
NW1 7DZ
020 7485 0303
london.bureau@featurestory.com
www.fsntv.com
*TV news for north America, south-
east Asia, southern Africa*

UK Press
Unit 27, The Limehouse Cut
46 Morris Road,
London E14 6NQ
020 7515 3878
info@ukpress.com
www.ukpress.com
Europe/UK photography

Unique Entertainment News
50 Lisson Street, London NW1
5DF
020 7453 1650
amie.oconnor@unique.com
www.unique.com
*Nationwide general news and
features*

Universal Pictorial Press & Agency
29–31 Saffron Hill
London EC1N 8SW
020 7421 6000
contacts@uppa.co.uk
www.uppa.co.uk
*Press and worldwide commercial
photography*

Wales News & Picture Service
Market Chambers,
St Mary's Street
Cardiff CF10 1AT
029 2066 6366
news@walesnews.com
www.walesnews.com
Wales. General news and features

Warwickshire News & Picture Agency
41 Lansdowne Crescent
Leamington Spa CV32 4PR
01926 424181
barrie@tracynews.co.uk
*Midlands. General news, features
and pictures*

Wessex Features and Photos Agency
Neates Yard,
108 High Street
Hungerford
RG17 0NB
01488 686810
news@britishnews.co.uk
www.britishnews.co.uk
Women's news, nationwide

West Coast News
Renaissance House,
Parracombe
Barnstaple,
Devon EX31 4QH
01598 763296
westcoast.news@dial.pipex.com
Devon, Cornwall, west Somerset

White's Press Agency
446 London Road
Heeley,
Sheffield S2 4HP
0114 255 3975
newsdesk@press-agency.com
Men's sport, south Yorkshire

World Entertainment News Network
35 Kings Exchange
Tileyard Road,
London N7 9AH
020 7607 2757
sales@wenn.com
www.wenn.com
Worldwide entertainment & photos

Xinhua News Agency of China
8 Swiss Terrace,
Belsize Road
Swiss Cottage,
London NW6 4RR
020 7586 8437
xinhua@easynet.co.uk
www.xinhuanet.com

Picture libraries

A1PIX Digital Picture Library
Finsbury Business Centre
40 Bowling Green Lane
London EC1R 0NE
020 7415 7045
london@a1pix.com
www.a1pix.com
Travel, business, lifestyle, children, nature, animals & illustrations. Hi-res download facility, personal search service

Advertising Archives
45 Lyndale Avenue
London NW2 2QB
020 7435 6540
suzanne@advertisingarchives.co.uk
www.advertisingarchives.co.uk
British and American press ads, magazine illustration

Allstar Picture Library
20 Clifton Street
Scarborough YO12 7SR
01723 367264
library@allstarpl.com
www.allstarpl.com
Worldwide sports, politics, travel

Alvey & Towers
Springboard centre
Mantle Lane, Coalville
Leicestershire LE67 3DW
01530 450011
alveytower@aol.com
www.alveyandtowers.com
Transport

Andes Press Agency
26 Padbury Court
London E2 7EH
020 7613 5417
apa@andespressagency.com
www.andespressagency.com
Travel and social documentary worldwide, Latin America, UK, Middle East

AP Photo Archive
12 Norwich Street
London EC4A 1BP
020 7427 4263
london_photolibrary@ap.org
www.apwideworld.com
Archive of global news agency

Art Directors & Trip Photo Library
57 Burden Lane, Cheam
Surrey SM2 7BY
020 8642 3593
images@artdirectors.co.uk
www.artdirectors.co.uk
Worldwide countries and religion

Artbank Illustration Library
114 Clerkenwell Road
London EC1M 5SA
020 8906 2288
info@artbank.com
www.artbank.com
Online library

Aviation Images – Mark Wagner
42B Queens Road
Wimbledon, London SW19 8LR
020 8944 5225
pictures@aviation-images.com
www.aviation-images.com
Aviation and aerial photography

Aviation Picture Library
116 The Avenue
West Ealing, London W13 8JX
020 8566 7712
avpix@aol.com
www.aviationpictures.com
Aviation pictures

Axel Poignant Archive
115 Bedford Court Mansions
Bedford Avenue
London WC1B 3AG
020 7636 2555
Rpoignant@aol.com
Anthropology, ethnography

BBC Picture Archives
Room B116, Television Centre
Wood Lane, London W12 7RJ
020 8225 7193
research-central@bbc.co.uk
www.bbcresearchcentral.com
Worldwide

BFI Stills, Posters and Designs
21 Stephen Street
London W1T 1LN
020 7957 4797
stills.films@bfi.org.uk
www.bfi.org.uk/collections/stills
/index.html
Images, film and TV

British Library Picture Library
96 Easton Road
London NW1 2DB
020 7412 7614
imagesonline@bl.uk
www.bl.uk/imagesonline
*Images/maps/historical and
engravings*

Bryan & Cherry Alexander Photography
Higher Cottage
Manston Sturminster, Newton
Dorset DT10 1EZ
01258 473006
alexander@arcticphoto.co.uk
www.arcticphoto.co.uk
Arctic and Antarctic specialists

Camera Press
21 Queen Elizabeth Street
London SE1 2PD
020 7378 1300
a.golding@camerapress.com
www.camerapress.com
Worldwide photographic library

Cephas Picture Library
Hurst House, 157 Walton Road
East Moseley, Surrey KT8 0DZ
020 8979 8647
pictures@cephas.co.uk
www.cephas.com
*Wine and vineyards, whisky and
brandy, food and drink*

Chris Howes/Wild Places Photography
51 Timber Square
Cardiff CF24 3SH
029 2048 6557
photos@wildplaces.co.uk
*Travel, topography and natural
history, plus action sports and caving*

Christie's Images
1 Langley Lane, Vauxhall
London SW8 1TJ
020 7582 1282
imageslondon@christies.com
www.christiesimages.com
Fine and decorative art

Chrysalis Images
The Chrysalis Building
Bramley Road,
London W10 6SP
020 7314 1469
Tforshaw@chrysalisbooks.co.uk
www.chrysalisbooks.co.uk
*History, transport, cookery, crafts,
space*

Collections
13 Woodberry Crescent
London N10 1PJ
020 8883 0083
collections@btinternet.com
www.collectionspicturelibrary.com
*Britain and Ireland: people and
traditional culture*

Country Life Pictures/Library
Kings Reach Tower
Stamford Street,
London SE1 9LS
020 7261 6337
camilla_costello@ipcmedia.com
www.countrylifelibrary.co.uk
*Architecture, country pursuits,
gardens, crafts, 1897 black and white
pictures*

David Hoffman Photo Library
c/o 18 Vine Hill
London EC1R 5DZ
020 8981 5041
info@hoffmanphotos.com
www.hoffmanphotos.com
*Social issues, built from journalistic
work since 1970s*

Double Red Photographic
The Old School
Thorn Lane, Goxhill
Barrow upon Humber
DN19 7JE
01469 531416
doublered@atlas.co.uk
www.doublered.co.uk
Motorsport photography

E&E Picture Library (Religion)
Beggars Roost
Wooltackle Hill
Smeeth, Kent TN25 6RR
01303 812608
isobel@picture-library.
freeserve.co.uk
www.picture-library.
freeserve.co.uk
World religion

Edifice
14 Doughty Street
London WC1N 2PL
020 7242 0740
info@edificephoto.com
www.edificephoto.com
Buildings and architecture

Education Photos
April Cottage, Warners Lane
Albury Heath, Guildford
Surrey GU5 9DE
01483 203846
johnwalmsley@
educationphotos.co.uk
www.educationphotos.co.uk
Education, work, homes, signs

English Heritage Photo Library
23 Saville Row,
London W15 2ET
020 7973 3338
celia.sterne@english-
heritage.org.uk
www.english-heritage.org.uk
*English Heritage properties,
locations*

Exile Images
1 Mill Row, Weston Hill Road
Brighton, East Sussex BN1 3SU
01273 208741
pics@exileimages.co.uk
www.exileimages.co.uk
*Refugees, protest, asylum seekers,
conflict. Middle East, Balkans,
south-east Asia*

ffotograff
10 Kyveilog Street,
Cardiff CF11 9JA
029 2023 6879
ffotograff@easynet.co.uk
www.ffotograff.com
*Travel, exploration, arts,
architecture, culture, Wales, Middle
East, Far East*

Financial Times Pictures
1 Southwark Bridge
London SE1 9HL
020 7873 3000
photosynd@ft.com
www.ft.com
Business

Fogden Wildlife Photographs
16 Lochetort,
North Uist
Western Isles HS6 5EU
01876 580245
susan.fogden@virgin.net
www.fogdenphotos.com
Natural history

Food Features
5 Upper Church Lane
Farnham, Surrey
GU9 7PW
01252 735240
frontdesk@foodpix.co.uk
www.foodpix.co.uk
Food and drink

Forest Commission Life Picture Library
231 Corstorphie Road
Edinburgh EH12 7AT
0131 314 6411
neil.campbell@forestry.gsi.gov.uk
www.forestry.gov.uk
Image bank of the Forestry Commission

Frank Lane Picture Agency
Pages Green House, Pages Green
Wetheringsett, Suffolk IP14 5QA
01728 860789
pictures@flpa-images.co.uk
www.flpa-images.co.uk
Natural history, environment, pets, weather

Galaxy Picture Library
34 Fennels Way
Flackwall Heath
High Wycombe
Bucks HP10 9BY
01628 521338
robin@galaxypix.com
www.galaxypix.com
Astronomy & the sky

Garden Picture Library
Unit 12 Ransome Dock
35 Parkgate Road
London SW11 4MT
020 7228 4332
info@gardenpicture.com
www.gardenpicture.com
Gardening

Geo Aerial Photography
4 Christian Fields
London SW16 3JZ
020 8764 6292
geo.aerial@geo-group.co.uk
www.geo-group.co.uk
Aerial photographs

Geo Science Features Picture Library
6 Orchard Drive, Wye
Kent TN25 5AU
01233 812707
gsf@geoscience.demon.co.uk
www.geoscience.demon.co.uk
Natural science and natural history

Geoslides Photography
4 Christian Fields
London SW16 3JZ
020 8764 6292
geoslides@geo-group.co.uk
www.geo-group.co.uk
Landscape and human interest

Getty Images
116 Bayham Street
London NW1 1OG
0800 376 7981
allsportlondon@gettyimages.com
www.gettyimages.com

Heather Angel/Natural Visions
6 Vicarage Hill
Farnham, Surrey GU9 8HJ
01252 716700
info@naturalvisions.co.uk
www.naturalvisions.co.uk
Online images of worldwide wildlife

Holt Studios International
The Courtyard, 2499 High Street
Berkshire RG17 0NF
01488 683523
library@holt-studios.co.uk
www.holt-studios.co.uk
World agriculture and horticulture. Wildlife, pests and diseases

Hutchison Picture Library
65 Brighton Road,
Shoreham on sea
West Sussex BN43 6RE
01273 440113
library@hutchisonpictures.co.uk
www.hutchisonpictures.co.uk
Worldwide contemporary images

Images of Africa Photobank
11 The Windings, Lichfield
Staffordshire WS13 7EX
01543 262898
info@imagesofafrica.co.uk
www.imagesofafrica.co.uk
130,000 images of 20 African countries

Imperial War Museum Photograph Archive
Lambeth Road, London SE1 6HZ
020 7416 5333
photos@iwm.org.uk
www.iwm.org.uk/collections/photos.htm
20th- and 21st-century conflicts

International Photobank
Unit D, Roman Hill Business Park
Broadmayne, Dorset BT2 8LY
01305 854145
peter@internationalphotobank.co.uk
www.internationalphotobank.co.uk
400,000 travel images

Jacqui Hurst
66 Richford Street
London W6 7HP
020 8743 2315
jacquih@dircon.co.uk
www.jacquihurstphotography.co.uk
Designers and applied artists, regional food producers and markets

James Davis Worldwide
65 Brighton Road,
Shoreham on sea
West Sussex BN43 6RE
01273 452252
library@eyeubiquitous.com
www.eyeubiquitous.com
Travel collection

Jessica Strang Photo Library
504 Brody House,
London E1 7LQ
020 7247 8982
jessica.strang@virgin.net
Architecture, interiors and gardens

Jim Henderson Photographer & Publisher
Crooktree Lincardine O'Neil
Aboyne, Aberdeenshire
AB34 4JD
01339 882149
JHende7868@aol.com
www.jimhendersonphotography.com
Aberdeenshire, aurora borealis, ancient Egypt

Forthill Gifford
Nr Salisbury, Wiltshire SP3 6QW
01747 820320
cleare@btinternet.com
www.mountaincamera.com
Landscapes for UK and worldwide – mountains and trekking

John Heseltine Archive
Mill Studio, Frogmarsh Mills
South Woodchester
Gloucester GL5 5ET
01453 873792
john@heseltine.co.uk
www.heseltine.co.uk
Landscapes, architecture, food and travel: Italy and UK

David King Collection
90 St Pauls Road,
London N1 2QP
020 7226 0149
davidkingcollection@btopenworld.com
www.bapla.org
Soviet Union and other Communist movements

Kos Picture Source
7 Spice Court, Plantation Wharf
London SW11 3UE
020 7801 0044
images@kospictures.com
www.kospictures.com
Water-based images

Lebrecht Music and Art
58b Carlton Hill,
London NW8 0ES
020 7625 5341
pictures@lebrecht.co.uk
www.lebrecht.co.uk
Musical and art images

Lesley & Roy Adkins
10 Acre Wood, Whitestone
Exeter EX14 2HW
01392 811357
mail@adkinsarchaeology.com
www.adkinarchaeology.com
Archaeology and heritage

London Aerial Photo Library
Studio D, West Entrance
Fairoaks Airport, Chobham
Surrey GU24 8HU
01276 855997
info@londonaerial.co.uk
www.londonaerial.co.uk
Aerial imagery (oblique and vertical) covering most UK

Mary Evans Picture Library
59 Tranquil Vale, Blackheath
London SE3 0BS
020 8318 0034
pictures@maryevans.com
www.maryevans.com
Historical images

Monitor Picture Library
The Forge, Roydon
Essex CM19 5HH
01279 792700
info@monitorpicturelibrary.com
www.monitorpicturelibrary.com
UK and international personalities

Morocco Scapes
Seend Park, High Street
Seend, Wiltshire SN12 6NZ
01380 828533
chris@realmorocco.com
www.realmorocco.com
Collection of Moroccan material

National History Museum of London Picture Library
National History Museum
Cromwell Road,
London SW7 5BD
020 7942 5041
nhmpl@nhm.ac.uk
www.nhm.ac.uk/piclib
History of London, museum's collection

National Galleries of Scotland Picture Library
The Dean Gallery, Belford Road
Edinburgh EH4 3DS
0131 624 6260
picture.library@nationalgalleries.org
www.nationalgalleries.org
Art

National Portrait Gallery Picture Library
39–45 Orange Street
London WC2H 0HE
020 7312 2474
picturelibrary@npg.org.uk
www.npg.org.uk
Portraits

Nature Photographers
West Wit, New Road
Little London
Tadley, Hampshire RG26 5EU
01256 850661
info@naturephotographers.co.uk
www.naturephotographers.co.uk
Worldwide natural history

Nature Picture Library
Broadcasting House
White Lady's Road
Bristol BS8 2LR
0117 974 6720
info@naturepl.com
www.naturepl.com
Wildlife

Neil Williams Classical Collection
22 Avon Hockley,
Tamworth
Staffordshire B77 5QA
01827 286086
neil@classicalcollection.co.uk
Classical music

NHPA
57 Hish Street, Ardingley
West Sussex RH17 6TB
01444 892514
nhpa@nhpa.co.uk
www.nhpa.co.uk
Natural history

Novosti Photo Library
3 Rosary Gardens
London SW7 4NW
020 7370 1873
photos@novosti.co.uk
www.rian.ru
Russia

PA Photos
292 Vauxhall Bridge Road
London SW1V 1AE
020 7963 7990
paphotos@pa.press.net
www.paphotos.com
News, entertainment, celebrity and sports

Panos Pictures
Studio 3B,
34 Southwark Street
London SE1 1UN
020 7234 0010
pics@panos.co.uk
www.panos.co.uk
Documentary library specialising in developing world

Papilio
155 Station Road,
Herne Bay
Kent CT6 5QA
01227 360996
library@papiliophotos.com
www.papiliophotos.com
Natural history subjects worldwide

Phil Sheldon Golf Picture Library
40 Manor Road, Barnet
Herts EN5 2JQ
020 8440 1986
phil@philsheldongolfpics.co.uk
www.philsheldongolfpics.co.uk
More than 500,000 images of golf

Photofusion
17a Electric Lane, London
SW9 8LA
020 7733 3500
library@photofusion.org
www.photofusion.org
Contemporary social and environmental issues

Photogold
40 Dunvegan Place, Polmont
Falkirk FK2 0NX
01324 720038
sales@photogold.co.uk
www.castlepictures.com
Scotland

Photolibrary Wales
2 Bro-Nant, Church Road
Pentrych, Cardiff CF15 9QC
029 2089 0311
info@photolibrarywales.com
www.photolibrarywales.com
Wales

PPL Photo Agency
Bookers Yard, The Street, Walberton
Arundel, West Sussex BN18 0PF
01243 555561
ppl@mistral.co.uk
www.pplmedia.com
*Watersports, sub-aqua, business, travel
Sussex scenes and historical images*

Premaphotos Wildlife
1 Kirland Road, Bodmin
Cornwall PL30 5JQ
01208 78258
library@premaphotos.co.uk
www.premaphotos.com
Natural history worldwide

Raymond Mander & Joe Mitchenson Theatre Collection
Jerwood Library of Performing Art
Trinity College of Music
King Charles Court
Old Royal Naval College
London SE10 9JF
020 8305 4426
rmangan@tcm.ac.uk
www.mander-and mitchenson.co.u
Theatre

Redferns Music Picture Library
7 Bramley Road
London W10 6SZ
020 7792 9914
info@redferns.com
www.musicpictures.com
Music photography

Retna Pictures
West Complex, Pinewood Studio
Pinewood Road, Iver Heath
Bucks SL0 0NH
01753 785450
ukinfo@retna.com
www.retna.com
Celebrity music and lifestyle

Retrograph Archive Collection
10 Hanover Street, Brighton
East Sussex BN2 9SB
01273 687554
retropix1@aol.com
www.retrograph.com
*Vintage consumer advertising, art,
decorative art*

Robbie Jack Photography
45 Church Road,
London W7 3BD
020 8567 9616
robbie@robbiejack.com
www.robbiejack.com
Performing arts

Robert Forsythe Picture Library
16 Lime Grove, Prudhoe
Northumberland NE42 6PR
01661 834511
robert@forsythe.demon.co.uk
www.forsythe.demon.co.uk
*Original ephemera and
transparencies of industrial and
transport heritage*

**Royal Air Force Museum
Hendon**
Grahame Park Way, Hendon
London NW9 5LL
020 8205 2266
hendon@rafmuseum.org
www.rafmuseum.org.uk/
History of aviation

**Royal Collection Photographic
Services**
Windsor Castle, Berkshire SL4 1NJ
1753 868286
photoservices@royalcollection.org.uk
www.the-royal-collection.org.uk
Royal family

RSPB Images
POBox 7515, Billericay
Leeds CM11 1WR
01268 711471
rspb@thatsgood.biz
www.rspb-images.com
Wildlife

RSPCA Photolibrary
Wilberforce Way, South Water
Horsham
West Sussex RH13 9RS
0870 754 0150
pictures@rspcaphotolibrary.com
www.rspcaphotolibrary.com
Natural history

RO Mathews Photography
Little Pit Place, Brighstone
Isle of Wight PO30 4DZ
01983 741098
oliver@mathews-
photography.com
www.mathews-photography.com
Gardens, plants and landscapes

**Science & Society Picture
Library**
Science Museum, Exhibition Road
London SW7 2DD
020 7942 4400
piclib@nmsi.ac.uk
www.nmsi.ac.uk/piclib/
*Science museum, national railway
museum; photography, film and
television*

Skishoot-Offshoot
Hall Place, Upper Woolcott
Hampshire RG28 7TY
01635 255527
skishootsnow@aol.com
www.skishoot.net
Winter sports

Skyscan Photolibrary
Oak House, Coddington
Cheltenham
Gloucestershire GL54 5BY
01242 621357
info@skyscan.co.uk
www.skyscan.co.uk
Aviation & aerial sports

**Snookerimages (Eric Whitehead
Photography)**
25 Oak Street, Windermere
Cumbria LA23 1EN
015394 48894
eric@snookerimages.co.uk
www.snookerimages.co.uk
Snooker

SOA Photo Library
Lovelly Farm, Dark Lane
St Gregory, Taunton TA3 6EU
0870 333 6062
info@soaphotoagency.com
www.soaphotoagency.com
*Humour, sports, travel, modern
European*

Still Moving Picture Company
1c Castlehill, Doune
Edinburgh FK16 6BU
01786 842790
info@stillmovingpictures.com
www.stillmovingpictures.com
Scotland and sport

Still Pictures Photolibrary
199 Shooters Hill Road
London SE3 8UL
020 8858 8307
info@stillpictures.com
www.stillpictures.com
*Environment, nature, social and
third-world issues*

Stockfile
5 High Street, Sunningdale
Berkshire SL5 0LX
01344 872249
info@stockfile.co.uk
www.stockfile.co.uk
Mountain biking and cycling

Sylvia Cordaiy
45 Rotherstone, Devizes
Wiltshire SN10 2DD
01380 728327
info@sylvia-cordaiy.com
www.sylvia-cordaiy.com
*160 countries, from obscure to stock
images*

The National Archives
Kew, Richmond, Surrey TW9 4DU
020 8876 34444
image-library@
nationalarchives.gov.uk
www.nationalarchives.gov.uk
British and colonial history

True North Photo Library
26 New Road, Hebden Bridge
West Yorkshire HX7 8ER
07941 630420
john@trunorth.demon.co.uk
Landscape and life of the North

Ulster Museum Picture Library
Botanic Gardens, Belfast
BT9 5AB
028 9038 3000
patricia.mclean.um@nics.gov.uk
www.ulstermuseum.org.uk
*Art, archaeology, ethnography,
natural history, Irish history*

V&A Images
Victoria & Albert Museum
South Kensington, London
SW7 2RL
020 7942 2966
vaimages@vam.ac.uk
www.vandaimages.com
Design imagery

Valley Green
Barn Ley, Valley Lane, Buxhall
Stowmarket IP14 3EB
01449 736090
pics@valleygreen.co.uk
Perennials

**Vaughan Williams Memorial
Library**
Cecil Sharpe House
Regents Park Road
London NW1 7AY
020 7485 2206
library@efdss.org
www.efdss.org
Traditional music and culture

VinMag Archive
Vin May House, 84–90 Digby Road
London E9 6HX
020 8533 7588
piclib@vinmag.com
www.vinmagarchive.com
*20th-century history. Books, news-
papers, posters, adverts, photos, film,
ephemera*

Waterways Photo Library
39 Manor Court Road
Hanwell, London W7 3EJ
020 88401659
watphot39@aol.com
www.waterwaysphotolibrary.com/
Inland waterways

World Pictures
25 Gosfield Street
London W1W 6HA
020 7437 2121
worldpictures@btinternet.com
www.worldpictures.co.uk
Travel

York Archaeological Trust Picture Library
Cromwell House, 13 Ogleforth
York YO1 7FG
01904 663000
enquiries@yorkarchaeology.co.uk
www.yorkarchaeology.co.uk
Archaeology in York area

Media monitoring

BBC Monitoring
Marketing Dept, Caversham Park
Reading RG4 8TZ
0118 948 6289
marketing@mon.bbc.co.uk
www.monitor.bbc.co.uk
News, information and comment gathered from mass media around the world

BMC Extreme Information
89 Worship Street, London
E2A 2BF
020 7377 1742
info@extremeinformation.com
www.extremeinformation.com
European press monitoring

CIS Information Services
16 Hatton Wall, London
EC1N 8JH
020 7242 5886
info@cisclip.co.uk
www.cisclip.com
Press monitoring service

Daryl Willcox Publishing
Melrose House, 42 Dingwall Road
Croydon CR9 2DX
0870 774 0777
info@dwpub.com
www.dwpub.com
Information services for journalists and PR

DigiReels Media Monitoring
45 Fouberts Place
London W1F 7QH
020 7437 7743
info@digireels.co.uk
www.digireels.co.uk
Online database of TV, radio, poster and press ads

Durrants Press Cuttings
Discovery House
28–42 Benner Street
London EC1Y 8QE
020 7674 0200
contact@durrants.co.uk
www.durrants.co.uk
All print media plus internet, newswire and broadcast monitoring

International Press-Cutting Bureau
224–236 Walworth Road
London SE17 1JE
020 7708 2113
ipcb2000@aol.com
National, provincial, trade, technical and magazine press

John Frost Newspapers
22b Rosemary Avenue, Enfield
Middlesex EN2 0SS
020 8366 1392
andrew@johnfrostnewspapers.com
www.johnfrostnewspapers.co.uk
Original newspapers and press cuttings

Ludvigsen Library
Scoles Gate, Hawkedon
Bury St Edmonds IP29 4AY
01284 789246
library@ludvigsen.com
www.ludvigsen.com
Photographic archive and research facilities for writers and publishers

Media Tenor
Kurt-Schumacher-Strasse 2
D-53113 Bonn, Germany
00 49 228 93 444 31
f.blase@innovatio.de
www.mediatenor.com
Analysis of new and traditional media content

Melanie Wilson
72 High Street, Syston
Leicester LE7 1GQ
0116 260 4442
melaniewilson@bigfoot.com
Research service across all media; free worldwide booksearch service

PA News Library
The Press Association
292 Vauxhall Bridge Road
London SW1V 1AE
020 7963 7000
palibrary@pa.press.net
www.pa.press.net
Digital library

Parliamentary Monitoring Services
19 Douglas Street
London SW1P 4PA
020 7233 8283
info@parliamentary-monitoring.co.uk
www.parliamentary-monitoring.co.uk/
Confidential monitoring and research services

Romeike Media Intelligence
Romeike House, 290 Green Lane
London N13 5TP
0800 289543
info@romeike.com
www.romeike.com
Monitors all media; back research; analysis and editorial summary service

Television Research Partnership (TRP)
Nightingale Lodge, East Reach
Taunton TA1 3EN
01823 424260
partners@trponline.co.uk
www.trponline.co.uk
Media measurement information

Diversity Contacts

Media diversity associations

Age Concern
Astral House, 1268 London Road
London SW16 4ER
020 8765 7200
www.ageconcern.co.uk

Age Positive
Department for Work and
Pensions
Room W8d, Moorfoot
Sheffield S1 4PQ
agepositive@dwp.gsi.gov.uk
www.agepositive.gov.uk/
Age diversity in employment

Broadcaster and Creative Industries Disability Network
Employers' Forum on Disability
Nutmeg House
60 Gainsford Street
London SE1 2NY
020 7403 3020
enny.stevens@
employers-forum.co.uk
www.employers-forum.co.uk
Employers organisation

Commission for Racial Equality (CRE)
St Dunstan's House
201–211 Borough High Street
London SE1 1GZ
020 7939 0000
info@cre.gov.uk
www.cre.gov.uk

Creative Collective
239a Uxbridge Road
Shepherds Bush, London
W12 9DL
020 8576 6300
nfo@thecreativecollective.com
www.thecreativecollective.com
*Aims to develop social policy on
diversity and to empower
community groups to harness
media*

Cultural Diversity Network (CDN)
c/o Channel 4,
124 Horseferry Road
London SW1P 2TX
diversitydatabase@channel4.co.uk
www.cdndiversitydatabase.tv
*Database for ethnic minorities in
broadcasting*

Digital Media Access Group
Applied Computing
University of Dundee
Dundee DD1 4HN
01382 345050
info@dmag.org.uk
www.dmag.org.uk/aboutus
/default.asp
Promotes new media accessibility

Disability Rights Commission
Freepost MID02164
Stratford upon Avon CV37 9BR
0845 762 2633
enquiry@drc-gb.org
www.drc-gb.org

Diversity Database
BBC Television Centre
London W12 7RJ
020 8743 8000
diversity.database@bbc.co.uk
www.bbc.co.uk/info/policies
/diversity.shtml

Emma Awards
67–69 Whitfield Street
London W1T 4HF
020 7636 1233
mail@emma.tv
www.emma.tv
Multicultural media awards

Equal Opportunities Commission
Arndale House, Arndale Centre
Manchester M4 3EQ
0845 601 5901
info@eoc.org.uk
www.eoc.org.uk

International Association of Women in Radio and Television
Radio Norway International,
Norwegian Broadcasting NRK
0340, Oslo, Norway
00 47 230 48441
nik@netactive.co.za
www.iawrt.org

International Women's Media Foundation
1625K Street NW, Suite 1275
Washington, DC 20006, USA
00 1 202 496 1992
info@iwmf.org
www.iwmf.org

PressWise Trust
38 Easton Business Centre
Felix Road, Bristol BS5 0HE
0117 941 5889
pw@presswise.org.uk
www.presswise.org.uk
Independent media ethics charity

Society of Women Writers & Journalists
Calvers Farm, Thelveton
Diss IP21 4NG
01379 740 550
zoe@zoeking.com
www.swwt.co.uk

Spoken Word Publishing Association (SWPA)
c/o Macmillan Audio
20 New Wharf Road
London N1 9RR
020 7014 6041
audio@penguin.co.uk
www.swpa.co.uk

Women and Equality Unit
35 Great Smith Street
London SW1P 3BQ
0845 001 0029
info-womenandequalityunit@
dti.gsi.gov.uk
www.womenandequalityunit.gov.uk

Women in Film and Television
6 Langley Street
London WC2H 9JA
020 7240 4875
emily@wftv.org.uk
www.wftv.org.uk

Women in Journalism
wijUK@aol.com
www.womeninjournalism.co.uk

Women in Publishing
info@wipub.org.uk
www.wipub.org.uk

Women's Radio Group
27 Bath Road, London W4 1LJ
020 8995 5442
wrg@zelo.demon.co.uk
www.womeninradio.org.uk
*Training, info and production
facilities*

187

Minority press

Disability

Big Print
Big Print, 2 Palmyra Square North
Warrington WA1 1JQ
01925 242222
sales@big-print.co.uk
www.big-print.co.uk
Weekly. Large print news. Editor:
Trevor Buckley

Break Times
Winged Fellowship Trust
20–32 Pentonville Road
London N1 9XD
020 7833 2594
admin@wft.org.uk
www.wft.org.uk
2pa. Physical disabilities and
carers.
Editor: James Hale

Breathe Easy
The British Lung Foundation
73–75 Goswell Road
London EC1V 7ER
020 7688 5555
info@britishlungfoundation.com
www.lunguk.org/
Quarterly, Lung disease. Editor:
Humphrey Cochrane

Communication
The National Autistic Society
393 City Road,
London EC1V 1NG
020 7833 2299
publications@nas.org.uk
www.nas.org.uk
3pa. Autism. Editor: Anne Cooper

Devon Link
Devon County Council and
Torbay Council
Room A123
Social Services Directorate
County Hall, Topsham Road
Exeter EX2 4QR
01392 382332
joanne.white@devon.gov.uk
Quarterly. People with physical &
sensory disabilities, & carers.
Editor: Joanne White

Disability Now
Scope, 6 Market Road
London N7 9PW
020 7619 7323
editor@disabilitynow.org.uk
www.disabilitynow.org.uk
Monthly. Editor: Mary Wilkinson

Disability Times
112 Craven Road
London W5 2TL
020 8566 1202
dtnews@btclick.com
www.disabilitytimes.co.uk
9pa. Editor: Teresa Moore

Disabled and Supportive Carer
Euromedia Associates, Unit 8,
Chorley West Business Park
Ackhurst Road
Chorley PR7 1NL
0870 444 8955
editorial@euromedia-al.com
6pa. Editor: Richard Cheeseborough

Disabled Motorist
Cottingham Way
Thrapston NN14 4PL
01832 734724
LesleyEBrowne@aol.com
www.ddmc@ukonline.co.uk
Monthly. Editor: Lesley Browne

DISH Update
DISH, 45 Grosvenor Road
St Albans AL1 3AW
01727 813815
info@dish4info.co.uk
www.dish4info.co.uk
Quarterly. Hertfordshire. Editor:
Jane Fookes

Epilepsy Today
Epilepsy Action
New Anstey House
Gate Way Drive, Yeadon
Leeds LS19 7XY
0113 2108800
smitchell@epilepsy.org.uk
www.epilepsy.org.uk
Quarterly. Editor: Sue Mitchell

FreeHand
Abucon, 13 Vincent Square
London SW1P 2LX
020 7834 1066
info@abucon.co.uk
www.abucon.co.uk
6pa. Elderly disabled in their own
homes. Editor: Liza Jones

Jigsaw
DISH, 45 Grosvenor Road
St Albans AL1 3AW
01727 813815
info@dish4info.co.uk
www.dish4info.co.uk
Quarterly. Young people. Editor:
Jane Fookes

London Disability News
Greater London Action on
Disability
336 Brixton Road,
London SW9 7AA
020 7346 5800
b.humphreys@glad.org.uk
www.glad.org.uk
10pa. Editor: Michael Turner

Motability Lifestyle
CBC Media,
Unit 4–5 Greenwich Quay
Clarence Road, London SE8 3EY
020 8469 9700
mike.trounce@cbcmedia.co.uk
www.cbcmedia.co.uk
Quarterly. Motability vehicles.
Editor: Mike Trounce

MS Matters
MS Society, 372 Edgware Road
London NW2 6ND
020 8438 0700
info@mssociety.org.uk
www.mssociety.org.uk
6pa. Editor: Debbie Reeves

New Beacon
Royal National Institute of the Blind
Falcon Park, Neasden Lane
London NW10 1RN
020 7878 2307
beacon@rnib.org.uk
www.rnib.org.uk
11pa. For those with sight problems
Editor: Ann Lee

New Pathways
The MS Resource Centre
Unit 7, Peartree Business Centre
Peartree Road, Stanway
Colchester CO3 0JN
01206 505444
info@msrc.co.uk
www.msrc.co.uk
6pa. MS issues. Editor: Judy
Graham

Ouch!
Room 2507, BBC White City
201 Wood Lane
London W12 7TS
020 8450 1018
ouch@bbc.co.uk
www.bbc.co.uk/ouch
Website. Producer: Damon Rose

One in Seven Magazine
The Royal National Institute for
Deaf People
19–23 Featherstone Street
London EC1Y 8SL
020 7296 8000
oneinseven@rnid.org.uk
www.rnid.org.uk
6pa. For the deaf. Editor: Dawn
Egan

The Parkinson Magazine
Parkinson's Disease Society
of the UK
215 Vauxhall Bridge Road
London SW1V 1EJ
020 7931 8080
bcormie@parkinsons.org.uk
www.parkinsons.org.uk
Quarterly. Editor: Barbara Cormi

Pinpoint
Disability West Midlands
Prospect Hall, College Walk
Selly Oak, Birmingham B29 6LE
0121 414 1616
pinpoint@dwm.org.uk
www.dwm.org.uk
6pa. Editor: Pete Millington

Positive Nation
The UK Coalition of People Living
  with HIV and Aids (UKC)
250 Kennington Lane
London SE11 5RD
020 7564 2121
editor@positivenation.co.uk
www.positivenation.co.uk
10pa. Issues for people with HIV/
AIDS.
Editor: Amanda Elliott

Pure
The National Kidney
  Research Fund
Kings Chambers, Priestgate
Peterborough PE1 1FG
01733 704650
louisecox@nkrf.org.uk
www.nkrf.org.uk
Quarterly. Editor: Louise Cox

RADAR Bulletin
Royal Association for Disability
  and Rehabilitation
12 City Forum, 250 City Road
London EC1V 8AF
020 7250 3222
radar@radar.org.uk
www.radar.org.uk
4pa. Civil rights issues for the
disabled.
Editor: John Stanford

Soundaround
Soundaround Associations
34 Glentham Road, Barnes
London SW13 9JJ
020 8741 3332
Freephone for advice: 0800 917
6008
nigel@soundaround.org
www.soundaround.org
Monthly. Visually impaired,
worldwide. Editor: Nigel Vee

Stroke News
The Stroke Association
Stroke House, 240 City Road
London EC1V 2PR
020 7566 0300
www.stroke.org.uk
Quarterly

Talk
The National Deaf Children's
  Society
15 Dufferin Street,
London EC1Y 8UR
020 7490 8656
ndcs@ndcs.org.uk
www.ndcs.org.uk
6pa. For deaf children.
Editor: Jo Kelly

Talking Sense
Sense, National Deafblind and
  Rubella Association
11–13 Clifton Terrace,
Finsbury Park
London N4 3SR
020 7272 7774
enquiries@sense.org.uk
www.sense.org.uk
3pa. Deafblind.
Editor: Colin Anderson

Typetalk Update
Paver Downes Associates
2 Queens Square
Liverpool L1 1RH
0151 293 0505
hogan@paverdownes.co.uk
www.typetalk.org
6pa. Down's syndrome.
Editor: Rachel Brough

Viewpoint
Mencap, 123 Golden Lane
London EC1Y 0RT
020 7696 5599
viewpoint@mencap.org.uk
www.mencap.org.uk/viewpoint
6pa. Learning disabilities.
Editor: Faiza Fareed

Yes!
Yes! Promotions,
36–38 Avenue Road
Hartlepool TS24 8AT
01429 282009
enquiries@yesmagazine.org.uk
www.yesmagazine.org.uk
6pa. Disability positive thinking.
Editor: Stephen Wharton

Gay and lesbian

3sixty
Newsquest (Sussex), Argus House
Crowhurst Road, Hollingbury
Brighton BN1 8AR
01273 561618
info@3sixtymag.co.uk
www.3sixtymag.co.uk
Monthly. Editor: Geoff Tourle

Attitude
Northern and Shell
Northern and Shell Tower
4 Selsdon Way, London E14 9GL
020 7308 5090
attitude@nasnet.co.uk
Monthly. Editor: Adam Mattera

AXM
Blue Maverick Media
2 Charlotte Road,
London EC2A 3DH
020 7749 1970
mike@axm-mag.com
www.axm-mag.com
Monthly. Editor: Mike Dent

Bent
All Points North Publications
Walk 34, Middleton Road
Leeds LS27 8BB
0870 125 5555
editor@bent.com
www.bent.com
11–12pa. Editor: Christopher Amos

Boyz
PP and B
63–69 New Oxford Street
London WC1A 1DG
020 7845 4300
hudson@boyz.co.uk
www.boyz.co.uk
Weekly. Editor: David Hudson

Diva
Millivres-Prowler
Unit M, Spectrum House
32–34 Gordon House Road
London NW5 1LP
020 7424 7400
edit@divamag.co.uk
www.divamag.co.uk
Monthly. Editor: Jane Czyzselska

G3
G3 Magazine, Oxford House
49a Oxford Road,
London N4 3EY
020 7272 0093
info@g3magazine.co.uk
www.g3magazine.co.uk
Monthly. Editor: Sarah Garrett

Gay Times
Millivres-Prowler
Unit M, Spectrum House
32–34 Gordon House Road
London NW5 1LP
020 7424 7400
edit@gaytimes.co.uk
www.gaytimes.co.uk
Monthly. Editor: Vicky Powell

Gay.com UK
22–23 Carnaby Street
London W1F 7DB
020 7734 3700
info@uk.gay.com
www.uk.gay.com
Editor: Christine Townsend

Midlands Zone
What's On Magazine Group
5–6 Shoplatch
Shrewsbury SY1 1HF
01743 281777
info@zonemag.com
Monthly. Editor: Martin Monahan

Outnorthwest
Unity House
15 Pritchard Street
(off Charles Street)
Manchester M1 7DA
0161 235 8035
editor@outnorthwest.com
www.outnorthwest.com
Monthly free, published by the Lesbian and Gay Foundation. Editor: Grahame Robertson

Pink Paper
PP and B,
63–69 New Oxford Street
London WC1A 1DG
020 7845 4300
editorial@pinkpaper.co.uk
www.pinkpaper.com
Weekly. Editor: Tris Reid-Smith

Refresh
CBC Media
Unit 4–5 Greenwich Quay
Clarence Road,
London SE8 3EY
020 8469 9700
refresh@cbcmedia.co.uk
www.refreshmag.co.uk
Monthly. Editor: David Tickner

ScotsGay
Pageprint, PO Box 666
Edinburgh EH7 5YW
0131 539 0666
editorial@scotsgay.co.uk
www.scotsgay.co.uk
Monthly. Editor: John Hein

Stonewall Newsletter
Stonewall,
46 Grosvenor Gardens
London SW1W OEB
020 7881 9440
info@stonewall.org.uk
www.stonewall.org.uk
Quarterly. Editor: Jodie West

UKBlackOut.com
0870 204 8071
www.ukblackout.com
Website. For black lesbians and gays

Cultural and ethnic minorities

Ad-Diplomasi News Report
PO Box 138, Chelsea
London SW3 6BH
020 7286 1372
www.ad-diplomasi.com
Monthly. Arabic. Editor: Raymond Atallah

African Times
Ethnic Media Group
Unit 2 Whitechapel Technology Centre
65 Whitechapel Road
London E1 1DU
020 7650 2000
africantimes@ethnicmedia.co.uk
www.ethnicmedia.co.uk
Weekly. Editor: Eminike Pio

Al Arab
Al Arab Publishing House
159 Acre Lane,
London SW2 5UA
020 7274 9381
editor@alarab.co.uk
www.alarab.co.uk
Daily. Editor: As Elhouni

Al-Jamila
Saudi Research and Marketing UK
Arab Press House,
184 High Holborn
London WC1V 7AP
020 7831 8181
aljamila@hhsaudi.com
www.arab.net
Monthly. Upper and middle-income Arab women. Editor: Sanaa Al-Hadethee

Al-Majalla
Saudi Research and Marketing UK
Arab Press House,
184 High Holborn
London WC1V 7AP
020 7831 8181
al-majalla@hhsaudi.com
www.al-majalla.com
Weekly. Arab matters. Editor: Fahed Al-Tayash

Anglo–Hellenic Review
Anglo–Hellenic League
23 Jeffreys Street,
London NW1 9PS
020 7267 3877
paul.watkins@virgin.net
www.hellenicbookservice.com/ahr.htm
2pa. Cultural affairs covering Greece and Britain. Editor: Paul Watkins

Asharq Al-Awsat
Saudi Research and Marketing U
Arab Press House,
184 High Holborn
London WC1V 7AP
020 7831 8181
editorial@asharqalawsat.com
www.aawsat.com
Daily. Saudi Arabia. Editor: Mohammed Alutam

Asian Express
Smart Asian Media,
211 Picadilly
London W1J 9HF
020 7917 2744
info@asianxpress.newspapers.cc
www.asianxpressnewspaper.cor
Weekly. Editor: Vallabh Kaviraj

Asian News
01706 898933
www.theasiannews.co.uk
Website. Editor: Steve Hammond

Asian Times
Ethnic Media Group
Unit 2 Whitechapel Technology Centre
65 Whitechapel Road
London E1 1DU
020 7650 2000
asiantimes@ethnicmedia.co.uk
www.ethnicmedia.co.uk
Weekly. Editor: Isaac Hamza

Asians in Media
243 North Hyde Lane
Southall, Middlesex UB2 5TE
020 7737 0749
sunny.hundal@asiansinmedia.or
www.asiansinmedia.org
Weekly. Guide to the British Asian media industry. Editor: Sunny Hundal

barfiCulture
www.barficulture.com
Website. British Asians. Editor: Sunny Hundal

Blacknet
46 Deptford Broadway
London SE8 4PH
0870 746 5000
information@blacknet.co.uk
www.blacknet.co.uk
Community website for black peo in Britain. Editor: Junior Wilson

Black Information Link
Suite 12, 9 Cranmer Road
London SW9 6EJ
020 7582 1990
blink1990@blink.org.uk
www.blink.org.uk
Website

Canada Post
RoseMaple Media, PO Box No 2
No. 4 Circular Road
London W5 2QA
020 7840 9765
info@canadapost.co.uk
www.canadapost.co.uk
Monthly. Editor: Paula Adamick

Caribbean Times
Ethnic Media Group
Unit 2 Whitechapel Technology
  Centre
65 Whitechapel Road
London E1 1DU
020 7650 2000
caribbeantimes@ethnicmedia.co.uk
www.ethnicmedia.co.uk
Weekly. Editor: Ron Shillingford

Chinatown
CTM Publishing, Enterprise Centre
14a Rochdale Road
Manchester M4 4JR
0161 839 5400
enquiries@
  chinatownthemagazine.com
www.chinatownthemagazine.com
*Bi-monthly. English-language for
Chinese*

Clickwalla.com
MeMedia, Clerkenwell House
57 Clerkenwell Road
London EC1R 5BL
020 7693 8400
info@memediagroup.com
www.clickwalla.com
Website

Daily Jang London
Jang Publications
1 Sanctuary Street
London SE1 1ED
020 7403 5833
editor@jang.globalnet.co.uk
www.jang.com.pk
Daily. Asian. Editor: Zahoor Niazi

Des Pardes
1 The Crescent,
Southall UB1 1BE
020 8571 1127
despadesuk@btconnect.com
*Weekly. Indian expatriates. Editor:
GS Virk*

Dziennik Polski
The Polish Daily (Publishers)
63 Jeddo Road,
London W12 9ED
020 8740 1991
editor@dziennikpolski.co.uk
www.polishdailynews.com
*Daily. Polish community in UK.
Editor: Jaroslaw Kovninski*

Eastern Eye
65 Whitechapel Road
London E1 1DU
020 7650 2000
aeditor@easterneyeuk.co.uk
www.ethnicmedia.co.uk
*Weekly. Second- and third-
generation UK Asians. Editor:
Aram Singh*

Eikoku News Digest
News Digest International
8–10 Long Street,
London E2 8HQ
020 7749 8000
info@newsdigest.co.uk
www.newsdigest.co.uk
*Weekly. Japanese. Editor: Mikiko
Toshima*

Filipino Observer
PO Box 20376,
London NW11 8FE
020 8731 7195
editor@filipino.co.uk
Monthly. Editor: Bong Forrouzan

Garavi Gujarat
1 Silex Street,
London SE1 0DW
020 7928 1234
garav@gujarat.co.uk
www.gg2.net
Weekly. Editor: Ramniknal Solanki

Gujarat Samachar
Asian Business Publications
8–12 Hoxton Market,
off Coronet Street
London N1 6HG
020 7749 4080
support@abplgroup.com
www.gujarat-samachar.com/
Weekly. Editor: C Patel

Hia
Saudi Research and Marketing UK
Arab Press House,
184 High Holborn
London WC1V 7AP
020 7831 8181
hia@hhsaudi.com
*Monthly. Arab women. Editor: Mai
Badr*

India weekly
Ethnic Media Group
White Chapel Technology Centre
65 Whitechapel Road
London E1 1DU
020 7650 2000
newsdesk@indiaweekly.co.uk
www.indiaweekly.co.uk
Weekly. Editor: Dr Premenaddy

Irish Post
Cambridge House
Cambridge Grove
Hammersmith, London W6 OLE
020 8741 0649
irishpost@irishpost.co.uk
www.irishpost.co.uk
Weekly. Editor: Frank Murphy

Irish World
934 North Circular Road
London NW2 7JR
020 8453 7800
sales@theirishworld.com
www.theirishworld.com
Weekly. Editor: Donal Mooney

Janomot Bengali Newsweekly
Creative Media Publications
Unit 2, 20B Spelman Street
London E1 5LQ
020 7377 6032
janomot@easynet.co.uk
*Weekly. Older Bangladeshi
immigrants. Editor: Nabob Udden*

Jewish Chronicle
25 Furnival Street,
London EC4A 1JT
020 7415 1500
webmaster@thejc.co.uk
www.jchron.co.uk
Weekly and website

Jewish Telegraph
Maccabi Complex, May Terrace
Glasgow G46 6LD
0141 621 4422
mail@jewishtelegraph.com
www.jewishtelegraph.com
Weekly. Editor: Paul Harris

La Voce degli Italiani
Scalabrine Fathers
20 Brixton Road
London SW9 6BU
020 7735 5164
redaction@lavoce.com
www.lavoce.com
*55pa. Italians in Europe. Editor:
Cari Lettori*

London Turkish Gazette
177 Green Lanes, Palmers Green
London N13 4UR
020 8889 5025
news@londragazete.com
www.londragazete.com
Weekly. Editor: Artun Goksan

London Welsh Magazine
London Welsh Association
157–163 Gray's Inn Road
London WC1X 8UE
020 7837 3722
gethinest@aol.com
Quarterly. Editor: Gethin Williams

Maghreb Review
45 Burton Street,
London WC1H 9AL
020 7388 1840
maghrab@maghrabreview.com
www.maghrabreview.com
*Quarterly. North Africa, Sub
Sahara Africa, Middle East &
Islam. Editor: Mohammed Ban-
madani*

MIL Matchmaker Magazine
Matchmaker International
PO Box 430, Pinner HA5 2TW
020 8868 1879
info@perfect-partner.com
www.perfect-partner.com
*Quarterly. Asians seeking partners.
Editor: Mr Bharat Raipthatha*

Mauritian Abroad
Sankris Publishing,
32 Ethelbert Road
Faversham ME13 8SQ
01795 539499
eveer77807@aol.com
Quarterly. Editor: Krish Veeramah

Mauritius News
583 Wandsworth Road
London SW8 3JD
020 7498 3066
editor@mauritiusnews.co.uk
www.mauritiusnews.co.uk
Monthly. Editor: Mr Chellen

Milap Weekly
Masbro Centre,
87 Masbro Road
London W14 0LR
020 7385 8966
*Weekly. Urdu-speaking
community.
Editor: Ramesh Soni*

Muslim News
Visitcrest, PO Box 380
Harrow HA2 6LL
020 8863 8586
editor@muslimnews.co.uk
www.muslimnews.co.uk
Monthly. Editor: A. Versi

Navin Weekly
Masbro Centre, 87 Masbro Road
London W14 0LR
020 7385 8966
*Weekly. South Asian community.
Editor: Ramesh Soni*

NetAsia.co.uk
www.netasia.co.uk
Website

New Nation
Ethnic Media Group
Unit 2 Whitechapel Technology
Centre
65 Whitechapel Road
London E1 1DU
020 7650 2000
newsdesk@newnation.co.uk
www.ethnicmedia.co.uk
*Weekly. Black news. Editor: Michael
Eboda*

New Zealand News UK
Southern Link Media, 2nd Floor
Quadrant House
250 Kennington Lane
London SE11 5RD
020 7820 0885
editor@southernlink.co.uk
www.nznewsuk.co.uk
Weekly. Editor: Rachael Walsh

Noticias Latin America
PO Box 34783,
London N7 7WD
020 7686 1633
informacion@noticias.co.uk
www.noticias.co.uk
Monthly. Editor: Albrairto Rojas

Notiun Din Bengali Newsweekly
Din Publishers
46g Greatorex Street
London E1 5NP
020 7247 6280
news@notiundin.dlus.com
Weekly. Editor: Mohib Choudhury

Occasions Magazine
Ethnic Media Group
Unit 2, 65 White Chapel Road
Edgware, London E1 1DU
020 7650 2000
reva@dircon.co.uk
www.occasions.co.uk
*Quarterly. Asians worldwide.
Editor: Terry Tan*

Parikiaki
534a Holloway Road
London N7 6JP
020 7272 6777
parikiakinews@yahoo.co.uk
*Weekly. Cypriots in UK.
Editor: Bambos Charalambous*

Perdesan Monthly
PTI Media, 24 Cotton Brook Road
Sir Francis Ley Industrial Estate
Derby DE23 8YJ
01332 372851
punjabtimes@aol.com
*Monthly. Asian community. Editor:
Mr Purewal*

Punjab Times International
PTI Derby Media
24 Cotton Brook Road
Sir Francis Ley Industrial Estate
Derby DE23 8YJ
01332 372851
punjabtimes@aol.com
*Weekly. Punjabi community in UK.
Editor: A Purewal*

Red Hot Curry
Unit 9, Fulton Close,
Argyle Way
Stevenage, Herts SG1 2AF
01438 365582
www.redhotcurry.com
*Website. Asian community website.
Editor: Mrs Lopa Patel*

Sayidaty
Saudi Research and Marketing UK
Arab Press House,
184 High Holborn
London WC1V 7AP
020 7831 8181
sayidaty@hhsaudi.com
www.sayidaty.net
*Weekly. Arab issues. Editor: Hani
Nakshbandi*

Sikh Courier International
The World Sikh Foundation
88 Mollison Way, Edgware
Middlesex HA8 5QW
020 8864 9228
thesikhcourier@aol.com
www.sikhfoundation.org
2pa. Sikhs. Editor: Sukhbir Singh

Snoop
Britasian Media, 5a High Street
Southall UB1 3HA
020 8571 7700
raj@snooplife.co.uk
www.snooplife.com
*Monthly. Second- and third-
generation UK Asians. Editor: Raj
Kaushal*

SomethingJewish.co.uk
PO Box 1554, Hanwell
London W7 1ZF
07976 220273
editor@somethingjewish.co.uk
www.somethingjewish.co.uk
*Web. UK Jewish website. Editor:
Leslie Bunder*

TNT Magazine
Trader Media Group
14–15 Child's Place
Earls Court, London SW5 9RX
020 7373 3377
ian.wakeling@tntmag.co.uk
www.tntmagazine.com
*Weekly. International travellers.
Editor: Lyn Eyb*

Ukrainian Thought
Association of Ukrainians in GB
49 Linden Gardens
London W2 4HG
020 7229 8392
*Weekly. Ukrainian. Editor:
Dr Swiatomyr Forstun*

Ultra Journey
Japan Journals
93 Newman Street
London W1T 3EZ
020 7255 3838
info@japanjournals.com
www.japanjournals.com
*Monthly. Japanese. Editor: Ko
Tejima*

Weekly Gleaner
Unit 220–223, Elephant and Castle
  Shopping Centre
London SE1 6TE
020 7277 1714
editorial@gleaner1.demon.co.uk
http://jamaica-gleaner.com
*Weekly. Caribbean and Jamaican.
Editor: Michael Oban*

Weekly Journey
Japan Journals
93 Newman Street
London W1T 3EZ
020 7255 3838
ina@japanjournals.com
www.japanjournals.com
*Weekly. Japanese in Britain.
Editor:
K Tejima*

oneast
Elm Media Communications
4th Floor, 44 Gerrard Street
London W1D 5QG
020 7439 2288
oneast@hotmail.com
*Monthly. Chinese in Europe. Editor:
Mrs Lei Wang*

eligion
- -

ll The World
The Salvation Army
101 Queen Victoria Street
London EC4P 4EP
020 7332 0101
kevin-sims@salvationarmy.org
www.salvationarmy.org
Quarterly. Editor: Kevin Sims

mar Deep Hindi Weekly
Chepstow Road
London W7 2BG
020 8840 3534
lphabet@globalnet.co.uk
*Weekly. India and diaspora. Editor:
H Kaushal*

Baptist Times
Baptist Times, PO Box 54
129 Broadway, Didcot OX11 8XB
01235 517670
btadmin@bluecom.net
*Weekly. Church leaders. Editor:
Hazel Southam*

Catholic Herald
Herald House, Lambs Passage
London EC1Y 8TQ
020 7588 3101
editorial@catholicherald.co.uk
www.catholicherald.co.uk
Weekly. Acting Editor: Luke Coppen

Catholic Times
Gabriel Communications, 1st Floor
St James' Buildings, Oxford Street
Manchester M1 6FP
0161 236 8856
kevin.flaherty@the-universe.net
www.ctonline.org
Weekly. Editor: Mark Moretti

Challenge
Authentic Media, PO Box 300
Carlisle CA3 0QS
01228 554320
steven.bunn@whsmithnet.co.uk
www.paternoster-publishing.com
*Monthly. Christian. Editor: Debbie
Bunn*

Christian Aid News
Christian Aid, PO Box 100
London SE1 7RT
020 7620 4444
press@christian-aid.org
www.christian-aid.org.uk
Quarterly. Editor: Susan Roberts

Christian Herald
Christian Media Centre
Garcia Estate, Canterbury Road
Worthing, West Sussex
BN13 1EH
01903 821082
editor@christianherald.org.uk
www.christianmedia.org.uk
*Weekly. Evangelical Christian
community. Editor: Russ Bravo*

Christianity and Renewal
Premier Media Group (PMG)
PO Box 17911, London
SW1P 4YX
020 7316 1450
john.buckeridge@premier.org.uk
www.christianityandrenewal.com
Monthly. Editor: John Buckeridge

Daily Bread
Scripture Union Publishing
207–209 Queensway, Bletchley
Milton Keynes MK2 2EB
01908 856000
laurels@scriptureunion.org.uk
www.dailybread.org.uk
*Quarterly. Adult Bible readers.
Editor: James Davies*

Home and Family
The Mothers' Union
Mary Sumner House,
24 Tufton Street
London SW1P 3RB
020 7222 5533
homeandfamily@
  themothersunion.org
www.themothersunion.org
Quarterly. Editor: Jill Worth

Jewish Chronicle
25 Furnival Street
London EC4A 1JT
020 7415 1500
webmaster@thejc.co.uk
www.jchron.co.uk
Weekly and website

Jewish Telegraph
Maccabi Complex, May Terrace
Glasgow G46 6LD
0141 621 4422
mail@jewishtelegraph.com
www.jewishtelegraph.com
Weekly. Editor: Paul Harris

Jewish.net
07976 220273
admin@jewishnet.net
www.jewishnet.net
Website. Director: Don Winer

The Life
Scripture Union Publishing
207–209 Queensway, Bletchley
Milton Keynes MK2 2EB
01908 856000
media@scriptureunion.org.uk
www.scriptureunion.org.uk/thelife
Quarterly. Editor: Adam Pettrie

Life and Work
Board of Communications
121 George Street
Edinburgh EH2 4YN
0131 225 5722
magazine@lifeandwork.org
www.lifeandwork.org
*Monthly. Church of Scotland.
Editor: Lynne Robertson*

The Muslim News
Visitcrest, PO Box 380
Harrow HA2 6LL
020 8863 8586
editor@muslimnews.co.uk
www.muslimnews.co.uk
Monthly. Editor: A Versi

New Day
The Leprosy Mission,
Goldhay Way
Orton, Goldhay
Peterborough PE2 5GZ
01733 370505
post@tlmew.org.uk
www.leprosymission.org
2pa. Editor: Mr Simon Watkinson

Presbyterian Herald
Church House, Fisherwick Place
Belfast BT1 6DW
028 9032 2284
herald@presbyterianireland.org
www.presbyterianrianireland.org
Monthly. Presbyterian. Editor: Rev
Arthur Clarke

Scottish Catholic Observer
19 Waterloo Street,
Glasgow G2 6BT
0141 221 4956
editorial@
  scottishcatholicobserver.com
www.scottishcatholicobserver.com
Weekly. Editor: Harry Conroy

Sikh Courier International
World Sikh Foundation
33 Wargrave Road
Harrow HA2 8LL
020 8864 9228
thesikhcourier@aol.com
www.sikhfoundation.org
2pa. Editor: Sukhbir Singh

SomethingJewish.co.uk
PO Box 1554, Hanwell
London W7 1ZF
07976 220273
editor@somethingjewish.co.uk
www.somethingjewish.co.uk
Web. UK Jewish website. Editor:
Leslie Bunder

Ummah.com
info@ummah.com
www.ummah.org.uk
Website. Muslim/Islam

The Universe
Gabriel Communications
1st Floor, St James' Building
Oxford Street,
Manchester M1 6FP
0161 236 8856
newsdesk@the-universe.net
www.totalcatholic.com
Weekly. Roman Catholics and
Ireland.
Editor: Joe Kelly

War Cry
101 Newington Causeway
Elephant and Castle
London SE1 6BN
020 7367 4900
warcry@salvationarmy.org.uk
www.salvationarmy.org.uk/warcry
Monthly. Christian current affairs.
Editor: Major Nigel Bovey

TV journalism

MAIN BBC ADDRESSES

Television Centre
Wood Lane
London
W12 7RJ

BBC White City
201 Wood Lane
London
W12 7TS

Broadcasting House
Portland Place
London
W1A 1AA
www.bbc.co.uk
020 8743 8000

BBC News
Television Centre
020 8743 8000
http://news.bbc.co.uk
Director of BBC News:
Helen Bowden; deputy director
of BBC News: Mark Damazer;
head of communications:
Janie Ironside Wood

BBC Television News
Room 1502, Television Centre
020 8624 9043
Head of television news:
Roger Mosey;
deputy: Rachael Attwell

Radio News
020 8743 8000
Head of radio news:
Stephen Mitchell;
head of radio current affairs:
Gwyneth Williams

BBC Newsgathering
020 8743 8000
Head of newsgathering:
Adrian Van Klaveren

Current affairs
Head of current affairs:
Peter Horrocks

Political programmes unit
BBC Westminster
4 Millbank
London
SW1P 3JA
020 7973 6000
Head of political programmes:
Fran Unsworth; political editor:
Andrew Marr

BBC News Online
Television Centre
http://news.bbc.co.uk
Head of new media: Richard
Deverell

BBC EDITORS & CORRESPONDENTS

Home editor: Mark Easton
Political editor: Andrew Marr
Business editor: Jeff Randall
World affairs editor: John Simpson
Diplomatic editor: Brian Hanrahan

HOME AND ABROAD

Home affairs: Margaret Gilmore;
education: Mike Baker; health:
Karen Allen; social affairs: Daniel
Sandford; royal: Nicholas Witchell,
Peter Hunt; political: Laura
Trevelyan; defence: Paul Adams;
security: Frank Gardner; rural
affairs: Tom Heap; diplomatic:
Bridget Kendall, James Robbins;
environment and science: David
Shukman; media: Torin Douglas;
technology (BBC News Online):
Alfred Hermida, Mark Ward

Special correspondents
Jeremy Bowen, Fergal Keane,
Gavin Hewitt; TV news: Ben Brown;
BBC News 24: Philippa Thomas

WORLD

World affairs
Peter Biles

Europe
Europe: Tim Franks, Chris Morris,
Stephen Sackur; Paris: Allan Little,
Caroline Wyatt; Berlin: Ray Furlong;
Rome: David Willey; Greece:
Richard Galpin; Moscow: Damian
Grammaticas; south Europe: Brian
Barron; central Europe: Nick Thorpe

Middle East
Orla Guerin, James Reynolds,
Paul Wood; Turkey: Jonny Dymond

Americas
Washington: Nick Bryant, Matt
Frei, Jon Leyne, Clive Myrie, Ian
Pannell, Justin Webb; California:
David Willis; Mexico and central
America: Claire Marshall; South
America: Elliott Gotkine

Other
Africa: Hilary Andersson; east
Africa: Andrew Harding; south
Asia: Adam Mynott; south-east
Asia: Kylie Morris; central Asia:
Monica Whitlock; world media:
Sebastian Usher; also Dominic
Hughes, Jill McGivering, Rageh
Omaar, Matthew Price

Press contacts : **Section 4**

195

Flagship news and politics programmes

020 8743 8000

Breakfast
Room 1605, News Centre,
Television Centre
020 8624 9700
breakfasttv@bbc.co.uk
*Editor: Richard Porter; presenters:
Dermot Murnaghan, Natasha
Kaplinsky*

Newsnight
Television Centre
020 8624 9800
*Editor: George Entwhistle;
presenters: Jeremy Paxman, Kirsty
Wark, Gavin Esler*

Panorama
Room 1118, BBC White City
020 8752 7152
panorama@bbc.co.uk
*Editor: Mike Robinson; deputy
editors: Andrew Bell and Sam
Collyns*

Politics Show
4 Millbank
London
SW1P 3JQ
020 7973 6199
politicsshow@bbc.co.uk
Presenter: Jeremy Vine

Question Time
Mentorn, 43 Whitfield Street
London
W1T 4HA
020 7258 6800
Presenter: David Dimbleby

Six O'Clock News
Television Centre
020 8624 9996
*Presenters: George Alagiah, Sophie
Raworth*

Ten O'Clock News
Television Centre
020 8624 9999
*Editor: Kevin Bakhurst; presenters:
Huw Edwards, Fiona Bruce*

Today programme (Radio 4)
Room G630, Stage 6
Television Centre
W12 7RJ
020 8743 8000
www.bbc.co.uk/radio4/today
*Editor: Kevin Marsh; presenters:
John Humphrys, James Naughtie,
Ed Stourton, Sarah Montague*

BBC nations and regions

BBC Scotland
0141 339 8844
www.bbc.co.uk/scotland

BBC Wales
029 2032 2000
www.bbc.co.uk/wales

BBC Northern Ireland
028 9033 8000
www.bbc.co.uk/northernireland

BBC East
01603 619 331
www.bbc.co.uk/england/lookeast

BBC East Midlands
0115 955 0500
www.bbc.co.uk/england/
eastmidlandstoday

BBC London
020 7224 2424
www.bbc.co.uk/london

BBC North
0113 244 1188
www.bbc.co.uk/england/
looknorthyorkslincs

BBC North East and Cumbria
0191 232 1313
www.bbc.co.uk/england/
looknorthnecumbria

BBC North West
0161 200 2020
www.bbc.co.uk/manchester

BBC South
02380 226201
www.bbc.co.uk/england/
southtoday

BBC South East
01892 670000
www.bbc.co.uk/england/
southeasttoday

BBC South West
01752 229201
www.bbc.co.uk/england/spotlight

BBC West
0117 973 2211
www.bbc.co.uk/england/
pointswest

BBC West Midlands
0121 567 6767
www.bbc.co.uk/birmingham

BBC TV channels

BBC1
020 8743 8000
www.bbc.co.uk/bbcone

BBC2
020 8743 8000
www.bbc.co.uk/bbctwo

BBC3
020 8743 8000
www.bbc.co.uk/bbcthree

BBC4
020 8576 3193
www.bbc.co.uk/bbcfour

CBBC
020 8743 8000
www.bbc.co.uk/cbbc

CBeebies
020 8743 8000
www.bbc.co.uk/cbeebies

BBC America
00 1 301 347 2222
www.bbcamerica.com

BBC Canada
00 416 934 7800
www.bbccanada.com

BBC Food
020 8433 2221
www.bbcfood.com

BBC News 24
020 8743 8000
bbcnews24@bbc.co.uk
www.bbc.co.uk/bbcnews24
Editoral director: Mark Popescu

BBC Parliament
020 7973 6216
parliament@bbc.co.uk
www.bbc.co.uk/bbcparliament

BBC Prime
020 8433 2221
www.bbcprime.com

BBC World
020 8576 2308
www.bbcworld.com
Editorial director: Sian Kevill

ITV Network

200 Gray's Inn Road
London
WC1X 8HF
020 7843 8000
*Controls commissioning and
scheduling across entire ITV
network, including non-ITV plc
regions*

ITV channels

ITV1
020 7843 8000
www.itv.com/itv1

ITV2
020 7843 8000
www.itv.com/itv2
*Channel editor: Zai Bennett,
020 7843 8129; controller of
commissioned programmes:
Daniella Neumann, 020 7843 8101*

ITV News
200 Gray's Inn Road
London
WC1X 8XZ
020 7833 3000
press: itvplanning@itn.co.uk
www.itv.com/news
Editor-in-chief: David Mannion

ITV plc
London Television Centre
Upper Ground
London
SE1 9LT
*Chief executive: Charles Allen;
chairman: Sir Peter Burt
Controls 11 of the 15 ITV franchises*

ITV News Group
020 7396 6000
*Chief executive: Clive Jones
Includes ITV1's national and
international news output, and
regional news for ITV plc
franchises; plus ITV plc's 40% stake
in ITN*

ITV News

ITN, 200 Gray's Inn Road
London
WC1X 8XZ
020 7833 3000

*Editor-in-chief: David Mannion;
editor: Deborah Turness; deputy
editor: Jonathan Munro; managing
editor: Robin Elias; head of ITV News
channel: Dominic Crossley-Holland*

*Key presenters: Sir Trevor McDonald;
Mary Nightingale; Katie Derham;
Mark Austin; Nicholas Owen;
Alastair Stewart*

Editors and correspondents
*UK editor: Tom Bradby; political
editor: Nick Robinson; consumer
affairs editor: Chris Choi;
international news editor: Bill Neely;
business and economics editor:
Caroline Kerr; science editor:
Lawrence McGinty;
sports editor: Tim Ewart;
senior correspondent: James Mates*

Home and abroad
*News correspondents: Shiulie Ghosh,
Joyce Ohajah, Mark Webster, Helen
Wright; news reporters: Catherine
Jacob, Philip Reay-Smith, Romilly
Weeks; political: Angus Walker,
Libby Wiener; north of England:
Tim Rogers; south of England:
Adrian Britton; Wales and west of
England: Geraint Vincent; Scotland:
Martin Geissler; medical: Sue
Saville; crime: Dan Rivers;
media and arts: Nina Nannar;
sport: Felicity Barr*

World
*International news: Andrea
Catherwood; Europe: Juliet Bremner;
Washington: Robert Moore;
Middle East: Julian Manyon;
Africa: Neil Connery;
Asia: John Irvine
Press officer: Saskia Wirth
020 7430 4825
saskia.wirth@itn.co.uk*
Press releases to:
itvplanning@itn.co.uk

ITV regions

OWNED BY ITV PLC

ITV Anglia
01603 615151
firstname.lastname@itv.com
www.angliatv.com
News at Anglia
0870 240 6003
news@angliatv.com
*Controller of news: Guy Adams
Cambridge regional office*
01223 467076
Chelmsford regional office
01245 357676
Ipswich regional office
01473 226157
Luton regional office
01582 729666
Northampton regional office
01604 624343
Peterborough regional office
01733 269440

ITV Border
01228 525101
www.border-tv.com
Head of news: Ian Proniewicz

ITV Central
0121 643 9898
firstname.lastname@itv.com
www2.itv.com/central/
*Editor Central News West:
Dan Barton
Central News East*
0115 986 3322
*News editor: Mike Blair
Studios marked for closure;
operation to move to Birmingham
office
Central News South*
01235 554123
News editor: Ian Rumsey

ITV Granada
0161 832 7211
firstname.lastname@itv.com
www.granadatv.com
*News editor: Cerys Griffiths
Blackburn regional news centre*
01254 690099
Chester regional news centre
01244 313966
Lancaster regional news centre
01524 60688

ITV London
020 7620 1620
firstname.lastname@itv.com
www2.itv.com/london/
Managing director: Christy Swords
London News Network
020 7430 4000
firstname.lastname@
itvlondon.com
www.itvlondon.co.uk
Head of news: Stuart Thomas; news editors: Brendan McGowan and Robin Campbell

ITV Meridian
023 8022 2555
news@meridiantv.com;
firstname.lastname@
granadamedia.com
www.meridiantv.co.uk
Head of news: Guy Phillips
Maidstone news office
01622 882244
Newbury news office
01635 552266

Tyne Tees Television
0191 261 0181
news@tynetees.tv;
firstname.lastname@itv.com
www.tynetees.tv
Head of news: Graham Marples
Tees Valley & North Yorkshire news office
Newsroom: 01642 566999
newstoday@tynetees.tv
Senior editor: Bill Campbell

ITV Wales
029 2059 0590
info@itvwales.com;
news@itvwales.com;
firstname.lastname@itvwales.com
www.itvwales.com
Head of news: John G Williams
Carmarthen news office
01267 236809
West Wales correspondent: Giles Smith
Colwyn Bay news office
01492 513888
colwyn@itvwales.com
North Wales correspondents: Carole Green and Ian Lang

Newtown news office
01686 623381
Mid-Wales correspondent: Rob Shelley
Wrexham news office
01978 261462
North Wales correspondent: Paul Mewies

ITV West
0117 972 2722
reception@itv.com;
firstname.lastname@itv.com
www.itv1west.com
Newsdesk
0117 972 2151/2152
itvwestnews@itv.com
Head of news: Steve Egginton
Press office
0117 972 2214

ITV Westcountry
01752 333333
firstname.lastname@itv.com
www.westcountry.co.uk
Main newsdesk
01752 333329
news@westcountry.co.uk
Controller of news: Phil Carrodus
Barnstaple news office
01271 324244
Exeter news office
01392 499400
Penzance News Office
01736 331483
Taunton news office
01823 322335
Truro news office
01872 262244
Weymouth news office
01305 760860

ITV Yorkshire
0113 243 8283
firstname.lastname@itv.com
www.yorkshiretv.com
Calendar (ITV Yorkshire News programme)
0845 121 1000
calendar@yorkshiretv.com
Head of news: Will Venters,
0113 222 8822
Grimsby office
01469 510661

Hull office
01482 324488
Lincoln ofice
01522 530738
Sheffield office
0114 272 777
York office
01904 610066
Press office
0113 222 7129
Press officer: Jo Gough

OWNED BY SCOTTISH MEDIA GROUP

Grampian TV
01224 848848
firstname.lastname@smg.plc.uk
www.grampiantv.co.uk
Head of news: Henry Eagles

Scottish TV
0141 300 3000
firstname.lastname@smg.plc.uk
www.scottishtv.co.uk
press office
0141 300 3670
Press officer: Kirsten Elsby
newsdesk
0141 300 3360
Head of news: Paul McKinney

INDEPENDENTLY OWNED

Channel Television
01534 816816; news room:
01534 816688
broadcast@channeltv.co.uk
www.channeltv.co.uk
Guernsey office
01481 241888
broadcast.gsy@channeltv.co.uk
London office
020 7633 9902

UTV
028 9032 8122
firstinitiallastname@utvplc.com
www.u.tv
Head of news: Rob Morrison

Channel 4

124 Horseferry Road
London
SW1P 2TX
Tel: 020 7396 4444
News and current affairs department:
Head: Dorothy Byrne 020 7306
8588 (assistant: Louise Platel 020
7306 8132)
Editors: Kevin Sutcliffe
(investigations) 020 7306 1068;
Mark Rubens 020 7306 8771

Channel 4 News

ITN, 200 Gray's Inn Road
London
WC1X 8XZ
020 7833 3000
www.channel4.com/news
*Editor: Jim Gray; deputy editor:
Martin Fewell; managing editor:
Gay Flashman*
Newsdesk
020 7430 4601
Press
020 7430 4220
Fiona.Railton@itn.co.uk
*Press & publicity manager:
Fiona Railton*
Presenters
*Anchor: Jon Snow; noon anchor:
Krishnan Guru-Murthy; Sue Turton,
Samira Ahmed*
Editors
*Senior home news editor:
Yvette Edwards
Political editor: Elinor Goodman
Senior foreign news editor:
Deborah Rayner
International editor:
Lindsey Hilsum
Commissioning editor, independent
productions: Fiona Campbell*
Correspondents
*Chief correspondent: Alex Thomson;
home affairs: Simon Israel; political:
Gary Gibbon; social affairs: Victoria
Macdonald; science: Tom Clarke;
science/defence: Julian Rush;
economics: Liam Halligan; arts:
Nicholas Glass; Midlands: Carl
Dinnen; Scotland: Sarah Smith;
foreign affairs: Jonathan Miller;
Washington: Jonathan Rugman;
Asia: Ian Williams; reporters:
Katie Razzall, Stephen Smith,
Darshna Soni; sport: Sue Turton*

Five

22 Long Acre
London
WC2E 9LY
020 7550 5555
firstname.lastname@five.tv
www.five.tv
*Five, address as above;
Tel: 020 7550 5551; head of sales:
Nick Milligan; email:
nick.milligan@five.tv*
five news
Until 2005: ITN
200 Grays Inn Road
London
WC1X 8XZ
020 7833 3000
www.itn.co.uk/fivenews
*Editor: Gary Rogers; political
editor: Andy Bell; presenters:
Kirsty Young, Charlie Stayt,
Rob Butler, Katie Ledger
Defence and foreign affairs
correspondent: James Bays;
consumer: Charlotte Hume; north of
England: Ben Scotchbrook; senior
reporters: Ben Ando, Mark Jordan;
reporters: Colin Campbell, Keith
Doyle, Catherine Jones*
From January 2005: Sky News
(see right)

ITN

200 Gray's Inn Road
London
WC1X 8XZ
020 7833 3000
www.itn.co.uk
*Chief executive: Mark Wood;
director of corporate affairs: Sophie
Cohen; managing director,
multimedia content: Nicholas
Wheeler; head of production, ITN
Factual: Marilyn Bennett; head of
ITN factual: Philip Dampier;
managing director, ITN Archive:
Alwyn Lindsay*

BSkyB

British Sky Broadcasting
Grant Way
Isleworth
TW7 5QD
0870 240 3000
www.sky.com
*Chief executive: James Murdoch;
chief operating officer: Richard
Freudenstein: managing director,
sales, marketing & interactive: Jon
Florsheim; managing director, Sky
Sports: Vic Wakeling; director of
corporate communications: Julian
Eccles*

Sky News
www.skynews.co.uk
*Head of Sky News: Nick Pollard
Key presenters
Afternoon: Kay Burley, Mark
Longhurst; Live at Five: Anna
Botting, Jeremy Thompson
Correspondents
Political: Adam Boulton, Jon Craig,
Jenny Percival, Peter Spencer, Glen
O'Glaza; business: Michael Wilson,
Heather Scott, Juliet Errington,
Alex Crawford; crime: Martin
Brunt; health: Nicola Hill, Thomas
Moore; foreign: Richard Bestic,
Colin Brazier, Keith Graves, Emma
Hurd, Laurence Lee, Tim Marshall,
Stuart Ramsay, Dominic Waghorn,
Andrew Wilson; entertainment:
Georgie Arnold, Neil Sean, Matt
Smith; royal: Geoff Meade; other:
David Bowden, David Chater,
Michelle Clifford, Lisa Holland,
Peter Sharp; also regional bureaux
and 25 other reporters*

Radio journalism

BBC radio

Broadcasting House
Portland Place
London
W1A 1AA
020 8743 8000
Director of radio and music: Jenny Abramsky; head of radio news; Stephen Mitchell; head of radio current affairs: Gwyneth Williams

BBC radio stations

BBC Radio 1
W1A 4DJ
08700 100100
www.bbc.co.uk/radio1
Controller: Andy Parfitt; breakfast show: Chris Moyles

BBC Radio 2
W1A 4WW
08700 100200
www.bbc.co.uk/radio2
Controller: Lesley Douglas; breakfast show: Terry Wogan

BBC Radio 3
W1A 1AA
08700 100300
www.bbc.co.uk/radio3
Controller: Roger Wright

BBC Radio 4
W1A 1AA
08700 100400
www.bbc.co.uk/radio4
Controller: Helen Boaden

Today programme
W12 7RJ
020 8743 8000
www.bbc.co.uk/radio4/today
Editor: Kevin Marsh; presenters: John Humphrys, James Naughtie, Ed Stourton, Sarah Montague

BBC Radio Five Live & Five Live Sports Extra
W12 7RJ
08700 100500
www.bbc.co.uk/fivelive
Controller: Bob Shennan

BBC 1Xtra
W1N 6AJ
020 8743 8000
1xtra@bbc.co.uk
www.bbc.co.uk/1xtra
Controller: Andy Parfitt; breakfast show: Rampage

BBC 6 Music
W1A 1AA
08700 100600
www.bbc.co.uk/6music
Controller: Lesley Douglas; head of programmes: Ric Blaxill; breakfast show: Phill Jupitus

BBC Asian Network
LE1 3SH
020 8743 8000
www.bbc.co.uk/asiannetwork/
Controller: Bijay Sharma; breakfast: Gagan Grewal

BBC 7
W1A 1AA
08700 100700
www2.thny.bbc.co.uk/bbc7
Controller: Helen Boaden

BBC World Service
WC2B 4PH
020 7557 2941
www.bbc.co.uk/worldservice
Director, World Service: Richard Sambrook

BBC Radio Scotland
0141 339 8844
www.bbc.co.uk/scotland
News editor: Blair Jenkins
92–95 FM; 810 AM

BBC Radio Nan Gaidheal
01851 705000
www.bbc.co.uk/scotlandalba/radio
News editor: Norrie Maclennan
103–105 FM

BBC Radio Wales/Cymru
0870 010 0110
www.bbc.co.uk/radiowales
Head of news: Geoff Williams
93–104 FM

BBC Radio Ulster
028 9033 8000
www.bbc.co.uk/radioulster
Head of news: Andrew Colman
92–95.4 FM

BBC Radio Foyle
028 7137 8600
www.bbc.co.uk/radiofoyle
Head of radio: Ana Leddy; head of news: Eimear O'Callaghan
792 AM; 93.1 FM

BBC local radio

BBC Radio Berkshire
0118 946 4200
www.bbc.co.uk/berkshire
Editor: Marianne Bell; breakfast show: Jim Cathcart/Maggie Filburn
104.1 FM; 95.4 FM; 104.4 FM; 94.6 FM

BBC Radio Bristol and Somerset Sound
01179 741111
www.bbc.co.uk/radiobristol and www.bbc.co.uk/bristol
Managing editor, Bristol: Jenny Lacey; assistant editors: Dawn Trevett (Bristol), Simon Clifford (Somerset Sound); breakfast show: Nigel Dando/Rachael Burden
95.5, 94.9 FM; 1548, 1566 AM

BBC Radio Cambridgeshire
01223 259696
www.bbc.co.uk/cambridgeshire
News editor: Alison Daws; managing editor: David Martin; breakfast show: Trevor Dann & Emma McLean
96 FM; 95.7 FM

BBC Radio Cleveland
01642 225211
www.bbc.co.uk/tees
Managing editor: Andrew Glover; news editor: Peter Harris; breakfa. show: Ken Snowdon
95 FM

BBC Radio Cornwall
01872 275421
www.bbc.co.uk/cornwall
Managing editor: Pauline Causey news editor: Ed Goodrich; breakfo show: Pam Spriggs & James Churchfield
103.9 FM; 95.2 FM

BBC Radio Cumbria
01228 592444
www.bbc.co.uk/radiocumbria
Managing editor: Nigel Dyson;
news editor: Tom Stight; breakfast
show: Richard Corrie & Richard
Nankivell
95.6 FM; 96.1 FM; 104.1 FM

BBC Radio Derby
01332 361111
www.bbc.co.uk/radioderby
Managing editor: Simon Cornes;
news editor: John Atkin; breakfast
show: Andy Whitaker
1116 AM; 104.5 AM; 95.3 FM;
96FM

BBC Radio Devon
01752 260323
www.bbc.co.uk/devon
Managing editor: Sarah Softley;
news editor: David Farwig;
breakfast show: Monica Ellis
103.4 FM

BBC Essex
01245 616000
www.bbc.co.uk/essex
Managing editor: Margaret Hyde;
news editor: Alison Hodgkins-
Brown; breakfast show: Etholle
George & John Hayes
103.5 FM; 95.3 FM; 765 AM; 1530
AM; 729 AM

BBC Radio Gloucestershire
01452 308585
www.bbc.co.uk/gloucestershire
Managing editor: Mark Hurrell;
news editor: Ivor Ward-Davis;
breakfast show: Vernon Harwood
104.7 FM; 1413 AM

BBC GMR
0161 200 2000
www.bbc.co.uk/england/gmr
Managing editor: Mike Briscoe;
news editor: Matt Elliott; breakfast
show: Heather Stott & Mark
Edwardson
95.1 FM; 104.6 FM

BBC Radio Guernsey
01481 200600
www.bbc.co.uk/guernsey
Managing editor: Rod Holmes;
news editors: Simon Alexander &
Kay Longlay; breakfast show:
Adrian Gidney
93.2 FM; 1116 AM

BBC Hereford and Worcester
01905 748485
www.bbc.co.uk/worcester or
/hereford
Managing editor: James Coghill;
news editor: Jo Baldwin; breakfast
show: Mike George
104 FM; 104.6 FM; 94.7 FM

BBC Radio Humberside and
BBCi Hull
01482 323232
www.bbc.co.uk/humber
Managing editor: Simon Pattern;
news editor: Mike Morris;
breakfast show: Andy Comfort
95.9 FM; 1485 AM

BBC Radio Jersey
01534 870000
www.bbc.co.uk/jersey
Managing editor: Denzil Dudley;
news editor: Sarah Scriven;
breakfast show: Colin Bray
88.8 FM

BBC Radio Kent
01892 670000
www.bbc.co.uk/kent
Managing editor: Robert Wallace;
news editors: Sally Dunk &
Simon Longprice; breakfast show:
Steve Ladner
96.7 FM; 97.6 FM; 104.2 FM

BBC Radio Lancashire and BBC
Open Centre
01254 262411
www.bbc.co.uk/lancashire
Managing editor: John Clayton;
news editor: Chris Rider; breakfast
show: Mike West
95.5 FM

BBC Radio Leeds
0113 244 2131
www.bbc.co.uk/leeds
Managing editor: John Ryan; news
editor: Andy Evans; breakfast
show: Andrew Edwards & Liz
Rhodes
92.4 FM

BBC Radio Leicester
0116 251 6688
www.bbc.co.uk/leicester
Managing editor: Kate Squire;
breakfast show: Ben Jackson
104.9 FM

BBC Radio Lincolnshire
01522 511411
www.bbc.co.uk/lincolnshire
Managing editor:
Charlie Partridge; news editor:
Andy Farrant; breakfast show:
William Wright
94.9 FM; 1368 FM; 104 FM

BBC London 94.9
020 7224 2424
www.bbc.co.uk/london
Managing editor: David Robey;
breakfast show: Danny Baker
94.9 FM

BBC Radio Merseyside and
BBC Open Centre
0151 708 5500
www.bbc.co.uk/liverpool
Managing editor: Mick Ord;
news editor: Lee Bennion; breakfast
show: Linda McDermot &
Andy Ball
95.8 FM

BBC Radio Newcastle
0191 232 4141
www.bbc.co.uk/england/
radionewcastle
Managing editor: Sarah
Drummond; news editor: Doug
Morris; breakfast show: Mike Parr
95.4 FM

BBC Radio Norfolk
01603 617411
www.bbc.co.uk/norfolk
Managing editor: David Clayton;
news editor: Sarah Kings; breakfast
show: Graham Barnard
104.1 FM; 95.1 FM; 855 AM;
873 AM

BBC Radio Northampton
01604 239100
www.bbc.co.uk/
northamptonshire
Managing editor: Laura Moss;
news editor: Mark Whall; breakfast
show: Liz Caroll-Wheat
104.2, 103.6 FM

BBC Radio Nottingham
0115 955 0500
www.bbc.co.uk/nottingham
Managing editor: Mike Bettison;
news editor: Steve Beech; breakfast
show: Karl Cooper
103.8 FM

BBC Radio Oxford
01865 311444
www.bbc.co.uk/radiooxford
Managing editor: Steve Taschini;
news editor: Neil Bennett
95.2 FM

BBC Radio Sheffield and BBC
Open Centre
0114 273 1177
www.bbc.co.uk/england/
radiosheffield
Managing editor: Angus Moorat;
news editor: Mike Woodcock;
breakfast show: Everard Davy
88.6 FM

BBC Radio Shropshire
01743 248484
www.bbc.co.uk/shropshire
Managing editor: Tim Pemberton;
news editor: John Shone; breakfast
show: Eric Smith
96 FM; 95.7 FM

BBC Radio Solent
02380 631311
www.bbc.co.uk/radiosolent
Managing editor: Mia Costello;
breakfast show: Julian Clegg
96.1 FM

BBC Southern Counties Radio
01483 306306
www.bbc.co.uk/southerncounties
Managing editor: Mike Hapgood;
news editor: Mark Carter;
breakfast show: Sarah Gorrell,
Ed Douglas, John Radford
104–104.8 FM; 95–95.3 FM

BBC Radio Stoke and BBC Open Centre
01782 208080
www.bbc.co.uk/stoke
Managing editor: Sue Owen; news
editor: Roy Hill; breakfast show:
Kevin Fernihough, Janine Machin
94.6 FM

BBC Radio Suffolk
01473 250000
www.bbc.co.uk/suffolk
Managing editor: Gerald Main;
news editor: Lis Henderson;
breakfast show: Mark Murphy
105.5 FM; 104.5 FM; 103 FM

BBC Radio Swindon
01793 513626
www.bbc.co.uk/wiltshire
Managing editor: Tony Worgan;
news editor: Kirsty Ward; breakfast
show: Peter Heaton-Jones
103.6 FM

BBC Three Counties Radio
01582 637400
www.bbc.co.uk/threecounties
Managing editor: Mark Norman;
breakfast show: Roberto Perrone
95.5 FM; 104.5 FM; 103 FM

BBC Radio Wiltshire
01793 513626
www.bbc.co.uk/wiltshire
Managing editor: Tony Worgan;
news editor: Kirsty Ward; breakfast
show: Sue Davies
103.5 FM; 104.3 FM; 104.9 FM

BBC WM (Birmingham)
0121 432 9000
www.bbc.co.uk/birmingham;
www.bbc.co.uk/blackcountry
Managing editor: Keith Beech;
breakfast show: Adrian Goldberg

BBC WM (Coventry)
02476 860086
www.bbc.co.uk/coventry
Managing editor: David Clargo;
breakfast show: Ann Othen,
Colin Hazelden, Sandie Dunleavy
103.7 FM; 94.8 FM; 104 FM

BBC North Yorkshire – Radio York
01904 641351
www.bbc.co.uk/northyorkshire
Managing editor: Matt Youdale;
news editor: Elly Fiorentini;
breakfast show: Allan Watkiss,
Anna Wallace
1260 AM; 666 AM; 104.3 FM;
103.7 FM; 95.5 FM

Commercial Radio

Main commercial radio groups

CN Group
01228 612600
news@cumbrian-newspapers.co.uk
www.cumbria-online.co.uk

Capital Radio
020 7766 6000
info@capitalradio.com
www.capitalradio.plc.uk

Chrysalis Radio Group
020 7221 2213
info@chrysalis.com
www.chrysalis.com

Classic Gold Digital
01582 676200
www.classicgolddigital.com

Emap Performance Network
020 7436 1515
www.emap.com

GWR Group
0118 928 4313
www.gwrgroup.musicradio.com

Lincs FM
01522 549900
enquiries@lincsfm.co.uk
www.lincsfm.co.uk

SMG
0141 300 3300
www.smg.plc.uk

Scottish Radio Holdings
0141 565 2200
www.srhplc.com

The Wireless Group
020 7959 7800
www.talksport.net

Tindle Radio Holdings
01252 735667
www.tindleradio.com

UKRD Group
01209 310435
enquiries@ukrd.co.uk
www.ukrd.com

Online news

Ananova
Marshall Mill, Marshall Street
Leeds
LS11 9YJ
0113 367 4600
www.ananova.com

Bbc.co.uk
Bush House
The Strand
London
WC2B 4PH
020 8743 8000
www.bbc.co.uk

Belfast Telegraph
Independent News and Media
(Northern Ireland), Internet
Department
124–144 Royal Avenue
Belfast
BT1 1EB
028 9026 4000
www.belfasttelegraph.co.uk

FT
One Southwark Bridge
London
SE1 9H2
020 7873 3000
joanna.manning-cooper@ft.com
www.ft.com

Guardian Unlimited
3–7 Ray Street
London
EC1R 3DR
020 7278 2332
editor@guardianunlimited.co.uk
www.guardian.co.uk

The Independent
Independent House
191 Marsh Wall
London
E14 9RS
020 7005 2000
www.independent.co.uk

ITN
200 Gray's Inn Road
London
WC1X 8X2
020 7430 4700
editor@itn.co.uk
www.itn.co.uk

Online Mirror
MGN
1 Canada Square, Canary Wharf
London
E14 5AP
020 7293 3000
www.mirror.co.uk

Reuters
85 Fleet Street
London
EC4P 4AJ
020 7250 1122
simon.walker@reuters.com
www.reuters.co.uk

Scotsman
Barclay House
108 Holyrood Road
Edinburgh
EH8 8AS
0131 620 8620
enquiries@scotsman.com
www.scotsman.com

Sun Online
Level 6
1 Virginia Street
London
E98 1SN
020 7782 4000
corporate.info@the-sun.co.uk
www.thesun.co.uk

Telegraph
1 Canada Square
Canary Wharf
London
E14 5DT
020 7538 5000
corporate.affairs@telegraph.co.uk
www.telegraph.co.uk

Times
1 Pennington Street
Wapping
London
E98 1TA
020 7782 5000
www.timesonline.co.uk

Press contacts : **Section 4**

Press awards

Amnesty International Media Awards
020 7814 6278
www.amnesty.org.uk/
mediaawards
Human rights journalism

British Garden Writers Guild
020 7245 6943
www.gardenwriters.co.uk/awards

British Press Awards
020 8565 4392
www.britishpressawards.com
Organised by Press Gazette

British Society of Magazine Editors
020 8906 4664
www.bsme.com

Emmas (Ethnic Multicultural Media Academy awards)
020 7636 1233
www.emma.tv
Multicultural media

Foreign Press Association Annual Media Awards
020 7930 0445
www.foreign-press.org.uk
International journalism by British media

Glenfiddich Food & Drink awards
020 8334 1235
www.glenfiddich.com/food
anddrink

Guardian Student Media Awards
020 7278 2332
www.media.guardian.co.uk/
studentmediaawards
Student journalists, designers and photographers

The Herald Scottish Student Press Awards 2003
0141 302 7000
www.theherald.co.uk
Open to full-time students in Scotland

ICIJ Award for Outstanding International Investigative Reporting
00 1 202 481 1234
www.icij.org

Local Reporting Awards
020 7636 7014
www.newspapersoc.org.uk
Under-30s

Medical Journalism Awards
023 8035 4728
www.norwichunion.co.uk/
medical_journalism_awards

NetMedia European Online Journalism Awards
020 7637 7097
www.net-media.co.uk

Newspaper Awards
01869 340788
www.newspaperawards.
newstech.co.uk
Technical innovation in newspaper and new media production

Observer Hodge Award
01727 799987
www.observer.co.uk/hodgeaward
Young photographers

Picture Editors' Awards
administrator@pictureawards.net
www.pictureawards.net
Photographic journalism

Plain English Media Awards
01663 744409
www.plainenglish.co.uk/
mediaawards
Campaign against gobbledygook

PPA Awards
020 7404 4166
www.ppa.co.uk
Magazines

PPAi interactive Awards
020 7400 7532
www.ppai.co.uk
Online publishing

Press Gazette Student Journalism Awards
020 8565 3056
www.pressgazette.co.uk
Open to students enrolled on a journalism course

Race in the Media Awards
020 7939 0000
www.cre.gov.uk
Organised by Commission for Racial Equality

Regional Press Awards
020 8565 3056
www.regionalpressawards.co.uk
Organised by Press Gazette

What the Papers Say Awards
Fax: 0870 7058562
www.whatthepaperssay.co.uk
National newspaper journalists

Training bodies

Broadcast Journalism Training Council
The Secretary
18 Miller's Close
Rippingale
Lincolnshire
PE10 0TH
01778 440025
Sec@bjtc.org.uk
www.bjtc.org.uk
Accredits courses

City & Guilds
1 Giltspur Street
London
EC1A 9DD
020 7294 2800
enquiry@city-and-guilds.co.uk
www.city-and-guilds.co.uk
Vocational qualifications

National Council for the Training of Journalists
Latton Bush Centre
Southern Way
Harlow
Essex
CM18 7BL
01279 430009
info@NCTJ.com
www.nctj.com
Runs schemes for print journalists.
Accredits courses

Periodicals Training Council
Queens House
28 Kingsway
London
WC2B 6JR
020 7404 4166
info1@ppa.co.uk
www.ppa.co.uk/ptc
Training arm of PPA

Anglia Polytechnic University
East Road, Cambridge, CB1 1PT
or Bishop Hall Lane, Chelmsford,
Essex, CM1 1SQ
01223 363271
answers@apu.ac.uk
www.apu.ac.uk
BA (Hons) writing (combined award); BA (Hons) communication studies.

Barnsley College
PO Box 266, Church Street
Barnsley
S70 2YW
01226 216569/216287
programme.enquiries@
barnsley.ac.uk
www.barnsley.ac.uk
Foundation degree journalism & media production (with University of Huddersfield).

Bell College
Almada Street
Hamilton, Lanarkshire
ML3 0JB
01698 283100
enquiries@bell.ac.uk;
r.bergman@bell.ac.uk
www.bell.ac.uk
HND/BA journalism.
PGDip in broadcast journalism (BJTC).

Bournemouth University
Bournemouth Media School,
Weymouth House, Fern Barrow
Poole, Dorset
BH12 5BB
01202 524111
bms@bournemouth.ac.uk
www.bournemouth.ac.uk
BA multimedia journalism (NCTJ, BJTC, PTC); MA/PGDip multimedia journalism (BJTC).

Brighton, University of
Mithras House, Lewes Road
Brighton
BN2 4AT
01273 600900
admissions@brighton.ac.uk
www.brighton.ac.uk
BA (Hons) sports journalism (NCTJ).

Buckingham University
Hunter Street
Buckingham
MK18 1EG
01280 814080
admissions@buckingham.ac.uk
www.buckingham.ac.uk
BA (Hons) English literature/English studies with multimedia journalism.

Canterbury Christ Church University College
Department of Media, North
Holmes Road
Canterbury, Kent
CT1 1QU
01227 767700
admissions@cant.ac.uk
www.cant.ac.uk
MA journalism.

Cardiff University
Dept of Journalism and Media
Studies, PO Box 927
King Edward VII Avenue, Cardiff
CF10 3NB
029 2087 4000
jomec@cardiff.ac.uk
www.cardiff.ac.uk/jomec
PGDip magazine/newspaper journalism; MA journalism studies, European journalism, international journalism.
BA (Hons) journalism, film and media (single and joint); PGDip broadcast journalism.

Cardonald College
690 Moss Park Drive
Glasgow
G52 3AY
0141 272 3333
enquiries@cardonald.ac.uk
www.cardonald.ac.uk
HND practical journalism (NCTJ).

Central England in Birmingham, University of
Corporation Street
Birmingham
B4 7DX
0121 331 5000
media@uce.ac.uk
www.uce.ac.uk
BA (Hons) media and communication (culture and society/ journalism/ media photography); MA international press journalism.
PGDip broadcast journalism (BJTC); MA international broadcast journalism.
BA (Hons) media and communication (multimedia).

Central Lancashire, University of
Department of Journalism
Preston, Lancashire
PR1 2HE
01772 894730
meward@uclan.ac.uk
www.ukjournalism.org
BA (Hons) journalism (NCTJ, BJTC) (single and combined)/ journalism and English/ international journalism/ sports journalism (seeking NCTJ); PGDip newspaper journalism (NCTJ); MA newspaper journalism (NCTJ)/ international journalism/ magazine journalism (seeking NCTJ).
PGDip/MA broadcast journalism (BJTC).
MA online journalism (BJTC).

University College Chester
Parkgate Road
Chester
CH1 4BJ
01244 375444
enquiries@chester.ac.uk
www.chester.ac.uk
BA journalism (NCTJ) (single and combined); BA media (multimedia journalism) (single and combined). BA media (commercial music production/ multimedia journalism/ radio production/ TV production) (single and combined). BA media (multimedia journalism/ web production) (single and combined).

City Literary Institute
Stukeley Street
London
WC2B 5LJ
020 7430 0542
www.citylit.ac.uk
Short courses: introduction to freelance journalism, freelance journalism stage 2, travel journalism, freelance writing for newspapers and magazines.

City Of Wolverhampton College
Wulfrun Campus, Paget Road
Wolverhampton
WV6 0DU
01902 836000
mail@
  wolverhamptoncollege.ac.uk
www.wolverhamptoncollege.ac.uk;
www.mediacove.com
Pre-entry journalism (NCTJ); BA (Hons) journalism and editorial design (W'ton Uni).
Fdg broadcast journalism (W'ton Uni).

City University, London
Department of Journalism,
Northampton Square
London
EC1V 0HB
020 7040 5060;
journalism dept: 020 7040 8221
ugadmissions@city.ac.uk
www.city.ac.uk
BA journalism with social science/contemporary history; PGDip newspaper journalism/ magazine journalism (PTC); PGDip/MA international journalism; MA creative writing; doctorate journalism.
PGDip broadcast journalism (BJTC)/ TV current affairs journalism (BJTC).
MA publishing studies; MA/MSc electronic publishing.

Cornwall College
Trevenson Campus, Pool
Redruth, Cornwall
TR15 3RD
01209 611611
enquiries@cornwall.ac.uk
www.cornwall.ac.uk
Fdg newspaper and magazine journalism; PGDip journalism (NCTJ).
Fdg multimedia design.

Coventry University
Priory Street
Coventry
CV1 5FB
024 7688 7050
rao.cor@coventry.ac.uk
www.coventry.ac.uk
PGCert/PGDip/MA automotive journalism/ international media journalism.
BA multimedia & communication design; PGCert/PGDip/MA design and digital media.

Crawley College
College Road, Crawley
West Sussex
RH10 1NR
01293 442200
information@
  crawley-college.ac.uk
www.crawley-college.ac.uk
Pre-entry newspaper journalism (NCTJ).

Cumbria Institute of the Arts
Brampton Road, Carlisle
Cumbria
CA3 9AY
01228 400300
info@cumbria.ac.uk
www.cumbria.ac.uk
BA (Hons) journalism (NCTJ).

Darlington College Of Technology
Cleveland Avenue, Darlington
County Durham
DL3 7BB
01325 503127
enquire@darlington.ac.uk
www.darlington.ac.uk
Pre-entry and PG journalism (NCTJ); Fdg journalism (University of Teesside).
Pre-entry and PG digital photo-journalism (NCTJ).

De Montfort University
The Gateway
Leicester
LE1 9BH
0116 255 1551
enquiry@dmu.ac.uk
www.dmu.ac.uk
BA (Hons) multimedia design (single and joint).

Dublin Institute of Technology
Fitzwilliam House, 30 Upper
Pembroke Street
Dublin 2
00 353 1 402 3000
(school of media: 00 353 1 402 3098)
www.dit.ie
BA/MA journalism.

University of East London
Docklands Campus,
Longbridge Road
Dagenham
E16 2RD
020 8223 3000
admiss@uel.ac.uk
www.uel.ac.uk
BA (Hons) journalism.

East Surrey College
Reigate School of Art Design
and Media, Gatton Point,
Claremont Road
Redhill, Surrey
RH1 2JX
01737 772611
studentservices@esc.ac.uk
www.esc.ac.uk
*C&G Dip media techniques –
journalism; PGDip journalism
(NCTJ).*

Edge Hill College of Higher Education
St Helen's Road, Ormskirk
Lancashire
L39 4QP
01695 584274
enquiries@edgehill.ac.uk
www.edgehill.ac.uk
BA (Hons) journalism (NCTJ).

Falmouth College of Arts
Woodlane Campus, Falmouth
Cornwall
TR11 4RH
01326 370400
admissions@falmouth.ac.uk
www.falmouth.ac.uk
*BA (Hons) journalism/ English
with media studies; PgDip/MA
professional writing.
PgDip/MA broadcast journalism
(BJTC)*

Fife College of Further Education
St Brycedale Avenue, Kirkcaldy
Fife, Scotland
KY1 1EX
01592 268591
enquiries@fife.ac.uk
www.fife.ac.uk
*HNC/HND practical journalism.
AdvDip interactive graphic design.*

Glasgow Caledonian University
70 Cowcaddens Road
Glasgow
G4 0BA
0141 331 3000
enquiries@gcal.ac.uk
www.gcal.ac.uk
*BA/BA (Hons) journalism (seeking
NCTJ); PGDip journalism studies
(NCTJ).
MA digital media design.*

Glasgow College of Building and Printing
60 North Hanover Street
Glasgow
G1 2BP
0141 332 9969
enquiries@gcbp.ac.uk
www.gcbp.ac.uk
*HNC/HND journalism: broadcast
and print.
HNC/HND digital media for
publishing and print/ multimedia
design and production.*

Gloucestershire University
The Park
Cheltenham
GL50 2QF
01242 532700
gthatcher@glos.ac.uk
www.glos.ac.uk
*BA/BSc (Hons) creative writing; BA
(Hons) journalism and
professional writing.
BA (Hons) broadcast journalism
BA design for interactive media.*

Goldsmiths College
Dept of Media and
Communications, University of
London
New Cross, London
SE14 6NW
020 7919 7171
media-comms@gold.ac.uk
www.goldsmiths.ac.uk
*MA journalism (PTC)/
comparative international
journalism/ script writing.
MA radio (BJTC, NUJ)/ TV
journalism (BJTC)*

Greenwich University
Old Royal Naval College
Park Row
Greenwich, London
SE10 9LS
020 8331 8000
courseinfo@greenwich.ac.uk
www.gre.ac.uk
*HND professional writing; BA
creative writing (with options)/
media writing (with options).
HND/BA graphic and digital
design; BA 3D digital design.*

Grimsby College
Nuns Corner
Grimsby
DN34 5BQ
01472 311222
infocent@grimsby.ac.uk
www.grimsby.ac.uk
*BA (Hons) digital media
production
(journalism/photography) (with
Lancaster University).*

Harlow College
Velizy Avenue, Town Centre
Harlow, Essex
CM20 3LH
01279 868000
full-time@harlow-college.ac.uk
www.harlow-college.ac.uk
*Pre-entry newspaper journalism
(NCTJ); BA (Hons) journalism
(PTC and Middlesex University);
PG pre-entry newspaper
journalism (NCTJ)/ magazine
journalism (NCTJ, PTC).*

Harrow College
Brookshill, Harrow Weald
Middlesex
HA3 6RR
020 8909 6000
www.harrow.ac.uk
NCTJ journalism.

Hertfordshire, University of
College Lane
Hatfield
AL10 9AB
01707 284000
admissions@herts.ac.uk
www.herts.ac.uk
BA (Hons) journalism (combined).

Highbury College, Portsmouth

Dept. of Media and Journalism,
Dovercourt Road
Portsmouth, Hampshire
PO6 2SA
023 9238 3131
info@highbury.ac.uk
www.highbury.ac.uk
*Pre-entry newspaper journalism
(NCTJ)/ magazine journalism
(PTC); HND media (journalism).
PGDip in broadcast journalism
(BJTC).*

Hopwood Hall College

St Mary's Gate
Rochdale
OL12 6RY
01706 345346
enquiries@hopwood.ac.uk
www.hopwood.ac.uk
*Fdg new media design (Manchester
Metropolitan University).*

University of Huddersfield

Queensgate
Huddersfield
HD1 3DH
01484 422288
admissions@hud.ac.uk
www.hud.ac.uk
*BA(Hons) media and print
journalism.
BA(Hons) media and radio
journalism.*

Journalism Training Centre

Unit G, Mill Green Business Park,
Mill Green Road
Mitcham, Surrey
CR4 4HT
020 8640 3696
info@jtctraining.com
www.jtctraining.ac.uk
*Short courses: sports writing,
subediting, feature writing; PGDip
journalism (acc. PTC, approved by
NUJ).*

Kensington and Chelsea College

Hortensia Road
London
SW10 0QS
020 7573 3600
l.gibbons@kcc.ac.uk
www.kcc.ac.uk
*Cert/Dip media studies –
introduction to
journalism/screenwriting (with
Birkbeck College).*

Kingston University

River House, 53–57 High Street
Kingston-upon-Thames, Surrey
KT1 1LQ
020 8547 2000
admissions-info@kingston.ac.uk
www.kingston.ac.uk
*BA(Hons) journalism (combined);
MA writing for the contemporary
media.
BA(Hons) film studies (combined)/
TV studies (combined); BA
(Hons)/DipHE/CertHE audio tech
and music industry studies; MA
production design for film and TV/
screen design for film and TV
(motion graphics)/ film studies/
composing for film and TV;
MA/DPhil media, film and drama
(by research).*

Lambeth College

Belmore Street, Wandsworth
Road
London
SW8 2JY
020 7501 5010
courses@lambethcollege.ac.uk
www.lambethcollege.ac.uk
*Fdg journalism (London
Metropolitan University); pre-
entry newspaper journalism
(NCTJ).
BTEC FirstDip multimedia and
photography.*

Leeds Trinity & All Saints University College

School of Media, Brownberrie
Lane, Horsforth
Leeds
LS18 5HD
0113 283 7100
enquiries@tasc.ac.uk
www.tasc.ac.uk
*BA business journalism/ lifestyle
journalism; BSc psychology with
journalism; MA/PgDip print
journalism (NCTJ).
MA/PgDip in bimedia journalism
(BJTC)/ radio journalism (BJTC).*

Lincoln, University of

Brayford Pool
Lincoln
LN6 7TS
01522 882000
enquiries@lincoln.ac.uk
www.lincoln.ac.uk
*BA (Hons) journalism – print,
internet, radio and TV; MA
journalism (from Sep 2005).*

Liverpool Community College

Journalism School, The Arts
Centre, 9 Myrtle Street
Liverpool
L7 7JA
0151 252 1515
www.liv-coll.ac.uk
*NCTJ prelimCert print journalism/
fast track/ periodical journalism/
day release.
FCert broadcast journalism (BJTC
provisional).*

Liverpool John Moores University

JMU Tower, 24 Norton Street
Liverpool
L3 8PY
0151 231 5090
recruitment@livjm.ac.uk
www.livjm.ac.uk
*BA/BA (Hons)/MA journalism/
international journalism.*

London College of Communication, School of Media

Elephant & Castle
London
SE1 6SB
020 7514 6569
info@lcc.arts.ac.uk
www.lcc.arts.ac.uk
*Fdg/BA (Hons)/MA journalism;
PGCert periodical journalism.
PGDip broadcast journalism; MA
documentary research.*

London College of Fashion

20 John Prince's Street
London
W1G 0BJ
020 7514 7344
enquiries@fashion.arts.ac.uk
www.fashion.arts.ac.uk
*BA (Hons) fashion promotion –
pathways in journalism; PGCert
fashion: fashion and lifestyle
journalism; MA fashion
journalism.*

London Metropolitan University

31 Jewry Street
London
EC3N 2EY
020 7320 1616
enquiries.city@londonmet.ac.uk
www.londonmet.ac.uk
*Fdg journalism; BA (Hons)
journalism studies.*

London South Bank University
103 Borough Road
London
SE1 0AA
020 7928 8989
enquiries@lsbu.ac.uk
www.lsbu.ac.uk
BA (Hons) writing for media arts;
MA media writing.

Luton, University of
Park Square
Luton, Beds
LU1 3JU
01582 734111
enquiries@luton.ac.uk
www.luton.ac.uk
BA (Hons) journalism/ journalism
studies and PR.
Fdg digital imaging and design for
media (at Milton Keynes College);
MA new media and internet
technologies.

Mid-Cheshire College
Hartford Campus, Chester Road
Northwich, Cheshire
CW8 1LJ
01606 744444
info@midchesh.ac.uk
www.midchesh.ac.uk
NCFE multimedia design.

Middlesex University
White Hart Lane
London
N17 8HR
020 8411 5000
admissions@mdx.ac.uk
www.mdx.ac.uk
BA (Hons) journalism/ journalism
and communication studies (single
and joint)/ creative and media
writing (single and joint); MA
writing.

Napier University
School of Communication Arts,
Craighouse Campus
Craighouse Road, Edinburgh
EH10 5LG
0131 455 6150
www.napier.ac.uk
Short courses: design for print/
intro to journalism/ intro to print
process/ journalism and media/
writing for specialists/ writing for
press and broadcast media/
intermediate subediting/ refresher
for journalists/ subediting for
beginners; BA/BA (Hons)/
PGDip/MSc journalism;
PGDip/MSc international English
language journalism.
Short course: writing for the press
and broadcast media.
Short course: new media writing.

National Broadcasting School
The Innovation Centre, University
of Sussex
Brighton
BN1 9SB
01273 704510
www.nationalbroadcasting
school.com
Cert radio presentation and
programming (CRCA)/ radio
journalism and news presentation
(CRCA/NCTJ).

Northbrook College Sussex
Little Hampton Road, Worthing
West Sussex
BN12 6NU
01903 606060
admissions@nbcol.ac.uk
www.nbcol.ac.uk
BA (Hons) digital journalism
(subject to validation).

Northumbria University
Ellison Place
Newcastle Upon Tyne
NE1 8ST
0191 232 6002
ca.marketing@northumbria.ac.uk
www.northumbria.ac.uk
MA creative writing.
BA (Hons) multimedia design.

**Norwich School of Art and
Design**
St George Street, Norwich
Norfolk
NR3 1BB
01603 610561
info@nsad.ac.uk
www.nsad.ac.uk
MA writing the visual.

noSweat Journalism Training
25b Lloyd Baker Street
London
WC1X 9AT
020 7713 1000
info@nosweatjt.co.uk
www.nosweatjt.co.uk
NCTJ PrelimCert (reporters) p/t,
f/t, intakes Sep & Mar; magazine
journalism (working towards acc.
PTC), p/t, f/t, intakes Feb, Jun &
Oct.
Short courses: feature writing,
Quark subbing, travel writing,
sports reporting etc.
Course director: Stephen Ward -
steve@nosweatjt.co.uk

Nottingham Trent University
Burton Street
Nottingham
NG1 4BU
0115 941 8418
cbj@ntu.ac.uk
www.ntu.ac.uk
PGDip/MA newspaper journalism/
newspaper journalism
(international). PGDip/MA TV
journalism/ TV journalism
(international)/ radio journalism/
radio journalism (international).
PGDip/MA online journalism/
online journalism (international).

Oxford Brookes University
Gypsy Lane Campus, Headington
Oxford
OX3 0BP
01865 484848
admissions@brookes.ac.uk
www.brookes.ac.uk
MA interactive media publishing.

Peterborough Regional College
Park Crescent
Peterborough
PE1 4DZ
01733 767366
info@peterborough.ac.uk
www.peterborough.ac.uk
C&G 7790 journalism (media
techniques); HNC/HND
journalism; Fdg print journalism.

Portsmouth, University of
University House, Winston
Churchill Avenue
Portsmouth, Hampshire
PO1 2UP
023 9284 8484
info.centre@port.ac.uk
www.port.ac.uk
BA (Hons) media studies with
creative writing.

**The Press Association/Editorial
Centre**
Hanover House, Marine Court, St
Leonards-on-Sea
Hastings, East Sussex
TN38 0DX
01424 435991
editorial-centre@mistral.co.uk
www.editorial-centre.co.uk
Combined Dip journalism and
NVQ Level 4 journalism; PADip
subediting.

Ravensbourne College of Design and Communication
Walden Road, Chislehurst
Kent
BR7 5SN
020 8289 4900
info@rave.ac.uk
www.ravensbourne.ac.uk
PG digital, new media and online journalism.

Robert Gordon University
School Hill
Aberdeen
AB10 1FR
01224 262000
admissions@rgu.ac.uk
www.rgu.ac.uk
BA/BA (Hons) publishing with journalism.

Roehampton University of Surrey
Erasmus House
Roehampton Lane
London
SW15 5PU
020 8392 3000
enquiries@roehampton.ac.uk
www.roehampton.ac.uk
BA journalism and news media/creative writing; MA creative writing and professional writing.
BA journalism and news media.

Salford, University of
Salford
Greater Manchester
M5 4WT
0161 295 5000
ugadmissions-exrel@
  salford.ac.uk
www.salford.ac.uk
BA (Hons) journalism and design studies/English/ languages/politics/sociology (NCTJ); BSc (Hons) journalism and broadcasting (NCTJ).
BSc (Hons) journalism and broadcasting (NCTJ).

Sheffield College
The Norton Centre, Dyche Lane
Sheffield
S8 8BR
0114 260 3603
mail@sheffcol.ac.uk
www.sheffcol.ac.uk
NCTJ journalism/ reporter; NCTJ journalism/ photography; NCTJ pre-entry journalism/ photography.

Sheffield Hallam University
Psalter Lane Campus
Sheffield
S11 8UZ
0114 225 5555
admissions@shu.ac.uk
www.shu.ac.uk
PGCert/PGDip/MA writing.
PGCert/PGDip/MA broadcast journalism/ film and digital production.

Sheffield University
Department of Journalism
Studies, 18–22 Regent Street
Sheffield
S1 3NJ
0114 222 2500
journalism@sheffield.ac.uk
www.sheffield.ac.uk/journalism
BA (Hons) journalism studies (NCTJ, BJTC)/ journalism and French/ Germanic studies/ Hispanic studies/ Russian; PGDip/MA print journalism (NCTJ).
PGDip/MA broadcast journalism (BJTC).
MA web journalism.

Solihull College
Blossomfield Road
Solihull
B91 1SB
0121 678 7001
enquiries@solihull.ac.uk
www.solihull.ac.uk
HNC/HND photography and digital imaging.

South East Essex College
Carmarvon Road
Southend-on-Sea
Essex
SS2 6LS
01702 220400
marketing@southend.ac.uk
www.southend.ac.uk
BA (Hons) journalism.

South Nottingham College
Greythorn Drive, West Bridgford
Nottingham
NG2 7GA
0115 914 6464
enquiries@
  south-nottingham.ac.uk
www.south-nottingham.ac.uk
HNC/HND photography and digital imaging/ print, media and digital design.

South Thames College
Wandsworth High Street
London
SW18 2PP
020 8918 7777
studentservices@
  south-thames.ac.uk
www.south-thames.ac.uk
Short course: intro to journalism.

Southampton Institute
East Park Terrace, Southampton
Hampshire
SO14 0RB
023 8031 9000
fmas@solent.ac.uk
www.solent.ac.uk
BA (Hons) journalism (NCTJ, PTC, BJTC)/ media writing/ writing fashion and culture.

St Helen's College
St Helens
Merseyside
WA10 1PZ
01744 623580
enquire@sthelens.ac.uk
www.sthelens.ac.uk
BTEC HND media (writing); Fdg vocational writing (subject to validation).

St Mary's College
Waldegrave Road
Twickenham
TW1 4SX
020 8240 4000
recruit@smuc.ac.uk
www.smuc.ac.uk
BA (Hons) professional and creative writing.

Staffordshire University, Faculty of Arts, Media and Design
College Road, Stoke-on-Trent
Staffordshire
ST4 2XW
01782 294869
amdadmissions@staffs.ac.uk
www.staffs.ac.uk
BA (Hons) journalism/sports journalism (NCTJ).
BA (Hons) broadcast journalism (NCTJ); MA broadcast journalism (NCTJ).

Stirling, University of
Stirling
FK9 4LA
01786 467046
recruitment@stir.ac.uk
www.stir.ac.uk
BA (Hons) journalism studies (single and combined).
BA (Hons) journalism studies.

Strathclyde, University of
16 Richmond Street, Glasgow,
G1 1XQ; 0141 552 4400
Scottish Centre for Journalism
Studies, Crawfurd Building,
Jordanhill Campus, 76 Southbrae
Drive, Glasgow G13 1PP; 0141
950 3281
www.strath.ac.uk
*BA in journalism and creative
writing; PgDip/MLitt in
journalism studies (NCTJ).*

Sunderland, University of
Langham Tower, Ryhope Road
Sunderland
SR2 7EE
0191 515 2000 (media dept:
0191 515 2112)
student-helpline@
  sunderland.ac.uk
www.sunderland.ac.uk
*BA (Hons) journalism (routes inc
newspaper and magazine) (NCTJ);
PGDip/MA journalism (NCTJ).*

**Surrey Institute of Art and
Design**
Falkner Road, Farnham
Surrey
GU9 7DS
01252 722441
registry@surrart.ac.uk
www.surrart.ac.uk
*BA (Hons) journalism (PTC, BJTC,
recognised by NCTJ)/ fashion
journalism.*

Sutton Coldfield College
34 Lichfield Road, Sutton
Coldfield
West Midlands
B74 2NW
0121 355 5671
infoc@sutcol.ac.uk
www.sutcol.ac.uk
*Cert newspaper journalism
(NCTJ).*

Tameside College
Beaufort Road, Ashton-under-
Lyne
Greater Manchester
OL6 6NX
0161 908 6600
www.tameside.ac.uk
*Fdg new media design (with
Manchester Metropolitan
University).*

Thames Valley University
London College of Music & Media,
St Mary's Road
Ealing, London
W5 5RF
0800 036 8888
www.tvu.ac.uk
*BA (Hons) digital broadcast media/
new media journalism.*

Ulster, University of
Cromore Road
Co Londonderry, Northern Ireland
BT52 1SA
0870 040 0700
online@ulster.ac.uk
www.ulster.ac.uk
*BA (Hons) combinations with
media, journalism & publishing,
English, languages; PGDip/MA
newspaper journalism.
BA (Hons) combinations with
media, journalism & publishing,
English, French, German, Irish,
Spanish.*

University College Northampton
Boughton Green Road
Northampton
NN2 7AL
01604 735500
study@northampton.ac.uk
www.northampton.ac.uk
BA (Hons) journalism.

**University College Winchester
(formerly King Alfred's College)**
Hampshire
SO22 4NR
01962 841515
admissions@winchester.ac.uk
www.winchester.ac.uk
*MA contemporary popular
knowledges/ creative and critical
writing/ writing for children.*

**University of Wales Institute,
Cardiff**
PO Box 377, Western Avenue
Cardiff
CF5 2YB
029 2041 6070
uwicinfo@uwic.ac.uk
www.uwic.ac.uk
*BA (Hons)/BA/BSc (Hons) design
for interactive media.*

University of Wales, Bangor
Gwynedd
LL57 2DG
01248 351151
admissions@bangor.ac.uk
www.bangor.ac.uk
*BA (Hons) cyfathrebu a
newyddiaduraeth (communication
& journalism);
anrhydedd cymraeg gyda
newyddiaduraeth (journalism
with history/English/Welsh)/
PGDip newyddiaduraeth
ymarferol (practical journalism);
MPhil/PhD creative & critical
writing.*

University of Wales, Newport
Caerleon Campus, PO Box 179
Newport, South Wales
NP18 3YG
01633 430088
uic@newport.ac.uk
www.newport.ac.uk
*BA (Hons) new media publishing
(subject to validation); MA
animation/ design (new media and
tech).*

University of Wales, Swansea
Singleton Park
Swansea
SA2 8PP
01792 205678
admissions@swansea.ac.uk
www.swansea.ac.uk
*MA comparative journalism/
creative and media writing.*

Wakefield College
Margaret Street, Wakefield
West Yorks
WF1 2DH
01924 789789
info@wakcoll.ac.uk
www.wakcoll.ac.uk
Fdg multimedia and web design.

Warwick, University of
Coventry
CV4 7AL
024 7652 3523
www.warwick.ac.uk
BA English and creative writing.

Warwickshire College
Leamington Centre
Warwick New Road
Leamington Spa
Warwickshire CV32 5JE
0800 783 6767
www.warkscol.ac.uk
PG journalism (NCTJ).

West Herts College
Hampstead Road
Watford WD17 3EZ
01923 812000
admissions@westherts.ac.uk
www.westherts.ac.uk
*Fdg media, design and production
– graphics and new media design.*

West Kent College
Brook Street, Tonbridge
Kent TW9 2PW
01732 358101
marketing@wkc.ac.uk
www.wkc.ac.uk
*Pre-entry newspaper journalism
(NCTJ).
BA (Hons) broadcast journalism.*

Westminster, University of
309 Regent Street
London W1B 2UW
020 7911 5000
www.wmin.ac.uk
*BA media studies with pathway in
journalism/ medical journalism;
PGDip periodical journalism; MA
journalism (for international
students)/ journalism studies.
PGDip broadcast journalism
(BJTC).
BSc digital and photographic
imaging/ multimedia computing;
MSc digital and photographic
imaging/ interactive multimedia/
computer animation.*

Wolverhampton, University of
Wulfruna Street
Wolverhampton WV1 1SB
01902 321000
enquiries@wlv.ac.uk
www.wlv.ac.uk
*BA (Hons) journalism and
editorial design (NCTJ)/ creative
and professional writing.
Fdg broadcast journalism.*

Archant
Prospect House, Rouen Road
Norwich
Norfolk NR1 1RE
01603 772803/628311
david.allison@archant.co.uk
www.archant.co.uk

Bristol United Press
Bristol United Press
Temple Way
Bristol BS99 7HD
0117 934 3000
a.ocallaghan@bepp.co.uk
www.thisisbristol.com
Owned by Northcliffe since 2000

Johnston Training Centre
Upper Mounts
Northampton NN1 3HR
01604 467755
ilvi.smith@northantsnews.co.uk
www.johnstonpress.co.uk

Midland News Association
MNA Training Centre
Rock House, Old Hill
Tettenhall
Wolverhampton WV6 8QB
01902 742126
c.clark@expressandstar.co.uk
www.expressandstar.com
*Mostly in-house but takes a few
non-company trainees*

Newsquest Media Group
58 Church Street
Weybridge
KT13 8DP
01932 821212
ebudiar@newsquest.co.uk
www.newsquest.co.uk

Press Association
The Press Association
292 Vauxhall Bridge Road
London
SW1V 1AE
020 7963 7000
information@pa.press.net
www.pa.press.net

Trinity Mirror Training Centre
Trinity Mirror Editorial Training
Thomson House
Groat Market
Newcastle-upon-Tyne
NE1 1ED
0191 201 6043
tony.johnston@ncj.media.co.uk